CW01573029

OXFORD THEOLOGY AND RELIGION MONOGRAPHS

OXFORD THEOLOGY AND RELIGION MONOGRAPHS

Bede's Temple

An Image and its Interpretation

CONOR O'BRIEN

OXFORD
UNIVERSITY PRESS

OXFORD

UNIVERSITY PRESS

Great Clarendon Street, Oxford, OX2 6DP,
United Kingdom

Oxford University Press is a department of the University of Oxford.
It furthers the University's objective of excellence in research, scholarship,
and education by publishing worldwide. Oxford is a registered trade mark of
Oxford University Press in the UK and in certain other countries

First Edition published in 2015

Impression: 2

Published in the United States of America by Oxford University Press
198 Madison Avenue, New York, NY 10016, United States of America

British Library Cataloguing in Publication Data
Data available

Library of Congress Control Number: 2015933283

ISBN 978-0-19-874708-6

Printed and bound by
CPI Group (UK) Ltd, Croydon, CR0 4YY

For my parents

Acknowledgements

This study has its origins in my undergraduate degree at Cork where I was first introduced to Bede and his exegesis of the temple. The influence of my inspiring teachers there, Jennifer O'Reilly and Diarmuid Scully, can be seen on every page that follows; I am very grateful to both for giving me the opportunity to first embark on this journey and for being highly supportive ever since.

If the foundations were laid in Cork, most of the construction work for this book was done in Oxford. There I benefited greatly from the presence of a host of dedicated scholars who gave generously of their time: John Blair, Mark Edwards, Matthew Kempshall, Henry Mayr-Harting, Christopher Rowland, Richard Sowerby, and the late Bernard Green—to all I am most obliged. My doctoral work at Oxford was supported financially by the Oxford Faculty of Theology, the Crewdson Trust, and the National University of Ireland. Throughout my years in Oxford I profited especially from the exceptional supervision and support of Sarah Foot; she gave invaluable assistance and advice at every step of the way, without which this work would have been less well researched, less well written, and much, much longer in the making. I was lucky to have two great and generous scholars as my examiners: Thomas Charles-Edwards and Alan Thacker. This study has gained much from their insight and suggestions. The Queen's College provided me with a happy home during my studies and I thank my colleagues in the Middle Common Room there for making the process so enjoyable.

It is a pleasure to acknowledge those academics who kindly shared their work with me, often pre-publication: Celia Chazelle, Samuel W. Collins, Paul Hilliard, Oliver Pengelley, Diarmuid Scully, and Lesley Smith. This research would have ended very differently without the inspiring questions of Kirsty March. My thanks to Paul Doolan for help with reading Dutch, to OUP's anonymous reader for their supportive comments, and to the members of the Institute of Historical Research's Earlier Middle Ages seminar, who kindly received a shortened version of Chapter 3. The staff of the Biblioteca Medicea Laurenziana assisted me in obtaining permission to reproduce the most vital images from the Codex Amiatinus. Zoë Sternberg provided me with linguistic assistance, many dinners, companionship, and encouragement over the past four years; I look forward to becoming increasingly indebted to her over the years to come.

I am very grateful to the University of Sheffield for generously agreeing to assist with the cost of publishing the images from the Codex Amiatinus and to the staff at Oxford University Press for their efficiency in dealing with the manuscript.

Needless to say, my debts to all of those who have contributed to this study leave me with little but the errors to claim as my own.

Finally, I must thank my mother and father, without whom even the least of my achievements would have been impossible. They have tirelessly supported me, emotionally and materially, at every stage of my education and career. My debt to my parents cannot be repaid but, for what it is worth, I dedicate this work to them.

Conor O'Brien
October 2014

Contents

List of Illustrations

Readers may find high-quality colour reproductions of the entire first quire of the Codex Amiatinus in Celia Chazelle, 'Christ and the Vision of God: The Biblical Diagrams of the Codex Amiatinus', in *The Mind's Eye: Art and Theological Argument in the Middle Ages*, eds Jeffrey F. Hamburger and Anne-Marie Bouché (Princeton NJ, 2006), pp. 84–111.

Abbreviations

Abac.	Bede, *Expositio in Canticum Abacuc Prophetae*, ed. J. E. Hudson, CCSL 119B, pp. 377–409.
Act.	Bede, *Expositio Actuum Apostolorum*, ed. M. L. W. Laistner, CCSL 121, pp. 3–99.
Apoc.	Bede, *Expositio Apocalypseos*, ed. Roger Gryson, CCSL 121A.
ASE	*Anglo-Saxon England.*
Augustine, *DCD*	Augustine, *De Civitate Dei*, eds B. Dombart and A. Kalb, CCSL 47–8.
Cant.	Bede, *In Cantica Canticorum*, ed. D. Hurst, CCSL 119B, pp. 167–375.
CCSL	Corpus Christianorum, Series Latina (Turnhout).
CSEL	Corpus Scriptorum Ecclesiasticorum Latinorum (Vienna).
DST	Bede, *De Schematibus et Tropis*, ed. Calvin B. Kendall, CCSL 123A, pp. 142–71; trans. Tannenhaus = Gussie Hecht Tannenhaus (trans.), 'Bede's *De Schematibus et Tropis*—a translation', *Quarterly Journal of Speech* 48 (1962), pp. 237–53.
DTR	Bede, *De Temporum Ratione*, ed. Charles W. Jones, CCSL 123B; trans. Wallis = Faith Wallis (trans.), *Bede: On the Reckoning of Time* (Liverpool, 1999).
EME	*Early Medieval Europe.*
EpCath.	Bede, *In Epistulas Septem Catholicas*, ed. D. Hurst, CCSL 121, pp. 181–342.
EpEcg.	Bede, *Epistola ad Ecgbertum Episcopum*, eds and trans. Christopher Grocock and I. N. Wood, *Abbots of Wearmouth and Jarrow* (Oxford, 2013), pp. 123–61.
Ezra.	Bede, *In Ezram et Neemiam*, ed. D. Hurst, CCSL 119A, pp. 235–392; trans. DeGregorio = Scott DeGregorio (trans.), *Bede: On Ezra and Nehemiah* (Liverpool, 2006).
Gen.	Bede, *In Principium Genesis*, ed. Charles W. Jones, CCSL 118A; trans. Kendall = Calvin B. Kendall (trans.), *Bede: On Genesis* (Liverpool, 2008).
HA	Bede, *Historia Abbatum*, eds and trans. Christopher Grocock and I. N. Wood, *Abbots of Wearmouth and Jarrow* (Oxford, 2013), pp. 21–75.
HE	Bede, *Historia Ecclesiastica Gentis Anglorum*, eds and trans. B. Colgrave and R. A. B. Mynors, *Bede's Ecclesiastical History of the English People* (Oxford, 1969).

Hom.	Bede, *Homiliarum Euangelii*, ed. D. Hurst, CCSL 122, pp. 1–403; trans. Martin and Hurst = Lawrence T. Martin and David Hurst (trans.), *Bede: Homilies on the Gospels*, 2 vols (Kalamazoo MI, 1991).
JEH	*Journal of Ecclesiastical History.*
JTS	*Journal of Theological Studies.*
Luc.	Bede, *In Lucae Euangelium Expositio*, ed. D. Hurst, CCSL 120, pp. 5–425.
Marc.	Bede, *In Marci Euangelium Expositio*, ed. D. Hurst, CCSL 120, pp. 431–648.
MGH	Monumenta Germaniae Historica (Berlin and Munich).
PL	*Patrologia Latina*, ed. J.-P. Migne (Paris).
Prov.	Bede, *In Proverbia Salomonis*, ed. D. Hurst, CCSL 119B, pp. 23–163.
RB	*Revue bénédictine.*
Reg.	Bede, *In Regum Librum XXX Quaestiones*, ed. D. Hurst, CCSL 119, pp. 289–322; trans. Foley = W. Trent Foley (trans.), *Thirty Questions on the Book of Kings*, in *Bede: A Biblical Miscellany* (Liverpool, 1999), pp. 81–143.
Ret.	Bede, *Retractatio in Actus Apostolorum*, ed. M. L. W. Laistner, CCSL 121, pp. 103–63.
Sam.	Bede, *In Primam Partem Samuhelis*, ed. D. Hurst, CCSL 119, pp. 5–287.
Tab.	Bede, *De Tabernaculo et Vasis eius ac Vestibus Sacerdotum*, ed. D. Hurst, CCSL 119A, pp. 1–139; trans. Holder = Arthur G. Holder (trans.), *Bede: On the Tabernacle* (Liverpool, 1994).
Temp.	Bede, *De Templo*, ed. D. Hurst, CCSL 119A, pp. 141–234; trans. Connolly = Seán Connolly (trans.), *Bede: On the Temple* (Liverpool, 1995).
VCeol.	*Vita Ceolfridi*, eds and trans. Christopher Grocock and I. N. Wood, *Abbots of Wearmouth and Jarrow* (Oxford, 2013), pp. 76–121.
VCP	Bede, *Vita Sancti Cuthberti*, ed. and trans. Bertram Colgrave, *Two Lives of Saint Cuthbert* (Cambridge, 1942), pp. 142–306.
VIII Q.	Bede, *VIII Quaestiones*, ed. Michael Gorman, 'Bede's *VIII Quaestiones* and Carolingian Biblical Scholarship', *RB* 109 (1999), pp. 32–74, at 62–74.
VW	Stephen, *Vita Wilfridi*, ed. and trans. Bertram Colgrave, *The Life of Bishop Wilfrid by Eddius Stephanus* (Cambridge, 1927).

Unless otherwise indicated, when citing the Bible I use the Vulgate for the Latin: *Biblia Sacra Iuxta Vulgatam Versionem*, ed. R. Weber et al., 2 vols (Stuttgart, 1969); and the Douay-Rheims version for the English: *The Holy Bible: Douay Version* (London, 1956).

Fig. 1. The Tabernacle image from the Codex Amiatinus: Florence, Biblioteca Medicea Laurenziana, MS Amiatino 1, fols IIv–IIIr; reproduced by permission of MiBACT. Further reproduction by any means is forbidden.

CODICIBVS SACRIS HOSTILI CLADE PERVSTIS
ESDRA DO FERVENS HOC REPARAVIT OPVS

Fig. 2. The Ezra portrait from the Codex Amiatinus: Florence, Biblioteca Medicea Laurenziana, MS Amiatino 1, fol. Vr; reproduced by permission of MiBACT. Further reproduction by any means is forbidden.

Fig. 3. The *Maiestas Domini* from the Codex Amiatinus: Florence, Biblioteca Medicea Laurenziana, MS Amiatino 1, fol. 796v; reproduced by permission of MiBACT. Further reproduction by any means is forbidden.

Possible Chronology of the Works of Bede

The most recent attempts to date Bede's corpus have been made by George Hardin Brown, *A Companion to Bede* (Woodbridge, 2009), pp. 13–15 and Michael Lapidge, 'Introduzione', in *Beda: Storia degli Inglesi*, ed. Michael Lapidge and trans. Paolo Chiesa, vol. 1 (Rome, 2008), pp. xlviii–lviii. Neither is perfect, however. Poor editing vitiates the usefulness of Brown's summary, which contradicts comments he makes elsewhere in the volume. Lapidge's study does not engage with some recent attempts to date certain works, resulting in some very conservative conclusions. The dating suggestions offered by M. L. W. Laistner and H. H. King, *A Hand-List of Bede Manuscripts* (Ithaca NY, 1943) have in many cases now been superseded by the editions and translations of individual works, to which the reader should turn in the first instance for much of what follows.[1] I have cited secondary literature where relevant in the main text.

pre-703?	*On the Holy Places*
703	*On the Nature of Things* and *On Time*
c.703	*Explanation of the Apocalypse*
c.705	*Verse Life of Cuthbert* (first recension)
708	*Letter to Plegwin*
c.710	*On Acts*
c.710	*Commentary on 1 John* (part of *On the Seven Catholic Epistles*)
post-710?	*On the Art of Metre* and *On Schemes and Tropes*
710–715	*On Luke*
c.715	*Thirty Questions on the Book of Kings*
715–717	*On 1 Samuel*
c.716	Letters to Acca: *On the Resting-Places* and *On What Isaiah Said*
pre-716?	*On the Song of Songs*
pre-716?	*On Proverbs*
716–717?	*History of the Abbots of Wearmouth and Jarrow*
710–720	Book One of *On Genesis*
c.720	Book Two of *On Genesis*

---

[1] Laistner and King's discussion of the manuscript transmission of Bede's works is wholly superseded by Michael Lapidge, 'Beda Venerabilis', in *La Trasmissione dei Testi Latini del Medioevo/Medieval Latin Texts and their Transmission*, eds Paolo Chiesa and Lucia Castaldi, vol. 3 (Florence, 2008), pp. 44–137—but not for Bede's exegesis, none of which is included.

c.720	*Prose Life of Cuthbert* and *Verse Life of Cuthbert* (second recension)
721–725?	*On the Tabernacle*
722–725?	Books Three and Four of *On Genesis*
pre-725	*Letter to Helmwald*
725	*On the Reckoning of Time*
post-725	*Letter to Wicthed*
c.725–731?	*On Mark*
725–731	*Retraction on Acts*
725–731	*Martyrology*
729–731	*On the Temple*
725–731?	*On Ezra and Nehemiah*
731	*The Ecclesiastical History of the English People* (with probable additions later)
734	*Letter to Ecgberht*

The following works all predate the *Ecclesiastical History* but cannot be more specifically dated:

The Gospel Homilies

On the Canticle of Habakkuk

On Tobit

Hymns and *Epigrams*

The Passion of St Anastasius

The Life of St Felix

Excerpts from the Works of Saint Augustine on the Letters of the Blessed Apostle Paul

On Orthography (in the past believed to be a very early work—but such assumptions are no longer secure)

Undated, but possibly from after 731: *Eight Questions*

1

Studying Bede's Temple

In the summer of AD 70, after years of Jewish insurrection, a Roman army under the future emperor Titus entered Jerusalem. A hard-fought, slow advance through the city reached its climax when the torching of the temple gates combined with the scorching summer heat to destroy the entire temple complex on the ninth day of the Hebrew month of Av (itself the anniversary of the destruction of Solomon's temple by the Babylonians). The destruction of the Jewish holy site may have been accidental, but its effects proved dramatically permanent.[1] The place of God's dwelling amongst his chosen people would never in fact be rebuilt, despite the hopes and dreams of many. But its power was not destroyed: the next two millennia saw the image of the Jewish temple exert an influence over many minds, Christian as well as Jewish.[2] Thus, when, at the beginning of the eighth century, a Christian monk at the northern edges of the former Roman Empire first sat down to write about the Bible, the image of the temple, despite the building's destruction, could still inspire him.

BEDE AND THE TEMPLE

The Venerable Bede (c.672–735) declared that 'the temple of the Lord had once been placed upon the earth ... but now the Church, the temple of the living God, whose way of life is in heaven' had replaced it; while the former had hidden the Ark of the Covenant behind a veil, the latter revealed the Lord's incarnation to the whole world.[3] Bede began his exegetical career as he

[1] Martin Goodman, *Rome and Jerusalem: The Clash of Ancient Civilisations* (London, 2008), pp. 23–9, 440–4.

[2] E.g. William J. Hamblin and David Rolph Seely, *Solomon's Temple: Myth and History* (London, 2007).

[3] *Apoc.*, p. 385 'Templum domini quondam in terra positum arcam testamenti sub uelamine mystico clausam tegebat. Nunc autem in ecclesia, quae est templum dei uiui [2 Corinthians 6.16], cuius conuersatio in caelis est [Philippians 3.20], uelo templi ueteris et medio pariete macheriae domini sanguine descisso [Ephesians 2.14], arca incarnationis eius toto iam panditur orbi'.

was to continue it—convinced of the relevance of the temple image even in a time and place far distant from the site of ancient Jewish worship. Bede would become one of the most significant intellectual figures in the Latin West of his day; his achievements substantially rest on the biblical commentaries which he wrote over thirty years, starting with his *Explanation of the Apocalypse*. In that extraordinary output the place of the temple image grew from occasional references to become the focus of self-consciously original works on Moses' tabernacle and the temple in Jerusalem.[4] Bede believed that God had allowed him 'not only to grasp the ancient offerings . . . but also to discover new ones beneath the veil'; that is, to build from the patristic tradition an original and uniquely detailed Christian exegesis of the temple.[5]

This work studies that exegesis in its entirety for the first time. It does so from the conviction that understanding Bede's use of the temple sheds significant light on the world view of this most important early medieval English author.[6] Bede's significance needs no defence: his *Ecclesiastical History of the English People* remains a major work, the pre-eminent source for the study of early Anglo-Saxon England, and has earned him a reputation as the father of English history. But his scriptural commentary reveals much more concerning the contours of Bede's mind and significance for his own time than does the *Ecclesiastical History* read in isolation. Exegesis provided the major form of intellectual discourse in the early Middle Ages. Intellectuals rarely wrote free-standing theological or academic treatises in this period because exegesis was an encyclopaedic endeavour, drawing on all spheres of knowledge. Scholars now recognize that 'exegesis and biblical commentary were often the field [sic] where political, philosophical and theological matters were discussed'.[7] Bede wrote about the temple image not from antiquarian interest, but convinced of its continuing relevance; as a consequence, his use of the image opens a window on what mattered to him about the nature of time and space, Christ, the Church as an institution, and the individual's relationship with God.

A trilogy of major commentaries on the temple image dominates Bede's mature output: *On the Tabernacle*, *On the Temple*, and *On Ezra and*

---

[4] *Temp.*, p. 144.

[5] *Ezra.*, p. 392 'amorem dedisti et auxilium . . . non solum uetera amplectendi uerum et noua sub uelamine ueterum donaria inueniendi'; trans. DeGregorio, p. 226. See Matthew 13.52.

[6] The best basic introduction to Bede and his work is now Scott DeGregorio (ed.), *The Cambridge Companion to Bede* (Cambridge, 2010). See also George Hardin Brown, *A Companion to Bede* (Woodbridge, 2009) and Benedicta Ward, *The Venerable Bede*, 2nd ed. (London, 1998).

[7] Ineke van 't Spijker, 'Introduction', in *The Multiple Meaning of Scripture: the Role of Exegesis in early Christian and Medieval Culture*, ed. Ineke van 't Spijker (Leiden, 2009), pp. 1–12, at 1. Also Thomas O'Loughlin (ed.), *The Scriptures and Early Medieval Ireland* (Turnhout, 1999); Celia Chazelle and Burton Van Name Edwards (eds), *The Study of the Bible in the Carolingian Era* (Turnhout, 2003).

Nehemiah, all three written during the latter half of Bede's career. These provide an insight into his developed thought and reveal an experienced author experimenting with exegetical tradition. *On the Tabernacle* and *On the Temple* are both formally unusual—thematically organized exegetical treatises, focusing narrowly on the details of the construction of the desert tabernacle and Solomon's temple. *On the Tabernacle* deals with the relevant texts from Exodus 24.12–30.21; *On the Temple* draws on 3 Kings 5–7 (Bede skipped over descriptions of Solomon's palace as irrelevant to his purposes), with additional material from 2 Paralipomenon 2–4. While *On Ezra and Nehemiah* provides a more traditional line-by-line commentary of an entire book of the Bible, it too broke new ground by dealing with the previously unexamined book of Esdras.[8] A propensity to understand architectural details and descriptions of construction work as symbolic of the Church unites the trilogy; beginning from the assumption that the temple image represented the entire reality of the Church, Bede explored the institutional, personal, historical, and spiritual ramifications of the image throughout these commentaries.

While this trilogy alone would justify scholarly interest, it does not exhaust Bede's use of the temple. He dealt with the image across different genres—as well as his commentaries, three of Bede's homilies concentrate on the temple: *Homily* II.1 (on John 2.12–22), II.24 (John 10.22–30), and II.25 (Luke 6.43–8); a fourth, *Homily* II.19 (on Luke 1.5–17), also dedicates much space to the image. If Bede's temple commentaries asserted the relevance of the image to all aspects of the life of the Church, in the homilies Bede spoke directly to his contemporaries of that relevance: 'we ourselves, who come together in the Lord's name, are...his temple'.[9] The homilies may date, along with the temple trilogy, from Bede's maturity but Bede's exegesis featured the temple image from the very beginning. Regardless of subject, his interest in it kept breaking through. Bede noted that Luke's gospel both begins and ends in the temple precincts—*On Luke* thus returns to the temple image repeatedly.[10] His exegesis of the tower of Babel contains a comparison with the temple of Jerusalem using much of the architectural approach familiar from the temple commentaries.[11]

No previous Christian author devoted the same degree of sustained focus to the image as Bede did; unsurprisingly, his works on the topic were to prove influential in England and throughout Europe long after his own time.[12] His

---

[8] Modern Bibles tend to treat Ezra and Nehemiah as two books, but in the Vulgate they form a single book: Esdras.

[9] *Hom.*, II.24, p. 359 'ipsi qui in nomine domini conuenimus... templum eius et appellemur et simus'; trans. Martin and Hurst, II, p. 242.

[10] *Luc.*, pp. 424–5; *Apoc.*, p. 283; see Ch. 8 within this volume, 'Diachronic overview', pp. 183–4.

[11] *Gen.*, pp. 157–62.

[12] Iain M. Douglas, 'Bede's *De Templo* and the Commentary on Samuel and Kings by Claudius of Turin', in *Famulus Christi: Essays in Commemoration of the Thirteenth Centenary*

On the Tabernacle and *On the Temple* inaugurated a new genre of themed
exegetical treatises, focusing on biblical structures, which reached its apogee in
the twelfth century.[13] The *Glossa Ordinaria*—the great collated biblical commentary that dominated the twelfth century—reveals the influence of Bede's
writings on medieval views of the temple. They provided most of the *Glossa's*
material on the building of the tabernacle and Solomon's temple and
all of the material on Ezra and Nehemiah and the account of the rebuilding
of the temple.[14]

The importance of Bede's work on the temple image in particular mirrored
the influence of his exegesis in general.[15] Shortly after his death his monastery
of Wearmouth-Jarrow already had to respond to a significant demand for
Bede's writings, coming especially from the Anglo-Saxon missionaries at work
in continental Europe.[16] The activity of these figures, and that of his fellow
Northumbrian Alcuin (*c*.740–804), rapidly made Bede a major intellectual
influence on the Carolingian renaissance, which in turn fuelled his importance
in later Anglo-Saxon England.[17] Bede's exegesis remained popular up until the
birth of Scholasticism and beyond, until well after the Reformation—
unsurprisingly given that he was accorded patristic status.[18] Not only did
Bede himself feel connected with the Church Fathers, but the Carolingian

---

of the Birth of the Venerable Bede, ed. Gerald Bonner (London, 1976), pp. 325–33; Valery
V. Petroff, 'The *De Templo* of Bede as the Source of an Ideal Temple Description in Eriugena's
Aulae Siderae', *Recherches de théologie et philosophie médiévales* 65 (1998), pp. 97–106; Joanna
Kramer, '"Ðu eart se weallstan": Architectural Metaphor and Christological Imagery in the Old
English *Christ I* and the Book of Kells', in *Source of Wisdom: Old English and Early Medieval
Latin Studies in Honour of Thomas D. Hill*, eds Charles D. Wright et al. (Toronto, 2007),
pp. 90–112. For the influence of *On the Tabernacle* and *On the Temple*: Arthur G. Holder,
'Bede's Commentaries on the Tabernacle and the Temple' (PhD dissertation, Duke University,
1987), pp. 141–8.

[13] Henri de Lubac, *Exégèse médiévale: les quatres sens de l'Écriture*, 2 parts in 4 vols (Paris,
1959–64), II.1, p. 406.

[14] Lesley Smith, *The* Glossa Ordinaria: *The Making of a Medieval Bible Commentary* (Leiden,
2009), pp. 45, 47, 55, 80–81.

[15] Dorothy Whitelock, *After Bede*, Jarrow Lecture (Jarrow, 1960); J. E. Cross, 'Bede's Influence
at Home and Abroad: An Introduction', in *Beda Venerabilis: Historian, Monk & Northumbrian*,
eds L. A. J. R. Houwen and A. A. MacDonald (Groningen, 1996), pp. 17–29; Brown, *Companion*,
pp. 117–34.

[16] M. Tangl (ed.), *Die Briefe des Heiligen Bonifatius und Lullus*, MGH Epistolae Selectae
1, 75–6 pp. 156–9; 91 pp. 206–8; 116 pp. 250–52; 125–7 pp. 262–5; Malcolm Parkes,
The Scriptorium of Wearmouth-Jarrow, Jarrow Lecture (Jarrow, 1982), pp. 12–16.

[17] Joyce Hill, *Bede and the Benedictine Reform*, Jarrow Lecture (Jarrow, 1998); David Rollason, *Bede and Germany*, Jarrow Lecture (Jarrow, 2001); Joshua A. Westgard, 'Bede and the
Continent in the Carolingian Age and Beyond', and Sharon M. Rowley, 'Bede in later Anglo-
Saxon England', both in *Cambridge Companion*, ed. DeGregorio, pp. 201–15 and 216–28,
respectively.

[18] Joyce Hill, 'Carolingian Perspectives on the Authority of Bede', in *Innovation and Tradition in the Writings of the Venerable Bede*, ed. Scott DeGregorio (Morgantown WV, 2006),
pp. 227–49; Richard W. Pfaff, 'Bede Among the Fathers? The Evidence from Liturgical Commemoration', *Studia Patristica* 28 (1993), pp. 225–9.

Council of Aachen named him in 836 as the 'venerable and admirable teacher of modern times', effectively recognizing him as a Father of the Church.[19] When Charlemagne (742–814) ordered the Lombard scholar Paul the Deacon (*c.*720–99) to compile a homiliary from the words of the Catholic Fathers, he derived almost a quarter of his material from Bede's writings—more than from any other source.[20] The Middle Ages paid its supreme compliment to Bede: dozens of works which he never actually wrote circulated under his name. Scientific works proved especially prone to gain authority from ascription to him, but the fact that penitentials and large quantities of exegesis shared the same fate indicates Bede's status as a major authority.[21]

No one idea or image can encapsulate everything worth understanding about a writer of such stature. But the broad and substantially original coverage of the temple image in Bede's corpus makes it perhaps the best entrance into his world view. Bede saw the wandering tabernacle and the various permutations of the temple in Jerusalem as closely related, all essentially the same house of God.[22] These Jewish holy sites also contained elaborately described altars and decorations, and priests dressed in distinctive vestments performing cult acts for the worship of God. This matrix of interlinking images cannot be separated from the idea of the temple complex; thus I use the phrase 'temple image' in this broader sense, rather than simply referring to the stones and mortar of a single building. This image combined the static architecture of the temple with the dynamic ritual of its priests, thus allowing Bede to speak about both the eternal reality of the Church and the lived experience of its members through a single divinely sanctioned image.

Addressing such a wide subject in a large body of literature, this study, while not claiming to be exhaustive, provides an extensive tour of Bede's thinking on the temple. I have chosen a thematic structure (focusing on possible interpretations of the temple image) which moves from the macrocosm of the temple as history and cosmos, through the temple as Christ and his body the Church, to the microcosm of the temple as individual. The impossibility of providing a convincing chronology for the whole corpus of Bede's works has led me to eschew a chronological structure—although a diachronic overview of Bede's use of the temple image does appear in the final chapter. That

---

[19] *Concilia Aevi Karolini I*, ed. A. Werminghoff, MGH Legum Sectio 3 Concilia 2, p. 759. For Bede's perspective: Jan Davidse, 'The Sense of History in the Works of the Venerable Bede', *Studi Medievali* 23 (1982), pp. 647–95, at 654–6; Roger Ray, 'Who Did Bede Think He Was?', in *Innovation and Tradition*, ed. DeGregorio, pp. 11–35.

[20] Cyril Smetana, 'Paul the Deacon's Patristic Anthology', in *The Old English Homily & its Backgrounds*, eds Paul E. Szarmach and Bernard F. Huppé (Albany NY, 1978), pp. 75–97, at 79–80.

[21] Michael Gorman, 'The Canon of Bede's Works and the World of Ps. Bede', *RB* 111 (2001), pp. 399–445; Charles W. Jones, *Bedae Pseudepigrapha: Scientific Writings Falsely Attributed to Bede* (Ithaca NY, 1939); Allen J. Frantzen, 'The Penitentials Attributed to Bede', *Speculum* 58 (1983), pp. 573–97.

[22] See Ch. 3 within this volume, 'The house made by human hands', pp. 47–9.

overview provides important clues as to the reasons for Bede's interest in the temple image, but given the repetitive nature of the monk's corpus, to provide a detailed examination of each work in turn would be tedious, even if possible. I follow the example of other recent synthetic studies of Bede's writings in pursuing a thematic approach while remaining sensitive to issues of chronology[23]—an approach made necessary by the free and open-ended nature of Bede's exegesis.[24]

Bede's methodology opened up rather than limited possible meanings. Since this study explores the use to which Bede put the image of the temple, one must start by acknowledging that he did not interpret that image in any one single way. Depending on the circumstances in which he discussed it, the temple could mean any of a host of different things. A thematic approach, therefore, succeeds in giving a sense of the multiplicity of meanings and ideas Bede explored through the temple. I have chosen the sequence employed (moving from macrocosm to microcosm) more for its own inner logic than to imply any hierarchy of meaning in Bede's mind. Although I will draw out common threads that link different interpretations of the temple, seeking to sketch out the world view which underpins Bede's work, to start from the assumption that one single interpretation explains all of his approaches to the temple image would simply mislead the reader.

Chasing one of Bede's favourite images through its plurality of interpretations means that we can gain important insights into numerous aspects of his thought—from his comparatively well-studied ecclesiology to his almost completely neglected Christology.[25] Scholars have recognized the wide significance of the temple throughout Bede's corpus and my work depends to a great extent on that completed previously by scholars such as Arthur Holder, Jennifer O'Reilly, and Scott DeGregorio.[26] But as the first thematic synthesis of Bede's

---

[23] E.g. Peter Darby, *Bede and the End of Time* (Farnham, 2012); Giovanni Caputa, *Il Sacerdozio dei Fedeli secondo San Beda: un itinerario di maturità cristiana* (Vatican City, 2002).

[24] See Ch. 2 within this volume, 'The intellectual context at Wearmouth-Jarrow', pp. 28–9.

[25] Surveys of Bede's ecclesiology: Johannes Beumer, 'Das Kirchenbild in den Schriftkommentaren Bedas des Ehrwürdigen', *Scholastik* 28 (1958), pp. 40–56; Sarah Foot, *Bede's Church*, Jarrow Lecture 2012 (Jarrow, 2013). I know of no overview of Bede's ideas on Christ, but recent work has made some contributions: e.g. Arthur G. Holder, 'The Feminine Christ in Bede's Biblical Commentaries', in *Bède le Vénérable entre tradition et postérité: The Venerable Bede. Tradition and Posterity*, eds Stéphane Lebecq et al. (Lille, 2005), pp. 109–18.

[26] E.g. Arthur G. Holder, 'New Treasures and Old in Bede's "De Tabernaculo" and "De Templo"', *RB* 99 (1989), pp. 237–49; Arthur G. Holder, 'Allegory and History in Bede's Interpretation of Sacred Architecture', *American Benedictine Review* 40 (1989), pp. 115–31; Arthur G. Holder, 'The Venerable Bede on the Mysteries of Our Salvation', *American Benedictine Review* 421 (1991), pp. 140–62. Jennifer O'Reilly, 'Introduction', in *Bede: On the Temple*, trans. Seán Connolly (Liverpool, 1995), pp. xxvii–lv; Jennifer O'Reilly, 'The Library of Scripture: Views from Vivarium and Wearmouth-Jarrow', in *New Offerings, Ancient Treasures: Studies in Medieval Art for George Henderson*, eds Paul Binski and William Noel (Stroud, 2001), pp. 3–39; Jennifer O'Reilly, 'The Multitude of Isles and the Corner-stone: Topography, Exegesis, and the Identity of the *Angli* in Bede's *Historia Ecclesiastica*', in *Anglo-Saxon Traces*, eds Jane Roberts

use of the temple image this study makes an important new contribution. Across many scriptural commentaries Bede would often repeat or contradict himself; only the holistic approach adopted here allows us to see which of the writer's statements were exceptional and which part of Bede's long-term world view. We might understand Bede's condemnation of constructing rich churches differently, for example, when aware that he also interpreted the temple as symbolizing the church building.[27]

I argue, therefore, that Bede's temple is a multifaceted image which, nonetheless, teaches us much about the structure of Bede's thought. Across different texts the temple image reveals the consistent importance of unity to Bede's world view and the theological importance of Christ as the guarantor and enabler of that unity. Bede's use of the temple does not provide access to the purely personal thinking of one mind, however exceptional. His approach to the image arose from a long-standing Christian tradition and more importantly, I argue, an immediate environment of monastic discourse and exegetical discussion. In other words, context matters. I consistently aim to set Bede's statements in their context, especially, though not exclusively that at Wearmouth-Jarrow.

Luckily we possess a contemporary representation of the temple image which we can compare with Bede's interpretation. The Bible created at Wearmouth-Jarrow during Bede's own lifetime, known as the Codex Amiatinus, contains, amongst other illuminations, a magnificent image of the tabernacle in the desert on one bifolium.[28] This provides important evidence for interest in and engagement with the temple image in the religious community to which Bede belonged. Reading Bede's work in relationship with the codex helps us to understand something of the factors forming Bede's thought on the temple. By offering a rare insight into the thought world of Wearmouth-Jarrow which does not come from the pen of the monastery's most famous member, the codex allows us to catch glimpses of the ways in which communal interpretation and ideology may have influenced Bede—thus potentially affecting our understanding of Bede as an author and an individual.

The importance of contextualizing Bede's writings with reference to the books and artefacts he knew, the events and institutions that shaped him, arises from the fact that, in truth, we know very little about Bede the man.[29] Central to our knowledge is that he entered Wearmouth-Jarrow at the age of

---

and Leslie Webster (Tempe AZ, 2011), pp. 201–27. Scott DeGregorio, '"Nostrorum socordiam temporum": the Reforming Impulse of Bede's Later Exegesis', *EME* 11 (2002), pp. 107–22; Scott DeGregorio, 'Bede's *In Ezram et Neemiam* and the Reform of the Northumbrian Church', *Speculum* 79 (2004), pp. 1–25.

[27] See Ch. 8 within this volume.

[28] Florence, Biblioteca Medicea Laurenziana, MS Amiatino 1, fols IIv–IIIr (Fig. 1). For a full discussion of the codex with bibliography see Ch. 4 within this volume, 'The Codex Amiatinus'.

[29] N. J. Higham, *(Re-)Reading Bede: The Ecclesiastical History in Context* (London, 2006), pp. 6–20.

seven and spent the rest of his life (about fifty-five years) there. If we hope to
understand Bede as a thinker we can never afford to forget the communal and
religious environment in which he lived. The importance of seeing Bede in a
communal context arises from the fact that the literature concerning him has
often been shaped by the ideal of the heroic individual, the genius, the 'great
man'. Research on Bede presents something of a paradox—although the
subject of a long and distinguished tradition of English-language scholarship,
Bede has very rarely been studied as a religious thinker until quite recently.[30]
The scholar who writes about Bede as an exegete both inherits a large body of
literature and simultaneously works in a relatively recent area of research.

HISTORIOGRAPHICAL OVERVIEW

Within the limits of this introduction a full analysis of the long tradition of
writing about Bede cannot be undertaken. I have, consequently, chosen to
focus on two particular themes in the modern historiography of Bede and
to trace their development over the past century or so. These are: the image of
Bede the man; and the scholarly engagement with the religious aspects of
Bede's writings, that is, with Bede as a theologian and exegete. Both provide
particularly important and relevant backgrounds to this work.

The link between the study of Bede's work and the celebration of a certain
image of Bede the man has long existed, and its longevity reveals the power of
many ideas concerning Bede's personality. The influence of Charles Plummer,
Bede's first great modern editor and commentator, remains particularly important for framing, at the dawn of the twentieth century, how the monk came
to be interpreted. A wide and sensitive reader of Bede's corpus, Plummer was
convinced that his reading had allowed him an insight into the author's
nature.[31] He derived a clear picture of a humble, pious, hard-working, sens-
ible, doggedly English figure: 'the very model of the saintly scholar-priest; a
type in which the English Church has never, thank God, been deficient'.[32] In
part Plummer may have had grounds for seeing Bede's writings as a window
on the author's personality; but those writings also reflected an awful lot of
Plummer and his contemporary interests back at him. His keenness for the
virtue of intellectual humility, something, it appears, that the chaplain of an
Oxford college especially needed to emphasize, seems to explain his conviction
that it was central to Bede's nature.[33]

---

[30] Higham, *(Re-)Reading Bede*, pp. 32–40.
[31] Charles Plummer, *Venerabilis Baedae Opera Historica*, 2 vols (Oxford, 1896), I, p. iii.
[32] Plummer, *Opera Historica*, I, pp. lxxviii–lxxix.
[33] Plummer, *Opera Historica*, I, p. lxvi.

This image of Bede, however, with the related certainty that the modern scholar could know Bede as a individual, did not belong to Charles Plummer alone. It dominated scholarship on Bede in the early twentieth century and has had a long influence until very recently. This image of the man towered over his works, even though it looks, retrospectively, like nothing more than the personification of the virtues (and sometimes vices) associated with the devout Christian, the scholar, and the Englishman.[34] Bede was brilliant, but unoriginal, deeply religious, but with the historian's commitment to truth. This image, that of a man who embodied timeless qualities, meant that historians frequently presented Bede as at one remove from his own barbarous age. The great power of this vision can be seen from the fact that historians, including those not themselves Bede experts, could speak of him with absolute certainty of understanding him as a person; Benedicta Ward thought that 'it is possible to know Bede more intimately than any other man of his time'.[35]

The dominant role of the study of Bede's historical writings in the earlier twentieth century substantially explains this focus on his exceptionalism and timelessness. Increased interest in and access to his more clearly religious writings (especially with the publication of new critical editions from the 1950s onwards) had an effect on this.[36] The institution of the Jarrow Lecture in 1958, held annually on the Friday closest to the Feast of St Bede, indicates the great respect for Bede the saintly scholar. But the lecture series helped to keep interest in Bede fresh and opened up the study of new areas in Bedan studies, with Gerald Bonner giving the first lecture on Bede's exegesis in 1966.[37] This fitted into a process of putting Bede in increasingly wider contexts (not just the histories, but the exegesis, not just England, but all of Europe), noticeable also in the volume produced to commemorate the thirteen-hundredth anniversary of his birth.[38]

Increased contextualization meant that the *Ecclesiastical History*'s failure always to reflect reality accurately became increasingly evident, along with the mismatch between much in Bede's thought and the rest of Anglo-Saxon culture. As a result even when a highly sympathetic reader of Bede came to write a major study of Christianity in early Anglo-Saxon England in the 1970s,

---

[34] E.g. Herbert Hensley Henson, 'Introduction', in *Bede: His Life, Times, and Writings*, ed. A. Hamilton Thompson (Oxford, 1935), pp. xiii–xvi, at xiv.

[35] Ward, *Venerable Bede*, p. 2. See David Knowles, *Saints and Scholars: Twenty-five Medieval Portraits* (Cambridge, 1962), pp. 12–18; R. W. Southern, *Medieval Humanism and Other Studies* (Oxford, 1970), pp. 1–8.

[36] Plummer, unusually, had read all of Bede's works and stressed the importance of the theology in understanding the history: *Opera Historica*, I, p. ii.

[37] The Jarrow Lectures for 1958–1993 are brought together in Michael Lapidge (ed.), *Bede and His World*, 2 vols (Aldershot, 1994), but I cite all lectures individually.

[38] Gerald Bonner, 'Introduction', in *Famulus Christi*, ed. Bonner, pp. 1–4; Peter Brown, 'What's in a name?', <http://www.ocla.ox.ac.uk/pdf/brown_what_in_name.pdf> pp. 10–11 [accessed 10 April 2013].

he saw the monk as primarily a religious writer, aiming to build up the Church, rather than straightforwardly to record truth.[39] A new image of Bede the man was forged, that of Bede as an idealist—an interpretation perhaps associated with Patrick Wormald above all.[40] This perspective saw Bede as an individual opposed to the general culture of his own day; driven by a devotion to Christianity, the monk had striven to change a materialist society according to a higher set of values. Bede was understood to have sought to reshape reality, rather than to describe it. Alan Thacker built on this tradition in revealing the reformist impulses behind much of Bede's work.[41]

This increased sensitivity to the degree to which Bede differed from modern historians combined with general changes in scholarly taste to emphasize the importance of Bede as a creative author. The linguistic turn and postmodern mood of the 1980s informed Walter Goffart's controversial *The Narrators of Barbarian History*.[42] Goffart placed Bede's historical literature within the context of other contemporary Northumbrian writings and saw these works as part of a textual battle in a wider war involving Church politics of the time. Few genuinely contested the conclusion that Bede as a historian had sometimes misled; but Goffart's image of the man proved divisive—in this case the image of a self-consciously political and partisan historian. Many of the subsequent debates over Goffart's thesis orbited around the question of whether Bede was worldly or idealistic. Both sides actually agreed (much more than they seem to have realized) on the essential point that Bede could not always be trusted—the question remained whether politics or religion dominated his outlook.[43] Interestingly, the debate often shifted to one concerning Bede's personal morality: whether he should be seen as 'Machiavellian' or 'innocent'.[44]

---

[39] Henry Mayr-Harting, *The Coming of Christianity to Anglo-Saxon England*, 3rd ed. (London, 1991; 1st ed. 1972). The work of James Campbell was also important in exploring the purposes and flaws of the *Ecclesiastical History*: James Campbell, *Essays in Anglo-Saxon History* (London, 1986), pp. 1–84.

[40] The most important expression of Wormald's interpretation probably appears in his 1978 'Bede, *Beowulf* and the Conversion of the Anglo-Saxon Aristocracy', repr. in *The Times of Bede*, ed. Stephen Baxter (Oxford, 2006), pp. 30–105.

[41] Alan Thacker, 'Bede's Ideal of Reform', in *Ideal and Reality in Frankish and Anglo-Saxon Society: Studies presented to J. M. Wallace-Hadrill*, eds Patrick Wormald et al. (Oxford, 1983), pp. 130–53.

[42] Walter Goffart, *The Narrators of Barbarian History (A.D. 550–800): Jordanes, Gregory of Tours, Bede and Paul the Deacon*, 2nd ed. (Notre Dame IN, 2005), with comments on the first edition's (1988) reception at pp. xxvii–xxviii.

[43] Henry Mayr-Harting, 'Bede's Patristic Thinking as an Historian', in *Historiographie im frühen Mittelalter*, eds A. Scharer and G. Scheibelreiter (Vienna, 1994), pp. 367–74; Walter Goffart, 'Bede's History in a Harsher Climate', in *Innovation and Tradition*, ed. DeGregorio, pp. 203–26.

[44] Mayr-Harting, 'Patristic Thinking', p. 373; Goffart, 'Harsher Climate', p. 207.

Goffart based his approach entirely on reading Bede's historical works—the reluctance to set them in the context of the larger, especially exegetical corpus now appears rather old-fashioned. At the same time, the image of Bede as idealist tended to overemphasize his distance from contemporary society. The recent flourishing of scholarship on Bede has tended towards integrating both approaches: portraying Bede as a devout Christian who cared about the realities of contemporary affairs, and all of whose work (exegesis and history) shared a common aim of promoting ecclesiastical reform.[45] The other main thrust of contemporary Bedan studies emphasizes the originality of his work. Close study of the scriptural commentaries since the 1980s has allowed the old belief in Bede's lack of originality to be cast aside and given new life to the even older respect for Bede as an exceptional writer. The new Bede is more original and more socially engaged than the old, but he remains a genius.[46]

Much, therefore, has changed in the representation of Bede since the days of Charles Plummer, but a common thread running throughout the period has assigned great importance to Bede as an individual. Of course, recent studies do a much better job of locating Bede in his wider world than those of the past. In particular there has been especially important work on Wearmouth and Jarrow as monastic institutions in the past few years, which opens the way for a reappraisal of the community there.[47] However, the increased focus on Bede as an innovator has also fed the traditional bias towards thinking of him as exceptional. The general belief that his works give access to Bede himself, his insights and ideas, has in fact grown with the recent emphasis on originality. Previous scholarship has investigated the possibility that the *Ecclesiastical History* represents something other than Bede's unalloyed personal opinion, but little comparable analysis of the exegesis exists.[48] The question of whether the uses of the temple image that we find in his writings should be entirely ascribed to Bede alone is one to which this study returns on a number of occasions.

From the Reformation onwards the most striking use of Bede as a religious writer has been to promote the claims of one or other Christian confession.[49]

---

[45] This viewpoint is not simply a post-Goffart synthesis, however, as its origins lie in Thacker, 'Ideal of Reform'.

[46] Scott DeGregorio, 'Introduction: The New Bede', in *Innovation and Tradition*, ed. DeGregorio, pp. 1–10.

[47] Christopher Grocock and I. N. Wood, *Abbots of Wearmouth and Jarrow* (Oxford, 2013), pp. xiii–lxiv.

[48] Higham, *(Re-)Reading Bede*, pp. 194–7; D. P. Kirby, 'King Ceolwulf of Northumbria and the *Historia Ecclesiastica*', *Studia Celtica* 14–15 (1979–80), pp. 168–73. But see D. P. Kirby, *Bede's Historia Ecclesiastica Gentis Anglorum: Its Contemporary Setting*, Jarrow Lecture (Jarrow, 1992), which concludes (p. 15) that the *Ecclesiastical History* is Bede's personal 'idiosyncratic' take on Anglo-Saxon history.

[49] John William Houghton, 'St. Bede among the Controversialists: A Survey', *American Benedictine Review* 50 (1999), pp. 397–422.

Even into the twentieth century Bede was used to establish the inherently Roman Catholic or Anglican nature of early English Christianity. Naturally the grounds for contemporary confessional debates tended to dominate such uses of his writings, sometimes obscuring his own theological interests. Bedan studies have always attracted a large number of scholars in religious communities or holy orders—and it would be exceptionally foolish to deny the value of many of these scholars' contributions. However, even as late as the 1940s and the publication of the first major study of his religious thought, a present-centred confessional viewpoint still framed the approach to Bede's theological writings.[50] Indeed for many scholars contemporary judgements led them to ignore the most explicitly religious writings in the Bedan corpus.

The allegorical method of exegesis fell out of fashion in nineteenth- and early twentieth-century scriptural commentary; scholars often dismissed Bede's commentaries as dull, silly even, and not worthy of serious study. They sought to avoid wasting time on works for which they had so little sympathy.[51] Even the classic English-language monograph on medieval biblical studies skipped over the early Middle Ages as quickly as possible; Beryl Smalley preferred to focus on the origins of the modern, text-critical study of the Bible from the twelfth century onwards.[52] The overwhelming interest in Bede's historical writings exacerbated this bias against the study of his exegesis. If Bede as a theologian had nothing to contribute to the present day, as an historian scholars deemed him to be proto-modern. Such a narrow focus meant that Bede's use of miracle stories disturbingly contradicted historians' image of him as a historical rather than religious thinker.[53]

Protestant attitudes to scriptural study may have partially inspired the antipathy to allegorical exegesis amongst Anglophone scholars. Certainly the study of Bede as a theologian benefited from the increased interest in patristic and early medieval theology driven initially by continental Roman Catholic

---

[50] Mary Thomas Aquinas Carroll, *The Venerable Bede: His Spiritual Teachings* (Washington DC, 1946), framed a study of Bede's theological corpus in terms of the scholastic tradition of systematic theology: see pp. 107–31 for her contribution to the long-running confessional debate over whether Bede believed in transubstantiation.

[51] Claude Jenkins, 'Bede as Exegete and Theologian', in *Life, Times and Writings*, ed. Thompson, pp. 152–200.

[52] Beryl Smalley, *The Study of the Bible in the Middle Ages*, 3rd ed. (Oxford, 1983), pp. 1–36. In this 3rd ed. Smalley acknowledged the limitations of her original (1940) approach: p. viii. Glenn W. Olsen, 'From Bede to the Anglo-Saxon Presence in the Carolingian Empire', *Settimane di studio del Centro italiano di studi sull'alto medioevo* 32 (1984), pp. 305–82, at 330–34, contrasts Smalley critically with Lubac, *Exégèse médiévale*.

[53] Hence the large bibliography on Bede and the miraculous: Bertram Colgrave, 'Bede's Miracle Stories', in *Life, Times and Writings*, ed. Thompson, pp. 201–29; Benedicta Ward, 'Miracles and History: A Reconsideration of the Miracle Stories used by Bede', in *Famulus Christi*, ed. Bonner, pp. 70–6; William D. McCready, *Miracles and the Venerable Bede* (Toronto, 1994).

writers such as Henri de Lubac, Jean Daniélou, and Jean Leclercq.[54] The latter's work, especially, generated much scholarly interest in a specifically monastic spirituality, centred on the liturgy of the Divine Office and *lectio divina*.[55] Such developments throughout the middle decades of the twentieth century combined with the growth of the image of Bede as an idealist, already outlined, to create a new interest in Bede's exegetical and religious writings. Frequently non-British scholars showed the greatest tendency to study Bede for his theology; British academics remained likely to use the exegesis as a way of helping them understand Bede as a historian.[56]

Not that such an approach should be denigrated. Scholars such as Henry Mayr-Harting and Roger Ray, by asserting the links between the *Ecclesiastical History* and Bede's commentaries, laid the groundwork for a really serious study of Bede's work as an integrated whole.[57] By the 1980s usable critical editions of the majority of Bede's exegesis became available for the first time effectively, which resulted in a flourishing in the study of these texts. The first major studies of Bede's use of the temple image appeared in this context. Arthur Holder shone light on the sources and themes of *On the Tabernacle* and *On the Temple*, exploring Bede's pastoral theology in particular.[58] Jennifer O'Reilly built on Mayr-Harting's initial contribution by exploring the rich patristic underpinning of Bede's historical work, revealing how the themes of the *Ecclesiastical History* and *On the Temple* overlap.[59] Both these contributions informed Scott DeGregorio's study of *On Ezra and Nehemiah* as a commentary reflective of the pastoral and reforming themes significant in Bede's later works.[60] The attempt to understand the monk's different writings as an integrated whole clearly has provided an important context for all this work on his exegesis.

My work, with its aim of undertaking a synthetic study of a particular scriptural image across Bede's work, fits into this current trend in the historiography. Much of the work of the past two decades has been devoted to

---

[54] E.g. Lubac, *Exégèse médiévale*; Jean Daniélou, *From Shadows to Reality: Studies in the Biblical Typology of the Fathers*, trans. Wulstan Hibberd (London, 1960).

[55] Esp. Jean Leclercq, *The Love of Learning and the Desire for God: A Study of Monastic Culture*, trans. Catherine Misrahi, 3rd ed. (New York, 1982).

[56] Compare, for example, Claudio Leonardi, 'Il Venerabile Beda e la Cultura del Secolo VIII', *Settimane di studio del Centro italiano di studi sull'alto medioevo* 20 (1973), pp. 603–58, with Judith McClure, 'Bede's Old Testament Kings', in *Ideal and Reality*, eds Wormald et al., pp. 76–98.

[57] Mayr-Harting, 'Patristic Thinking'; Mayr-Harting, *The Venerable Bede, The Rule of St Benedict, and Social Class*, Jarrow Lecture (Jarrow, 1976); Roger D. Ray, 'Bede, the Exegete, as Historian', in *Famulus Christi*, ed. Bonner, pp. 125–40; Roger D. Ray, 'What do we know about Bede's Commentaries?', *Recherches de Théologie ancienne et médiévale* 49 (1982), pp. 5–20.

[58] Holder, 'Commentaries on the Tabernacle and the Temple'.

[59] O'Reilly, 'Introduction', esp. pp. xxxiv–xxxix.

[60] DeGregorio, 'Reforming Impulse', pp. 113–21; DeGregorio, 'Reform of the Northumbrian Church'.

elucidating individual commentaries—necessary work considering the substantial neglect of Bede's religious works up until quite recently. But that does mean that scholars have undertaken few large-scale studies of any single idea in Bede's corpus. This work attempts to put the theory of the integrity of that corpus into practice. We must also acknowledge that much work still remains to be done on many aspects of Bede's theology. The increased interest in religion, arising from the influence of anthropology and cultural history that has marked late antique studies, amongst many other historical fields, has influenced early medievalists. But while late antiquity (broadly speaking, the third to the sixth centuries) possesses a rich literature on patristic theology, early medieval religion still requires much attention. In examining Christology and ecclesiology as part of this study, I focus on theological issues that mattered just as much to Bede as they did to the early Church Fathers.

BEDE'S WORLD

Bede lived in a world very different from that of the Fathers. With an unbroken line of Christian kings only beginning in 634 at the accession of Oswald, Northumbria had been converted comparatively recently and the process probably continued for some time after that.[61] Some scholars have traditionally looked for signs of pagan survivals into the eighth century and have portrayed the process of Christianization as shallow and ineffective in changing the lives of the masses.[62] But we should not see everything pre-Christian as necessarily anti-Christian; Christianity adapted in the face of new cultures just as much as it forced cultures to adapt to it (Roman missionaries to the Anglo-Saxons taking a noticeably syncretic approach), but adaptation does not equate to dilution.[63] Certainly some of the clergy, Bede among them, were not slow to condemn practices that fell outside their vision of correct Christianity. But no real evidence exists to suggest that the people who participated in such practices considered themselves anything other than Christian.[64]

---

[61] Mayr-Harting, *Coming of Christianity*, remains perhaps the most readable account of the conversion of the Anglo-Saxons. For more recent interpretations, from different points of view: N. J. Higham, *The Convert Kings: Power and Religious Affiliation in early Anglo-Saxon England* (Manchester, 1997); Marilyn Dunn, *The Christianization of the Anglo-Saxons c.597–c.700: Discourses of Life, Death and Afterlife* (London, 2009).

[62] E.g. Rosalind Hill, 'Bede and the Boors', in *Famulus Christi*, ed. Bonner, pp. 93–105.

[63] I am greatly influenced by R. A. Markus, *The End of Ancient Christianity* (Cambridge, 1990), pp. 1–17; see also James C. Russell, *The Germanization of Early Medieval Christianity* (Oxford, 1994).

[64] John Blair, *The Church in Anglo-Saxon Society* (Oxford, 2005), pp. 166–81; Helen Foxhall Forbes, *Heaven and Earth in Anglo-Saxon England: Theology and Society in an Age of Faith* (Farnham, 2013), p. 57.

While organized polytheism probably presented no living threat to the Church during the lifetime of Bede, the level of catechetical instruction no doubt varied widely throughout the Northumbrian countryside and then, as now, the Church would have contained a wide diversity of attitudes to both belief and practice. People probably accessed the reality of Christianity in a variety of ways, mirrored in the varying interpretations of modern historians. For some, standing crosses might have represented displays of patristic learning, for others signs of wealth and power, and for yet others they could have had supernatural powers.[65] In this way, serving a diversity of needs and interests, Christianity came to be rooted in Northumbrian society. The evidence indeed suggests that the Anglo-Saxon elites keenly embraced the exotic new religion which had come to them from the wider world, and made it work for them within their own context, this process of adaptation beginning well before formal conversion to Christianity in many cases.[66]

The major growth of monasticism that marked Bede's own lifetime provides one measure of the zeal with which the aristocratic rulers of Northumbria, like many of the other Anglo-Saxon kingdoms, took to Christianity. The world of religious communities that Bede and his contemporaries inhabited was financed by noble and royal wealth. Investing in such communities had many advantages for the aristocracy. Monasteries combined devotional and commemorative functions with an innovative legal status, whereby landed resources could be retained for eternity—at least in theory.[67] As in Frankia and Ireland, monasticism in late seventh-century Anglo-Saxon England came to further the prestige and spiritual and material wealth of noble families.[68] Ruling dynasties, never sure of their worldly permanence, tried to gain some part of the sacred and the eternal through monasteries designed for burial and

---

[65] Paul Meyvaert, 'A New Perspective on the Ruthwell Cross: Ecclesia and Vita Monastica', in *The Ruthwell Cross: Papers from the Colloquium sponsored by the Index of Christian Art, Princeton University, 8 December 1989*, ed. Brendan Cassidy (Princeton NJ, 1992), pp. 95–166; Fred Orton and Ian Wood with Clare A. Lees, *Fragments of History: Rethinking the Ruthwell and Bewcastle Monuments* (Manchester, 2007), esp. p. 202; Carol Neuman de Vegvar, 'Converting the Anglo-Saxon Landscape: Crosses and their Audiences' in *Text, Image, Interpretation: Studies in Anglo-Saxon Literature and its Insular Context in Honour of Eamonn Ó Carragáin*, eds Alastair Minnis and Jane Roberts (Turnhout, 2007), pp. 407–29.

[66] Peter Brown, *The Rise of Western Christendom: Triumph and Diversity, A.D. 200–1000*, 2nd ed. (Oxford, 2003), pp. 340–44; Blair, *Anglo-Saxon Society*, pp. 51–7.

[67] For the variety of reasons for founding a religious house: Sarah Foot, *Monastic Life in Anglo-Saxon England, c.600–900* (Cambridge, 2006), pp. 77–87. Much work has been done on the elite engagement with Northumbrian monasticism, especially in relation to land tenure: e.g. Patrick Wormald, 'Bede and the Conversion of England: The Charter Evidence', repr. in *Times of Bede*, ed. Baxter, pp. 135–66; Ian Wood, 'Monasteries and the Geography of Power in the Age of Bede', *Northern History* 45 (2008), pp. 11–25.

[68] Blair, *Anglo-Saxon Society*, pp. 84–91; Brown, *Western Christendom*, pp. 252–5; Richard Sharpe, 'Some Problems concerning the Organization of the Church in Early Medieval Ireland', *Peritia* 3 (1984), pp. 230–70, esp. 258–9, 263–5.

memorial purposes. We see this most clearly perhaps in those establishments, containing both male and female religious, ruled over by princess-abbesses.[69]

As a consequence of this material dependence on the aristocracy, Northumbrian religious communities seem to have been primarily aristocratic in terms of personnel and culture. Elite pastimes, including the pleasures of the table and the hunt, proved popular in these societies.[70] Monastic egalitarianism had to deal with patrician pride;[71] in fact there is no recorded senior Northumbrian cleric or religious for whom peasant birth can be proved, although Anglo-Saxon monasteries probably contained many servants and slaves.[72] The difficulty of differentiating religious and secular households of the time from the archaeological evidence alone proves the similarities between them.[73] One reason why monasticism proved so amenable to Anglo-Saxon culture may well have been the similarities between it and the close-knit, single-sex communities in which the native warrior elite spent their youth.[74] However, we should not assume that secular and religious households differed not at all; even the inhabitants of the worldliest establishments seem to have recognized the existence of a distinctive monastic way of life.[75]

Historians have often distinguished Bede's Wearmouth-Jarrow from the mass of such aristocratic establishments. Certainly the evidence suggests that it came much closer to an ideal of Benedictine piety than most Northumbrian houses.[76] Nonetheless, we should consider whether, at the time, distinguishing Wearmouth-Jarrow materially from a family-based religious community may have proved difficult.[77] Its founder Benedict Biscop (*c*.628–89) was noble-born and many of his assistants and successors seem to have come from amongst his kin; there is even a possibility that Bede himself was a relative.[78] While the

[69] Barbara Yorke, *Nunneries and the Anglo-Saxon Royal Houses* (London, 2003). For a discussion of female monasticism at this time more generally: Sarah Foot, *Veiled Women. Volume I: The Disappearance of Nuns from Anglo-Saxon England* (Aldershot, 2000), pp. 35–60.

[70] Foot, *Monastic Life*, pp. 236–46; James Campbell, 'Elements in the Background to the Life of St Cuthbert and his Early Cult', in *St Cuthbert, His Cult and His Community until AD 1200*, eds Gerald Bonner et al. (Woodbridge, 1989), pp. 3–19; Wormald, 'Bede, *Beowulf*', pp. 50–58.

[71] Mayr-Harting, *Rule of St Benedict, and Social Class*.

[72] Foot, *Monastic Life*, pp. 179–83; Caedmon was probably the sole peasant named by Bede, only becoming a monk thanks to miraculous powers of song: *HE*, IV.24 pp. 414–21.

[73] Foot, *Monastic Life*, pp. 96, 247–8; Christopher Loveluck, 'Cædmon's World: Secular and Monastic Lifestyles and Estate Organization in Northern England, A.D. 650–900', in *Cædmon's Hymn and Material Culture in the World of Bede*, eds Allen J. Frantzen and John Hines (Morgantown WV, 2007), pp. 150–90.

[74] See Brown, *Western Christendom*, p. 348.   [75] Blair, *Anglo-Saxon Society*, pp. 105–7.

[76] Foot, *Monastic Life*, pp. 22, 55; Patrick Wormald, 'Bede and Benedict Biscop', repr. in *Times of Bede*, ed. Baxter, pp. 3–29.

[77] Ian Wood, 'The Gifts of Wearmouth and Jarrow', in *The Languages of Gift in the Early Middle Ages*, eds Wendy Davies and Paul Fouracre (Cambridge, 2010), pp. 89–115, at 95–6.

[78] Ian Wood, 'The Foundation of Bede's Wearmouth-Jarrow', in *Cambridge Companion*, ed. DeGregorio, pp. 84–96, at 88; Alan Thacker, 'Bede and the Ordering of Understanding', in *Innovation and Tradition*, ed. DeGregorio, pp. 37–63, at 39–40.

latter argument is often contested, Bede was certainly born on land which later became part of his monastery.[79] Wearmouth and Jarrow had been founded with royal support and Jarrow seems to have belonged to a network of high-status sites near the mouth of the Tyne. The monastery probably overlooked a busy harbour in which it may have had an economic stake, and certainly controlled extensive landholdings.[80] Bede and his abbots communicated with generations of Northumbrian kings, regularly engaging in forms of gift exchange indicative of elite relationships.[81] The one thing that set Wearmouth-Jarrow apart from other houses was probably its wealth and size; in a context where most religious communities probably numbered between five and twenty members, Wearmouth-Jarrow's six hundred brothers in 716 seems astounding, even if most of these were not strictly monks.[82]

Bede's own community thus lay in the mainstream of Northumbrian monasticism; however, diversity not uniformity defined that mainstream.[83] The imposition of Benedictine seclusion as the one correct form of monasticism had to wait until the tenth-century reform movement in England.[84] Abbots chose the rules for their communities and the word *monasterium* seems to have referred to a whole variety of institutions whose inhabitants differed in gender, clerical status, and lifestyle, for which reason some scholars prefer to call early Anglo-Saxon religious houses *minsters* rather than monasteries.[85] While Bede did not believe that all such communities deserved the name, the modern scholar should be cautious of differentiating 'real' from 'false' monasteries.[86] Perhaps because of their very adaptability and diversity, these establishments could meet many societal functions: the high-status functions previously outlined were important, but religious houses also existed as central places in the landscape, with economic, pastoral, and charitable roles.[87]

---

[79] Grocock and Wood, *Abbots*, pp. xvii–xviii, lxii–lxiii; *HE*, V.24 pp. 566–7.

[80] For the location of Jarrow: Ian Wood, 'Bede's Jarrow', in *A Place to Believe In: Locating Medieval Landscapes*, eds Clare A. Lees and Gillian R. Overing (University Park PA, 2006), pp. 67–84. Royal support and endowment: *HA*, 4 pp. 30–3, 7 pp. 36–9; *VCeol.*, 7 pp. 84–7, 11 pp. 88–9; *Hom.*, I.13 p. 91.

[81] *HA*, 9 pp. 44–5, 15 pp. 58–9; *VCeol.*, 12 pp. 90–91; *HE*, praef. pp. 2–3.

[82] Foot, *Monastic Life*, pp. 172–4; *HA*, 17 pp. 64–5; *VCeol.*, 33 pp. 112–13.

[83] Foot, *Monastic Life*, pp. 10, 48–60. [84] Foot, *Monastic Life*, pp. 12–20.

[85] Foot, *Monastic Life*, p. 6; Blair, *Anglo-Saxon Society*, p. 3. For a defence of the term *monastery*: Wood, 'Geography of Power', p. 13, n. 20; for contemporary terminology: Sarah Foot, 'Anglo-Saxon Minsters: a Review of Terminology', in *Pastoral Care before the Parish*, eds John Blair and Richard Sharpe (Leicester, 1992), pp. 212–25.

[86] *EpEcg.*, 10 pp. 142–3.

[87] Foot, *Monastic Life*, pp. 283–336; Blair, *Anglo-Saxon Society*, pp. 141–65, 251–61. The 1990s saw a major debate over the role of monastic communities in pastoral care in this period: Sarah Foot, 'The Role of the Minster in Earlier Anglo-Saxon Society', and David Rollason, 'Monasteries and Society in Early Medieval Northumbria', both in *Monasteries and Society in Medieval Britain: Proceedings of the 1994 Harlaxton Symposium*, ed. Benjamin Thompson

This variety in the forms which religious life took in Bede's Northumbria mirrors and is in part explained by a wider diversity in the culture of that time and place. The late seventh and early eighth centuries saw a cultural efflorescence in Northumbria, marked by an artistic style combining Anglo-Saxon, Irish, Roman, Frankish, and more exotic features.[88] The art-historical term for this cosmopolitan style, Insular, has come to indicate the shared culture of the British Isles during this period—a culture that we cannot neatly subdivide on straightforwardly ethnic or national lines.[89] Northumbria especially was open to a number of influences. For roughly thirty years, until the Synod of Whitby in 664, the Northumbrian Church belonged to the Columban network controlled from Iona.[90] A number of key aristocratic figures, including Bishop Wilfrid (c.634–710) and Benedict Biscop, imported 'Roman' ecclesiastical concepts and promoted an ideology of unity with the wider Catholic Church; although this is sometimes painted as a nativist drive to replace foreign ecclesiasts with locals, and certainly was linked to political desires for religious independence from Iona, the Romanist party included Irish clerics and had wide links throughout the Christian world.[91] Northumbria lay at the edge of Europe, but trade and economic exchange linked it to continental routes which carried wealth, art, and ideas over long distances.[92]

While older studies presented this mixture of cultures primarily in terms of a conflict between 'Celtic' and 'Roman' churches, recent scholarship emphasizes synthesis—a 'middle party' seems to have occupied the Northumbrian mainstream.[93] The religious communities mentioned by Bede seem to have been largely connected by networks of personnel and ideas.[94] Bede is often seen as viewing Wilfrid with distaste, but Ceolfrith (642–716, abbot of Wearmouth-Jarrow for much of Bede's life) had belonged to Wilfrid's monastic *familia* and the bishop himself clearly visited the monastery as a

---

(Stamford, 1999), pp. 35–58 and 59–74 respectively; see also Ch. 5 within this volume, 'The priesthood of all believers', p. 114.

[88] Carol Neuman de Vegvar, *The Northumbrian Renaissance: A Study in the Transmission of Style* (London, 1987); Michelle P. Brown, *The Lindisfarne Gospels: Society, Spirituality and the Scribe* (London, 2003).

[89] For the unity (and diversity) of the British Isles: Thomas Charles-Edwards, 'Conclusion', in *After Rome*, ed. Thomas Charles-Edwards (Oxford, 2003), pp. 259–70, at 266–70.

[90] Máire Herbert, *Iona, Kells, and Derry: The History and Hagiography of the Monastic Familia of Columba* (Oxford, 1988), pp. 41–60; Thomas Charles-Edwards, *Early Christian Ireland* (Cambridge, 2000), pp. 308–43.

[91] E.g. *HE*, III.25 pp. 294–7.

[92] Richard Morris, *Journeys from Jarrow*, Jarrow Lecture (Jarrow, 2004). For Northumbria's trade links with the continent: J. R. Maddicott, 'Two Frontier States: Northumbria and Wessex, c.650–750', in *The Medieval State: Essays Presented to James Campbell*, eds J. R. Maddicott and D. M. Palliser (London, 2000), pp. 25–45, at 38–40.

[93] Charles-Edwards, *Early Christian Ireland*, pp. 336–43.

[94] Mayr-Harting, *Coming of Christianity*, pp. 164–7.

friend on occasion.[95] While Lindisfarne's connections to Iona might seem to have set it against the ultra-Roman Wearmouth-Jarrow, in fact the evidence points to close cooperation between the two monasteries in the early eighth century.[96] Even Iona's great abbot Adomnán (*c.*628–704) visited the community in Bede's lifetime and was remembered with warmth by both Bede and Ceolfrith.[97] When Northumbria gained its ecclesiastical independence from Iona at Whitby in 664 interest in the island monastery did not end; Anglo-Saxons continued to seek the conversion of the Columbans to Roman ways through domination or persuasion.[98]

We should not impose an image of irenic Christian charity on the real divisions in the Northumbrian Church. The wealth and aristocratic links of most monasteries would have naturally drawn them into the world of politics. The arguments between Ionan- and Roman-leaning clergy left genuine wounds and these were exacerbated by the upheaval of Wilfrid's career: twice expelled from his episcopal office, he met attempts by kings to wrest some of the vast wealth of his monastic network from him with successful appeals to papal judgement, which the Anglo-Saxon hierarchy, in turn, mostly ignored.[99] These factors all seem to have led to a real sense of insecurity and, therefore, to competition between the major Northumbrian religious communities during Bede's lifetime. The attempts to form cults around major figures such as Cuthbert and Wilfrid, and especially the hagiographies associated with such cults, form the best evidence of such competition.[100]

We can see this interaction of unity and division played out in Bede's own community at Wearmouth-Jarrow also—a monastery actually consisting of two monasteries. Biscop founded the establishment at Wearmouth in 674; seven years later King Ecgfrith (*c.*646–85) founded (apparently without the practical involvement of Biscop) that at Jarrow with Ceolfrith as abbot. The death of Ecgfrith in battle within a month of the dedication of St Paul's at

[95] *VCeol.*, 3 pp. 80–1; *HE*, IV.19 pp. 390–3. Ian Wood, *The Most Holy Abbot Ceolfrid*, Jarrow Lecture (Jarrow, 1995), pp. 6–7.

[96] Brown, *Lindisfarne Gospels*, pp. 53–66, 407–8; *VCP*, prol. pp. 142–7.

[97] *HE*, V.21 pp. 550–51; Barbara Yorke, 'Adomnán at the court of King Aldfrith', and Clare Stancliffe, '"Charity with Peace": Adomnán and the Easter Question', both in *Adomnán of Iona: Theologian, Lawmaker, Peacemaker*, eds Jonathan M. Wooding et al. (Dublin, 2010), pp. 36–50 and 51–69, respectively.

[98] Charles-Edwards, *Early Christian Ireland*, pp. 432–5. See Ch. 3 in this volume, 'The house made by human hands', pp. 60–62.

[99] See now on Wilfrid: N. J. Higham (ed.), *Wilfrid: Abbot, Bishop, Saint; Papers from the 1300th Anniversary Conferences* (Donington, 2013).

[100] Alan Thacker, 'Lindisfarne and the Origins of the Cult of St Cuthbert', in *St Cuthbert*, eds Bonner et al., pp. 103–22; D. P. Kirby, 'The Genesis of a Cult: Cuthbert of Farne and Ecclesiastical Politics in Northumbria in the Late Seventh and Early Eighth Centuries', *JEH* 46 (1995), pp. 383–97; David Rollason, 'Hagiography and Politics in Early Northumbria', in *Holy Men and Holy Women: Old English Prose Saints' Lives and Their Contexts*, ed. P. E. Szarmach (Albany NY, 1996), pp. 95–114; Brown, *Lindisfarne Gospels*, pp. 9–10, 64–6; Goffart, *Narrators*, pp. 259–95.

Jarrow probably left the monastery directionless and forced it to seek closer relations with Wearmouth. Hence, Bede and the author of the *Life of Ceolfrith* may have insisted that Wearmouth and Jarrow had always been a single unit, inseparable as head and body, so fiercely because the issue was open to question.[101] The continuous need to emphasize the unity of Wearmouth-Jarrow seems defensive, and we know that Biscop's brother certainly tried to inherit Wearmouth against the founder's wishes.[102]

Despite this, Wearmouth-Jarrow did present a clear and distinctive culture to the outside world, a culture reified in the material of the buildings themselves.[103] The grand stone churches of St Peter and St Paul were partially a typical Anglo-Saxon use of monumentalism to display wealth and prestige, but they also followed distinctively foreign and late Roman models—a symbolic declaration of union with the Church of Rome.[104] Benedict Biscop, like Wilfrid, chose to construct his churches in the 'Roman fashion';[105] this required skilled workers in stone and stained glass to be imported, for use of these materials was unknown in native Anglo-Saxon construction.[106] The churches at both Wearmouth and Jarrow contained religious images and holy relics carried from Rome.[107]

Wearmouth-Jarrow thus contained a self-consciously cosmopolitan community, living in buildings constructed with foreign expertise, filled with foreign objects, and protected by papal privileges.[108] But it also participated in Northumbrian society: female bodies in the cemetery and phraseology in Bede's homilies which may imply the presence of the unbaptized in church suggest that the monastery did not hold itself aloof from the lay communities surrounding it.[109] It may indeed have performed a pastoral role, at least towards the individuals who must have lived on the lands owned by the house.[110] These factors should be taken into account when considering whether Bede was a figure isolated from society. His immersion in the communal life of Wearmouth-Jarrow would have necessitated an awareness of the Northumbrian world insofar as it made an impact on the monastery.

---

[101] Head and body: *HA*, 7 pp. 38–9.

[102] Wood, 'Foundation'. Biscop's brother: *HA*, 11 pp. 48–9.

[103] Rosemary Cramp et al., *Wearmouth and Jarrow Monastic Sites*, 2 vols (Swindon, 2005–2006) provides a complete summary of the archaeological and material evidence for Wearmouth-Jarrow.

[104] Alecia Arceo, 'Rethinking the Synod of Whitby and Northumbrian Monastic Sites', *Haskins Society Journal* 20 (2008), pp. 19–30; Cramp, *Wearmouth and Jarrow*, I, pp. 358–9.

[105] *HA*, 5 pp. 32–3 'iuxta Romanorum . . . morem'; *VW*, XVII pp. 34–7, XXII pp. 44–7.

[106] *HA*, 5 pp. 32–3; *VCeol.*, 7 pp. 86–7.

[107] *HA*, 6 pp. 34–7, 9 pp. 44–5; *VCeol.*, 9 pp. 86–7.   [108] *Hom.*, I.13 p. 93.

[109] Cramp, *Wearmouth and Jarrow*, I, p. 84; *Hom.*, II.6 p. 222; A. G. P. van der Walt, 'The Homiliary of the Venerable Bede and Early Medieval Preaching' (PhD thesis, University of London, 1980), pp. 56–8.

[110] Alan Thacker, 'Monks, Preaching and Pastoral Care in early Anglo-Saxon England', in *Pastoral Care*, eds Blair and Sharpe, pp. 137–70, at 140–42.

Unsurprisingly, therefore, scholars have noted Bede's Northumbrian bias or patriotism.[111] For all of Bede's lifetime Northumbria remained a major player in British power politics, although no longer enjoying the hegemony which the kingdom had commanded around the middle of the seventh century. The monk thus genuinely cared about the power and security of the kingdom and will no doubt have been aware of and possibly disturbed by the signs of increased political upheaval in the early eighth century; his comments on Ecgfrith's loss to the Picts, the state of Britain in 731, and the possibility of 'barbarian' invasion all imply concern for Northumbria's military fortunes.[112] Crises associated with the royal succession seem to have taken place in 705, 716, and 729–31, although it is unclear how much of a negative impact these would have had on the wider life of the kingdom. Ceolfrith, who resigned the abbacy of Wearmouth-Jarrow in 716 (the same year that King Osred was killed), may have played an important role in Northumbrian diplomacy—just as Biscop had regularly attended King Ecgfrith's councils.[113] The political unrest of this period may possibly have some connection with the dramatic changes that the establishment of the Northumbrian Church, and in particular the significant endowment of religious communities brought about in aristocratic society.[114]

Power and politics formed only part of Bede's world, however, and fail by themselves to explain his exegetical writings. While they should constantly be kept in mind when reading the analysis of Bede's use of the temple image which follows, we require additional context before undertaking that analysis. Life in most Northumbrian monastic houses would not have matched that in secular households exactly. Communal prayer structured both day and night; some form of work was expected of all individuals, usually manual labour but those with more specialized skills may have been allowed to concentrate on their strengths.[115] Roman-leaning monasteries, including Wearmouth-Jarrow, appear to have been particularly keen on perfecting liturgical song and ritual.[116] Bede situated his scholarship within this environment of monastic routine and communal worship: 'amid the observance of the discipline of the Rule and the daily task of singing in the church, it has always been my delight

---

[111] Goffart, *Narrators*, pp. 240, 252–3; Higham, *(Re-)Reading Bede*, pp. 145–6.

[112] *HE*, IV.26 pp. 428–9, V.23 pp. 560–1; *EpEcg.*, 11 pp. 144–5.

[113] Ceolfrith's communication with the Pictish King Nechtan and Adomnán (*HE*, V.21 pp. 532–53) suggests links with the royal court: Higham, *(Re-)Reading Bede*, pp. 129, 190. Biscop at royal councils: *VCeol.*, 12 pp. 90–91.

[114] Orton and Wood, *Fragments of History*, pp. 199–201; N. J. Higham, *The Kingdom of Northumbria: AD 350–1100* (Stroud, 1993), pp. 132–9, 147, argues that the endowment of monasteries caused Northumbria's political decline.

[115] Foot, *Monastic Life*, pp. 186–226.

[116] *HA*, 6 pp. 34–7; *VCeol.*, 9 pp. 86–9, 14 pp. 92–5; *Hom.*, I.13 p. 92; *VW*, XLVII pp. 98–9. Wood, *Ceolfrid*, pp. 16–18.

to learn or to teach or to write'.[117] Bede may have had an educational role at Wearmouth-Jarrow, and the nature of the personal possessions that he gave away on his deathbed (pepper, incense, and *oraria*—possibly clothes or vestments—all with probable liturgical functions) suggest that he frequently performed his priestly duty of celebrating Mass.[118]

In other words, the spiritual, sacramental, and communal were all realities that impinged daily on Bede. Locating him politically or socially involves imaginatively reconstructing Bede's participation in certain groupings of kin, class, and ethnicity. But the monastic liturgy and the performance of the Mass located Bede spiritually, whether in the brotherhood of religious at Wearmouth-Jarrow or in the cosmic body of Christ. We must seek to reconstruct his participation in these communities. The dominant ideology of Wearmouth-Jarrow may not quite deserve the definition 'countercultural' which some have given it—but in living there Bede did participate in realities separate and sometimes opposed to those of Northumbria's secular aristocracy.[119] In studying Bede's use of the temple image we can see just how much membership of the body of Christ mattered to him, and, I argue, we can discern how the communal spirituality of Wearmouth-Jarrow may have shaped his ideas.

One activity in which Bede engaged would certainly have set him apart from most of the secular elite: the extensive reading and detailed note-taking that must lie behind his exegesis.[120] The post-Goffart emphasis on Bede as socially engaged has often defined itself in opposition to the idea, enunciated by Wormald and Mayr-Harting, that Bede's world was a 'world of books'.[121] Obviously such a phrase is potentially reductive (one should consider, say, how Bede's world of books was financed and sustained), but it should be nuanced, not rejected. As Alan Thacker's work has subtly shown, we can understand Bede as an idealist informed by a world view significantly derived from books and as an individual aware of and reacting to his wider society.[122] If Bede built his temple in eighth-century Northumbria, its foundations were laid in the books he read, and it is to this intellectual context which I now turn.

---

[117] *HE*, V.24 pp. 566–7 'inter obseruantiam disciplinae regularis, et cotidianam cantandi in ecclesia curam, semper aut discere aut docere aut scribere dulce habui'.

[118] Faith Wallis, *Bede: On the Reckoning of Time* (Liverpool, 1999), pp. xxx–xxxiv; Daniel J. Heisey, 'Bede's Pepper, Napkins, and Incense', *Downside Review* 129 (2011), pp. 16–30.

[119] Olsen, 'From Bede', p. 317. For the ideology of Wearmouth-Jarrow as classless: Mayr-Harting, *Rule of Benedict and Social Class*; for the possibility that while Bede himself was critical of aristocratic culture, other Wearmouth-Jarrow monks were more positive: Wood, 'Gifts of Wearmouth and Jarrow', p. 114.

[120] Aldfrith's learning proves that members of secular society could be highly literate too, but he, in fact, had probably received a clerical education: Barbara Yorke, *Rex Doctissimus: Bede and King Aldfrith of Northumbria*, Jarrow Lecture (Jarrow, 2009), pp. 5–6.

[121] Wormald, 'Bede, *Beowulf*', p. 63; Mayr-Harting, 'Patristic Thinking', p. 373.

[122] Thacker, 'Ideal of Reform', p. 130; Thacker, 'Monks', p. 169.

2

Bede's Temple in its Intellectual Context

To understand Bede, as any author, we need to locate him as a writer and to put his work into its wider context. Bede's own autobiographical comments in the *Ecclesiastical History* bring two important contexts to our attention. Firstly, Benedict Biscop and Ceolfrith educated Bede at Wearmouth-Jarrow, where he read and wrote all his life and for whose members he produced his exegesis; secondly, that exegesis self-consciously drew on the works of the early Church Fathers.[1] Recent scholarship has demonstrated convincingly that Bede did more than merely copy what he found in the patristic tradition—but his claim to 'follow in the footsteps of the Fathers' is not just a modesty topos.[2] Rather, it reminds us of the important links which Bede himself saw between the Fathers and his own work. This chapter, then, examines these two contexts, focusing primarily on Bede's reading as the necessary starting point for understanding Bede's writing. Firstly, I examine the intellectual resources available at Wearmouth-Jarrow and how they would have conditioned Bede's exegetical methodology; I then provide an overview of the Christian interpretations of the temple image which Bede inherited.

THE INTELLECTUAL CONTEXT AT WEARMOUTH-JARROW

Before he founded a monastery at Wearmouth, Benedict Biscop had gathered a large number of books during his fourth visit to Rome (*c.*671) and indeed it was partially these books that inspired King Ecgfrith to donate land to him.[3]

---

[1] *HE*, V. 24 pp. 566–7.
[2] See the papers by Ray, Thacker, and DeGregorio in *Innovation and Tradition in the Writings of the Venerable Bede*, ed. Scott DeGregorio (Morgantown WV, 2006). Also within this chapter, 'The temple in the Christian tradition before Bede', p. 45 and Ch. 7 within this volume, 'Imitation', p. 168.
[3] *HA*, 4 pp. 30–31.

After the monastery had been built, Biscop returned to Rome (this time accompanied by Ceolfrith, during 679–80) and obtained 'a countless number of books'.[4] Sometime after the establishment of Jarrow, Biscop visited Rome for a sixth time and once again brought back many volumes.[5] In a society still in the comparatively early stages of literacy this importation of books is striking; Biscop's pride in the library he had built up made him fearful of its division after his death, as other aristocrats might worry about the dismemberment of the land they had accumulated.[6] Instead, according to Bede, the library doubled in size under Ceolfrith's abbacy.[7] The founders of Wearmouth and Jarrow were stereotypical Anglo-Saxon aristocrats in their commitment to gathering treasure, though it consisted of parchment rather than gold. Like gold, manuscripts had an economic value and Ceolfrith could exchange a volume from his library for land if need be.[8]

Fortunately for Bede, therefore, he had access to possibly the largest library ever collected in Anglo-Saxon England.[9] The founders' hoard of books having long vanished, we can only reconstruct this library from the evidence of Bede's own writings, which reveal an extraordinary amount of reading. The four Fathers of the Latin Church, whom Bede played a major role in popularizing in the West, appear to have dominated: Ambrose, Augustine, Jerome, and Gregory the Great.[10] Bede did not have equal access to all their works—he may have only read a small amount of Ambrose's (d. 397) corpus, for example, though he certainly had access to the bishop's commentary on Luke, *De Fide*, *De Spiritu Sancto*, and possibly the *Exameron*.[11] He had, however, read quite substantial quantities of Jerome (d. 419/420) and Augustine's colossal output. The evidence for his knowledge of Augustine (354–430) may be skewed by the fact that Bede used Eugippius' *Excerpta* of quotations from the Augustinian corpus. Nonetheless, he clearly had read many of Augustine's writings in their entirety, including some of the largest works: *De Civitate Dei*, *De Genesi ad Litteram*, *De Trinitate*, the commentaries on John's gospel and on the Psalms, and at least the first three books (and probably all) of *De Doctrina*

---

[4] *HA*, 6 pp. 34–5 'innumerabilem librorum omnis generis copiam apportauit'; *VCeol.*, 9 pp. 86–7.

[5] *HA*, 9 pp. 44–5.   [6] *HA*, 11 pp. 48–9.

[7] *HA*, 15 pp. 56–7; *VCeol.*, 20 pp. 98–9.   [8] *HA*, 15 pp. 58–9.

[9] M. L. W. Laistner, 'The Library of the Venerable Bede', in *Life, Times, and Writings*, ed. Thompson, pp. 237–66, and M. L. W. Laistner, 'Bede as a Classical and a Patristic Scholar', *Transactions of the Royal Historical Society* 4th series 16 (1933), pp. 69–94, remain the essential starting point. Also Michael Lapidge, *The Anglo-Saxon Library* (Oxford, 2006), pp. 34–7, 191–228; Rosalind Love, 'The library of the Venerable Bede', in *The Cambridge History of the Book in Britain. Volume 1: c.400–1100*, ed. Richard Gameson (Cambridge, 2012), pp. 606–32.

[10] Bernice M. Kaczynski, 'Bede's Commentaries on Luke and Mark and the Formation of a Patristic Canon', in *Anglo-Latin and its Heritage: Essays in Honour of A. G. Rigg on his 64th Birthday*, eds Siân Echard and Gernot R. Wieland (Turnhout, 2001), pp. 17–26.

[11] Dabney Anderson Bankert et al., *Ambrose in Anglo-Saxon England with Pseudo-Ambrose and Ambrosiaster*, Old English Newsletter Subsidia 25 (Kalamazoo MI, 1997).

Christiana.[12] Bede certainly had all of Gregory's (*c*.540–604) major works available to him (especially the *Regula Pastoralis, Moralia in Iob*, and the homilies on the gospels and Ezekiel) and indeed the writings of the pope left a definite impression on him, playing a central role in shaping his mindset.[13]

Along with this key patristic core, Biscop and Ceolfrith had imported many of the classics of Christian Latin culture. Bede's reading included poetry (Sedulius and Arator, for example), hagiography (the *vitae* of Martin and Antony, for example), and monastic texts (Cassian's *Conferences* and the Benedictine Rule, for example), as well as major biblical commentaries.[14] In comparison to this wealth of Latin texts, Bede did not have access to a large quantity of Greek patristic thought. Nonetheless, he did have Latin translations of a few works, especially Rufinus' version of Eusebius' *Ecclesiastical History*. Bede did not limit his reading to Christian sources either; his writings show a deep familiarity with the works of Virgil, despite the common Christian claims to reject classical literature and secular rhetoric.[15] And Bede had access to scientific material coming from Ireland—indeed while rejecting the Easter calculation associated with Iona, he relied heavily on a dossier of computistical materials first collected in Ireland.[16]

The availability of so many texts notwithstanding, Bede's life and Wearmouth-Jarrow's culture remained dominated by a single book: the Bible. Ceolfrith expanded his library not simply by collecting, but also by creating new books—especially copies of a Bible text newly edited at Wearmouth-Jarrow from a variety of exemplars.[17] Because of this project Bede had access to numerous biblical texts, including at least some of the

[12] Love, 'Library', pp. 624–5; Alan Thacker, *Bede and Augustine of Hippo: History and Figure in Sacred Text*, Jarrow Lecture (Jarrow, 2005), p. 5; François Dolbeau, 'Bède, lecteur des Sermons d'Augustin', *Filologia Mediolatina* 3 (1996), pp. 105–33, at 106–8.

[13] Paul Meyvaert, *Bede and Gregory the Great*, Jarrow Lecture (Jarrow, 1964); Scott DeGregorio, 'The Venerable Bede and Gregory the Great: Exegetical Connections, Spiritual Departures', *EME* 18 (2010), pp. 43–60.

[14] While Wearmouth-Jarrow did not follow the Benedictine Rule exclusively, Bede knew it very well: A. D. P. van der Walt, 'Reflections of the Benedictine Rule in Bede's Homiliary', *JEH* 37 (1986), pp. 367–76; Scott DeGregorio, 'Bede and Benedict of Nursia', in *Early Medieval Studies in Memory of Patrick Wormald*, eds Stephen Baxter et al. (Farnham, 2009), pp. 151–63.

[15] Neil Wright, 'Bede and Vergil', *Romanobarbarica* 6 (1982), pp. 361–79. For the Christian tradition condemning the secular classics and the continuing monastic use of the same works: Jean Leclercq, *The Love of Learning and the Desire for God: A Study of Monastic Culture*, trans. Catherine Misrahi, 3rd ed. (New York, 1982), esp. pp. 112–25; George Hardin Brown, 'Ciceronianism in Bede and Alcuin', in *Intertexts: Studies in Anglo-Saxon Culture Presented to Paul E. Szarmach*, eds Virginia Blanton and Helene Scheck (Tempe AZ, 2008), pp. 319–29, at 319–23.

[16] Jean-Michel Picard, 'Bède et ses sources irlandaises', in *Bède le Vénérable entre tradition et postérité: The Venerable Bede. Tradition and Posterity*, eds Stéphane Lebecq et al. (Lille, 2005), pp. 43–61; Dáibhí Ó Cróinín, 'The Irish Provenance of Bede's *Computus*', *Peritia* 2 (1983), pp. 238–42.

[17] Richard Marsden, *The Text of the Old Testament in Anglo-Saxon England* (Cambridge, 1995), pp. 140–201.

New Testament in Greek. It appears that he taught himself enough Greek to engage intelligently with this version towards the end of his life.[18] Bede certainly worked with a variety of scriptural manuscripts, often displaying an interest in comparing different translations and versions of the text.[19] But the ideology of Wearmouth-Jarrow promoted respect for Jerome's Vulgate above all, for Ceolfrith's Bible text consisted of a complete edition of that work. Hence, despite his penchant for textual criticism, Bede accorded the Vulgate a special status. It was the *hebraica veritas*—the Hebrew truth. As Bede himself did not independently know any Hebrew, Jerome's *Hebrew Names* and the Latin translation of Josephus' *Jewish Antiquities* were vital for his understanding of the Old Testament.[20] Indeed, Bede probably cited *Hebrew Names* more than any other patristic work[21]—proof that the need to understand the Bible dominated his reading above all.

All of Bede's intellectual endeavours orbited, at greater or lesser distances, the Bible—unsurprisingly when we consider the type of education he would have received at Wearmouth-Jarrow. The cultural efflorescence in late seventh- and early eighth-century Anglo-Saxon England depended on a Christian and almost wholly monastic education system.[22] Children educated in monasteries, like Bede, would have initially learnt Latin through the liturgy, memorizing and internalizing the Psalter through the performance of the monastic Offices.[23] Religious schools carried on the traditions of late Roman grammatical education in the ways students were subsequently trained in reading and understanding Latin texts.[24] Traditionally grammar had been taught through the use of the secular classics as examples of perfect Latin style. This certainly did continue in the Christian context: Bede's own *Verse Life of Cuthbert* shows his familiarity with Virgil, Lucan, and Claudian.[25]

---

[18] Kevin M. Lynch, 'The Venerable Bede's Knowledge of Greek', *Traditio* 39 (1983), pp. 432–9; Anna Carlotta Dionisotti, 'On Bede, Grammars, and Greek', *RB* 92 (1982), pp. 111–41.

[19] Paul Meyvaert, 'Bede the Scholar', in *Famulus Christi: Essays in Commemoration of the Thirteenth Centenary of the Birth of the Venerable Bede*, ed. Gerald Bonner (London, 1976), pp. 40–69, at 47–51; Marsden, *Text of the Old Testament*, pp. 202–19.

[20] E. F. Sutcliffe, 'The Venerable Bede's Knowledge of Hebrew', *Biblica* 16 (1935), pp. 300–306; Damian Fleming, '"The Most Exalted Language": Anglo-Saxon Perceptions of Hebrew' (PhD thesis, University of Toronto, 2006), pp. 53–79.

[21] Lapidge, *Anglo-Saxon Library*, p. 217.

[22] Pierre Riché, *Education and Culture in the Barbarian West: from the Sixth through Eighth Century*, trans. John J. Contreni (Columbia SC, 1978), pp. 369–99; Patrick Sims-Williams, *Religion and Literature in Western England, 600–800* (Cambridge, 1990), ch. 7–11; Michael Lapidge, 'Anglo-Latin Literature', in *Anglo-Latin Literature 600–899* (London, 1996), pp. 1–36, at 1–5.

[23] Lapidge, 'Anglo-Latin', pp. 1–2; Benedicta Ward, *Bede and the Psalter*, Jarrow Lecture (Jarrow, 1991).

[24] Martin Irvine, 'Bede the Grammarian and the Scope of Grammatical Studies in eighth-century Northumbria', *ASE* 15 (1986), pp. 15–44.

[25] Lapidge, *Anglo-Saxon Library*, pp. 107–15.

However, his grammatical and educational works show the reorientation of late Roman grammar towards the study of the Bible. Scripture had become the new 'classic' studied and interpreted in the classroom.[26] While some have argued for the centrality of rhetoric, especially as evidenced by Cicero, to Bede's writings, it seems that grammar was the mainstay of his education.[27]

The attitudes long held by grammarians towards secular literature, therefore, provide the context for Bede's Christian approach to the Bible: texts demanded interpretation, and were approached from the reader's, rather than the author's, point of view.[28] The Anglo-Saxons' predilection for riddles reveals a delight in the double meanings of words; this native tradition possibly played a part in life at Wearmouth-Jarrow, if the riddles of Eusebius are indeed the work of Bede's contemporary, and abbot of Wearmouth-Jarrow from 716, Hwaetberht.[29] Bede's grammatical writings show his awareness of the twists and turns of scriptural language, the ways in which words can mean something other than what they say—that for him was the definition of allegory.[30] This interpretative approach to the text is commonly associated with the four senses of scripture: the historical, allegorical (here narrowly defined as referring to Christ and the Church), tropological (moral), and anagogical (heavenly or eschatological) senses. Bede, it has been claimed, 'coined the definitive formula for the fourfold sense'.[31] In *On Schemes and Tropes* Bede outlined all four, illustrating them using the image of the temple of Jerusalem:[32]

> According to the historical fact the temple of the Lord is the house which Solomon built; allegorically, it is the body of the Lord, about which He said: *Destroy this temple; and in three days I will raise it up.* Or it is his Church, which was addressed as follows: *For the temple of God is holy, which you are.* Through the tropological interpretation it signifies some one of the faithful, who are

[26] Margot H. King, '*Grammatica Mystica*: A Study of Bede's Grammatical Curriculum', in *Saints, Scholars, and Heroes: Studies in Medieval Culture in Honour of Charles W. Jones*, eds Margot H. King and Wesley Stevens, 2 vols (Collegeville MN, 1979), I, pp. 145–59; Carmela Vircillo Franklin, 'Grammar and Exegesis: Bede's *Liber de schematibus et tropis*', in *Latin Grammar and Rhetoric: From Classical Theory to Medieval Practice*, ed. Carol Dana Lanham (London, 2002), pp. 63–91.

[27] Roger Ray, 'Bede and Cicero', *ASE* 16 (1987), pp. 1–15; Gabriele Knappe, 'Classical Rhetoric in Anglo-Saxon England', *ASE* 27 (1998), pp. 5–29.

[28] Irvine, 'Bede the Grammarian', pp. 27, 41. Frances M. Young, *Biblical Exegesis and the Formation of Christian Culture* (Cambridge, 1997), throughout argues that patristic authors used the methodology of secular exegesis.

[29] *Aenigmata Eusebii*, ed. F. Glorie, CCSL 133, pp. 209–71.

[30] *DST*, II.12 p. 161 'Allegoria est tropus quo aliud significatur quam dicitur...'.

[31] Henri de Lubac, *Medieval Exegesis: The Four Senses of Scripture*, trans. Mark Sebanc and E. M. Macierowski, 2 vols (Edinburgh, 1998–2000), II, p. 213. Lubac's study is only partially translated into English: see *Exégèse médiévale: les quatres sens de l'Écriture*, 2 parts in 4 vols (Paris, 1959–64) for the complete work.

[32] Bede's application of the four senses to the temple clearly adapts the earlier application to Jerusalem (e.g. John Cassian, *Collationes*, ed. M. Petschenig, CSEL 13, XIV.VIII.4 p. 405), which he used at *Cant.*, p. 260.

addressed as follows: *Know you not that you are the temple of God, and that the Spirit of God dwelleth in you?* Through the anagogical interpretation it signifies the joys of the heavenly dwelling for which that man longed who said: *Blessed are they that dwell in thy house, O Lord . . .*[33]

As scholars have long recognized, like his predecessors, Bede did not apply the senses in such a systematic way to every verse on which he commented; discussing the four senses in *On the Tabernacle*, he chose to explain each with a different verse.[34] The senses rather pointed towards the diversity of possible meanings which a text could contain; they existed to open up and not to limit the interpretation of the Bible.[35] In practice then we will look in vain for hard and fast 'rules' of interpretation in Bede's exegesis—neither the senses, nor Tyconius' seven rules ('a systematisation of an essentially arbitrary process') supply such a need.[36] Bede learned the art of interpretation from reading the Latin Fathers and from them, especially from Gregory, he would have learned about the infinity of scripture. The Bible shaped itself according to the reader, expanding and contracting with the needs of one's mind. There was nobody so simple that they could learn nothing from it, nobody so wise that they could ever exhaust its meanings.[37] The four senses and other such schemes simply alerted the exegete to the possible ways one could read scripture, revealing that one should penetrate beyond the surface of the letter and into the inner spiritual meaning.[38]

Therefore, speaking of Bede's use of allegory does not imply any codified system of one-to-one meanings that unlocked the real significance of a biblical text. An image can change meaning a number of times throughout the course of a commentary or can have multiple possible meanings simultaneously.[39] Bede could produce diverse interpretations for a single verse: the twelve stones

---

[33] *DST*, II.12 pp. 168–9 'templum Domini iuxta historiam domus quam fecit Salomon; iuxta allegoriam corpus Dominicum de quo ait: "Soluite templum hoc, et in tribus diebus excitabo illud," siue ecclesia eius, cui dicitur: "templum enim Dei sanctum est, quod estis uos"; per tropologiam quisque fidelium, quibus dicitur: "An nescitis quia corpora uestra templum est Spiritus sancti qui in uobis est"; per anagogen supernae gaudia mansionis, cui suspirabat qui ait: "Beati qui habitant in domo tua, Domine . . . "'; adapted from trans. Tannenhaus, p. 252.

[34] *Tab.*, p. 25.

[35] Charles W. Jones, 'Some Introductory Remarks on Bede's Commentary on Genesis', *Sacris Erudiri* 19 (1969–70), pp. 115–98, at 135–40.

[36] *Apoc.*, pp. 223–31; Augustine, *De Doctrina Christiana*, ed. and trans. R. P. H. Green (Oxford, 1995), III.92–133 pp. 172–95. The quotation is from Young, *Biblical Exegesis*, p. 205.

[37] Gregory, *Homiliae in Hiezechihelem Prophetam*, ed. M. Adriaen, CCSL 142, I.VII.8 p. 87; Gregory, *Moralia in Iob*, ed. M. Adriaen, CCSL 143+A+B, Epistola ad Leandrum IV p. 6; Lubac, *Medieval Exegesis*, I, pp. 75–82, II, pp. 204–7.

[38] The importance of the spiritual core: *Ezra.*, p. 237; *Marc.*, p. 524; *Ret.*, p. 163; *Hom.*, II.2 p. 196.

[39] Augustine, *Doctrina*, III.84 p. 168; Jennifer O'Reilly, 'Exegesis and the Book of Kells: The Lucan Genealogy', in *The Book of Kells: Proceedings of a Conference at Trinity College Dublin, 6–9 September 1992*, ed. Felicity O'Mahony (Aldershot, 1994), pp. 344–97, at 377.

on the high priest's breastplate symbolize faith in the Trinity being preached in the four parts of the world; that a teacher ought to combine that faith with the four virtues; and, Bede declared a little later, the zodiac because the 'Sun of righteousness is going to fill all our times and all regions of our world with his light, after the pattern of the mundane sun'.[40] Artistry clearly played a role in all this; exegetical exuberance could provide pleasure: 'if it pleases you to hear something new ...'.[41]

Nor did Bede restrict any meaning to a single word or image. While the portico of the temple signified the faithful before the incarnation, the Sanctuary represented those after the incarnation, and the Holy of Holies the heavenly reward shared by both, Bede saw no problem with also, apparently inconsistently, applying the same interpretations to the materials (stone, wood, and gold) from which all three locations were built: 'For in the different materials there is a manifold repetition of the same figures'.[42] Thus Bede's commentaries tend to be highly repetitious: in different contexts the same basic interpretations come up repeatedly. In such repetition, rather than in striking once-off statements, we can see Bede's major interests coming to the surface.[43] The content of the biblical text can seem secondary to the exegete's own ideas in these cases, although Bede could be sensitive and drawn to the 'plot' of a book of the Bible when it suited.[44] Bede in this respect again followed the example of Gregory whose 'free-wheeling' exegesis tended to produce religious treatises, rather than textual commentaries per se.[45] While extensive Gregorian tangents appear comparatively rarely in Bede's work, his exegesis shines far more light on his own world view than it does on the Bible.

Of course, Bede did not conceive of all readings of scripture as equally justified. While Kendall's argument that Bede differentiated between signs consecrated by God and symbols devised by human intelligence does not convince, I do agree with him that Bede saw Augustine's law of charity as the determinant of true exegesis.[46] Bede, Augustine, and most Christian interpreters held that correct exegesis had to take place within the Church, being circumscribed by the limits of orthodox faith as handed down (which

---

[40] *Tab.*, p. 112 'sol iustitiae cuncta nostra tempora cunctas orbis nostri plagas sua esset luce repleturus in exemplum solis mundani'; trans. Holder, p. 129.

[41] *Tab.*, p. 54 'Aut si noui aliquid audire delectat ...'; trans. Holder, p. 59.

[42] *Temp.*, p. 175 'Multiplex namque est in diuersis rebus earundem repetitio figurarum'; trans. Connolly, p. 42.

[43] Meyvaert, 'Bede the Scholar', p. 46.

[44] Scott DeGregorio, *Bede: On Ezra and Nehemiah* (Liverpool, 2006), pp. xxx–xxxii.

[45] R. A. Markus, *Signs and Meanings: World and Text in Ancient Christianity* (Liverpool, 1996), pp. 48–70 (quotation at p. 50). For just how free Bede's methodology could be: Jones, 'Introductory Remarks', pp. 151–60.

[46] Calvin B. Kendall, 'The Responsibility of *Auctoritas*: Method and Meaning in Bede's Commentary on Genesis', in *Innovation and Tradition*, ed. DeGregorio, pp. 101–19; Augustine, *Doctrina*, I.86–88 pp. 48–51.

Augustine summarized as love of God and neighbour).[47] Thus Bede would have approached the Bible from the conviction that he already knew essentially what it meant—exegesis simply showed how every scriptural text upheld orthodox Christianity. Hence, for Bede, Jews could never really understand the Bible, which had meaning solely in Christ.[48] Scripture spoke only of the correct Christian faith and those who rejected this closed off the possibility of an accurate, spiritual exegesis; the unfaithful (whether Jews or heretics) as a consequence gained nothing from their reading of scripture.[49]

Bede's conviction that the Bible should be read spiritually need not suggest that he held the literal or historical aspects of the text in contempt. Some scholars have made an especial effort to highlight Bede's interest in the historical and textual questions that arise in exegesis.[50] Sometimes this has led to misleading attempts to portray Bede as a historical exegete opposed to allegorical tendencies, as Lapidge for example has argued: 'By nature Bede favours philological and historical exposition and avoids the wilder excesses of allegorical interpretation'.[51] Traditionally, historians of Christian exegesis have distinguished 'Alexandrian' (allegorical/spiritual in nature, deriving from Origen, and dominant in the West) from 'Antiochene' exegesis (opposed to Origen, focused on literal, historically contextualized interpretation).[52] Bischoff influentially suggested that 'Antiochene' interpretation dominated in the Canterbury school of Theodore of Tarsus (602–90); the recent explosion of work on Theodore and Canterbury has strengthened this impression that an 'Antiochene' literal approach to the Bible characterized that school.[53]

This has naturally led to questions as to what extent Canterbury's literalism influenced Bede—Benedict Biscop after all had close connections with

---

[47] Young, *Biblical Exegesis*, pp. 17–21; Lubac, *Medieval Exegesis*, I, pp. 25–7.

[48] See R. A. Markus, 'The Jew as a Hermeneutic Device: The Inner Life of a Gregorian Topos', in *Gregory the Great: A Symposium*, ed. John C. Cavadini (London, 1995), pp. 1–15, at 1–4; John William Houghton, 'Bede's Exegetical Theology: Ideas of the Church in the Acts Commentaries of St. Bede the Venerable' (PhD dissertation, University of Notre Dame, 1994), pp. 70–2; Lubac, *Medieval Exegesis*, I, pp. 225–41.

[49] *Apoc.*, p. 267; *Abac.*, p. 406; *Prov.*, pp. 95–6. Sharon M. Rowley, 'Reassessing Exegetical Interpretations of Bede's *Historia Ecclesiastica Gentis Anglorum*', *Literature and Theology* 17 (2003), pp. 227–43, at 233.

[50] E.g. Meyvaert, 'Bede the Scholar'.

[51] Lapidge, 'Anglo-Latin', p. 16.

[52] Beryl Smalley, *The Study of the Bible in the Middle Ages*, 3rd ed. (Oxford, 1983), pp. 1–36; Manlio Simonetti, *Biblical Interpretation in the Early Church: An Historical Introduction to Patristic Exegesis*, trans. John A. Hughes, eds Anders Bergquist and Marcus Bockmuehl (Edinburgh, 1994).

[53] Bernhard Bischoff, 'Turning-Points in the History of Latin Exegesis in the Early Middle Ages', trans. Colm O'Grady, in *Biblical Studies: The Medieval Irish Contribution*, ed. Martin McNamara, Proceedings of the Irish Biblical Association 1 (Dublin, 1976), pp. 74–160; Bernhard Bischoff and Michael Lapidge, *Biblical Commentaries from the Canterbury School of Theodore and Hadrian* (Cambridge, 1994), pp. 243–9; Jane Stevenson, *The 'Laterculus Malalianus' and the School of Archbishop Theodore* (Cambridge, 1995), pp. 43–7.

Theodore and Canterbury.[54] I would be cautious about overstating the importance of the Canterbury evidence for a number of reasons. Firstly, patristic scholars increasingly question the binary opposition of 'Alexandrian' and 'Antiochene' exegesis on which so much has been based, becoming more wary of its utility as a frame of reference.[55] Secondly, no exegetical work analogous to that of Bede survives from Canterbury: the majority of the evidence derives from surviving biblical glosses.[56] The gloss is a distinct genre, separate from the commentary, and always more likely to focus on the literal meaning of the text—it does not necessarily imply rejection of spiritual readings.[57] Thirdly, although Bede did once cite Theodore, he did so to dismiss the archbishop's interpretation of the verse in question.[58] Finally, while Bede obviously valued understanding the historical dimensions of scripture, there is nothing surprising about this; his reading of Augustine and Jerome, as well as Gregory, alone suffices to explain his interpretive approach.

Christian hermeneutics approached the Bible as speaking of real historical events which themselves had spiritual meaning, prefiguring other real historical events. The inspired authors had recorded the history of Israel which God himself had authored to refer to Christ's saving work.[59] Any human text could contain 'allegory in words'; the Bible also contained 'allegory in deeds'.[60] Augustine and Jerome rendered this approach authoritative for the Latin West, since their work came increasingly to stress the historical reality of the Old Testament.[61] At prayer in the church at Jarrow, Bede found himself surrounded by this approach to scripture, reified in the pictures that paired events from the Old and New Testaments.[62] Therefore, Bede knew that the

---

[54] Bischoff, 'Turning-Points', pp. 74–7; James Siemens, *The Christology of Theodore of Tarsus: The* Laterculus Malalianus *and the Person and Work of Christ* (Turnhout, 2010), p. 180; Paul Hilliard, 'The Venerable Bede as Scholar, Gentile and Preacher', in *Ego Trouble: Authors and their Identities in the Early Middle Ages*, eds Richard Corradini et al. (Vienna, 2010), pp. 101–9, at 105–6.

[55] Young, *Biblical Exegesis*, pp. 120–2, 161–85; Elizabeth A. Clark, *Reading Renunciation: Asceticism and Scripture in Early Christianity* (Princeton NJ, 1999), pp. 70–8.

[56] Michael Gorman, 'Theodore of Canterbury, Hadrian of Nisida and Michael Lapidge', *Scriptorium* 50 (1996), pp. 184–92, at 189.

[57] Lubac, *Medieval Exegesis*, II, pp. 214–16.

[58] *VIII Q.*, III p. 65. Also Helen Conrad-O'Briain, 'The Harrowing of Hell in the Canterbury Glosses and its Context in Augustinian and Insular Exegesis', in *Text and Gloss: Studies in Insular Learning and Literature Presented to Joseph Donovan Pheifer*, eds Helen Conrad-O'Briain et al. (Dublin, 1999), pp. 73–88, at 87–8.

[59] Lubac, *Medieval Exegesis*, II, pp. 41–98; Erich Auerbach, '"Figura"', trans. Ralph Manheim, in *Scenes from the Drama of European Literature* (Manchester, 1984), pp. 11–76.

[60] *DST*, II.12 p. 164 'allegoria aliquando factis, aliquando uerbis tantummodo fit'; *Tab.*, p. 25.

[61] Markus, *Signs and Meanings*, pp. 5–11; Simonetti, *Patristic Exegesis*, pp. 99–108. For the link between Augustine's methodology and Bede's attitude to the temple: Thacker, *Bede and Augustine*, pp. 17–25, 31–3.

[62] *HA*, 9 pp. 44–5. For exegesis in a liturgical context: Benedicta Ward, *The Venerable Bede*, 2nd ed. (London, 1998), pp. 44–6.

history of the Old Testament was both true and spiritually significant. He could take details unrecorded in the Bible from Josephus, because he was interpreting not just the scriptural account of the temple, but also the physical temple itself.[63]

Bede believed that any use of allegory that denied the reality of Old Testament history, which recounted God's work in this world, could damage faith: 'But it must be carefully observed, as each one devotes his attention to the allegorical senses, how far he may have forsaken the manifest truth of history by allegorical interpretation'.[64] He did not believe that allegory was itself wrong, but that Christian allegory should never undermine the believer's faith in sacred history. Bede would never use allegory or indeed history to explain away a scriptural miracle, indeed he disagreed with Theodore when the latter attempted to use 'historical' knowledge to explain what was, interpreted literally, a miracle;[65] but Bede would use allegory to make historical facts spiritually useful to contemporary readers.[66] The exegete could only fruitfully interpret the tabernacle once he had its physical dimensions clear.[67] It was (usually[68]) impossible to have a spiritual interpretation without the foundation of the historical one; but equally philological or historical analysis of the Bible alone was fruitless. Hence, Bede habitually referred to the meaning of Hebrew words or alternative versions of a text simply to make a spiritual point.[69]

Discussion of different methodologies can disguise the fact that Bede would simply have viewed his exegesis as biblical and derived from the principles asserted by Paul. Bede quoted Paul to explain why everything in the Old Testament had a meaning relevant to contemporary Christians: 'all these things happened to them in figure; and they are written for our correction'.[70] Every biblical detail of space and time was important for Bede, not because he drew on classical rhetoric's *circumstantiae*, but because of his traditional

---

[63] Samuel W. Collins, *The Carolingian Debate over Sacred Space* (New York, 2012), pp. 18–21. See also Arthur G. Holder, 'Allegory and History in Bede's Interpretation of Sacred Architecture', *American Benedictine Review* 40 (1989), pp. 115–31, at 127–31.

[64] *Gen.*, p. 3 'Sed diligenter intuendum ut ita quisque sensibus allegoricis studium impendat, quatenus apertam historiae fidem allegorizando derelinquat'; trans. Kendall, p. 69.

[65] William D. McCready, *Miracles and the Venerable Bede* (Toronto, 1994), pp. 62–4.

[66] For example, *Sam.*, p. 9.

[67] *Tab.*, pp. 43–4. Bede's literal exegesis of the tabernacle is much briefer than that of Augustine: *Quaestiones in Heptateuchum*, ed. J. Fraipont, CCSL 33, II.177 pp. 152–74.

[68] Traditionally, Christian exegetes decreed the Song of Songs to have no literal meaning: *Cant.*, p. 337.

[69] Hebrew etymology: *Temp.*, pp. 152, 155; *Ezra.*, p. 353; *Tab.*, pp. 18–19. Textual comparison: *Ret.*, p. 138; *Apoc.*, p. 285. See Tristan Major, 'Words, Wit, and Wordplay in the Latin Works of the Venerable Bede', *Journal of Medieval Latin* 22 (2012), pp. 185–219, at 210–18.

[70] 1 Corinthians 10.11: *Temp.*, p. 148; *Gen.*, p. 188; *Reg.*, XVI p. 310; *Tab.*, p. 5. Bede used Romans 15.4 to make a similar point: *Temp.*, p. 143; *Sam.*, p. 9 (quotes both verses).

understanding of Paul's exegesis.[71] Similarly, Bede frequently would use scripture to explain scripture. Scholars see this as a particularly monastic type of exegesis where the individual drew on their extensive memory of the biblical text, connecting similar words or phrases.[72] Bede's second homily on the dedication of a church, where he commented on the parable of the man who built his house on a rock, provides a good example of the kind of exegesis to which such an approach led. Bede interpreted the man building a house as Christ in his guise as mediator—using, it seems, the word 'man' (*homo*) which is common to Luke 6.48 and 1 Timothy 2.5. He went on to link the discussion of building upon a rock in Luke's gospel with a discussion of building upon a rock in Matthew's gospel, and thus interpreted the house as the Church, following the words: 'thou art Peter; and upon this rock I will build my Church'.[73] Once again a single word (*petra*) connected the two separate parts of the Bible and thereby allowed Bede to interpret the verse before him. Having linked the two gospels, Bede connected the flood which the house built upon rock resists in Luke with the gates of hell which cannot prevail against the Church in Matthew. In the midst of all this, 'and the rock was Christ' (1 Corinthians 10.4) clearly influenced Bede, though he never explicitly quoted it.[74]

If we call Bede a 'monastic exegete' based on this methodology and intellectual background, does that mean Bede was a monk writing for brother-monks? Bede wrote exegesis for members of the Wearmouth-Jarrow community, explicitly stating that he worked 'for my own benefit and that of my brothers', but many of his commentaries (such as *On Luke* and Book One of *On Genesis*) were requested by his diocesan bishop, Acca of Hexham (d. 740), who encouraged Bede's exegetical activities in general.[75] Recent work has highlighted the probable importance of a clerical audience with pastoral duties to whom Bede provided necessary materials; hence the moral emphasis of Bede's exegesis: the focus on spiritual meanings which require realization in action.[76] A clerical audience, however, does not rule out a monastic one. While the community at Hexham had a bishop and that at Wearmouth-Jarrow did not, they probably overlapped in many other features.[77] In the context of an

---

[71] Roger Ray, 'What do we know about Bede's Commentaries?', *Recherches de Théologie ancienne et médiévale* 49 (1982), pp. 5–20, at 16–18; Lubac, *Exégèse médiévale*, II, pp. 2, 62–4.

[72] Leclercq, *Love of Learning*, pp. 73–7; Scott DeGregorio, 'Bede, the Monk, as Exegete: Evidence from the Commentary on Ezra-Nehemiah', *RB* 115 (2005), pp. 343–69, at 367–8.

[73] Matthew 16.18.   [74] *Hom.*, II.25 pp. 372–3.

[75] *HE*, V.24 p. 566 'meae meorumque necessitati'; *Act.*, p. 3.

[76] Judith McClure, 'Bede's *Notes on Genesis* and the Training of the Anglo-Saxon Clergy', in *The Bible in the Medieval World: Essays in Memory of Beryl Smalley*, eds Katherine Walsh and Diana Wood (Oxford, 1985), pp. 17–30; DeGregorio, 'Exegetical Connections', pp. 55–60; Arthur G. Holder, 'Bede and the Tradition of Patristic Exegesis', *Anglican Theological Review* 72 (1990), pp. 399–411.

[77] Sarah Foot, *Monastic Life in Anglo-Saxon England, c.600–900* (Cambridge, 2006), pp. 61–9.

Anglo-Saxon monasticism not yet characterized exclusively by cloistered contemplation, this 'pastoral' element in Bede's thought does not contradict a monastic concentration on the Bible.[78]

The Bible thus lay at the heart of Bede's education and intellectual endeavours. As we will see shortly, Bede's interpretations of the temple image derive from the use of that image within scripture itself. But often such interpretations were also patristic commonplaces. Centuries of Christian scholarship had been devoted to the Bible before Bede. A monk's exegesis depended almost as much on his memory of the writings of the Fathers as on that of the sacred text.[79] We cannot discuss Bede's 'methodology' without acknowledging the importance of his patristic reading, for, as already seen, he often simply had learned that methodology from the Fathers. Thus, before embarking on a detailed study of Bede's use of the temple image, we must look at how it was used in the Christian tradition before him.

THE TEMPLE IN THE CHRISTIAN TRADITION BEFORE BEDE

In this section, I locate Bede within the extensive tradition of Christian interpretation of the temple image. The sheer bulk of Christian material before Bede making reference to the temple image mocks any attempt at synthesis or summary.[80] I confine myself, therefore, to emphasizing writers and themes that may have influenced Bede, identifying particularly important sources (including some not previously recognized)—without striving for exhaustive coverage. Readers who wish to examine Bede's sources in detail are well advised to go first to the work of Holder and DeGregorio whose English translations of *On the Tabernacle* and *On Ezra and Nehemiah* respectively provide critical appartuses that improve dramatically on those in the original Latin critical editions.[81]

Christianity initially arose in the shadow of the temple at Jerusalem and both Jesus and his early followers continued to worship there. In such circumstances, the image of the temple features frequently in the New Testament—though some of its uses may not refer exclusively to the Jewish

---

[78] DeGregorio, 'Bede, the Monk', p. 362.   [79] Leclercq, *Love of Learning*, p. 89.

[80] Other overviews of this topic: Arthur G. Holder, 'Bede's Commentaries on the Tabernacle and the Temple' (PhD dissertation, Duke University, 1987), pp. 151–79; Jennifer O'Reilly, 'Introduction', in *Bede: On the Temple*, trans. Seán Connolly (Liverpool, 1995), pp. xxiii–xxviii; Christiana Whitehead, *Castles of the Mind: A Study of Medieval Architectural Allegory* (Cardiff, 2003), pp. 10–18.

[81] See also Arthur G. Holder, 'New Treasures and Old in Bede's "De Tabernaculo" and "De Templo"', *RB* 99 (1989), pp. 237–49.

temple: gentile Christians were also familiar with pagan temples.[82] Perhaps most obviously, the temple image appears as a description of the Christian community, a topos possibly derived from similar language in other first-century Jewish groupings.[83] Architectural language appears repeatedly in the New Testament: the Church appears as a temple or building; Christian leaders are pillars; the cornerstone symbolizes Christ; the apostles and prophets form the foundation (although elsewhere Christ is the foundation); and individual Christians become 'living stones'.[84] The work of Christ tears down the 'middle wall of partition' which separated Jews and gentiles—a possible reference to the barrier separating the court of the gentiles from the rest of the temple complex.[85] While Paul's letters argued for the interpretation of the community as a temple, Paul further suggested that the body of the individual Christian formed a temple.[86] Through Christ all individual Christians had become priests and sacrifices.[87]

While some Christian texts sought to commandeer the image of the temple for the Church, others intended to denigrate it by emphasizing how Christ had superseded the old Jewish cult and holy place. The Gospel of John identified Jesus' body with the temple, and seems indeed to have presented the incarnate Word as replacing the temple as the means of God's communication with his people.[88] Related ideas appear in the other gospels where the destruction of the temple veil marks Christ's death; in Matthew's gospel Christ declared himself 'greater than the temple'.[89] Christians interpreted Jesus' death on the cross as an act of sacrifice on the model of Jewish cult.[90] The Letter to the Hebrews provides the most detailed use of such an idea, presenting Christ's death not simply as superior to the Jewish sacrifices of the Old Testament but in fact as

---

[82] E. P. Sanders, 'Jerusalem and its Temple in Early Christian Thought and Practice', in *Jerusalem: Its Sanctity and Centrality to Judaism, Christianity, and Islam*, ed. Lee I. Levine (New York, 1999), pp. 90–103; Christopher Rowland, 'The Temple in the New Testament', in *Temple and Worship in Biblical Israel*, ed. John Day (London, 2005), pp. 469–83. For the significance of temples in the pagan world: Gregory Stevenson, *Power and Place: Temple and Identity in the Book of Revelation* (Berlin, 2001), pp. 37–114.

[83] R. J. McKelvey, *The New Temple: The Church in the New Testament* (Oxford, 1969); Timothy Wardle, *The Jerusalem Temple and Early Christian Identity* (Tübingen, 2010). Elisabeth Schüssler Fiorenza, 'Cultic Language in Qumran and in the NT', *Catholic Biblical Quarterly* 38 (1976), pp. 159–77.

[84] 1 Corinthians 3.16–17; 2 Corinthians 6.16; Ephesians 2.21; Galatians 2.9; Apocalypse 3.12; Ephesians 2.20; 1 Corinthians 3.11; 1 Peter 2.5.

[85] Ephesians 2.14.

[86] 1 Corinthians 6.19. While Jewish writers had thought of the soul or mind as a temple of God, the identification with the body was original: Schüssler Fiorenza, 'Cultic Language', p. 172.

[87] 1 Peter 2.5, 2.9; Apocalypse 1.6; Romans 12.1. Schüssler Fiorenza, 'Cultic Language', pp. 174–5.

[88] John 2.19–21 (see also Matthew 26.61, 27.40; Mark 14.58, 15.29). See Paul M. Hoskins, *Jesus as the Fulfillment of the Temple in the Gospel of John* (Milton Keynes, 2006), pp. 10–18.

[89] Matthew 27.51; Luke 23.45; Mark 15.38; Matthew 12.6.

[90] 1 Corinthians 5.7; Ephesians 5.2.

their completion and perfection with Christ as the true high priest.[91] The work of Christ had rendered the old mediation of the temple priesthood unnecessary. Hence, in the New Jerusalem there will be no temple because the Lord God 'is the temple'.[92] Stephen's diatribe in Acts indicates that some Christians condemned the temple as something always nigh-idolatrous in its attempt to localize and limit the transcendent God.[93]

The Letter to the Hebrews may also display a cosmological reading of the tabernacle similar to that presented by first-century Jewish authors such as Philo (d. *c*.50) and Josephus (d. 95)—the Holy of Holies represents heaven which Christ has entered by his sacrifice, though such language may be as much metaphorical as genuinely cosmological.[94] John's Apocalypse similarly depicts heaven as a temple where God sits enthroned, worshipped by priestly angels.[95] Christian longing for the New Jerusalem, the house not made by hands, replaced the old Jewish longing for Zion. In this great variety of New Testament sources lies the origin of Bede's 'rather exceptionally architectural approach to Revelation'.[96]

Broadly speaking, Bede interpreted the temple image in those ways established by the New Testament. Indeed, when outlining the multiplicity of possible meanings for the temple, he listed those interpretations which appear in the Bible: the temple as Church, as Christ's body, as the individual believer, as heaven.[97] And Bede cited the appropriate New Testament texts to back up these interpretations—the uses from John's gospel and 1 Corinthians of course, but also 1 Peter (on 'living stones') and Ephesians (Christ as cornerstone).[98] While he also made use of the Letter to the Hebrews and the related ideas of Christ's replacement of the temple cult, Bede seems to have rarely used Stephen's condemnation of the temple 'made by hands' and, interestingly, never seems to have independently cited Stephen's proof text, Isaiah 66.1–2's attack on the temple.[99] The virulent polemic which the image of the temple incited in some early Christian writers, who attacked the material

---

[91] Hebrews 7–10; Marie E. Isaacs, *Sacred Space: An Approach to the Theology of the Epistle to the Hebrews* (Sheffield, 1992); Kenneth L. Schenck, *Cosmology and Eschatology in Hebrews: The Settings of the Sacrifice* (Cambridge, 2007).

[92] Apocalypse 21.22.

[93] Acts 7.47–50. Rowland, 'Temple in the New Testament', pp. 473–4; Wardle, *Jerusalem Temple*, pp. 197–202.

[94] Hebrews 9.24; Jean Daniélou, 'La Symbolique du Temple de Jerusalem chez Philon et Josephe', in *Le Symbolisme Cosmique des Monuments Religieux*, ed. Giuseppe Tucci (Rome, 1957), pp. 83–90; Schenck, *Cosmology and Eschatology*, pp. 180–81.

[95] Apocalypse 4–5, 11.19, 15.5–8. See also 2 Corinthians 5.1.

[96] Jones, 'Introductory Remarks', p. 169.

[97] *DST*, II.12 pp. 168–9; *Temp.*, p. 147; *Ezra.*, p. 300; *Hom.*, II.1 pp. 189–90; *Gen.*, p. 213.

[98] John 2.19; 1 Corinthians 3.16–17; 1 Peter 2.5; Ephesians 2.20. See the *Indices Scriptorum* of the relevant CCSL volumes.

[99] *Act.*, p. 37; see Ch. 3 within this volume, 'The house made by human hands', p. 54.

temple as having always been opposed to God's plan, never reached him.[100] The New Testament provided a variety of interpretations of the temple image, and Bede clearly preferred some to others.

Centuries of patristic thought had mediated and refined such interpretations. One of the most important figures in this process, as in Christian exegesis more generally, was Origen (185–254). Variations on the temple image regularly appear throughout his extensive exegetical corpus, including the standard Pauline interpretation of the temple as the individual and the Johannine reading of Christ's human body as the true temple.[101] Origen considered the destruction of the physical temple of great importance, not simply from a supercessionist perspective, but from an exegetical one: by rendering Jewish cult impossible to fulfil literally, God had shown that it ought to be interpreted spiritually.[102] Hence, Origen's fascination with the Old Testament accounts of the tabernacle in particular. He read the description of the ancient Jewish sacrifices in the light of the Letter to the Hebrews: these presented types of Christ's own saving work.[103] Origen interpreted the tabernacle itself on two levels. Firstly, the tabernacle represented the Church, built up by the teachers of the faith (an idea central to Bede's exegesis);[104] secondly, the individual Christian could become a tabernacle through the virtues.[105] God desires the individual to move from earthly to heavenly things and be transformed into a higher being in the heavenly Holy of Holies.[106]

The diversity and range of Origen's use of the temple image anticipated its importance in Bede's work.[107] Did Bede, however, actually know Origen's exegesis, as represented in Rufinus' Latin translations? Bede and Origen

---

[100] *Epistle of Barnabas*, ed. and trans. Michael W. Holmes, *The Apostolic Fathers: Greek Texts and English Translations*, 3rd ed. (Grand Rapids MI, 2007), 16 pp. 428–33; Justin Martyr, *Dialogue with Trypho*, trans. G. Reith, *The Writings of Justin Martyr and Athenagoras* (Edinburgh, 1867), XXII p. 115.

[101] Individual as temple: Origen/Rufinus, *In Genesim Homiliae*, ed. W. A. Baehrens, *Origenes Werke* 6 (Leipzig, 1920), I.17 p. 22; Christ as temple: Origen/Rufinus, *In Exodum Homiliae*, ed. Baehrens, *Origenes Werke* 6, VI.12 pp. 202–3.

[102] Origen/Rufinus, *In Numeros Homiliae*, ed. W. A. Baehrens, *Origenes Werke* 7 (Leipzig, 1921), XXIII.1 pp. 210–11; C. P. Bammel, 'Law and Temple in Origen', in *Templum Amicitiae: Essays on the Second Temple presented to Ernst Bammel*, ed. William Horbury (Sheffield, 1991), pp. 463–76.

[103] Origen/Rufinus, *In Leviticum Homiliae*, ed. Baehrens, *Origenes Werke* 6, IV.8 p. 327, IX.5 pp. 424–8.

[104] Origen/Rufinus, *In Exodum*, IX.3 pp. 239–40, XIII.4 p. 276.

[105] Origen/Rufinus, *In Exodum*, IX.4 pp. 240–44.

[106] Origen/Rufinus, *In Exodum*, IX.4 pp. 243–4; Origen/Rufinus, *In Leviticum*, IX.11 pp. 438–40. Rowan A. Greer, *The Captain of Our Salvation: A Study in the Patristic Exegesis of Hebrews* (Tübingen, 1973), pp. 18–22.

[107] For Bede following in Origen's footsteps: Jennifer O'Reilly, 'The Library of Scripture: Views from Vivarium and Wearmouth-Jarrow', in *New Offerings, Ancient Treasures: Studies in Medieval Art for George Henderson*, eds Paul Binski and William Noel (Stroud, 2001), pp. 3–39, at 19–21.

quoted many of the same biblical texts on the tabernacle as the Church (Psalms 11.7; Galatians 2.9; Ecclesiastes 4.12) but rarely to the same effect and the evidence for knowledge of Origen at Canterbury (the Anglo-Saxon centre most likely to be familiar with the Greek author) is rather vague.[108] Hurst identified Origen's homily on the tabernacle as a source for *On the Tabernacle*, but Arthur Holder has demonstrated convincingly that Hurst's citations consist of, at best, vague reminiscences of Origen which do not suggest that Bede had access to the work.[109] However, Bede did directly quote from a homily of Origen's concerning the temple on at least one occasion: in *On Luke* Bede, repeating Rufinus' translation of Origen, explained that the temple was destroyed by God to prevent the external ceremonies of its cult from enrapturing those weak in the faith.[110] This proves nothing about his wider access to Origen's corpus, but possibly other snippets from it reached Bede, who cited Origen by name in *On Genesis*.[111]

The temple image played its part in the controversies which disturbed the Church in the Greek-speaking world of the fourth and fifth centuries. To speak of the humanity assumed by the second person of the Trinity as the temple was 'typical' of the so-called 'Antiochene' theologians, who favoured a two-natures Christology.[112] A close reading of John 2.19 ('Destroy this temple; and in three days I will raise it up'), they argued, showed a clear distinction between the temple/humanity to be destroyed and the divine Word promising to raise it up.[113] Suspicion eventually fell on the 'Antiochene' school due to association with the heretical Nestorius (d. 450), who shared this understanding of the temple as the human nature assumed by God;[114] in the long run, many of the 'Antiochene' thinkers were condemned. Describing Christ's body as the temple was never condemned, though such language came to be used only cautiously in the Greek East. The Formula of Reunion, signed by the patriarchs of Alexandria and Antioch in 433, spoke of the Word uniting himself to the temple he took from Mary and so the expression was canonized.[115] While

---

[108] *Tab.*, pp. 64, 74, 91. Bischoff and Lapidge, *Biblical Commentaries*, pp. 219–20.

[109] Holder, 'New Treasures and Old', pp. 245–8; Holder has similarly dealt with the suggestion that Origen was a direct source for *On the Song of Songs*: 'The Patristic Sources of Bede's Commentary on the Song of Songs', *Studia Patristica* 34 (2001), pp. 370–75.

[110] *Luc.*, p. 364; compare Origen/Rufinus, *In Leviticum*, X.1 pp. 441–2. Conor O'Brien, 'A Quotation from Origen's *Homilies on Leviticus* in Bede's Commentary on Luke's Gospel', *Notes and Queries* 60 (2013), pp. 185–6.

[111] *Gen.*, p. 111.

[112] Greer, *Captain of Our Salvation*, pp. 280–81; J. N. D. Kelly, *Early Christian Doctrines*, 5th ed. (London, 1977), p. 329.

[113] Paul B. Clayton, *The Christology of Theoderet of Cyrus: Antiochene Christology from the Council of Ephesus (431) to the Council of Chalcedon (451)* (Oxford, 2007), p. 144; Frederick G. McLeod, *Theodore of Mopsuestia* (London, 2009), p. 146.

[114] John A. McGuckin, *St. Cyril of Alexandria: The Christological Controversy: Its History, Theology, and Texts* (Leiden, 1994), p. 366; Greer, *Captain of Our Salvation*, p. 311.

[115] McGuckin, *Cyril of Alexandria*, p. 345.

Bede condemned Nestorius, he often used the temple image to stress Christ's human body, as we shall see.[116]

Many of the 'Antiochene' writers also ended up associated with another distinctive use of the temple image: the belief in a tabernacle-shaped physical universe. Of course, cosmological interpretations of the tabernacle long played a part in the tradition, arising from Jewish exegesis, but only Theodore of Mopsuestia's (d. 428) followers came to view the tabernacle as a literal image of the world. What had previously been symbolic became scientific.[117] The *Christian Topography* of Cosmas Indicopleustes, a Nestorian and flat-earther, provides the most elaborate defence of this belief in a tabernacle-shaped universe.[118] While 'Antiochene' uses of the temple image may seem far removed from Wearmouth-Jarrow, many of these writers were known in Anglo-Saxon England. The output of the school of Canterbury, which explicitly cites Cosmas, for example, reveals the influence of the works of Theodore of Mopsuestia and his followers. It remains difficult, however, to determine whether this reflects Archbishop Theodore's personal learning or the existence of actual copies of such works in England.[119]

The vast majority of Bede's exegetical education came directly from the Latin Fathers; even a figure such as Ambrose, of whose work Bede only had access to a small amount, probably proved more important than any Greek theologian. Ambrose frequently interpreted the Old Testament priesthood in a distinctly clerical light, but Bede was more likely to know his interpretation of the robes of the Aaronic high priest as symbolizing the union of faith and works.[120] Soteriologically, Ambrose often emphasized Christ's status as priest and victim, a status particularly linked to his humanity; Christ did not 'sacrifice for us in temples made by hand, but in the temple of his body'.[121] In addition, the bishop of Milan liked the image of the temple Church being built up from living stones—an image that he shifted towards emphasizing the election of the gentiles, a concern that Bede would also share.[122]

[116] On Nestorius: *Act.*, p. 83; *EpCath.*, p. 311; *Luc.*, p. 32. See Ch. 5 within this volume, 'The temple as Christ', p. 101–5.

[117] Wanda Wolska, *La Topographie Chrétienne de Cosmas Indicopleustès: Théologie et Science au VIe siècle* (Paris, 1962), pp. 113–18; Arthur G. Holder, 'The Mosaic Tabernacle in Early Christian Exegesis', *Studia Patristica* 25 (1993), pp. 101–6.

[118] For Cosmas' intellectual outlook: Wolska, *La Topographie Chrétienne*.

[119] Bischoff and Lapidge, *Biblical Commentaries*, pp. 205–33; Lapidge, *Library*, p. 33. See Ch. 4 within this volume, 'Bede's use of the cosmic interpretation', p. 74.

[120] Roger Gryson, 'Les Lévites, Figure du Sacerdoce Véritable, selon Saint Ambrose', *Ephemerides Theologicae Lovanienses* 56 (1980), pp. 89–112. For the High Priest's vestments: Ambrose, *De fide*, ed. O. Faller, CSEL 78, II.prol.11–13 pp. 61–2 (compare *Tab.*, p. 106).

[121] Ambrose, *De fide*, III.XI.86–7 pp. 139–40; Ambrose, *Expositio Evangelii Secundum Lucam*, ed. M. Adriaen, CCSL 14, prol.7 p. 5, I.23 p. 18; Ambrose, *De Spiritu Sancto*, ed. O. Faller, CSEL 79, I.prol.4 p. 17. Roger Gryson, *Le Prêtre selon Saint Ambroise* (Louvain, 1968), pp. 45–62.

[122] Ambrose, *Expositio Evangelii*, II.75 pp. 62–3 (compare *Luc.*, pp. 77–8), VII.169 p. 273, IX.1 p. 333.

While Paul, breaking new ground, declared the body to be the temple of God, the Church Fathers received their education in a classical tradition which saw the soul as the only part of a human that one could consider divine; Ambrose, along with Jerome, thus displayed a tendency towards speaking of the soul, rather than the body, as God's dwelling place.[123] When they did speak of the body as the temple, they generally sought to condemn sexual sin and to celebrate the uncontaminated virgin body—an interpretation for which scriptural justification did exist.[124] Bede thus inherited a tradition that had shifted the image of the temple-as-individual in a more spiritual direction, away from Paul's focus on the body.

Jerome's primary interpretation of the temple image remained ecclesiological. Indeed, he stated that one should understand any mention of building Jerusalem or its temple in the Old Testament as referring to the growth of the Church, on an institutional or individual level, in the current age.[125] A concern to refute so-called Jews and 'Judaizers', who read such passages as prophecies to be literally fulfilled in the future, seems to have driven Jerome.[126] He believed that the universal spread of the gospel had superseded the limitations of the material temple; the individual believer had become the locus of God's presence and thus heaven was just as easily accessible from Britain as from Jerusalem.[127] Jerome's interpretation of Ezekiel's temple provided a model for Bede's exegesis, interweaving textual criticism with mystical exegesis, requiring both linguistic competence and number symbolism.[128]

Augustine was unusual in the degree to which he saw the Old Testament Jewish cult as an explicitly good thing. God had ordered blood sacrifices and the temple ritual not because of the weakness of a carnal people, but because these things bore a genuine sacramental relationship to the true sacrifice of Christ on the cross. God had intended the Jews to practise physical sacrifice

---

[123] Ambrose, *Expositio Evangelii*, X.6 p. 347, X.17 pp. 350–1; Ambrose, *Exameron*, ed. C. Schenkl, CSEL 32, VI.6.39 p. 231. Gryson, *Le Prêtre*, pp. 77–84, does not discuss this quotation as part of his study of Ambrose's use of the temple image. Jerome, *Epistulae*, ed. I. Hilberg, CSEL 54, LVIII.7 p. 536, CSEL 55, CVII.4 p. 293; Jerome, *In Matheum*, eds D. Hurst and M. Adriaen, CCSL 72, p. 148.

[124] Ambrose, *De Virginibus*, ed. and trans. Franco Gori, *Verginità e Vedovanza*, 2 vols (Milan, 1989), II, pp. 18, 180; Jerome, *Epistulae*, CSEL 54, XXII.6 p. 150, LV.2 p. 489. For the tendency to relate the Jewish priesthood and cult to the position of virgins in the Church: Clark, *Reading Renunciation*, pp. 208–32.

[125] Jerome, *In Amos*, ed. M. Adriaen, CCSL 76, p. 346.

[126] Robert L. Wilken, '*In novissimis diebus*: Biblical Promises, Jewish Hopes and Early Christian Exegesis', *Journal of Early Christian Studies* 1 (1993), pp. 1–19; Michael Graves, '"Judaizing" Christian Interpretations of the Prophets as seen by Saint Jerome', *Vigiliae Christianae* 61 (2007), pp. 142–56.

[127] Jerome, *In Esaiam*, ed. M. Adriaen, CCSL 73+A, pp. 86, 585, 634, 694; Jerome, *Epistulae*, CSEL 54, LVIII.3 p. 531.

[128] Jerome, *Commentarii in Hiezechielem*, ed. F. Glorie, CCSL 75, XII pp. 549–604.

and approved when they did so in the period before the Passion.[129] This approach clearly influenced Bede, who repeatedly quoted Augustine that, while there was a diversity of sacraments on account of the difference of times, the faith had been one always.[130] Augustine's positive view of the temple cult derived from the centrality of Christ's sacrifice to his view of salvation, and, while not alone in this, he was probably the most influential theologian to transmit this view to Bede. In the form of the incarnation Christ existed as true mediator, priest, and sacrifice.[131] He had offered the Church, in the form of his body, up to God in sacrifice; since Christ's own body was the temple, it followed that so, too, was the Church.[132]

The temple image, therefore, proved primarily Christocentric for Augustine: Christians participate in Christ as parts of his body; Christ dwells within Christians as God in his temple.[133] Consequently, Augustine (like Bede) was fond of applying architectural imagery to the Church.[134] The temple image represented unity for Augustine: the unity of the individual with Christ, but also of all Christians with each other through charity.[135] In his preaching Augustine tended towards emphasizing the bodily nature of the individual temple, for reasons of moral exhortation.[136] He both dismissed the idea that God's temple was the human mind and declared that the bodies of married women were temples of God just as much as those of virgins.[137] But, of course, the body of fallen humanity did not deserve this dignity

---

[129] Augustine, *DCD*, X.5 pp. 276–8; Augustine, *Contra Faustum*, ed. J. Zycha, CSEL 25, XIX.16–17 pp. 512–16, XX.18 pp. 558–9, XX.22 pp. 565–6. Paula Fredriksen, *Augustine and the Jews: A Christian Defense of Jews and Judaism* (New York, 2008), esp. ch. 9–10.

[130] *Act.*, pp. 26, 66–7; *Tab.*, p. 86; *Cant.*, p. 190; *Hom.*, II.3 p. 204; compare Augustine, *Epistulae*, ed. A. Goldbacher, CSEL 57, CXC.6 p. 142. See Ch. 3 within this volume, 'The house made by human hands', p. 53.

[131] Augustine, *DCD*, X.6 p. 279, X.20 p. 294; Augustine, *De Trinitate*, ed. W. J. Mountain, CCSL 50, IV.14 pp. 186–7. Gerald Bonner, 'The Doctrine of Sacrifice: Augustine and the Latin Patristic Tradition', in *Sacrifice and Redemption: Durham Essays in Theology*, ed. S. W. Sykes (Cambridge, 1991), pp. 101–17; Earl C. Muller, 'The Priesthood of Christ in Book IV of the *De trinitate*', in *Augustine: Presbyter Factus Sum*, eds Joseph T. Lienhard et al. (New York, 1993), pp. 135–49.

[132] Augustine, *Sermones post Maurinos Reperti*, ed. G. Morin, *Miscellanea Agostiniana*, vol. 1 (Rome, 1930), III.4 pp. 598–9.

[133] Augustine, *Enarrationes in Psalmos*, ed. E. Dekkers and J. Fraipont, CCSL 38–40, CXXXI.3 p. 1913; Augustine, *In Iohannis Evangelium Tractatus*, ed. R. Willems, CCSL 36, XXVII.6 p. 272, CXI.6 pp. 632–3.

[134] Dominique Sanchis, 'Le symbolisme communautaire du temple chez Saint Augustin', *Revue d'Ascétique et de Mystique* 37 (1961), pp. 3–30, 137–47; Finbarr G. Clancy, 'Augustine's Sermons on the Dedication of a Church', *Studia Patristica* 38 (2001), pp. 48–55.

[135] Augustine, *Enarrationes*, X.7 pp. 79–80, CXXX.1 p. 1898; Augustine, *Sermones*, PL 38, XV.1 col. 116; Augustine, *Epistulae*, CLXXXVII.38 p. 115.

[136] Augustine, *Sermones*, IX.15 col. 86–87, CLXI.2 col. 878–879, CCLXXVIII.7 col. 1271.

[137] Augustine, *Sermones*, LXXXII.13 col. 512; Augustine, *De Bono Viduitatis*, ed. J. Zycha, CSEL 41, VI.8 pp. 312–13.

automatically—individuals only became the temple of God once they had received the grace of baptism.[138]

This idea was not unique to Augustine. The liturgical forms preserved in the Gelasian Sacramentary, probably known to Bede and his contemporaries in Anglo-Saxon England, declare that the Christian becomes a temple of God through baptism.[139] This reminds us that exegesis and theological writings did not provide Bede's only sources for Christian views of the temple. The Gelasian liturgy of church dedication speaks of the church building as a temple, and the link between churches and the Jerusalem temple appears frequently, either in their design or through inscriptions and commemorative verses.[140] Anglo-Saxon Christians made the link in their own writings— Stephen's account of Wilfrid's church at Ripon, for example, compared it to both the temple and the tabernacle, while Aldhelm's verses on the dedication of churches frequently describe the church building as *templum*.[141] Great preachers such as Augustine and Caesarius of Arles (d. 542) made use of this tradition in sermons and homilies to mark the dedication or anniversary of the dedication of a physical church. They used Christian architectural language to direct moral exhortations to their congregation or to speak about the congregation as the true temple.[142] Bede himself participated in this tradition, taking exactly the same kind of approach in his *Homilies* II.24 and II.25 for the feast of a church's dedication.

While all the Fathers had a claim on Bede's devotion, Gregory the Great, the 'Apostle of the English', had a special influence over the Northumbrian. One of Gregory's letters (known to Bede) concerning the mission to the Anglo-Saxons comments interestingly on ancient Jewish cult. Suggesting that the Church reuse the sites of old pagan shrines, Gregory put forward the unAugustinian argument that God ordered the Jews to sacrifice animals because they were already familiar with such a rite from paganism and it

---

[138] Augustine, *Epistulae*, CLXXXVII.31–33 pp. 108–11; Augustine, *Contra Iulianum*, PL 44, VI.XIV.42–43 col. 846–847.

[139] *Liber Sacramentorum Romanae Aeclesiae Ordinis Anni Circuli*, eds Leo Cunibert Mohlberg et al. (Rome, 1960), LXXV.607 p. 95, also LXXXVIII.700 pp. 109–10, XXXIII.294 p. 45. Richard W. Pfaff, *The Liturgy in Medieval England: A History* (Cambridge, 2009), pp. 40–45.

[140] *Liber Sacramentorum*, LXXXVIIII pp. 110–11. Marie-Pierre Terrian, 'Religious Architecture and Mathematics during the Late Antiquity', in *Mathematics and the Divine: A Historical Study*, eds T. Koetsier and L. Bergmans (Amsterdam, 2005), pp. 147–60, at 151–2; Helen Gittos, *Liturgy, Architecture, and Sacred Places in Anglo-Saxon England* (Oxford, 2013), pp. 37, 237, 244, 263–4, 276.

[141] *VW*, XVII pp. 34–7; Aldhelm, *Carmina Ecclesiastica*, ed. R. Ehwald, MGH Auctores Antiquissimi 15, I–III pp. 11–18.

[142] Ambrose, *Exhortatio Virginitatis*, ed. and trans. Franco Gori, *Verginità e Vedovanza*, II, 2.10 p. 206, 14.94 p. 270; Augustine, *Sermones*, CCCXXXVI–CCCXXXVII col. 1471–1478; Caesarius of Arles, *Sermones*, ed. G. Morin, CCSL 104, CCXXVIII–CCXXIX pp. 901–10. See Brian Repsher, *The Rite of Church Dedication in the Early Medieval Era* (Lampeter, 1998), esp. pp. 27–33.

would ease their progress to the true faith.[143] More commonly Gregory used temple imagery to advance his vision of clerical reform and pastoral purity. For example, he returned to the story of the cleansing of the temple repeatedly to condemn simony among the clergy;[144] he interpreted the details of the tabernacle and its priesthood as giving rules for the Christian pastor in a manner on which Bede later expanded.[145] The latter's interpretation of the Jewish priests' garments, in particular, depended to a large extent on Gregory.[146]

Gregory's *Homilies on Ezekiel* probably presented Bede with the most influential example of Christian exegesis of the temple. His own approach became infused with the language and themes of Gregory's interpretation. The role of preachers and teachers building the Church, seen as an institution with twin origins in the Jewish and gentile peoples, provided the ecclesiological focus of Gregory's work on Ezekiel's vision.[147] While love of neighbour builds up the Church in this life, the desire for perfect contemplation of God drives the faithful on towards heaven.[148] As elsewhere, Gregory's use of the temple-as-individual image tended to concentrate on the interior, the mind rather than body as the place of divine inhabitation.[149] As we shall see repeatedly, Bede built the edifice of his exegesis with words and imagery quarried from the Fathers, especially Gregory.

Christian exegesis, of course, did not only take place within the Mediterranean basin: the Insular world produced commentaries of its own, although the debate concerning the extent of that achievement rages on.[150] Certainly teachers explaining the Bible orally abounded, and at least on occasion, in Ireland as well as at Canterbury, had their ideas set down in texts.[151] The

[143] Gregory, *Registrum Epistularum*, ed. D. Norberg, CCSL 140+A, XI.56 pp. 961–2; *HE*, I.30 pp. 106–9. See Flora Spiegel, 'The *tabernacula* of Gregory the Great and the Conversion of Anglo-Saxon England', *ASE* 36 (2007), pp. 1–13.

[144] E.g. Gregory, *Registrum*, V.58 p. 355, VI.7 p. 376, IX.219 p. 784; Gregory, *Homiliae in Evangelia*, ed. R. Étaix, CCSL 141, I.IV.4 pp. 30–1, I.LXVII.13 pp. 126–7, II.XXXIX.6 p. 386; compare *Luc.*, p. 349; *Marc.*, p. 579; *Hom.*, II.1 pp. 186–7.

[145] Esp. Gregory, *Regula Pastoralis*, PL 77, II.2–7 col. 27–42, II.11 col. 48–50; Gregory, *Moralia*, XXV.XVI.39 pp. 1263–4; Gregory reused parts of the *Regula* such as at Gregory, *Registrum*, I.24 pp. 22–32.

[146] *Tab.*, pp. 95–124; Holder, 'New Treasures and Old', p. 243.

[147] Teachers: Gregory, *In Hiezechihelem*, II.I.17 p. 222, II.VI.6–8 pp. 297–300, II.IX.20–2 pp. 374–7. Jews and gentiles: II.V.2 p. 276, II.VI.20 p. 309, II.X.11 pp. 386–7.

[148] Gregory, *In Hiezechihelem*, II.I.5 p. 211, II.IV.3 p. 259, II.VII.5 p. 319, II.VIII.4 pp. 338–9, II.IX.10 p. 364.

[149] Gregory, *In Hiezechihelem*, II.II.5 p. 228, II.II.14 p. 234; Gregory, *Moralia*, XXIV.VIII.18 p. 1200; Gregory, *In Evangelia*, II.XXXIX.7 pp. 386–7. Carole Straw, *Gregory the Great: Perfection in Imperfection* (Berkeley CA, 1988), pp. 96–7, argues that Gregory did think of the body as the temple, at least in the case of saints.

[150] Michael Gorman, 'The Myth of Hiberno-Latin Exegesis', and Dáibhí Ó Cróinín, 'Bischoff's Wendepunkte Fifty Years On', *RB* 110 (2000), pp. 42–85 and 204–37, respectively.

[151] Michael W. Herren, 'Irish Biblical Commentaries before 800', in *Roma, Magistra Mundi: Itineraria Culturae Medievalis*, ed. Jacqueline Hamesse, vol. 1 (Louvain, 1998), pp. 391–407.

temple image fascinated Irish exegetes as it had the Church Fathers, and so we should think of Bede as part of an ongoing tradition of interpretation even if evidence concerning his dependence on Irish commentaries remains slight.[152] In a similar way to some of the grand claims made of the Canterbury school, so too the distinctiveness of Irish exegesis has been exaggerated.[153] Insular interpretation, including Bede's work on the temple image, existed in essential continuity with the patristic tradition which it inherited.

We must temper a modern interest in authorial originality with an appreciation of this continuity. Holder has sought to identify an original contribution to the tradition in Bede's contrast between the tabernacle and the temple— interpreted either as the Synagogue (the tabernacle entirely built by Jews) and the Church (the temple built by both Jews and gentiles), or as the pilgrim Church of this world and the triumphant Church in heaven.[154] The first of these two contrasts does appear original to Bede but the second proves rather more complicated. Behind it we may readily identify 2 Corinthians 5, which speaks of a 'house not made with hands, eternal in heaven' contrasted with the temporal life of those *in tabernaculo*.[155] While Paul probably meant the mortal body by 'tabernacle', rather than the earthly Church, he had already established Bede's basic contrast of two different dwellings. Centuries of patristic thought elaborated on this. Augustine particularly enjoyed contrasting the *tabernaculum* of the earthly Church with the *domus* of the heavenly one.[156] Of course, *tabernaculum* can simply mean 'tent' and often need not have explicitly referred to the tabernacle of Exodus. Bede himself applied the earthly interpretation to *tabernacula* other than that in which God dwelt;[157] but it is, nonetheless, clear that here lies the origin of the tabernacle/temple contrast.

Other exegetes before Bede seem to have touched on this contrast. Isidore of Seville (d. 636) did so implicitly, beginning his exegesis of the tabernacle by saying that it symbolized 'the Church established in the desert of this life', and that on the temple by linking 'he who built the most excellent temple for the Lord' with Christ 'who built a house for God in the heavens'.[158] Holder has

---

[152] For Irish use of the temple image: O'Reilly, 'Exegesis and the Book of Kells'. Bede may not have used Irish exegesis as much as once claimed: Roger Gryson, CCSL 121A, pp. 155–7; Giovanni Caputa, *Il Sacerdozio dei Fedeli secondo San Beda: un itinerario di maturità cristiana* (Vatican City, 2002), pp. 52–60.

[153] Clare Stancliffe, 'Early "Irish" Biblical Exegesis', *Studia Patristica* 12 (1975), pp. 361–70.

[154] Holder, 'New Treasures and Old', p. 239; Holder, 'Mosaic Tabernacle', p. 105. *Temp.*, pp. 147–8; *Tab.*, pp. 42–3; *Hom.*, II.25 p. 369.

[155] 2 Corinthians 5.1–4 'Scimus enim quoniam si terrestris domus nostra huius habitationis dissolvatur quod aedificationem ex Deo habeamus domum non manufactam aeternam in caelis . . . nam et qui sumus in tabernaculo ingemescimus gravati . . .'.

[156] Augustine, *Enarrationes*, XXX.8 pp. 218–19, CXXXI.10 p. 1916; Augustine, *In Iohannis Evangelium*, XXVIII.9 p. 282.

[157] *Ezra*, pp. 267–8; *Gen.*, pp. 138–9; *EpCath.*, pp. 265–6.

[158] Isidore of Seville, *Quaestiones in Vetus Testamentum*, PL 83, Exodus.L.1 col. 313 'Tabernaculum hoc per allegoriam Ecclesia est in hujus vitae eremo constituta' (compare *Tab.*, p. 128

argued that this work did not influence Bede, but similar ideas appear in works he certainly had read.[159] Cassiodorus (*c*.487–*c*.580) interpreted 'the place of the tabernacle' as 'the present Church', which he contrasted with 'that Jerusalem, which the Lord promised to his saints', home to the 'house of God of the world to come'.[160] An Irish commentary understood 2 Peter 1.13's tabernacle (a reference to the body) as being that of Exodus, contrasting it with the Jerusalem temple signifying heaven.[161] While Bede may have been the first to make this contrast clearly and explicitly, such 'originality' seems highly conservative—being nothing more than the development of a patristic commonplace.

Thus while we naturally seek to stress the differences between authors' uses of the temple image, we ought to remember that repetition is one of the most common features of these writings. Frequently, in fact, Bede directly borrowed the very words of previous writers—as much as ninety per cent of *On Luke* may consist of direct quotation from other authors.[162] This has often been linked to Bede's description of himself as 'following in the footsteps of the Fathers';[163] consequently scholars once saw him as a conduit of patristic learning to an otherwise ignorant Anglo-Saxon England.[164] But Bede's works, formed of a mosaic of biblical citations, patristic quotations and echoes, and original comments, display great deliberation in their manipulation of patristic learning and, thus, when Bede chose to use the words of earlier writers, he had made a calculated decision to do so.[165] No doubt he used the words of other men because they genuinely expressed his views. Traditional interpretations and images were not external presences in his writings—they formed part of his living thought.[166] Bede's authorial identity did not rest on modern conceptions of originality or individuality; in building his exegesis out

'per heremum huius uitae'), *Reg.*, III.II.1 col. 415 'Nam id, quod aedificavit templum excellentissimum Domino, et ibi Christum significat, qui aedificavit domum Deo in coelestibus'.

[159] Holder, 'New Treasures and Old', p. 248.

[160] Cassiodorus, *Expositio Psalmorum*, ed. M. Adriaen, CCSL 97–8, XLI.5 p. 382 '*in locum tabernaculi*; hoc est in Ecclesiam praesentem . . . illam Ierusalem, quam sanctis suis Dominus repromisit . . . De isto uero tabernaculo *usque ad* illam futuri saeculi *domum Dei* pius incola festinabat'; also XIV.1 p. 133.

[161] *Commentarius in Epistolas Catholicas Scotti Anonymi*, ed. R. E. McNally, CCSL 108B, p. 36. For Bede's knowledge of this work see Gryson's comments in CCSL 121A, p. 157, n. 20.

[162] Michael Gorman, 'Source Marks and Chapter Divisions in Bede's Commentary on Luke', *RB* 112 (2002), pp. 246–90, at 274.

[163] E.g. *Sam.*, p. 10; *Temp.*, p. 144; *Act.*, p. 3.

[164] Holder, 'Patristic exegesis', p. 400; Ray, 'Bede's Commentaries?', pp. 10–11. See *Gen.*, pp. 1–2; *Luc.*, pp. 5–7.

[165] Bede's thoughtful manipulation of his source materials has long been recognized: Ansgar Willmes, 'Bedas Bibelauslegung', *Archiv für Kulturgeschichte* 44 (1962), pp. 281–314, at 290–305; J. N. Hart-Hasler, 'Bede's Use of Patristic Sources: The Transfiguration', *Studia Patristica* 28 (1993), pp. 197–204.

[166] Hilliard, 'Bede as Scholar', p. 103.

of other authors' words he participated in a distinguished tradition of exegetical writing.[167] The communal context at Wearmouth-Jarrow had often mediated those words to Bede. For instance, his first encounter with the Church Fathers probably came via their use in the monastic liturgy.[168] Interaction with his brother monks thus framed Bede's understanding of patristic tradition. As I argue in what follows, Wearmouth-Jarrow's influence on Bede's temple probably went a lot further than simply providing a library on which the great author could draw.

[167] Mark Stansbury, 'Early-Medieval Biblical Commentaries, Their Writers and Readers', *Frühmittelalterliche Studien* 33 (1999), pp. 49–82.

[168] Caputa, *Sacerdozio dei Fedeli*, pp. 65–6.

3

Bede's Temple as History

Bede's claim to be *verax historicus* and subsequent reputation as the first English historian have cast a long shadow over the study of his writings;[1] despite an increasing recognition among scholars that he was much more than just a historian, he continues to be studied, taught, and thought of primarily as such—and not only in the public imagination. Since the temple was itself part of history, it seems appropriate to begin this study of Bede's use of the temple image by asking what it reveals about his ideas concerning time and the past. The importance of Bede's ideas about the historical temple lies in the fact that they relate to what he considered the key dynamic in human development: the movement between the old and the new dispensations brought about through the coming of Christ. Thinking about the temple image forced Bede to consider the relationship between the Jewish past and the Christian present, and even, when the temple was read as symbolic (rather than simply a part) of history, the relationship between past, present, and future. This chapter shows us how the temple image expressed Bede's vision of universal history, where the Old and New Testaments were linked in sight of the end.

THE HOUSE MADE BY HUMAN HANDS

Bede began his work on the image of the Jewish holy sites with a solid foundation (as he saw it) of historical details concerning the temple. Bede derived his image of the temple from a number of different holy structures that had existed in Israel's history and concerning which Bede could have told a detailed narrative pieced together from the accounts of the tabernacle in Exodus and Solomon's temple in Kings and Paralipomenon in particular. Bede's history would have begun at Mount Sinai when God instructed Moses to build the tabernacle, construct the cultic objects within it which

---

[1] *HE*, III.17 pp. 264–5.

would be used in worship, and institute the priesthood that would man its altars.[2] The tabernacle was in effect an elaborate tent, made of animal hides and wooden boards, designed to be transported by the Israelites on their journey to the Promised Land.[3] On arrival in Canaan the tabernacle continued to have a peripatetic existence, changing location on a number of occasions. The most sacred object in the tabernacle, the Ark of the Covenant (a great golden box containing the tablets of the Law and the rod of Aaron amongst other things, and providing a focus for the divine presence), often journeyed far and wide during Israel's long wars with the Philistines.[4]

It was David who eventually brought the ark into Jerusalem and conceived of the plan to build a temple, but it was left to his son Solomon to construct a permanent house of God in that city.[5] Solomon's temple of white stone was a magnificent, stationary, and (in intention at least) permanent replacement for the old tabernacle. But it, too, proved subject to the ravages of time; these could be repaired by later kings but eventually with the fall of Jerusalem to the Babylonians the entire temple was destroyed (Bede seems never to have addressed the question of what happened to the Ark of the Covenant at this point in the story).[6] After many years in exile in Babylon, the Jewish people began to return to Jerusalem with rebuilding the temple as one of their priorities.[7] Nonetheless, many years of trial passed before Solomon's work was replaced and it was never equalled.[8] From then on a temple continued to stand in Jerusalem, suffering or flourishing with the fluctuations in Israel's history, until the coming of Christ, who with his followers visited the temple, prayed there, and began the work of evangelization in its courtyards.[9] But Christ himself had predicted that the temple's days were numbered.[10] So, a few short decades after the crucifixion, the vengeance of God descended on stubborn Israel—the Romans took away the Jewish kingdom and destroyed Jerusalem and its temple.[11] Christians, of course, were not worried by this; as 2 Corinthians 5.1 declared, they awaited a house not made by human hands, eternal in the heavens. The eschatological temple was yet to come, but when

---

[2] Exodus 25–30; *Tab.*, pp. 12, 44, 95.   [3] *Tab.*, pp. 42–4; *Temp.*, pp. 147–8.

[4] The building of the ark: Exodus 25.10–22; its wanderings in Canaan: 1 Kings 4–7; *Sam.*, pp. 59–60; *VIII Q.*, VIII pp. 71–2. For doubts about the authenticity of the latter text: Eric Knibbs, 'The Manuscript Evidence for the *De Octo Quaestionibus* ascribed to Bede', *Traditio* 63 (2008), pp. 129–83.

[5] 2 Kings 6–7.13; 3 Kings 5.5–6.38; 1 Paralipomenon 15, 17.1–12, 22, 28.10–20; 2 Paralipomenon 2–7; *Luc.*, p. 21; *VIII Q.*, VIII p. 73.

[6] 4 Kings 25.9–17; 2 Paralipomenon 34.10, 36.18–19; *Ezra.*, pp. 241–2.

[7] 1 Esdras.   [8] *Ezra.*, pp. 280, 305; *Hom.*, II.24 pp. 363–4.

[9] Matthew 21; Mark 11; Luke 2.46, 24.53; John 7.14; Acts 3, 21.26; *Luc.*, pp. 424–5; *Abac.*, p. 385; *Act.*, p. 23; *Sam.*, p. 72 (= *Luc.*, p. 135; compare Jerome, *Liber de Viris Inlustribus*, ed. E. C. Richardson (Leipzig, 1896), II p. 7).

[10] Mark 13.1–2; Luke 21.5–6; Matthew 24.1–2; *Luc.*, p. 364; *Marc.*, p. 595.

[11] *DTR*, LXVI p. 498.

it did it would be the genuine, unmediated presence of God and not a physical shelter.[12]

The history of the temple that Bede could have recounted was clearly dynamic, a story of extensive change over time, but the different Jewish holy sites also had much in common with each other that provided the basis for the exegetical temple image with which he worked. All were based on concentric rings of holiness and exclusion. A barrier separated the entire complex from the world and inside it lay one (as in the tabernacle) or more courtyards;[13] in the Jerusalem temple each courtyard became progressively more restrictive (the court of gentiles was followed by that for women, men, and finally that reserved for priests) as one approached the building.[14] Inside the structure existed yet a further division: that between the outer room, the Sanctuary, and the inner Holy of Holies where the ark was placed, hidden from view behind a veil.[15]

The ark was not the only object within the temple complex, although it was the most sacred. The courtyard (of priests) surrounding the building contained water basins (in Solomon's temple also a great bronze 'sea') for washing the priests and animal sacrifices as well as two large bronze pillars in front of the Jerusalem temple.[16] Within the Sanctuary lay the table of the showbread and the great candelabrum.[17] The most important of all such liturgical objects were, of course, the altars—the larger one (the altar of holocausts) in the open air, intended for animal sacrifices, and a smaller altar on which incense was burnt within the Sanctuary before the Holy of Holies.[18] All of these cult objects were made of rich materials and precious metals, though Bede noted that the second temple used noticeably less fine materials than its predecessor.[19] Rich too were the vestments and tools of the priests who served in the temple complex.[20] David instituted a much more elaborate system of teams of priests for use in Jerusalem than had operated in the tabernacle in the desert—but in both cases only the high priest of the time could enter into the Holy of Holies to pray for the sins of Israel.[21]

---

[12] Apocalypse 21.22; *Luc.*, p. 207 (= *Marc.*, p. 544); *Hom.*, I.24 pp. 174–6; *Apoc.*, p. 561.

[13] Exodus 27.9–18; Josephus, *Jewish Antiquities*, eds and trans. H. St J. Thackeray et al., in *The Loeb Classical Library: Josephus*, 10 vols (Cambridge MA, 1926–1981), VIII.III.9, V, pp. 623–5. Bede had only the Latin translation of Josephus which still awaits a complete modern edition.

[14] *Temp.*, pp. 192–3; *Reg.*, XVIII pp. 311–12.

[15] Exodus 26.33; 3 Kings 6.16; *Hom.*, II.1 p. 190, II.25 pp. 375–6; *Temp.*, pp. 171–3, 176, 187; *Tab.*, pp. 70–3.

[16] Exodus 30.18–20; 3 Kings 7.15–39; 2 Paralipomenon 3.15–17, 4.1–6; *Temp.*, pp. 198–222; *Hom.*, II.25 p. 377.

[17] Hebrews 9.2; *Temp.*, pp. 227–32; *Tab.*, pp. 21–40.

[18] *Ezra.*, pp. 263–7; *Tab.*, pp. 76–83, 125–34; *Hom.*, II.19 pp. 323–4.

[19] *Tab.*, pp. 11, 30; *Temp.*, p. 233; *Ezra.*, p. 367.   [20] Exodus 28; *Tab.*, pp. 97–123.

[21] Josephus, *Jewish Antiquities*, VII.XIV.7, V, pp. 555–7; *Reg.*, XVIII pp. 312–13; *Hom.*, II.19 pp. 319–20; *Luc.*, p. 21.

Bede did not simply piece together these ideas about the history of the temple image from the scattered comments within the biblical books; he also drew on centuries of comment concerning the temple and especially on extra-biblical sources such as Josephus. This allowed him to assume that he could provide a convincing historical account of the temple and tabernacle and sometimes he took the time to go into detail with minute precision. It might seem strange that in exegetical works (some self-consciously allegorical) Bede would put so much effort into exploring historical details, grappling with exact measurements, or bringing together different scriptural descriptions to create a coherent picture of the real temple. Sometimes he was clearly concerned to prove that the word of God made no mistakes.[22] Hence, when the books of Kings and Paralipomenon seemed to give two radically different figures for the height of the temple, Bede carefully explained that in fact no contradiction existed. Kings had merely been describing the height to the first storey of the temple, whereas Paralipomenon gave the overall height of the building with its side chambers.[23] Although Bede's solution came from Josephus, no previous Christian writer seems to have examined the temple image in so much detail as to worry about this point.[24] Occasionally, Bede simply seems to have been particularly struck or fascinated by some of the facts he discovered in his reading. For example, the temple's flat roof interested him intensely, since he took the time repeatedly to explain to his readership that in fact flat roofs were common for buildings in Palestine and Egypt (unlike, one supposes, Anglo-Saxon England).[25] Above all, however, Bede cared about the historical details of the temple because they were the foundation on which rested his spiritual understanding.[26] Measurements and structures were interesting, but their meaning rested not in themselves but in the Christian messages that Bede could draw from them. In fact historical detail and spiritual interpretation became closely intermingled for Bede, because the one only existed for the sake of the other.

In the Book of Exodus, God showed Moses the pattern of the tabernacle and its objects on Mount Sinai: the mysteries of Christ and the Church, according to Bede.[27] This was not simply a figural reading of what happened to Moses. Rather, it seems Bede believed that Moses had personally foreseen the Christian dispensation to come and then built the historical tabernacle

---

[22] See also Paul Hilliard, 'Sacred and Secular History in the Writings of Bede (†735)' (PhD thesis, University of Cambridge, 2007), pp. 88, 194; William D. McCready, *Miracles and the Venerable Bede* (Toronto, 1994), pp. 220–29.

[23] 3 Kings 6.2; 2 Paralipomenon 3.4; *Temp.*, pp. 161, 166; *Reg.*, XI pp. 303–4; *Ezra.*, p. 293; *Hom.*, II.25 p. 375.

[24] Josephus, *Jewish Antiquities*, VIII.III.2, V, p. 605.

[25] *Reg.*, XIII p. 305; *Temp.*, p. 169; *Tab.*, p. 43; *Luc.*, p. 246.

[26] *Hom.*, II.19 p. 323; *Tab.*, p. 44; see Ch. 2 within this volume, 'The intellectual context at Wearmouth-Jarrow', pp. 31–2.

[27] Exodus 25.9, 25.40; *Tab.*, p. 40.

deliberately and knowingly as a figure of those realities.[28] Analogously, elsewhere in his corpus Bede stated that the great prophets and patriarchs of the
Old Testament had insight into the Christian revelation which the rest of the
contemporary Jewish nation lacked.[29] Bede emphasized, with similar overtones to his description of Moses' work on the tabernacle, that Solomon's
temple was *built as* a figure ('in figuram facta est') of the Church.[30] For Bede
the figural, Christian meaning of these Jewish structures formed as integral a
part of them as the wood and stone from which they were constructed. That
has potential consequences for how Bede would have thought of the temple
image as history. We have seen how some early Christians denigrated the
physical temple, in particular arguing that its destruction necessarily proved
accurate their own spiritual readings of Jewish cult.[31] As Bede stated, the
temple was meant to stand in Jerusalem 'until it fulfilled the task of the
heavenly figures imposed upon it'.[32] The transitory, historical nature of
the temple was essential to the reading that it only existed so as to signify
the mysteries of the Christian faith. Once these were revealed by Christ in his
incarnation and preaching, the Jewish temple could—indeed had to—be
destroyed.[33] The signifier (the Jewish temple and its cult) was condemned to
temporality, whereas the signified (Christianity) alone partook of eternity.

Understandably, Bede believed that the incarnation was a watershed in
human history which changed everything that had come before.[34] His works
teem with interpretations explaining how the new Christian priesthood replaced
the old priesthood and cult—this is what had been symbolized when in the New
Testament the high priest tore his vestments or when the family of Heli was
replaced by that of Samuel.[35] By virtue of his father, John the Baptist had the
right to become a priest offering sacrifice in the temple, but, prophetically, he
preferred to reject his family tradition to preach the coming of the one who
would render temple and sacrifices unnecessary.[36] The temporality of the
temple made it prone to vicissitudes, in particular the corruption of its priesthood and the desecration of its cult. Bede believed that Jewish devotional
practices were already corrupt by the time Christ was born—an idea we also
find in early Irish exegesis;[37] he frequently referred to the idols set up in the

---

[28] See Hilliard, 'Sacred and Secular History', pp. 90–1.

[29] *Cant.*, p. 332; *Temp.*, pp. 159, 223; *Tab.*, p. 31; *Hom.*, II.15 p. 241.

[30] *Temp.*, p. 147; *Luc.*, p. 363; *Hom.*, II.25 p. 368.

[31] See Ch. 2 within this volume, 'The temple in the Christian tradition before Bede', p. 37.

[32] *Temp.*, p. 148 'donec inditum sibi figurarum caelestium munus impleret'; trans. Connolly, p. 6.

[33] *Luc.*, pp. 363–4; *Sam.*, p. 254.

[34] Mary Thomas Aquinas Carroll, *The Venerable Bede: His Spiritual Teachings* (Washington
DC, 1946), pp. 72–3.

[35] *Act.*, p. 88; *Reg.*, I pp. 296–7; *Sam.*, pp. 31, 67.   [36] *Hom.*, II.19 p. 319.

[37] *Act.*, p. 62; *Luc.*, p. 29; *Sam.*, p. 34. *Tractatus Hilarii in Septem Epistolas Canonicas*, ed.
R. E. McNally, CCSL 108B, p. 82; see pp. xii–xvii in the same volume for evidence that Bede had
access to this work.

temple by both Jews and foreigners, a process which became more common after Christ had come.[38] History, from which it could not escape, severely weakened the temple's claim to be something special and holy, for God's eternity stood in stark contrast to the house made by merely human hands.

This could have led to a wholesale rejection of the temple cult. Bede did express doubts as to whether God had ever looked with favour on the material sacrifices of the Old Testament Jewish cult, offered through fear more than love.[39] In general, however, he believed that history had slowly taken its toll on the temple and, in practice, Bede seems to have been a little unsure as to what stage the Church had fundamentally rejected the Old Testament dispensation as belonging to the past.[40] The destruction of the temple certainly marked the end of the period when it was acceptable for Christians also to practice Jewish religion. But such a period had nonetheless existed after the incarnation when the Church was to a large extent Jewish and when the temple cult retained a genuine religious validity.[41] Christ himself had instructed a leper he healed to perform sacrifice in the temple precisely because (Bede explained in the words of Augustine) the time of the sacrifice of Christ's body had not yet come and thus the temple still provided a correct means of worship.[42] Elsewhere Bede argued that the faithful began to abandon sacrifices gradually from the time of Christ's baptism, rather than his passion, but the general thrust of his comments, like his recognition of Jesus and Mary's humble willingness to follow the Jewish Law and worship in the temple, argued that the material temple had been spiritually beneficial in its own time.[43] Christ submitted to the Law for the same reason that Paul continued to follow Jewish custom even while arguing that it should not be imposed on gentiles (an example concerning which Bede had been very influenced by Augustine's debate with Jerome concerning how the New Testament account of Peter and Paul's dispute over circumcision should be read). Both saviour and apostle intended to prove that, while no longer necessary for salvation, the divinely mandated old religion ought not to be condemned.[44]

---

[38] *Sam.*, p. 247; *Reg.*, XXVIII pp. 318–19; *Hom.*, II.24 p. 364.

[39] *Sam.*, p. 133; *Hom.*, I.21 p. 152; *Act.*, p. 36; *Marc.*, pp. 590–91; *Gen.*, pp. 181–2; *Luc.*, p. 272.

[40] John William Houghton, 'Bede's Exegetical Theology: Ideas of the Church in the Acts Commentaries of St. Bede the Venerable' (PhD dissertation, University of Notre Dame, 1994), pp. 121–8.

[41] Houghton, 'Exegetical Theology', pp. 111–21; Glenn Olsen, 'Bede as Historian: The Evidence from his Observations on the Life of the First Christian Community at Jerusalem', *JEH* 33 (1982), pp. 519–31, at 523–6. *Act.*, pp. 67–8; *HE*, III.25 pp. 300–3; *Gen.*, pp. 241–2.

[42] *Luc.*, p. 117 (= *Marc.*, pp. 451–2); compare Augustine, *Quaestiones Evangeliorum*, ed. A. Mutzenbecher, CCSL 44B, II.3 p. 44.

[43] *DTR*, IX pp. 308–9; *Hom.*, I.11 p. 75, I.18 pp. 128–9; *Ezra.*, p. 314. *Luc.*, p. 62 has a rather different variation on this trope, arguing that Jesus and Mary submitted themselves to the Law so that they might free us from its chains.

[44] *Act.*, pp. 85–6; Bede, *Excerpts from the Works of Saint Augustine on the Letters of the Blessed Apostle Paul*, trans. David Hurst (Kalamazoo MI, 1999), pp. 202–3.

This formed a key part of the Augustinian tradition which Bede had inherited. The temporal religion of the Old Testament was not just a typological shadow of true and eternal Christian practice—it, in fact, constituted the form that correct divine worship took in that period.[45] The change brought about via the incarnation was essentially one of grammatical tense: ancient Israel worshipped the Christ who was yet to come, modern Christians worshipped the Christ who had come.[46] The same faith flourished and the same Christ saved in both times. These Augustinian ideas heavily influenced Bede and, indeed, he seems to have taken them further than Augustine ever did by suggesting that Old Testament Judaism in its entirety, rather than individually faithful Hebrews, formed the City of God at that time.[47] Sometimes Bede's language even shifted into suggesting that rather than being the true fulfilment of the temple cult, the Church provided the means by which those who missed out on salvation through God's original dispensation could be saved.[48]

The Augustinian idea that historical change consists essentially of a shift in tense in relation to eternity allowed Bede to emphasize continuity across the otherwise stark divide of the incarnation. He spoke on occasion in the temple commentaries as if little religious difference divided the period of the Law from that of the Gospel—highlighting the continuities and connections in religious practice.[49] The God of the Old Testament seemed constantly to promise eternity to the temple cult and its priesthood and the literal untruth of this promise could be used to bolster the Christian claim that it was never really intended for the historical Jewish priesthood, their altars, and animal sacrifices.[50] However, Bede could use allegory not just to condemn the temple image to history, but also to rescue it from history. On a literal level the sons of Aaron clearly did not still tend the flames of the tabernacle's altars—but nonetheless God's instruction regarding that tabernacle 'continues to be everlasting'; Bede and his brothers fulfilled the eternal law God had given to Aaron and his descendants. Indeed, they were those descendants: 'We are not born of the lineage of Aaron, but we have believed in him in whom Aaron also, with the saints of that age, believed'.[51]

---

[45] See Ch. 2 within this volume, 'The temple in the Christian tradition before Bede', pp. 40–41.

[46] Augustine, *Contra Faustum*, ed. J. Zycha, CSEL 25, XIX.16 pp. 512–14; *Tab.*, p. 48; *Temp.*, pp. 182–3, 206; *Act.*, p. 26. Also Gregory, *Homiliae in Hiezechihelem Prophetam*, ed. M. Adriaen, CCSL 142, II.III.16–17 pp. 247–50.

[47] Houghton, 'Exegetical Theology', pp. 85–91; Georges Tugène, 'Le thème des deux peuples dans le *De Tabernaculo* de Bède', in *Bède le Vénérable entre tradition et postérité: The Venerable Bede. Tradition and Posterity*, eds Stéphane Lebecq et al. (Lille, 2005), pp. 73–84.

[48] *Temp.*, p. 158.

[49] *Temp.*, p. 175; *Hom.*, II.24 p. 358, II.25 pp. 376–7; *Ezra.*, p. 372. Diarmuid Scully, 'Introduction', in *Bede: On Tobit and On the Canticle of Habakkuk*, trans. Seán Connolly (Dublin, 1997), pp. 17–37, at 21.

[50] *Tab.*, p. 95; *Gen.*, p. 180.

[51] *Tab.*, p. 139 'Et si enim labrum siue altare quod fecit Moyses ablatum, si sacerdotium quod constituit nouo ecclesiae sacerdotio mutatum est, nihilominus sempiternum manet legitimum . . . Nam et nostra humilitas ad illud semen pertinet de quo dictum est quia *legitimum*

Bede, too good a historian to ignore the complete destruction of the temple cult, too orthodox a Christian to claim that the Old Testament Law still ruled the Church, naturally accepted that the temple was consigned to the past. But he could balance this out with a spiritual continuity that implied a belief in a gradual progression through human history, rather than a stark leap forward from shadows to light. His belief that the Church shed Jewish customs gradually rather than all at once provides a striking example of this approach. Important too is the fashion in which he explained Stephen's condemnation of the temple (Acts 7.44–50) in the context of historical progress: as the temple replaced the tabernacle, so too was the temple to be replaced in turn by something better.[52] This radically softened the tone of Stephen's polemic, indeed reversed its argument that the temple had been a move away from the divinely approved tabernacle;[53] Bede's argument allowed the temple's goodness within its historical context to be accepted while also explaining its eventual rejection.

Two things ensured that this theory of progress rose above a simple variation on the view of history which saw the incarnation as dismissing the shadows of the past. Firstly, Bede remained acutely aware that historical progress involved loss. His celebration of the priest Ezra for having rewritten scripture at the time of the building of the second temple existed alongside an appreciation that the job was only partially completed. Ezra never rewrote certain books that had been destroyed by the Babylonians and were therefore lost forever—Bede never provided a moral explanation for this, seemingly accepting it as a simple historical fact.[54] Similarly he could mention with apparent empathy the tears of the Jews who saw the final destruction of Jerusalem and its temple, while believing that, with their prophetic functions fulfilled, these material figures had no more role to play in history and so could be abandoned.[55]

Secondly, progress for Bede did not form a simple two-stage process from Jewish to Christian, from Old Testament to New. As his explanation of Stephen's speech makes clear, Old Testament history saw progress and development where knowledge of God grew over time—but Bede also applied this principle to the post-incarnation era: '*in both testaments* knowledge of the truth became known to the faithful more and more as time went by'.[56]

---

sempiternum erit ipsi et semini eius per successiones [Exodus 30.21] non quidem de Aaron stirpe nascendo sed credendo in eum in quem et Aaron cum sanctis illius aeui credidit'; trans. Holder, p. 162. Conor O'Brien, 'Bede on the Jewish Church', in *The Church on its Past*, eds Peter D. Clarke and Charlotte Methuen (Woodbridge, 2013), pp. 63–73.

[52] *Act.*, p. 37.
[53] Houghton, 'Exegetical Theology', p. 109.   [54] *Reg.*, VII pp. 301–2; *Ezra.*, pp. 307–8.
[55] *Sam.*, p. 254.
[56] E.g. *Tab.*, pp. 19–20: p. 20 '*in utroque testamenta* fidelibus magis ex tempore magisque cognitio ueritatis innotuit'; trans. Holder, p. 19 (my emphasis). Bede's source here seems to be

Progress before Christ could easily fit into the theory of the six world ages which Bede inherited from Augustine: the first five ages were all dedicated to pre-incarnational history, whereas the sixth age might seem like a single, undifferentiated Christian era.[57] Bede, however, complicated that view with his interpretation of the tabernacle's great candlestick in relation to human history. Christ was the centre point of history with three divisions before him (before the Law, under the Law, and under the prophets) and three after him (the primitive Jewish Church, the Church of the gentiles, and the conversion of the remnant of the Jews before the end).[58] The harmonious image of the candlestick seems to balance out the two periods—progress took place after Christ as before.[59] This idea is repeated elsewhere in the temple commentaries where Bede emphasized that the present Church represented one stage in an eschatological development which would end with many important aspects of Christian religion (such as scripture and the sacraments) being rendered entirely unnecessary.[60]

The similarity to Bede's view of the temple cult is striking, something which Bede himself recognized. Just as the material figures of the Law were abandoned after the incarnation, 'in the same way, when the mortal life is ended and the immortal follows, the works . . . that we now enjoy will for the most part cease'.[61] This constituted a historical argument for Bede, since he could only understand history in the light of its eschatological purpose. In that perspective the Christian Church was just a fleeting shadow, superior but similar to the Jewish shadows that preceded it.[62] By importing progress into the post-incarnation Church, even by accepting that Christ's coming did not instantly make old Jewish religious practices irrelevant, Bede rendered the abandonment of the temple less negative. Nonetheless, Bede did make many negative comments about the temple and ancient Hebrew religion. The Anglo-Saxon's attitude to the historical temple was complex and, if not carefully examined, apparently contradictory. I have argued elsewhere that Bede's thought on Old Testament Jewish religion in general

---

Gregory, *In Hiezechihelem*, II.IV.12 p. 267—but Gregory made no mention of progress in knowledge continuing in the New Testament; similarly Augustine, *DCD*, X.14 p. 288.

[57] On the theory of the world ages that Bede developed from Augustine: Peter Darby, *Bede and the End of Time* (Farnham, 2012), ch. 1–3.

[58] *Tab.*, pp. 33–4; Darby, *End of Time*, pp. 200–2.

[59] See also Jan Davidse, 'The Sense of History in the Works of the Venerable Bede', *Studi Medievali* 23 (1982), pp. 647–95, at 659–66.

[60] *Tab.*, pp. 28, 39, 94; *Hom.*, II.25 p. 376; *Temp.*, pp. 223–4. See within this chapter, 'History and the figural interpretation of the temple', p. 69.

[61] *Tab.*, pp. 38–9: p. 39 'litteralis obseruatio completa exordium gratiae mundo clarius fulgens exhibuit itemque finita mortali et succedente uita immortali cessabunt maxima ex parte opera . . . quibus nunc utimur'; trans. Holder, p. 42.

[62] See *Act.*, p. 30.

changed over time;[63] here I limit myself to making the case that he had a rather more positive attitude to the historical temple and its cult in the latter half of his career than he had in the earlier.

No radical differences between Bede's writings appear based on his attitude to the temple cult—the belief that this served a figural purpose foreshadowing the grace of the Christian Church is expressed in works from all stages of his career. The basic outlines of Bede's view of history did not change in anything he wrote, because they consisted of nothing more than the standard Christian ideas he inherited from tradition. What changed was the degree to which he emphasized the break between the temple cult and what followed. For example, in *On Luke* Bede discussed how the temple proved no longer necessary after Christ performed his saving sacrifice. Therefore, God brought it about that 'the temple and all those things were to be destroyed together lest by chance anyone immature in faith (if he had seen those things remain) might be swept away, astounded by that vision of the diverse appearances during the ceremony of the sacrifices, during the succession of the services'.[64] The statement implies that the purely external show of the temple cult could have delayed believers' acceptance of Christian grace. A decade or more later, commenting on Mark's gospel, Bede reproduced his earlier statement in part but changed his language in significant ways. Now God ensured that the

> formerly sacred temple with its ceremonies was to be destroyed lest by chance anyone immature in faith, regarding the worldly as holy, might little by little from the wholeness of the faith which is in Christ Jesus slip toward carnal Judaism if he saw those things remain which had been made by the holy prophets and established by the Lord.[65]

The lure of the temple in the later text seems more understandable because the building's genuinely divine origin has been acknowledged. In the early commentary on Acts, Bede suggested that Jewish customs, 'the shadows of the Law', were accepted for some time by the Church merely as a sop to the Jews, the apostles treating them 'as if they had at some time been established by the Lord'.[66] By the 720s (when *On Mark* was composed) Bede had abandoned that ambivalent

---

[63] O'Brien, 'Jewish Church', pp. 69–71. Hilliard, 'Sacred and Secular History', pp. 195–6, suggests that Bede may sometimes have responded to criticism of his positive attitudes to Judaism by making negative comments elsewhere.

[64] *Luc.*, p. 364 'diuina dispensatio procurauit ut et ciuitas ipsa et templum et omnia illa pariter subuerterentur ne qui forte adhuc paruulus et lactans in fide, si uiderit illa constare, dum sacrificiorum ritum dum ministeriorum ordinem attonitus stupet ipso diuersarum formarum raperetur intuitu'.

[65] *Marc.*, p. 595 'Diuinitus autem procuratum est ut... templum ipsum quondam augustum cum suis caerimoniis tolleretur ne qui forte adhuc paruulus ac lactans in fide, si uideret illa permanere quae a prophetis sanctis facta quae a domino sunt instituta, ammirando sanctum saeculare paulatim a sinceritate fidei quae est in Christo Iesu ad carnale laberetur Iudaismum'.

[66] *Act.*, p. 68 'Istae enim umbrae legales, quasi a domino aliquando constitutae, interdum ad apostolis sunt illis temporibus ob declinandam Iudaeorum perfidiam usurpatae...'.

'as if'; he expressed no doubt that the temple cult had been instituted by the Lord. In that same decade he also finished *On Genesis* with a consideration of the Church's historical need to reject the materialistic focus of Jewish religion—but made sure to state that the literal observance of carnal Jewish rites had been required up until the incarnation.[67] Indeed, in Book One of that work Bede suggested that the rebuilding of the material temple by the exiles returning from Babylon proved that their minds were on 'heavenly things'; Old Testament religion was certainly not too carnal here.[68] The date of this book of *On Genesis* is uncertain: Bede dedicated it to Bishop Acca, who only achieved the see of Hexham in 710, and the exegete had moved on to the next book of *On Genesis* by 720, so scholars have suggested a range of possible dates within that decade.[69] Nonetheless Bede's suggestion in Book One that the temple was the glory of the fourth age finds no parallel in his earliest discussions of the world ages (nor indeed in any of his sources on the world ages, apparently constituting an original contribution to the tradition), while matching what he said around 725 in *On the Reckoning of Time*.[70]

In both *On Genesis* and *On the Reckoning of Time* the monk even went so far as to declare that the Babylonian exile happened because the people of Israel had ignored the temple.[71] The comment seems ironic because in writings from the first half of his career Bede had explained the Jews' rejection of Christ and persecution of the apostles by reference to their fear that a decline in respect for the temple and the Law would lead to the destruction of their kingdom.[72] In this case it was their very actions to protect the earthly temple and kingdom that led inevitably to the loss of those material realities. Continuing Jewish devotion to the Old Testament religion was short-sighted, carnal in nature, and eventually self-defeating; Bede was convinced, like most Christian thinkers before him, that the destruction of the temple and Jerusalem was punishment for the sins of Israel, a conviction he never quite lost.[73] The historical desecrations of the temple could be read as a mockery of the Jewish obsession with protecting the purity of any material building. Bede's earlier works certainly make this implication, whereas *On Genesis* and *On the*

---

[67] *Gen.*, pp. 238–42 (esp. p. 242).

[68] *Gen.*, p. 38 'tota intentione caelestia petebant, ita ut etiam templum ac ciuitatem Dei reaedificare . . . niterentur'; trans. Kendall, p. 103.

[69] Calvin B. Kendall, *Bede: On Genesis* (Liverpool, 2008), pp. 45–53 has argued that it was composed around 717/718; Darby, *End of Time*, p. 82, has, more recently, wanted to push the date back closer to 710.

[70] *Gen.*, p. 37; *DTR*, X p. 311. Compare Bede, *De Temporibus*, ed. Charles W. Jones, CCSL 123, XVI pp. 600–1; Augustine, *DCD*, XXII.30 pp. 865–6; Isidore of Seville, *Etymologiae sive Origines*, ed. W. M. Lindsay, 2 vols (Oxford, 1911), V.XXXVIII.

[71] *Gen.*, p. 37; *DTR*, X p. 311.

[72] *Act.*, p. 86; *Sam.*, pp. 188, 242–3. See also *Prov.*, pp. 28–9.

[73] *DTR*, IX p. 308; *EpCath.*, pp. 218–19; *Luc.*, pp. 347, 367; *Prov.*, p. 31.

Reckoning of Time seem to suggest that the Jews of old had a point: at least at one time, devotion to the physical temple did have real material consequences.

Scully, however, has argued that the *Greater Chronicle* in *On the Reckoning of Time* underlines the disastrous decline of the Jewish nation with the coming of Christ, particularly by paralleling the first entrance of Britain into world and Christian history with the degradations suffered by the temple.[74] Certainly the same entry notes that Pompey desecrated the Holy of Holies and that Caesar conquered Britain—but no explicit link is made between the two facts.[75] Bede emphasized that Herod's rule brought the reign of the old Jewish priesthood to an end, but he never directly tied the incarnation to that fact as Isidore had when speaking of the end of the Jewish priesthood and the virgin birth in a single breath.[76] Had the Anglo-Saxon really wanted to highlight God's rejection of the temple in his chronicle, he could have included mention of Julian the Apostate's (331–63) attempt to rebuild it, stopped by divine intervention, but he never did.[77] That silence must be set beside ambiguous evidence such as an entry that mentions both Vespasian's activities in Britain and his role in the final destruction of the temple.[78] *On the Reckoning of Time* certainly records all the insults visited on the temple in its final years but Bede did not take the opportunity to openly relate this to the entrance of his own people into providential history.[79]

Certainly Bede had previously contrasted his own people's salvation with the material focus of the temple cult. His earlier writings show a particular contempt for the earthly riches of the temple (the gold, silver, and dressed stone which are described in such detail in the biblical account) and in the *Verse Life of Cuthbert*, Bede made a slighting comparison between Solomon's temple and Cuthbert's hermitage on Farne.[80] The temple may have glittered with gold and jewels, but it was still burnt to the ground, whereas the humble materials of the Anglo-Saxon hermitage survived to work miracles.[81] When Bede wrote Cuthbert's life in prose around 720 he dropped all mention of the

---

[74] Diarmuid Scully, 'Bede's *Chronica Maiora*: Early Insular History in a Universal Context', *Proceedings of the British Academy* 157 (2009), pp. 47–73, at 51–2, 56–7.

[75] *DTR*, LXVI p. 493.

[76] *DTR*, LXVI pp. 494–5; Isidore, *Chronica*, ed. Jose Carlos Martin, CCSL 112, pp. 114–15. I owe this reference to Jamie Wood, *The Politics of Identity in Visigothic Spain: Religion and Power in the Histories of Isidore of Seville* (Leiden, 2012), p. 203.

[77] See Isidore, *Chronica*, pp. 162–5.   [78] *DTR*, LXVI p. 498.

[79] *DTR*, LXVI pp. 480–81, 491, 493, 494, 497, 498.

[80] *Act.*, pp. 23–4, 37, 41 (compare Jerome, *Epistulae*, ed. I. Hilberg, CSEL 54, LIII.5 p. 452). The verse life is likely to have been broadly contemporary with *On the Acts of the Apostles*—both dating from the first decade of the eighth century: Michael Lapidge, 'Bede's Metrical *Vita S. Cuthberti*', in *St Cuthbert, His Cult and His Community until AD 1200*, eds Gerald Bonner et al. (Woodbridge, 1989), pp. 77–93, at 78–85; M. L. W. Laistner, *Bedae Venerabilis: Expositio Actuum Apostolorum et Retractatio* (Cambridge MA, 1939), pp. xv–xvii.

[81] Bede, *Vita Cuthberti (Metrica)*, ed. W. Jaager, *Bedas metrische Vita Sancti Cuthberti* (Leipzig, 1935), XLIV pp. 127–8.

temple from this story, merely contenting himself with stating that Cuthbert 'sought the splendour of a heavenly mansion rather than of an earthly habitation', while at the same time in *On Genesis* describing the gold and silver of the tabernacle as an example of how metalwork could be turned to a righteous purpose.[82] When, in *On the Temple*, Bede quoted Peter's description of the Christian faithful as 'a kingly priesthood, a holy nation', he pointed out that the 'ancient people of God was also singled out by the honour of this dignity';[83] in an earlier work he had emphasized that this 'testimony of praise' had been given to the Jews 'once' but 'now rightly' had been given to 'the gentiles, certainly because they believed in Christ'.[84] This has a supersessionist tone strikingly absent from *On the Temple*, where Bede seems to have been more interested in noting the parallel between the priesthood of the gentile Church and that of Israel than in celebrating the replacement of the latter by the former.

It seems unlikely that Bede's interest in emphasizing the election of his own people declined in the second half of his career; rather he found that continuity instead of rupture could be turned to this purpose. Something seems to have changed between Bede beginning Book Six of *On Luke* with an overwhelming emphasis on the temple as a fleeting figure to be destroyed when replaced and his completion of *On the Temple*, which, while entirely devoted to exploring the image's figural meaning, only makes one vague comment about the necessity of the temple's destruction.[85] Like many Christian exegetes before him, Bede spent most of his life reflecting on the relationship between the Old Testament and the New and, just like those earlier writers, Bede primarily used writing on the Jewish past as a way of commenting on the Christian present. We know that one event of great significance took place in the late 710s which I have argued can help explain the shift in Bede's thought: in 716 the monks of Iona accepted the Roman 'orthodox' Easter for the first time.[86] For Bede this constituted the climax of the Easter Question, a debate which, scholars have shown, relied heavily on an exegetical discourse that used the narrative of the rejection of ancient Jewish religion to argue for abandoning non-Roman Easter calculations.[87]

---

[82] *VCP*, XLVI pp. 302–3; *Gen.*, p. 88. For the evidence that Book Two of *On Genesis* can be securely dated to 720: Kendall, *Bede: On Genesis*, pp. 45–7, 322–6.

[83] *Temp.*, p. 194 '*Vos autem genus electrum regale sacerdotium gens sancta populus adquisitionis.* [1 Peter II.9; Exodus 19.6] *Cuius honore dignitatis etiam antiquus Dei populus erat insignitus*'; trans. Connolly, p. 68.

[84] *EpCath.*, p. 237 '*Vos autem genus electum, regale sacerdotium, gens sancta, populus adquisitionis. Hoc laudis testimonium quondam antiquo Dei populo per Moysen datum est quod nunc recte gentibus dat apostolus Petrus, quia uidelicet in Christum crediderunt*'.

[85] *Luc.*, pp. 364–5; *Temp.*, p. 148.

[86] O'Brien, 'Jewish Church', pp. 71–3.

[87] Mark Laynesmith, 'Anti-Jewish Rhetoric in the *Life of Wilfrid*', in *Wilfrid: Abbot, Bishop, Saint; Papers from the 1300th Anniversary Conferences*, ed. N. J. Higham (Donington, 2013),

The importance of rejecting the old, outdated, and materialist religion and embracing the true grace of the suffering Christ provided a message that could be used against followers of the Columban Easter who wanted to follow the traditions of their people, a desire which had distinctly 'Jewish' overtones in an exegetical context.[88] The conversion of Iona to the Roman Easter created a new situation for the Northumbrian Church; the polemical heat, the absolute need to separate right from wrong, had gone out of discussions concerning Iona and its Easter observance. The problem of the Northumbrian Church's origins in the mission of monks from that monastery when it had followed the incorrect Columban Easter remained, however. In this situation Bede's progressive vision of history, where the material temple could be viewed as divinely sanctioned but nonetheless consigned to the past, could easily be applied to his local Church. Its Ionan origins could be read positively but their abandonment at the Synod of Whitby for Roman orthodoxy remained historically essential. The assertion that Aidan followed an incorrect Easter dating but nonetheless shared the same faith in Christ as contemporary *Romani* clearly parallels the idea that the sacraments of the Old and New Testaments differed but both were based on a single faith in Christ.[89]

Thus, Bede's understanding of the history of the temple cult may have helped him express his thoughts on contemporary Northumbrian ecclesiastical affairs; and recent events in the Insular world may have led him to rethink some of his ideas about the Jewish past. Does this make Bede's ideas about the temple as history nothing more than another example of a personal weakness for obsessing over the date of Easter?[90] It seems much more likely that, in adopting this attitude, he reflected the outlook of a whole section of the Northumbrian Church, not just his own personal opinion. In particular it appears most probable that Bede cared about the Easter Question and assigned great importance to the conversion of Iona because his own community at Wearmouth-Jarrow did so: hence, while the conversion of Northumbria to the Roman Easter is the centre of the *Ecclesiastical History*, the conversion of Iona forms its climax.[91] Wearmouth-Jarrow was, as an institution, clearly involved in the campaign to spread the Roman Easter in the early eighth century. When

---

pp. 67–79; Robert W. Hanning, *The Vision of History in Early Britain: From Gildas to Geoffrey of Monmouth* (London, 1966), pp. 79–83; Jennifer O'Reilly, 'Introduction', in *Bede: On the Temple*, trans. Seán Connolly (Liverpool, 1995), pp. xxxv–xxxix. On the Easter Question and how it related to the Insular Church: Charles W. Jones, *Bedae Opera de Temporibus* (Cambridge MA, 1943), pp. 6–113; Thomas Charles-Edwards, *Early Christian Ireland* (Cambridge, 2000), pp. 391–415.

[88] *HE*, III.25 pp. 298–9 and V.21 pp. 550–51; W. Trent Foley and Nicholas J. Higham, 'Bede on the Britons', *EME* 17 (2009), pp. 154–85, at 162–4.

[89] *HE*, III.17 pp. 266–7; *Tab.*, p. 86; *Cant.*, p. 190.

[90] Charles Plummer, *Venerabilis Baedae Opera Historica*, 2 vols (Oxford, 1896), I, pp. xl–xli.

[91] *HE*, III.25 pp. 294–309, V.22 pp. 552–5; O'Reilly, 'Introduction', p. xxxvi; Archibald A. M. Duncan, 'Bede, Iona and the Picts', in *The Writing of History in the Middle Ages: Essays*

King Nechtan of the Picts (d. 732) decided to adopt the Dionysian Easter dating it was to Bede's abbot Ceolfrith that he turned to provide himself with weighty intellectual backing, albeit, it should be noted, retrospectively. Nechtan knew of Wearmouth-Jarrow as a centre of Romanist thought which would supply him with the spiritual arguments to support his decision.[92]

Some scholars have claimed that Bede wrote Ceolfrith's reply as preserved in the *Ecclesiastical History*, but we should be cautious in taking such ideas too far, Charles Jones having seen 'no justification' for the idea.[93] If Bede rewrote the letter when adding it to his history so that the language matched that of his own recent *On the Reckoning of Time*, this need not mean that he wrote the original missive. More to the point, we would certainly expect his words on the major ecclesiastical dispute of his youth to match those of the man he credited with teaching him. On the official level it was with Ceolfrith as abbot that Nechtan corresponded, requesting not just computistical advice but also builders for a stone church, and the exchange therefore indicates Wearmouth-Jarrow's involvement in the Easter dispute on an institutional level. The advice to Nechtan was part of a wider campaign to bring Iona into line with Rome since one of the consequences of the king's conversion was that he expelled recalcitrant Columban clergy from his lands.[94] The evidence is confusing, not least because the dates imply that Nechtan moved against the Ionans after the island monastery had itself actually accepted the Roman Easter.[95] Nonetheless it seems clear that Wearmouth-Jarrow was very much involved in the attempt to spread 'orthodoxy' deep into the Columban Church in the first half of the 710s.

Bede claimed that Northumbrian clerics convinced Adomnán of Iona (*c.*628–704) to accept the Roman Easter and tonsure when visiting the Anglo-Saxon kingdom and Ceolfrith's letter credits this achievement to Wearmouth-Jarrow's abbot himself.[96] Problems exist with this account but it clearly shows what Bede's monastery wanted to have happened.[97] Certainly Northumbrians were very deeply involved in the conversion of Iona with the

---

Presented to Richard William Southern, eds R. H. C. Davis and J. M. Wallace-Hadrill (Oxford, 1981), pp. 1–42, at 41–2.

[92] *HE*, V.21 pp. 532–53. Kenneth Veitch, 'The Columban Church in northern Britain, 664–717: a reassessment', *Proceedings of the Society of Antiquaries of Scotland* 127 (1997), pp. 627–47, at 635–6.

[93] Plummer, *Opera Historica*, II, p. 332; D. P. Kirby, 'Bede and the Pictish Church', *Innes Review* 24 (1973), pp. 6–25, at 9. Jones, *Opera de Temporibus*, p. 104, n. 4; also O'Reilly, 'Introduction', p. lv.

[94] Seán Mac Airt and Gearóid Mac Niocaill (eds and trans.), *The Annals of Ulster (to A. D. 1131)*, (Dublin, 1983), U717 p. 173.

[95] For discussion: Kirby, 'Bede and the Pictish Church'; Duncan, 'Bede, Iona and the Picts'.

[96] *HE*, V.15 pp. 504–7, V.21 pp. 550–51.

[97] Jean-Michel Picard, 'Bede, Adomnán, and the writing of history', *Peritia* 3 (1984), pp. 50–70.

final credit for the 716 acceptance of the Roman Easter going to Ecgberht (639–729), a Northumbrian cleric long living in exile in Ireland. His heroic status in Bede's writings makes it clear that this achievement mattered greatly to the northern Anglo-Saxons.[98] Ecgberht remained in contact with many communities within the Northumbrian monastic establishment during his time in Ireland;[99] while the importance of Cuthbert's old monastery of Melrose to Ecgberht's work converting the Columbans seems especially clear, Wearmouth-Jarrow was certainly also involved.[100] Ceolfrith's own brother had been one of the many Anglo-Saxons to journey to Ireland to study and had probably died there in Ecgberht's monastery of Rath Melsigi.[101] Bede's substantial knowledge of the missionary Willibrord (c.658–739), as opposed to his silence about the more famous Boniface (c.674–754), may have as much to do with Willibrord's membership of Ecgberht's evangelically minded community as his Northumbrian origins.[102]

The conversion of Iona therefore clearly did matter in the ecclesiastical circles that linked Wearmouth-Jarrow to other parts of the Insular Church; Abbot Ceolfrith was keen to claim credit for the spread of *Romanitas* to the Picts and Columbans. Indeed his swift departure from Wearmouth-Jarrow in June 716 on pilgrimage to Rome may not be entirely unrelated to the celebration of Easter according to the Roman date on Iona shortly before this. He carried with him on that occasion the Codex Amiatinus, the magnificent pandect (single-volume Bible) produced in his monastery, which displays a striking quantity of temple imagery. If, as I shall argue throughout this book, Bede's writings on the temple image were heavily influenced by the ideas that lay behind the Codex Amiatinus, then it makes sense that the ecclesiastical changes of recent years had an influence on his thinking on the historical temple.

Some might consider that the spread of the Roman Easter would have occasioned triumphalism at a monastery such as Wearmouth-Jarrow, where supersessionist contempt for the temple might have better matched attitudes to the old Columban traditions. Certainly, the excision of the Ionan mission to Northumbria from the historical record was one temptation to which Bede nearly succumbed: the *Greater Chronicle* in *On the Reckoning of Time* and the summary at the end of the *Ecclesiastical History* make almost no mention of the Ionan mission or figures central to it such as Aidan (d. 651)

---

[98] *HE*, III.27 pp. 312–15, IV.3 pp. 344–5, V.9–10 pp. 474–81, V.22 pp. 552–5, V.24 pp. 566–7; *DTR*, LXVI pp. 532–3.

[99] E.g. Æthelwulf, *De Abbatibus*, ed. A. Campbell (Oxford, 1967), VI pp. 10–17.

[100] On the Melrose connection: Kirby, 'Bede and the Pictish Church', pp. 10–12, 18–19.

[101] Dáibhí Ó Cróinín, 'Rath Melsigi, Willibrord, and the Earliest Echternach Manuscripts', *Peritia* 3 (1984), pp. 17–49, at 31.

[102] *DTR*, LXVI p. 529; *HE*, V.11 pp. 484–7. Ó Cróinín, 'Rath Melsigi'.

and Oswald (d. 642).[103] But such a strategy could not have proved acceptable to establishments such as Lindisfarne which had too much to lose by
that approach and Wearmouth-Jarrow's connections with Lindisfarne and
Melrose undoubtedly had an effect on attitudes there.[104] More generally
the Northumbrian Church as a whole was implicated in its Columban
past.[105] Heated rhetoric concerning the need to root out the Ionan element
in Northumbria must have been particularly strong before 716 (to which
period Stephen's *Life of Wilfrid*, with its particularly strong anti-Columban
tone, has now been entirely dated) but would have been no longer so necessary
once the Columban mother-house fell in line with Rome.[106] Wearmouth-
Jarrow's relationship with the past was deeply ambiguous—biblical exegesis of
the Christian relationship with ancient Judaism gave a language to express this
ambiguity. The history of the universal Church in the sixth age that Bede
outlined in *On the Tabernacle* neatly mimicked the history of his own local
Church: as the one began in Israel, extended through the calling of the gentiles,
and will one day receive the remainder of Israel, so too the other drew its
origins from Iona, moved on to become a universal institution, but eventually
the Columban remnant came into the fold.[107]

HISTORY AND THE FIGURAL
INTERPRETATION OF THE TEMPLE

Even when talking about the material temple, Bede's temple commentaries
looked towards the image's deeper meaning. As we have just seen, it was
primarily the temple image's significance for his own time that mattered to
Bede and spiritual interpretation provided the primary means of establishing
that significance. Christian spiritual exegesis always relied quite heavily on
history because to a large extent it depended on typologically linking two
historical events from different periods, one the promise and the other the
fulfilment.[108] This suggests a second sense of how Bede could have seen the

---

[103] N. J. Higham, *(Re-)Reading Bede: The* Ecclesiastical History *in Context* (London, 2006),
pp. 84–95 and 118–27. For possible reasons for Bede's silence about the Columbans in the
Chronicle: Scully, 'Chronica Maiora', pp. 71–2; Alan Thacker, 'Bede and the Irish', in *Beda
Venerabilis: Historian, Monk & Northumbrian*, ed. L. A. J. R. Houwen and A. A. MacDonald
(Groningen, 1996), pp. 31–59, at 51.

[104] See Ch. 1 within this volume, 'Bede's world', p. 19.

[105] Higham, *(Re-)Reading Bede*, p. 145.

[106] Clare Stancliffe, 'Dating Wilfrid's Death and Stephen's *Life*', in *Wilfrid*, ed. Higham,
pp. 17–26.

[107] *Tab.*, p. 34. See Scully, 'Introduction', pp. 35–7.

[108] See Ch. 2 within this volume, 'The intellectual context at Wearmouth-Jarrow', p. 31.

temple image as history—the temple was not just itself part of history, but also acted as a symbol of it, displaying the great sweep of time in its features.

Most straightforwardly, and in line with the classic line of Christian figural interpretation, the temple image symbolized Christ and his redemptive work in the New Testament. For example, the animal sacrifices of the temple cult were a type that found their fulfilment in Christ's self-sacrifice on the cross.[109] The common people brought offerings to the priests who could bring them to the altars of the temple on their behalf, just as the gentile Christians of the early Church gave charitable gifts to Paul and Barnabas to support the Church in Jerusalem that prayed on their behalf.[110] Even such a straightforward example from the history of the early Church shows that Bede looked beyond the life of Christ when seeking examples of the historical fulfilment of the figures within the temple image. After all, for Bede, the era which Christ inaugurated with his grace in the New Testament encompassed all subsequent time right up to the present day, as indicated by the AD (*Anno Domini*) dating system; Christ's coming in the flesh had consecrated the entire sixth age of the world.[111] In some respect then, all of that age could be considered as the fulfilment of the Old Testament.

Hence, Bede could easily slip between seeing the temple image as representing the life of the early Church detailed in the Acts of the Apostles and understanding it as symbolizing the early Church which he only knew about from extra-biblical sources. Amongst the craftsmen received by the Solomonic Christ (the peaceful rule of the Israelite king foreshadowing the Prince of Peace) were great preachers from the gentiles such as Dionysius the Areopagite and Cyprian (d. 258).[112] Bede, indeed, often saw the late antique and patristic Church as providing at the very least noteworthy examples of the realities about which the Old Testament text had prophesized. Thus if the treasures gifted from the riches of the king of Persia to the Jewish temple symbolized members of royal households who enter the religious life, one such treasure was Cassiodorus.[113] The outer layers of goat hides which protected the tabernacle represented the Fathers of the Church, such as Augustine and Gregory, who protected the faithful from the storms of heresy.[114] A noticeable cluster of interpretations that use examples from late antique heresies, Church councils, and ecclesiastical debates to show the fulfilment of biblical figures appears in *On Ezra and Nehemiah*.[115]

---

[109] *Tab.*, p. 71; *Ezra.*, pp. 306, 329; *Luc.*, pp. 350, 378 (= *Marc.*, p. 611). See Ch. 5 within this volume, 'The temple as Christ', p. 101–10.

[110] *Temp.*, pp. 195–6.

[111] Máirín Mac Carron, 'Bede, *Annus Domini* and the *Historia ecclesiastica gentis anglorum*', in *The Mystery of Christ in the Fathers of the Church: Essays in Honour of D. Vincent Twomey SVD*, eds Janet E. Rutherford and David Woods (Dublin, 2012), pp. 116–34; *DTR*, LXVI p. 495.

[112] *Temp.*, p. 149.   [113] *Ezra.*, p. 295.

[114] *Tab.*, p. 57.   [115] *Ezra.*, pp. 281–4, 295, 302.

Nor was Bede beyond suggesting that even comparatively recent events in Anglo-Saxon history fell within the scope of the figural prophecies in the temple image. The water basins in the court of the priests represented two types of preachers, those who built up the faith amongst their own people and those who travelled to bring it to unbaptized nations; this division could be seen 'when the blessed Pope Gregory recently in our own day ruled the Roman Church' and 'when the most venerable Fathers Augustine, Paulinus, and the rest of their companions . . . came to Britain at his command and a short while ago entrusted the word of God to unbelievers'.[116] Bede did not seem to think it inappropriate to suggest that the events he recounted in the *Ecclesiastical History* had been predicted in the mysteries of the Old Testament—after all many popes had made the same claim long before him.[117] Certainly such explicit statements were few and could possibly have appeared more often. Benedict Biscop would have been as good an example as Cassiodorus of someone who came from a king's household to enter the monastic life; Bede seems to have had the Christian emperors in mind, more so than Anglo-Saxon kings, when he spoke about secular rulers helping the work of conversion.[118] But Gregory the Great had himself inserted a discussion of the Rome of his day into his commentary on the temple image in Ezekiel, thereby providing Bede with an example to follow.[119] Condemning the failings of the present when interpreting the Bible was a common patristic trope, such as when Jerome declared that Jeremiah's condemnation of idols being placed in the temple had relevance for his own time whenever some new dogma was set up in the Church;[120] on a similar basis Bede asserted that the moral interpretations of the temple image spoke directly to the contemporary clerical failings which he confronted.[121] Thus it seems likely that, even when he did not specifically state this, he believed that biblical prophecies could be seen fulfilled both in the past and in his own time—something he explicitly stated in the case of Daniel's prophecy of the abomination of desolation being set up in the temple.[122]

---

[116] *Temp.*, p. 218 'cum nostris nuper temporibus beatus papa gregorius euangelicis roboratus eloquiis romanam rexit ecclesiam . . . cum reuerendissimi patres augustinus paulinus et ceteri socii eorum eisdem euangelicis confirmati oraculis iubente illo uenere brittanniam et uerbum dei incredulis dudum commisere gentibus'; trans. Connolly, p. 98.

[117] Georges Tugène, 'L'histoire "ecclésiastique" du peuple anglais: Réflexions sur le particularisme et l'universalisme chez Bède', *Recherches augustiniennes* 17 (1982), pp. 129–72, at 161–2; Jennifer O'Reilly, 'Islands and Idols at the Ends of the Earth: Exegesis and Conversion in Bede's *Historia Ecclesiastica*', in *Bède Le Vénérable*, eds Lebecq et al., pp. 119–45, at 121–6.

[118] *Ezra.*, pp. 284, 294, 318. Also *Temp.*, p. 149.

[119] Gregory, *In Hiezechihelem*, II.VI.22–24 pp. 310–13.

[120] Jerome, *In Heremiam Prophetam*, ed. S. Reiter, CCSL 74, VI.47 p. 343.

[121] *Tab.*, pp. 96, 119; *Temp.*, p. 207; *Reg.*, XXX pp. 320–21; Scott DeGregorio, '"Nostrorum socordiam temporum": the Reforming Impulse of Bede's Later Exegesis', *EME* 11 (2002), pp. 107–22, at 113–14.

[122] *DTR*, IX p. 309; Daniel 9.27. Presumably Bede here referred to the fact that the temple in Jerusalem had not been rebuilt following its destruction.

Often Bede understood scripture as symbolizing not discrete historical events, whether from the New Testament or subsequently, but general aspects of the life of the Church that were worked out through history. When the temple image symbolized the spread of the Church to all peoples and all places, Bede thought not of a single datable event, but of a long drawn-out process that began within the scriptural New Testament and extended right up until his own lifetime. It is primarily in this sense that Bede felt that he and his contemporaries could see their own lives reflected in the Bible, that the Anglo-Saxon Church was the fulfilment of scriptural prophecies. Some scholars have seen Bede as the heir of an understanding of Christian history championed by Eusebius (*c*.260–*c*.340) and Orosius (*fl. c*.375–418) which saw the fulfilment of Old Testament prophecy in the events of recent history, thus allowing him to discern confidently the actions of God in the present world where the Anglo-Saxons were a new Israel.[123] The British writer Gildas had applied this tradition to Insular history, influencing Bede with a reading of the history of the Anglo-Saxon invasions in the light of the Bible.[124] This has been contrasted to Augustine's vision of history in which all post-scriptural history remained opaque, since the word of God did not reveal the workings of providence, which went on behind human affairs.[125]

Recent work has substantially rejected the older, Orosian reading of Bede. The belief that his writings were a triumphalist assertion that the Anglo-Saxons were the new 'chosen people' promised glory in this world by the God of the Old Testament has now lost favour.[126] For Bede, Anglo-Saxon history was not *the* fulfilment of scriptural prophecy, but part of its ongoing fulfilment in the life of the Church; the Anglo-Saxons were not *the* chosen people, but one nation called to join the elect. Thus the temple image could represent aspects of the Anglo-Saxon Church, but largely as examples of the universal Church which in its totality fulfilled the Old Testament figures. Therefore, one cannot say that Bede had entirely imbibed a vision of history where the workings of providence in the present world could not be understood at all. The very fact that he saw the patristic era as fulfilling scripture in his interpretations in the temple commentaries shows that for Bede that age could be read with Christian eyes pretty unambiguously even if he

---

[123] For a recent example of such an interpretation: Mary Garrison, 'The Franks as the New Israel? Education for an identity from Pippin to Charlemagne', in *The Uses of the Past in the Early Middle Ages*, eds Yitzhak Hen and Matthew Innes (Cambridge, 2000), pp. 114–61, at 157.

[124] For the importance of Gildas as a conduit of this providential view of history to Bede: Hanning, *Vision of History*, ch. 1–3.

[125] R. A. Markus, *Saeculum: History and Society in the Theology of St Augustine*, rev. ed. (Cambridge, 1988), pp. 1–21.

[126] O'Reilly, 'Introduction', pp. xxxviii–xxxix; O'Reilly, 'Islands and Idols', p. 128; Hilliard, 'Sacred and Secular History', pp. 18, 126–7, 153, 218–19; George Molyneux, 'Did the English really think they were God's elect in the Anglo-Saxon period?', *JEH* 65 (2014), pp. 721–37, at 726–30.

might be cautious about predicting the result of actions in eighth-century Northumbria.[127]

Although Bede did not embrace a vision of history quite as shallow as that of Orosius this does not mean that he lacked absolute confidence in his ability to understand the workings of providential history. The prologue to *On the Temple*, probably written for Bishop Acca to console him in his exile, makes this clear.[128] It touches partially on the classic problem of why people suffer and while Bede did not make judgements about individual cases, he was clear that all suffering was providential and meaningful, something which his addressee would see from a perusal of scriptural history. Bede encouraged the reader to look for consolation in his allegorical interpretation of the temple image: 'If you read it attentively . . . the more liberally you see the gifts of God bestowed upon us in this present time or promised us in the future, the more tolerable and less worthy of concern will you consider both the favourable and unfavourable vicissitudes of perishable things'.[129] His exegesis of the temple presented all of human history as carefully authored by God from its beginning to its inevitable end—the construction of the temple represented the building up of the Church through time and its dedication symbolized the final judgement at which the elect will rise to eternal life.[130] Reflecting on the temple image's spiritual interpretation therefore was no different to meditating on the providential design of history.

Seen in this light, the temple can be contrasted with another famous building from Bede's corpus: the Anglo-Saxon king's hall through which a sparrow flies, symbolizing the swift and mysterious course of human life to a philosophically minded pagan thegn of Edwin's court.[131] The image of the hall emphasizes how little non-Christians understand what comes before or after their own brief period alive: 'what follows or indeed what went before, we know not at all';[132] the temple image reveals Christian self-knowledge as a stone built into the developing Church of Christ, an institution that stretches out into the future as well as the past, bringing comfort to mortals. In this light, there is nothing of historical agnosticism about Bede's outlook, which is not to say that his works claim insight into every event in post-biblical history. Many of the details remain opaque, but the outline of time was clear to Bede, as was

---

[127] See *HE*, V.23 pp. 560–61; R. A. Markus, *Bede and the Tradition of Ecclesiastical Historiography*, Jarrow Lecture (Jarrow, 1975), pp. 14–15.

[128] See Ch. 7 within this volume, 'Morality', p. 165–6.

[129] *Temp.*, p. 144 'Cuius lectioni intentus quanto plura christi et ecclesiae sacramenta antiquis indita paginis inueneris quanto ampliora ibi dei dona siue in praesenti nobis data seu in futuro promissa perspexeris tanto leuiora credo et minus curanda omnium labentium rerum et aduersa iudicabis'; trans. Connolly, p. 3.

[130] *Temp.*, pp. 147, 232–4. Also *Prov.*, p. 23; *Ezra.*, p. 306.

[131] *HE*, II.13 pp. 182–5.

[132] *HE*, II.13 pp. 184–5 'Ita haec uita hominum ad modicum apparet; quid autem sequatur, quidue praecesserit, prorsus ignoramus'.

much of the detail—the *Ecclesiastical History* does make frequent claims to discern the hand of God in recent events, for example, when it declares with absolute certainty that Coldingham monastery was burnt down because of God's punishment of its sins.[133] Analogous is Bede's attitude to the apocalypse. While eschewing any attempt to date the end of the world, he, nonetheless, remained very happy to map out in a great amount of detail the exact sequence of events that would occur when the end came.[134] Certainty rather than doubt is the predominant note in Bede's discussions of both time and history.

Augustine's caution about reading God's control of history into specific post-biblical events arose from his ecclesiology. All temporal societies were formed of a mixture of reprobate and elect, and that included the institution of the Church; the good and the evil would only be separated from each other at the end of time and until then one had to accept that only God could really understand the providential design of history.[135] This view set up an important distinction between the present (necessarily morally opaque to mortal eyes) and the future (where God will reveal the distinctions between the cities of God and the world, which currently lie hidden in history). Bede's strikingly frequent mention of the 'present Church' in contrast to the future life of Christians in heaven could appear to relate to this eschatological distinction between the Church pre- and post-judgement. Certainly, Gregory the Great seems to have predominantly used the expression 'present Church' to describe the institution where good and bad were all mixed together, only to be separated when the elect enter the kingdom of heaven.[136] Bede's fondness for the phrase, however, never takes on this sense of the Augustinian 'mixed Church' of both damned and elect.

Rather Bede tended to focus on the present Church as one of toil and exile in contrast to the rest in the heavenly homeland which awaits the Church. Paired images such as the tabernacle and the temple, or the Sanctuary and the Holy of Holies, express this idea where the tiresome burden of good works in the current Church is balanced out by the rewards and rest that will come in the future.[137] In this way the division between the present and future Churches easily slipped into being no different than that between the true Church on earth and that institution in heaven. In that sense there is nothing necessarily to do with time to the expression—as Bede himself recognized. He remained very much aware that the life of the righteous with Christ in heaven only existed in the future on an individual level since in reality heaven predated any

---

[133] *HE*, IV.25 pp. 420–21. For discussion: McCready, *Miracles*, pp. 29–32.

[134] Darby, *End of Time*, pp. 95–124.

[135] Augustine, *DCD*, XVIII.49 p. 647. Markus, *Saeculum*, pp. 58–63, 158–9.

[136] Gregory, *Homiliae in Evangelia*, ed. R. Étaix, CCSL 141, XII.2 p. 82, XXIV.3 p. 199, XXXVIII.7 p. 365. See also Augustine, *Sermones*, PL 38, CCXXIII.2 col. 1092.

[137] *Temp.*, pp. 148, 166; *Tab.*, p. 42; *Hom.*, II.25 pp. 375–6.

mortal's existence: 'the promised life in heaven which indeed precedes this life of our exile ... but it is later in time because it is after the labours of this world that we succeed in entering it'.[138] The distinction between the heavenly Church and the earthly Church is one we will explore in greater detail in the next chapter, but at the moment it seems sufficient to note an important eschatological element to it.[139] But the great event that the present Church awaits is not the judgement which will separate the wheat from the chaff within it, but rather the vision of God which currently it longs for but has not achieved.[140]

The present Church, for Bede, certainly represented the institutional Church since one entered into it through the sacraments.[141] There Christians still in the mortal life were supported by scripture, good works, and the sacraments, necessarily only temporary crutches that would not be needed in the future.[142] Bede, nonetheless, could speak vaguely about how the present Church was being built up from the very first of the elect until the end of time—suggesting that those predestined to be saved from before the incarnation shared the same 'present' as Christians of the sixth age.[143] The great divide between the present and future Churches then is death and little else; judgement does not seem to have loomed very large over Bede's thought on the present Church and he expressed little fear that those in it might not make it into the future Church. The present life of the Church is a preparation for that life which is yet to come; the move between the two seems pretty seamless in Bede's temple—a simple matter of going up from the ground floor to the first storey.[144]

I do not mean to dismiss the importance of the eschatological tone which this contrast between present and future gave to Bede's temple commentaries. The Anglo-Saxon understood time entirely as a preparation for eternity, the laborious change of the present encouraging the Christian soul to ache for perpetual rest.[145] Christians had to make sure that they would make it to the heavenly resting place, and therein lay the significance of judgement; as an author much concerned with the Day of Judgement he clearly believed eschatological reflection to be morally beneficial as a stimulus to penitence and renunciation of the world.[146] In practice the purpose of Bede's eschatology was exactly the same as that of Gregory the Great: to encourage the reader to

---

[138] *Temp.*, p. 171 'promissa uita in caelis anterior quidem hac conuersatione nostri exilii ... sed posterior tempore quia post huius saeculi labores ad illius ingressum perducimur'; trans. Connolly, p. 37.

[139] See Ch. 4 within this volume, 'Bede's use of the cosmic interpretation', p. 79–80.

[140] *Tab.*, p. 30; *Temp.*, pp. 176, 188.   [141] *Cant.*, p. 322; *Temp.*, p. 232.

[142] *Temp.*, pp. 171, 190; *Tab.*, p. 30; *Hom.*, II.25 p. 376.

[143] *Temp.*, p. 147; *Tab.*, p. 43.   [144] *Hom.*, II.1 p. 191; *Gen.* pp. 109–10.

[145] E.g. *DTR*, LXXI p. 544.

[146] *DTR*, LXVIII pp. 537–8; Bede, *De Die Iudicii*, ed. J. Fraipoint, CCSL 122, pp. 439–44.

turn to a holy life.[147] But, for Bede, the present Church already has the pledge of its future salvation in heaven and so already knows the outcome of any judgement.[148] It would be wrong to describe the Church of the present age as perfect, but only because no mortal is perfect: even the predestined elect require redemption from sins by Christ.[149]

This idea of the present Church seems close to the way in which Cassiodorus and the seventh-century Irish exegete Ailerán used the expression; for Ailerán the courts of the house of the Lord were the present Church, whereas the house itself constituted the future Church.[150] Present and future seem integrally linked, the one being merely the vestibule of the other. Exile and pilgrimage provided key images which Bede associated with the present Church, emphasizing that its purpose was to move into heaven in the future.[151] Augustine had interpreted the inn in the story of the good Samaritan as the Church where travellers are refreshed on their journey to the eternal homeland—Bede reused Augustine's interpretation verbatim, except for adding the detail that the inn was the *present* Church.[152] Bede's change seems to have come from a concern to highlight the essential continuity between the future life in heaven and the sacramental institution that is inevitably journeying towards eternity.

Here we see the two ways of reading the temple as history coming together: the progressive vision of the Church, which Bede presented when reflecting on the relationship between the old and new dispensations, appears again in the relationship between the present and the future Church. As Christ's Church fulfils the figural significance of the Jewish temple, life in heaven fulfils the purpose of the present Church. The forward, progressive thrust of Bede's history seems unavoidable—the serried rows of stones in the wall of the temple represent the generations of the faithful who succeed each other in the present Church in turn, each supported by those before them and supporting those after them until the wall reaches its appointed end.[153] In this section the emphasis on continuity rather than rupture between the present and future Churches seems as noticeable as that between the temple and Christianity in the previous section.

The universal scope of Bede's vision of history further links the two sections of the current chapter. The wall of the temple ceases to be built up when the

[147] R. A. Markus, 'Living within Sight of the End', in *Time in the Medieval World*, eds Chris Humphrey and W. M. Ormrod (York, 2001), pp. 23–34, at 31–4; Ralph Walterspacher, 'Book V of Bede's *Historia ecclesiastica gentis Anglorum*: Perspective on Salvation History and Eschatology', *Archa Verbi: Yearbook for the Study of Medieval Theology* 1 (2004), pp. 11–24.

[148] *Ezra.*, pp. 278, 310.   [149] *Tab.*, p. 133.

[150] Cassiodorus, *Expositio Psalmorum*, ed. M. Adriaen, CCSL 97–8, XLI.5 p. 382; Ailerán, *Interpretatio Mystica Progenitorum Domini Iesu Christi*, PL 80, col. 336.

[151] *Tab.*, p. 85; *Temp.*, p. 142.

[152] Augustine, *Quaestiones Evangeliorum*, II.19 p. 63; *Luc.*, p. 224.

[153] *Ezra.*, p. 365; *Temp.*, pp. 156, 169–70, 227–8; *EpCath.*, p. 234.

present and the future life are done away with and a single existence awaits the Church in the risen body and in the presence of God. If the first floor of the temple is the Church militant on earth and the second floor the Church triumphant in heaven, then the third storey is the resurrection that awaits both at the end of time.[154] In the temple commentaries number symbolism constantly makes reference to the whole scope of the ages. Almost every appearance of the numbers six, seven, and eight anywhere in Bede's temple commentaries ends up related to the ages of the world and the vast span of the Church through all mortal time and beyond.[155] In particular, the seven years Solomon took to build the temple represented the entirety of the temporal world through which Christ built his Church from living stones, row on row, generation on generation. The temple's dedication in its eighth year symbolized the eighth age, that of the resurrection, when all the elect will reign in the completed temple Church.[156]

Bede's temple stretched not just forwards in time to the end, but also backwards to incorporate the very origins of the Church. He developed from Gregory the idea that the entrance portico to the temple symbolized the elect who had come before the incarnation—as one walked through the portico towards the doors of the temple one actually journeyed through history from Abel to Simeon (as it were, the last stone before the door, which symbolized Christ).[157] Similarly, the entrance to the tabernacle represented the primitive Church of the Acts of the Apostles—and the back wall of the tabernacle's enclosure symbolized the completion of time, implying here again that the passage from one end of the holy structure to the other was a journey through history.[158] The different stages of true religion all fit into the temple image: the tabernacle signifies the pre-incarnation Synagogue, the temple, the post-incarnation Church of Jews and gentiles; the temple image as a whole thus covers the entire historical society of the elect.[159] The design of the temple image showed that the Church was a universal body that stretched across all of

---

[154] *Hom.*, II.1 p. 191, II.25 p. 375; *Temp.*, pp. 166–7; *Ezra.*, p. 301; *Gen.*, pp. 109–10; *Reg.*, XII p. 304.

[155] *Temp.*, p. 153; *Ezra.*, pp. 268, 363, 371; *Tab.*, pp. 66–7.

[156] *Hom.*, II.1 p. 191, II.24 pp. 364–5; *Temp.* pp. 196–7, 232–3; *Ezra.*, p. 241; *DTR*, LXVI p. 476. Bede developed the idea of eight world ages by differentiating (as Augustine had not) between the Sabbath rest of elect souls between their death and bodily resurrection (this seventh age therefore began with the death of Abel and exists concurrently with the six ages of the world that progress through history) and the age of the resurrection (the eighth age); see Darby, *End of Time*, pp. 65–74.

[157] *Temp.*, pp. 161–2; *Hom.*, II.25 pp. 376–7; compare Gregory, *In Hiezechihelem*, II.III.16 pp. 247–8. Christiana Whitehead, *Castles of the Mind: A Study of Medieval Architectural Allegory* (Cardiff, 2003), pp. 14, 17–18.

[158] *Tab.*, pp. 74, 65.

[159] *Tab.*, pp. 42–3; *Temp.*, pp. 148, 157. *Hom.*, II.25 p. 369, seems to suggest that the difference is between the two peoples called to Christ, Jews and gentiles, rather than the elect from two different eras—though the interpretations are close in practice.

history and thereby situated Christian Anglo-Saxons within a history much wider than their own. Bede's *Greater Chronicle* had a similar purpose: by eschewing the Eusebian approach of structuring universal history by paralleling the chronologies of different nations, it created a single history of all peoples under God, into which Insular history was seamlessly integrated.[160]

Thus when we look at the temple image to understand Bede's concept of history we see that he considered time a dynamic process through which the Church marches to salvation. The key development along the way was, of course, the incarnation of Christ, which to some extent revolutionized the human relationship with eternity. But progress did not only come about at this one historically discrete moment—as the master builder, constantly interfering in history, Christ constructed his temple 'from the first of the elect until the last to be born at the end of the world'.[161] Before his birth as a man, Christ had been present in history and remained so right up until Bede's own time, and indeed, would continue to be present in the future eternity awaiting the Church. The result was that history could be seen as a unified whole where the past did not need to be condemned by the present; within the confines of the temple Church those 'upon whom the ends of the ages have come' could embrace in loving affection 'those faithful who were in the beginning of the world'.[162] Ancient Israelites and contemporary Northumbrians were part of a single but constantly developing history, which awaited its inevitable conclusion in immortality.[163]

Thus when Bede engaged with the temple as history he did not distance himself, his time, or his people from it; rather he asserted its universal relevance both by connecting Jewish past and Christian present and by presenting a harmonious vision of salvation history (symbolized by the temple image) in which that connection took place. The universal relevance of the temple image appears when we study it through the lens of history—but not just that lens. For Bede, Christ's saving work took place in space just as much as in time and so we now turn to examine the ways in which Bede interpreted the temple as the cosmos. The next chapter will not only provide the spatial complement to this chapter's temporal focus, it will also further unpick the circumstances within Bede's community that influenced his outlook within the temple commentaries.

---

[160] Andrew Rabin, 'Historical recollections: rewriting the world in Bede's *De Temporum Ratione*', *Viator* 36 (2005), pp. 23–39, at 34–6; Scully, 'Bede's *Chronica Maiora*'.

[161] *Temp.*, p. 147 'quae a primo electo usque ad ultimum qui in fine mundi nasciturus est'; trans. Connolly, p. 5.

[162] *Tab.*, p. 62 'nos in quos fines saeculorum deuenerunt etiam eos qui in primordio saeculi fuerunt fideles sincero affectu diligamus'; trans. Holder, p. 69.

[163] See O'Brien, 'Jewish Church', p. 73.

4

Bede's Temple as Cosmos

Long before Bede, Jewish commentators had sought to make the sites of the Jewish national cult relevant to all peoples at all times by interpreting the temple image as symbolic of the entire cosmos and therefore of no mere local religious significance.[1] For Christians the Letter to the Hebrews suggested such a reading, speaking as it did of the tabernacle as just a shadow of the heavenly reality which had been shown to Moses.[2] This line of interpretation reached its most extreme end in the *Christian Topography* of Cosmas Indicopleustes, a sixth-century Egyptian monk who believed that the tabernacle replicated the physical structure of the universe: a cuboid cosmos, with a flat earth at its base, split vertically between heaven and earth.[3] One might imagine that Bede, separated in time and place from the site of the physical building, would have welcomed some such cosmic interpretation that would have made the temple image relevant to his world. As we shall see in this chapter, his use of the image does reveal ideas about the created world and the Anglo-Saxons' place within it that find a striking parallel in the Codex Amiatinus, suggestive of the communal background to Bede's writings on the temple image.

I use the word 'cosmos' here to refer to the whole created universe—both heaven and earth. It might seem strange to describe heaven as part of the same universe as the earth, but Bede clearly envisaged it this way. God had created heaven as the unchanging location where angels dwell in the light of the divine presence, along with the earth at the beginning of time.[4] Bede even seems to have assigned a spatial location to the higher heaven of the angels, suggesting that it had a physical relationship with earth.[5] Of course, Bede never sought

---

[1] E.g. Josephus, *Jewish Antiquities*, ed. Franz Blatt, *The Latin Josephus* (Copenhagen, 1958), III.VII.7 pp. 241–2. See Ch. 2 within this volume, 'The temple in the Christian tradition before Bede', p. 36.

[2] Hebrews 8.5, 9.23.

[3] Cosmas Indicopleustes, *Topographie Chrétienne*, ed. and trans. Wanda Wolska-Conus, 3 vols (Paris, 1968–73), II, pp. 38–74. See Ch. 2 within this volume, 'The temple in the Christian tradition before Bede', p. 39.

[4] *Gen.*, pp. 3–4.

[5] Bede, *De Natura Rerum*, ed. Charles W. Jones, CCSL 123A, VII pp. 197–8.

precisely to map that relationship or definitively to place heaven within the cosmos described in his scientific works. Confusion concerning the relationship between the spiritual heaven and the material world was not unusual in Anglo-Saxon England;[6] nonetheless, heaven certainly formed part of God's creation, as did earth.

BEDE'S USE OF THE COSMIC INTERPRETATION

Cosmas's *Christian Topography* was known at Canterbury, and Wearmouth-Jarrow possessed a cosmographical codex (later sold to King Aldfrith by Ceolfrith), which may have included the work[7]—but Bede would certainly have dismissed the ideas expressed therein had he known them, since he believed in the traditional cosmos of a spherical earth at the centre of a spherical universe. Bede left his students in no doubt as to the shape of the world:

> The reason why the same [calendar] days are of unequal length is the roundness of the Earth, for not without reason is it called 'the orb of the world' on the pages of Holy Scripture and of ordinary literature. It is, in fact, a sphere set in the middle of the whole universe. It is not merely circular like a shield [or] spread out like a wheel, but resembles more a ball, being equally round in all directions...[8]

Whether Bede's insistence on the point arose because he had to struggle against some alternative way of thinking that contradicted his teaching is unclear, although some scholars have argued that he faced 'real doubt and disbelief'.[9] Contemporary Irish cosmological texts suggest that some scholars had difficulties with the difference between a spherical and a merely circular world.[10] But the spherical earth clearly remained the dominant model in learned

---

[6] Jennifer Neville, *Representations of the Natural World in Old English Poetry* (Cambridge, 1999), pp. 23, 71, 142.

[7] Bernhard Bischoff and Michael Lapidge, *Biblical Commentaries from the Canterbury School of Theodore and Hadrian* (Cambridge, 1994), pp. 208–11; Michael Gorman, 'Theodore of Canterbury, Hadrian of Nisida and Michael Lapidge', *Scriptorium* 50 (1996), pp. 184–92, at 191–2; *HA*, 15 pp. 58–9. Henry Mayr-Harting suggested to me that Wearmouth-Jarrow might willingly have parted with a work whose thesis the community rejected, but on the manuscript see Paul Meyvaert, 'Discovering the Calendar (*Annalis Libellus*) attached to Bede's own Copy of *De Temporum Ratione*', *Analecta Bollandiana* 120 (2002), pp. 5–64, at 17–18.

[8] *DTR*, XXXII p. 380 'Causa autem inaequalitatis eorundem dierum terrae rotunditas est; neque enim frustra et in scripturae diuinae et in communium literarum paganis orbis terrae uocatur. Est enim re uera orbis idem in medio totius mundi positus, non in latitudinis solum giro quasi instar scuti rotundus sed instar potius pilae undique uersum aequali rotunditate persimilis'; trans. Wallis, p. 91.

[9] Calvin B. Kendall and Faith Wallis, *Bede: On the Nature of Things* and *On Times* (Liverpool, 2010), p. 162.

[10] Marina Smyth, *Understanding the Universe in Seventh-Century Ireland* (Woodbridge, 1996), pp. 271–9.

Anglo-Saxon writings during Bede's lifetime and for Bede himself the tabernacle could not possibly have provided a literal image of the cosmos.[11]

A comparison between Bede and Cosmas shows how they differed on this point. Cosmas described the table on which the showbread was set out as an image of the earth: its four corners referred to the four seasons of the year and the complicated pattern around the edge represented the encircling Ocean and the land beyond it.[12] Bede avoided such blatantly physical interpretations: the crown of the table represented the gospels (not the mountains that hold up heaven, as for Cosmas); its legs signified the four senses of scriptural interpretation.[13] The only cosmic element in Bede's interpretation of the table was the four corners, which symbolized the spread of the gospels throughout the world.[14] Nonetheless, Bede and Cosmas do seem to have shared some cosmological ideas. Bede happily stated that '[i]n the beginning God created heaven and earth like one house', and, 'although it is one house', he divided the entire world into two parts: 'so that the upper region would serve as a home for the angels and the lower for men'. He quoted the Pseudo-Clementine *Recognitions* here, but Cosmas also advanced the same idea.[15]

This is one of a few suggestive hints scattered throughout Bede's work of a cosmic temple or similar structure. Caedmon's divinely inspired hymn on creation quoted in the *Ecclesiastical History* refers to God building the firmament as a roof for men.[16] Bede opened *On Genesis* by comparing the creative work of God to that of a man setting about the construction of a stone building of some kind;[17] later he briefly but significantly linked God's rest on the seventh day to Solomon's dedication of the temple after its completion.[18] The concept of a 'cosmic hall' or world hall 'appears to be the only particularly Anglo-Saxon cosmological image that occurs in Old English poetry'.[19] Knowledge of Cosmas' cuboid world perhaps partly lay behind the 'cosmic hall' of vernacular works, but the sources of Old English verse remain to a large extent

---

[11] Gopa Roy, 'The Anglo-Saxons and the Shape of the World', in *Essays on Anglo-Saxon and Related Themes in Memory of Lynne Grundy*, eds Jane Roberts and Janet Nelson (London, 2000), pp. 455–81.

[12] Cosmas, *Topographie*, II, p. 62.   [13] *Tab.*, pp. 23–5.

[14] *Tab.*, p. 24; see within this chapter, 'The Anglo-Saxons' place in the world'.

[15] *Gen.*, p. 12 'In principio cum fecisset Deus caelum et terram, tamquam domum unam . . . ita totius mundi machinam cum una domus esset in duas diuisit regiones. Diuisionis autem haec fuit causa ut superna regio angelis habitaculum, inferior uero praeberet hominibus'; adapted from trans. Kendall, pp. 77–8; Pseudo-Clement/Rufinus, *Recognitiones*, eds Bernhard Rehm and Georg Strecker, *Die Pseudoklementinen II* (Berlin, 1994), I.27 pp. 23–4. Compare Cosmas, *Topographie*, I, pp. 322–4.

[16] *HE*, IV.24 pp. 416–17.

[17] *Gen.*, p. 3. Ruth Wehlau, '*The Riddle of Creation': Metaphor Structures in Old English Poetry* (New York, 1997), p. 7.

[18] *Gen.*, p. 33.

[19] Neville, *Representations*, p. 147. Also Wehlau, '*Riddle of Creation*', pp. 15–54.

obscure and the origin of this image cannot be asserted with certainty.[20] For Bede this imagery functioned as a metaphorical aid rather than as an alternative to the authoritative image of the spherical earth he obtained from classical sources.[21]

Bede knew of the common interpretation of the temple veil as heaven, even providing a 'literal' interpretation where the beauties of the firmament were symbolized by the colourful tapestry of the veil at one point, but he avoided using the cosmological reading of the veil which connected it, through its constituent colours, with the four elements that formed the basis for all creation.[22] Previous exegetes had often connected the four colours of the veil and the priestly vestments—purple, red, white (i.e. linen), and violet/blue (*hyacinthum*)—with the elements.[23] For Bede, as in much Insular writing on creation, the Christian universe followed classical cosmology and the elements remained the essential building blocks of the universe.[24] In the temple commentaries, however, Bede preferred moral interpretations of the four colours and focused discussion of the elements on the human body rather than the cosmos.[25] Only on one occasion did he link the colours of the high priest's robes with the four elements. By pointing out that 'the Hebrews say that the high priest carried the figure of all the elements in his vesture', Bede made the cosmic reading part of the Jewish letter which had to be interpreted and from which the Christian spirit arose.[26] This reveals Bede's standard approach to cosmological references in *On the Tabernacle*: they did not serve as final interpretations, but were rather the means to get to the spiritual understanding. For example, the uppermost layer of skins covering the tabernacle was blue because 'blue is the colour of heaven' but the significance of this lay in that it represented the virtue of those who 'live a pure heavenly life on earth'.[27] Similarly, the four rows of three stones on the priestly rational/breastplate

---

[20] Neville, *Representations*, p. 147.

[21] For examples of how the 'cosmic hall' may have influenced Bede's thought: Faith Wallis, 'Cædmon's Created World and the Monastic Encyclopedia', in *Cædmon's Hymn and Material Culture in the World of Bede*, eds Allen J. Frantzen and John Hines (Morgantown WV, 2007), pp. 80–110, esp. 98.

[22] Veil as heaven: *Sam.*, p. 67; *Tab.*, pp. 71, 130; *Temp.*, p. 187. Literal interpretation: *Tab.*, p. 71.

[23] E.g. Cosmas, *Topographie*, II, p. 62; Jerome, *Epistulae*, ed. I. Hilberg, CSEL 54, LXIV.18 p. 605; Ambrose, *De fide*, ed. O. Faller, CSEL 78, II.prol.12 pp. 61–2.

[24] DTR, XXXV pp. 391–5; Smyth, *Understanding the Universe*, pp. 47–87.

[25] *Tab.*, pp. 11, 89–90; *Temp.*, p. 188. For Bede's moral interpretation of the colours, see Ch. 7 within this volume, 'Morality', p. 162; for the four elements as the constituent parts of the human body: *Temp.*, p. 227; *Tab.*, pp. 61, 87.

[26] *Tab.*, p. 123 'aiuntque Hebraei quod ideo pontifex omnium figuram elementorum in suo habitu gestauerit'; trans. Holder, p. 142.

[27] *Tab.*, p. 58 'Hyacinthus namque caelestis est coloris... quid per pelles hyacinthinas nisi uirtus exprimitur illorum qui... caelestem quodam modo in terris uitam gerunt'; trans. Holder, p. 64.

clearly corresponded to the year, 'divided into four seasons of three months each'. The signified year, however, itself signifies 'the time of our salvation'.[28] In other words, Bede transferred the cosmological meanings of the Jewish holy objects to the literal level; such interpretations became, therefore, the basis for a spiritual reading which arose from them. In this approach Jerome, who had outlined the Jewish understanding of the priestly robes, before developing the deeper, Christian interpretation, undoubtedly influenced him.[29]

The key biblical verse for the cosmic interpretation (as emphasized in Hebrews 8.5) was the one in which Moses was told to make the tabernacle according to the pattern that had been shown to him on the mountain. According to Hebrews, Moses saw the heavenly reality, Cosmas believed that he saw the universe itself as made in Genesis 1, but Bede never suggested that Moses had been shown the structure of the cosmos.[30] Rather he proposed that the heavenly pattern may have represented a way of life (the love-filled existence of the angels that humans should imitate) or the secrets of Christ and the Church that the tabernacle typologically foretold.[31] The Egyptian monk had tried to find in scripture ways to describe locations, whereas the Northumbrian used it to talk about moral states. This becomes clear when one examines those instances where Bede did describe the temple image as representing heaven and earth. He followed Hebrews 7–10 in associating Christ's passion with entrance into the heavenly Holy of Holies through the veil. Hence, Bede interpreted the Holy of Holies as heaven where Christ reigns having passed from earth to his rest (the Ark of the Covenant being the body of the incarnate Christ) and the Sanctuary in front of the veil as the earth, where the Church militant draws near while still waiting to pass through the veil.[32] This reading placed heaven and earth within the temple horizontally, but they also appeared there vertically—thus problematizing the horizontal reading. In the last chapter we saw that Bede read the lower storey of the temple as the Church on earth, the middle storey as the Church currently at rest in heaven, and the upper storey as the Church of the resurrected at the end of time, thus providing a temporal as well as spatial progression through which the individual Christian can journey.[33]

---

[28] *Tab.*, p. 113 'Nam et hoc quod quattuor ordines in rationali ternos habebant lapides congruit anni uertentis ordini qui per ternos menses in quattuor tempora distinguitur. Annum autem in scripturis uocari totum hoc salutis nostrae tempus'; trans. Holder, p. 130.

[29] Jerome, *Epistulae*, LXIV.18 p. 605. See Arthur G. Holder, 'New Treasures and Old in Bede's "De Tabernaculo" and "De Templo"', *RB* 99 (1989), pp. 237–49, at 243.

[30] Cosmas, *Topographie*, I, pp. 448–50.

[31] *Tab.*, pp. 12, 40, 69–70.

[32] *Tab.*, pp. 72–3, 129–30; *Temp.*, pp. 171, 176–7; *Hom.*, II.1 p. 190, II.25 p. 376; *DTR*, VIII p. 303; *Reg.*, XIV p. 306. Also *Sam.*, p. 67; *Apoc.*, p. 301; *Luc.*, p. 362.

[33] See Ch. 3 within this volume, 'History and the figural interpretation of the temple', p. 71.

But in so far as both interpretations are cosmological, they contradict each other on the literal level: the Holy of Holies, heaven on the horizontal analysis, forms part of the earthly ground floor according to the vertical interpretation. Bede used number symbolism to back up his analysis and here too apparent contradictions arose: the Sanctuary measured forty cubits in length 'for this number is often used to signify the present labour of the faithful';[34] but the entire length of the temple (i.e. Sanctuary and Holy of Holies) is sixty cubits. That refers to the earth 'because the Lord completed the creation of the world in six days, and because there are six ages of this world'.[35] These different ways of dividing up the temple exist alongside the simple fact that the temple *tout court* could symbolize heaven.[36] All these interpretations had some justification depending on whether Bede sought to emphasize the relative holiness of the Church on earth and in heaven, the progression of the individual towards God, or the life of heaven as being a temple liturgy consisting of the sacrifice of praise.[37]

The difficulty arises, then, when one seeks to read these interpretations as descriptions of the literal structure of the cosmos and the physical relationship between heaven and earth, for on such a level they make no sense. Occasionally for Bede, the temple could symbolize the heavenly things that a Christian ought to contemplate or desire, rather than heaven itself. To be in the temple, therefore, meant that one concentrated on heavenly things—something that could be done while yet on the earth.[38] The hierarchy of holiness in the Church, which Bede mapped out using the temple courtyards, each more restrictive than the previous, does not form a literal description of the locations in heaven to which the various grades of Christian could expect to go, as Collins has argued.[39] The tone of Bede's language, with a focus on the life and works (preaching, alms-giving, fasting, etc.) of the various types of Christian, implies that he thought here of the current state of the soul, rather than its future destination.[40]

Bede did speak in *On the Tabernacle* in spatial terms of the disposition of the elect in heaven: 'the ones who endeavour to cleave to Christ higher up in

---

[34] *Temp.*, p. 172 'qui numerus saepe in significatione ponitur praesentis fidelium laboris'; trans. Connolly, p. 38.

[35] *Hom.*, II.25 pp. 374–5 'dominus sex diebus mundi ornamentum perfecit et sex sunt huius saeculi aetates'; trans. Martin and Hurst, II, p. 263. For the symbolism of the numbers four and forty see within this chapter, 'The Anglo-Saxons' place in the world', p. 82–3; for medieval number theory: Heinz Meyer and Rudolf Suntrup, *Lexikon der Mittelalterlichen Zahlenbedeutungen* (Munich, 1987).

[36] *Act.*, p. 24; *Luc.*, pp. 21–2, 61; *Hom.*, I.19 p. 135, II.16 p. 296, II.25 pp. 377–8.

[37] *Hom.*, I.11 p. 77, II.24 pp. 365–6; *Apoc.*, p. 301.

[38] *Sam.*, pp. 35, 39; *Luc.*, p. 29.

[39] Samuel W. Collins, *The Carolingian Debate over Sacred Space* (New York, 2012), pp. 30–3.

[40] *Temp.*, pp. 194–6.

this life will enjoy a closer vision of him in that life'.[41] In this case we could perhaps say that the candelabrum, which he here commented on, maps the position of souls in heaven. Certainly Bede believed that earthly holiness affected one's eventual celestial location; there were many mansions in the Father's house to match the different merits of the faithful.[42] The diversity of merits easily connected with ideas about hierarchy and Bede frequently read various architectural and design features of the temple image as referring to some hierarchical structuring of the Church.[43] But he did warn against seeking to discover the exact nature of those heavenly distinctions, stating that 'what the actual conditions and mode of life are like in that heavenly homeland, is clear only to those of its citizens who have gained entrance to it'.[44] The fact that the opposite walls of the temple symbolized the Jews and gentiles did not constitute proof that those peoples would be kept separate in heaven.[45] We should not search for any detailed images of the universe or heaven in Bede's use of the temple image, therefore. But Bede's temple does still speak of cosmic realities—in particular it sheds light on the spiritual relationship between heaven and earth.[46]

For Bede, heaven and earth were necessarily opposites and he used the temple image to explore the separation between the states associated with the two. The temple was built on a mountain top having been divinely inspired, but valley dwellers built its evil counterpart, the tower of Babel, with materials mined from the earth that symbolized their base minds.[47] Bede used the temple image to contrast the different states of the Church or individual Christian: the mobile tabernacle represented the 'exile' of this earthly life, one of struggle and suffering, the fixed mountain top temple the life to come, one of rest in the vision of God.[48] While the various locations of the ark's wanderings call to mind the diversity of the present life, its arrival in the Jerusalem temple symbolizes the departure from the body into heaven.[49] This

---

[41] *Tab.*, p. 32 'quanto quisque altius in hac uita Christo adhaerere curauerit tanto uicinior in illa uita eius uisione fruitur'; trans. Holder, p. 35.

[42] John 14.2. *Tab.*, p. 22; *Temp.*, pp. 233–4; *Ezra.*, pp. 376, 383; *Hom.*, II.24 p. 367; compare Gregory, *Homiliae in Hiezechihelem Prophetam*, ed. M. Adriaen, CCSL 142, II.IV.6 pp. 262–3.

[43] As well as *Temp.*, pp. 194–6, see *Temp.*, p. 163; *Tab.*, pp. 31–5. See Ch. 5 within this volume, 'The hierarchical body of Christ'; Arthur G. Holder, 'The Venerable Bede on the Mysteries of Our Salvation', *American Benedictine Review* 421 (1991), pp. 140–62, at 151–2.

[44] *Temp.*, p. 205 'status et conuersatio patriae illius caelestis quomodo sese habeat solis eis qui hanc intrare meruerunt eius ciuibus patet'; trans. Connolly, p. 82.

[45] *Temp.*, p. 181.

[46] See Holder, 'Mysteries of Our Salvation', pp. 159–61.

[47] *Gen.*, pp. 158–61. Also *Ezra.*, p. 247; *Apoc.*, p. 247.

[48] *Temp.*, pp. 147–8; *Tab.*, p. 42. Jennifer O'Reilly, 'Bede on Seeing the God of Gods in Zion', in *Text, Image, Interpretation: Studies in Anglo-Saxon Literature and its Insular Context in Honour of Eamonn Ó Carragáin*, eds Alastair Minnis and Jane Roberts (Turnhout, 2007), pp. 3–29, at 6–13.

[49] *Sam.*, pp. 59–60.

Augustinian contrast between the two states of the Church (the one a pilgrim on the earth and the other triumphant in heaven) clearly spoke deeply to Bede—perhaps because of the importance of religious exile in Insular culture.[50] Heaven and earth were different then—but not entirely incompatible since the Church existed simultaneously in both. The temple image consistently showed forth this message, because it contained both heaven and earth within its symbolism.

Bede's use of the temple image thus could frequently undermine the distinction between heaven and earth. The Church in this life may be the wandering tabernacle but it in fact carries the Christian, a citizen of heaven, homeward.[51] While the old temple was built on earth, the new temple of the living God, the Church, has its way of life in heaven.[52] The barrier before the Holy of Holies did not reach the Sanctuary roof but left a gap open through which the scent of sacrifices could waft as prayers made on earth can still reach God in heaven.[53] Angels in heaven and humans on earth both participate in the one temple Church.[54] Contemplation allows the perfect to draw near the veil and see part of the heavenly life—if not the ark itself, at least the poles extending from it.[55] Many holy people in this life have earthly bodies but heavenly minds; standing near the veil they are liminal figures encompassing in themselves both cosmic extremes.[56] While Cosmas' cosmology was based on a contrast between now and then, here and there, Bede saw the Church as coexisting in many times and places. Its members, despite their separation by time, place, or nature, were built together into the one temple.[57]

How did this unity of heaven and earth within the temple image come about? As we have seen, the house of God sat on a mountain: the incarnate Christ.[58] Christ can be portrayed as a mountain because, while born of the earth, through his incarnation his divine nature raised him up above all men.[59] Christ raised the Church along with himself; through his incarnation humanity has gained entrance to the heavenly temple.[60] This relates to a common

---

[50] E.g. *Hom.*, II.16 p. 294; *Cant.*, p. 237. M. A. Claussen, '"Peregrinatio" and "Peregrini" in Augustine's "City of God"', *Traditio* 46 (1991), pp. 33–75; Augustine, *DCD*, XV.1 p. 454, XIX.17 pp. 683–5; Augustine, *Enarrationes in Psalmos*, eds E. Dekkers and J. Fraipont, CCSL 38–40, CXXV.3 pp. 1846–7; Thomas Charles-Edwards, 'The Social Background to Irish *Peregrinatio*', *Celtica* 11 (1976), pp. 43–59.

[51] *Tab.*, pp. 42, 85; *Temp.*, pp. 160, 172–3; *Ezra.*, pp. 267–8, 369.

[52] *Apoc.*, p. 385; see also *Ezra.*, pp. 266, 327, 365. Philippians 3.20.   [53] *Temp.*, p. 172.

[54] *Tab.*, pp. 72–3; *Temp.*, pp. 147, 179–81; *Ezra.*, pp. 300, 371, 384.   [55] *Reg.*, XIV p. 307.

[56] *Tab.*, pp. 22, 58–9; *Ezra.*, p. 370. Gregory, *In Hiezechihelem*, II.X.21–2 pp. 395–6, presented the altar of incense as the saints who, while still in their bodies, draw near to Christ in heaven through love; Bede then expanded on this idea: *Temp.*, pp. 224–5.

[57] *Temp.*, p. 185; *Sam.*, p. 60; *EpCath.*, p. 235; *Tab.*, p. 48; compare Augustine, *DCD*, X.7 pp. 279–80.

[58] *Cant.*, pp. 245, 305–6; *Sam.*, p. 221; *Marc.*, pp. 527–8; *Tab.*, p. 21.

[59] *Temp.*, p. 158; also *Hom.*, II.15 p. 283; compare Gregory, *In Hiezechelem*, II.I.4 pp. 209–10.

[60] *Ezra.*, pp. 329–30, 351; *Hom.*, I.6 p. 41; *Temp.*, p. 187; *Tab.*, p. 12.

patristic topos that by lowering himself Christ raised up humanity; God became man so that man might become God.[61] The joining of paradoxical natures in Christ not only reversed the effects of the Fall but served to join the hitherto separated parts of the universe. For Bede, the Ark of the Covenant represented Christ's earthly body, his human nature, which now resided in heaven: the divine Christ had stooped down to earth to become incarnate and had then carried human flesh into heaven at his ascension.[62] The temple for Bede, just as for the Jews originally, proved that God 'ruled in heaven in such a way that he was nevertheless with his faithful on earth'.[63] That is, God transcended the cosmic divide through the incarnation and ascension— '[b]ecause he who was taken up into heaven is both God and a human being, he remains on the earth with the saints in the humanity which he took from the earth'.[64] The incarnation has two interlinking aspects: it allowed fallen humanity to regain connection with divinity by making the divine human, and it brought together the cosmic opposites of heaven and earth.

We saw earlier that, while elsewhere in *On the Tabernacle* Bede simply spoke of the elements as the constitutive parts of the human body, he did once provide the four elements with a cosmic meaning.[65] However, there too, after explaining that the elemental colours of the high priest's vestments suggest that his sacrifices had universal significance, Bede explained the link with the human body and that 'for this same reason, Greek natural science refers to the human being as a "microcosm", that is, a "little world"'.[66] This has obvious significance when one reads the Exodus text Christologically: 'But if we understand the high priest whom Moses consecrates as the Lord Saviour, it is quite right that he carries in his vesture a figure of the whole world, and of a human being as well'.[67] Bede then argued that this dual meaning of the

---

[61] E.g. Gregory, *Moralia in Iob*, ed. M. Adriaen, CCSL 143+A+B, XXII.XVII.42 pp. 1121–2; Augustine, *Sermones*, PL 38, CXCII.1 col. 1012. Carole Straw, *Gregory the Great: Perfection in Imperfection* (Berkeley CA, 1988), pp. 147–55; Gerald Bonner, 'Augustine's Conception of Deification', *JTS* 37 (1986), pp. 369–86.

[62] *Tab.*, pp. 13–17, 72; *Apoc.*, pp. 301, 385; *Reg.*, XIV p. 306; *Hom.*, II.25 p. 376. Primasius, *Commentarius in Apocalypsin*, ed. A. W. Adams, CCSL 92, III.11 p. 177; Gregory, *In Hiezechihelem*, II.X.21 p. 395; Ch. 5 within this volume, 'The temple as Christ', p. 107–8.

[63] *Ezra.*, p. 246 'ita in caelis regnare credidit ut nihilominus cum suis fidelibus esset in terra'; trans. DeGregorio, p. 15.

[64] *Hom.*, II.8 p. 235 'Quia enim ipse Deus et homo est adsumptus est in caelum humanitate quam de terra susceperat manet cum sanctis in terra'; trans. Martin and Hurst, II, p. 72.

[65] See within this chapter, p. 76.

[66] *Tab.*, p. 123 'Vnde et a physiologis Graece homo microcosmos, id est minor mundus, uocatur'; trans. Holder, p. 143. Jerome, *Epistulae*, LXIV.18 pp. 605–9, deals with the cosmic meaning of the elements, but does not go on to connect this to man as microcosm; Isidore of Seville is Bede's probable source for this language, e.g. *De Natura Rerum*, ed. and trans. Jacques Fontaine, *Traité de la Nature* (Bordeaux, 1960), IX.2 p. 207.

[67] *Tab.*, p. 123 'Quod si in pontifice quem consecrat Moyses dominum saluatorem intelligimus iure in habitu suo totius mundi figuram simul et hominis habet'; adapted from trans. Holder, p. 143.

vestments was appropriate since Christ rules the entire world and takes away
the sins of the world (John 1.29), by implication through his human nature.
The reference to the human body as microcosm suggests a link between
Christ's physical incarnation and his control over the entire macrocosmic
universe to which the four elements connected his body.[68] When Christ took
upon himself the physical elements he changed and redeemed them, as he
turned water into the means of baptismal grace when he stepped into it.[69]

THE ANGLO-SAXONS' PLACE IN THE WORLD

The incarnation sanctified all of the created cosmos then, transforming the
universe just as it had changed history by fulfilling the figures of the old
dispensation.[70] History obviously mattered a great deal to Bede, but as an
Anglo-Saxon perhaps the spatial extension of the Church mattered even more.
Bede's temple Church was truly cosmic because it was an entity that stretched
throughout the universe. This cosmic unity of the Church also justified its
earthly unity: just as one house of Christ encompassed both angels and
humans so too the churches of many peoples all formed part of one Catholic
Church throughout the world.[71] Bede's use of the temple image drew on a
wide Insular and patristic discourse to celebrate the Church's catholicity and,
although I began this chapter by stating that Bede would have dismissed
any idea of the earth as flat and rectangular, when drawing on that discourse
he seemingly appealed to this image repeatedly throughout the temple
commentaries.

In numerous places Bede spoke of the earth as represented by the number
four, talking of a square world, or simply of the four parts of the world.[72] He,
of course, had a good scriptural basis for doing so since the Bible regularly
described the earth with reference to its four corners.[73] The language is thus
highly stereotyped and primarily metaphorical; Bede did not reject the spherical earth but rather used an accepted image that could help explain the text he
had before him.[74] Here he was drawing on imagery common in Insular

---

[68] For the various fours (elements, humours, seasons) which link all of creation: *DTR*, XXXV
pp. 391–5.

[69] *Temp.*, p. 222. See Clare Stancliffe, 'Creator and Creation: A Preliminary Investigation of
Early Irish Views and their Relationship to Biblical and Patristic Traditions', *Cambrian Medieval
Celtic Studies* 58 (2009), pp. 9–27, at 21–5.

[70] See Ch. 3, within this volume.   [71] *EpCath.*, p. 235.

[72] *Tab.*, pp. 10, 112; *Temp.*, pp. 172, 213; *Luc.*, p. 132.

[73] E.g. Isaiah 11.12; Ezekiel 7.2; Matthew 24.31; Apocalypse 7.1.

[74] See Wallis, 'Caedmon's Created World', p. 99; Wanda Wolska, *La Topographie Chrétienne
de Cosmas Indicopleustès: Théologie et Science au VIe siècle* (Paris, 1962), pp. 133–6.

(especially Irish) exegesis, which tended to link the gospels with the four-fold world; Bede adapted this imagery, almost always referring it to the global mission or universal spread of Christianity.[75] When he could he interpreted circular objects as referring to this universal mission, but the simple fact is that such objects are rare in these texts (I have only found two references to the circular world in the context of universal mission in Bede's temple commentaries) and references to four or rectangular objects appear much more frequently.[76] For Bede's allegorical purposes the weight of biblical tradition won out over his own scientific knowledge.

The four-fold world may have been forced on Bede mainly by circumstances but the image also carried important symbolic resonances. It primarily referred to the four cardinal points, biblical shorthand for the whole earth and all peoples in it and thus often called upon when speaking of the universal spread of the Good News or the destruction of all things during the End Times. Isaiah 11.12's use of the cardinal points had referred to the return of the Jews from exile, but a letter from Pope Vitalian to Oswiu of Northumbria saw the spread of orthodoxy to the Anglo-Saxons as prophesied in scripture, quoting Isaiah 11.[77] Being associated in this way with the earth's extent, four, and as a consequence forty also, came to stand as symbolic shorthand for this world, the temporal and material earth as a place of penance and struggle.[78] When Bede spoke of the four-fold world, he thought not just of the created world, but of that place as the desert where the Church suffers and works.[79] All of human life therefore appeared as a journey towards heaven, a process of progression.[80] The four-fold world was also connected with the cosmic reach of the cross.[81] The laborious work of the Church in this world, as of Christ on the cross, consisted of the salvation of mankind—and thus the four-fold world became for Bede the allegorical location of evangelization.

In the temple commentaries the rectangular objects of Jewish cult (the altars for example) suggested the four corners of the world to which the four books of the gospel or faith in the Trinity would be taken by the missionary work of

[75] Jennifer O'Reilly, 'Patristic and Insular Traditions of the Evangelists: Exegesis and Iconography', in *Le Isole Britanniche e Roma in Età Romanobarbarica*, eds A. M. Luiselli Fadda and É. Ó Carragáin (Rome, 1998), pp. 49–94.

[76] Circular world: *Temp.*, pp. 183, 207. Fourfold world: *Temp.*, pp. 210, 221; *Luc.*, p. 86; *Marc.*, pp. 469–70; *Tab.*, pp. 16, 20, 77, 82.

[77] *HE*, III.29 pp. 318–21; Georges Tugène, 'L'histoire "ecclésiastique" du peuple anglais: Réflexions sur le particularisme et l'universalisme chez Bède', *Recherches augustiniennes* 17 (1982), pp. 129–72, at 161; see also Jerome, *In Esaiam*, ed. M. Adriaen, CCSL 73+A, pp. 154–6.

[78] Meyer and Suntrup, *Lexikon*, pp. 332–7, 710–14. Augustine was clearly influential in passing this idea to Bede: *Sermones*, CCLXIII.4 col. 211–212 appears at *Luc.*, p. 94; *Ret.*, p. 142; *Temp.*, p. 173.

[79] E.g. *Temp.*, pp. 172–3; *Hom.*, II.25 p. 376.   [80] O'Reilly, 'Seeing the God of Gods'.

[81] E.g. *Luc.*, p. 401 (compare Sedulius, *Carmen Paschale*, ed. J. Huemer, CSEL 10, V.188–195 p. 128); *Apoc.*, p. 311.

the Church.[82] One of the primary purposes of Bede's exegesis of the temple image was to prove that it depicted the universal mission of the Church; it represented a symbol of God's intention to save the gentiles, existing long before the coming of Christ in the flesh.[83] The wanderings of the Jewish ark provided a sign of the faith's progression from Israel to all the gentile nations.[84] When the veil ripped at Christ's death, the sacraments of the Law were uncovered and passed over to the gentiles.[85] The temple was to be built of living stones and the gentiles could rightly be represented by the stones they once worshipped; they were the stones that Christ turned into children of Abraham.[86] For Anglo-Saxon readers a pun on the name *Saxones* (*saxonus* = stony) may have made this imagery particularly relevant.[87] In a Bedan reading, the temple image never simply represented the site of a national religion; it was for all nations, a symbolic place reaching out to the ends of the earth.[88]

At every available opportunity Bede stated that Jews and gentiles were both called by God. While the temple image might seem to be exclusively Jewish, Bede's exegesis drew out the unity of the two peoples symbolized in its decorations. The two pillars at the entrance to Solomon's temple represented the teachers to the Jews and gentiles respectively; the temple was rebuilt from old and new stones, representing the Church's construction from both peoples.[89] Christ as the cornerstone of the temple Church linked the two nations through himself. Sometimes Bede emphasized that Christ the cornerstone was also the stone which the Jews rejected;[90] but the attempt to foil God's plan for universal salvation failed—both Jews and gentiles were joined together in the one Church of Christ.[91] Occasionally Bede seems to have been pleading almost as much for the place of Jews among the elect as for the other nations of the earth, but the calling of the gentiles consistently remained one of the most important themes

---

[82] *Tab.*, pp. 16, 77, 82; *Temp.*, pp. 210, 217; *Luc.*, p. 132; compare Gregory, *Regula Pastoralis*, PL 77, II.11 col. 49.

[83] *Temp.*, pp. 149, 182–3; *Ezra.*, p. 347; *Sam.*, p. 32.

[84] *Sam.*, pp. 43–6. Also *VIII Q.*, VIII pp. 71–2.

[85] *Luc.*, pp. 406–7 (= *Marc.*, p. 636); compare Jerome, *In Matheum*, eds D. Hurst and M. Adriaen, CCSL 77, p. 275.

[86] *Luc.*, pp. 78, 346 (compare Ambrose, *Expositio Evangelii Secundum Lucam*, ed. M. Adriaen, CCSL 14, II.75 pp. 62–3); *EpCath.*, p. 234. Luke 3.8; 1 Peter 2.5. Jennifer O'Reilly, 'The Multitude of Isles and the Corner-stone: Topography, Exegesis, and the Identity of the *Angli* in Bede's *Historia Ecclesiastica*', in *Anglo-Saxon Traces*, eds Jane Roberts and Leslie Webster (Tempe AZ, 2011), pp. 201–27, at 209–12.

[87] James Palmer, *Anglo-Saxons in a Frankish World, 690–900* (Turnhout, 2009), pp. 138–9; O'Reilly, 'Multitude of Isles', pp. 217–19.

[88] *Marc.*, p. 579; compare Jerome, *In Esaiam*, p. 635.

[89] *Temp.*, pp. 198–9; *Hom.*, II.25 p. 377; *Ezra.*, p. 291.

[90] *Luc.*, pp. 354–5 (= *Marc.*, p. 586); *Act.*, p. 26; *Hom.*, II.3 p. 204.

[91] *Tab.*, p. 76; *EpCath.*, pp. 233, 236; *Sam.*, pp. 64, 167; *Ezra.*, p. 352. Ephesians 2.20. O'Reilly, 'Multitude of Isles', pp. 219–24; the image was traditional in the Latin West: Gerhart B. Ladner, 'The Symbolism of the Biblical Corner Stone in the Mediaeval West', *Mediaeval Studies* 4 (1942), pp. 43–60, at 47–52.

in his writings.[92] One cannot read this material without the sense of the Anglo-Saxon monk arguing for his people's place, as the latest nation converted, within the temple.[93] Bede certainly identified closely with the gentiles throughout his exegesis: 'our Church' is very clearly that 'of the gentiles'.[94]

Explicit references to the conversion of the Anglo-Saxons are understandably rare in the exegesis on the Old Testament but do appear, such as the reference to the Roman mission to Britain in *On the Temple*, with Gregory, Augustine, and Paulinus named.[95] We ought to consider how imagery of the four corners of the world or of Christ as cornerstone may have spoken more subtly of the Anglo-Saxon situation of being *Angli* living in a corner (*angulus*) of the earth.[96] The southern wall of the tabernacle represented the Jewish people who came first to God, the northern wall the gentiles who had languished 'in the darkness and cold of unbelief right up to the time of the Lord's incarnation'.[97] While it might be a step too far to see this as a reference to chilly Northumbria, it calls to mind a similar use of the idea of the frozen north in terms of the coming of Christianity to Britain in Gildas.[98] Bede declared that 'we are rightly compared to the . . . north wall, for to us it was granted to know the light of truth after . . . the darkness of idolatry'.[99] He here expanded on the Greco-Roman association of the frozen north with uncivilized barbarians—a topos which papal writers had picked up on to refer to the pagans, appearing for example in a letter from Pope Boniface to Edwin, king of

[92] Diarmuid Scully, 'Introduction', in *Bede: On* Tobit *and On the* Canticle of Habakkuk, trans. Seán Connolly (Dublin, 1997), pp. 17–37. Paul Hilliard, 'Sacred and Secular History in the Writings of Bede (†735)', (PhD thesis, University of Cambridge, 2007), pp. 33–5, 56–9, 77–9, 104–6, 127–8.

[93] Charles W. Jones, 'Some Introductory Remarks on Bede's Commentary on Genesis', *Sacris Eruditi* 19 (1969–70), pp. 115–98, at 129. For the relevance of Bede's attitudes to the Jews to his ideas about the conversion of the Anglo-Saxons: Andrew P. Scheil, *The Footsteps of Israel: Understanding Jews in Anglo-Saxon England* (Ann Arbor MI, 2004), pp. 78–97; Scully, 'Introduction', pp. 30–37.

[94] *Sam.*, p. 204 'nostram, id est gentium . . . ecclesiam'.   [95] *Temp.*, p. 218.

[96] Gregory, *Registrum Epistularum*, ed. D. Norberg, CCSL 140+A, VIII.29 p. 551; Palmer, *Frankish World*, pp. 51–2; O'Reilly, 'Multitude of Isles', pp. 220–21. O'Reilly's article in part responds to the large literature (fitting into a larger discussion about the roots of English identity) on the word *Angli* and of Bede's influential choice of it over *Saxones* to describe his people: Patrick Wormald, 'The Venerable Bede and the "Church of the English"', repr. in *The Times of Bede: Studies in Early English Christian Society and its Historian*, ed. Stephen Baxter (Oxford, 2006), pp. 207–28; Sarah Foot, 'The Making of *Angelcynn*: English Identity before the Norman Conquest', *Transactions of the Royal Historical Society* 6th series 6 (1996), pp. 25–49; Nicholas Brooks, *Bede and the English*, Jarrow Lecture (Jarrow, 2000).

[97] *Tab.*, p. 64 'tenebris ac frigore infidelitatis usque ad tempus dominicae incarnationis'; trans. Holder p. 71.

[98] Gildas, *De Excidio Britanniae*, ed. and trans. Michael Winterbottom (London, 1978), pp. 18, 91.

[99] *Temp.*, p. 183 'secundo parieti, hoc est septemtrionali, recte comparamur quibus post figuram ac tenebras idolatriae lucem ueritatis cognoscere datum est'; trans. Connolly, p. 52; also *Temp.*, p. 221; *Hom.*, II.25 p. 377. Scheil, *Footsteps of Israel*, pp. 92–3.

Northumbria.[100] The two walls of the tabernacle, the two peoples, met in the western wall.[101] Bede probably hinted at the teleological progression where salvation moved from the East to the West: his contemporaries believed that the End Times would start in the West when the ends of the earth were converted to Christ.[102] Bede went out of his way to emphasize that the fact that scripture states that the western wall of the tabernacle 'looks to the sea' heightened this eschatological geography.[103]

Thus we have an image of the universal Church of the four-fold world, where the cold north is seen as the location of gentile would-be Christians and where the End will come about when the Church reaches a location in the west facing the sea. It does not seem far-fetched to suggest that Bede here drew on the standard tropes concerning the representation of Britain. The classical geographical tradition located Britain in the far north-west, either in ocean or on its edge, in either case removed from the rest of the world.[104] Greek or Roman authors who wrote of Britain, from Virgil on, saw it and its inhabitants at or near the ends of the earth in an *alter orbis*, another world.[105] Britain was remote, distant, other. Bede, like other educated Insular figures, inherited this tradition and seems to have had a strong sense of Britain's peripherality— portraying the island as lying in the distant north-west of Europe in the opening of the *Ecclesiastical History* for instance.[106] While Michelet has suggested that Anglo-Saxons cannot have genuinely felt peripheral, Bede certainly embraced such an idea for his own people.[107] Christianity justified this peripherality by situating the significance of the Anglo-Saxons' conversion in their status as a gentile people living in the isles at the end of the earth, thus making it a fulfillment of biblical prophecies and a key stage in the history of the sixth age of the world.[108] But Christianity also rendered peripherality unimportant, giving Bede the intellectual resources, such as Adomnán's

---

[100] *HE*, II.10 pp. 168–9. Gregory made use of this theme on a number of occasions: *In Hiezechihelem*, II.VI.20 p. 309; Gregory, *Moralia*, XXVII.XLIII.71 p. 1386 (compare *Act.*, p. 56); Diarmuid Scully, 'Location and Occupation: Bede, Gildas, and the Roman Vision of Britain' in *Anglo-Saxon Traces*, eds Roberts and Webster, pp. 243–72, at 253–7.

[101] *Tab.*, p. 65.

[102] Fabienne Michelet, *Creation, Migration, and Conquest: Imaginary Geography and Sense of Space in Old English Literature* (Oxford, 2006), pp. 158–9; Jan Davidse, 'The Sense of History in the Works of the Venerable Bede', *Studi Medievali* 23 (1982), pp. 647–95, at 665.

[103] *Tab.*, p. 66 'Respicit ergo mare plaga occidentalis tabernaculi'; trans. Holder, p. 73.

[104] Diarmuid Scully, 'Bede, Orosius and Gildas on the Early History of Britain', in *Bède le Vénérable entre tradition et postérité: The Venerable Bede. Tradition and Posterity*, eds Stéphane Lebecq et al. (Lille, 2005), pp. 31–42, at 32–5; Michelet, *Creation, Migration, and Conquest*, pp. 119–26. For Bede's use of classical geographical sources in *HE*, I.1 pp. 14–21: A. H. Merrills, *History and Geography in Late Antiquity* (Cambridge, 2005), pp. 249–68.

[105] E.g. Virgil, *Eclogues*, ed. and trans. Guy Lee (Liverpool, 1980), I.66 pp. 10–11.

[106] Merrills, *History and Geography*, pp. 254–60.

[107] Michelet, *Creation, Migration, and Conquest*, p. 126; e.g. *Hom.*, II.10 p. 252.

[108] O'Reilly, 'Islands and Idols'; Davidse, 'Sense of History', pp. 662–6.

work *On the Holy Places*, with which to overcome Britain's remoteness.[109] What could be more of a reminder of the Anglo-Saxons' peripheral place in the universal religion to which they had converted than the sites of Jewish cult? These were places no Anglo-Saxon had ever seen, belonging to a nation foreign to Britain, from which as gentiles Bede's people had been historically excluded: 'the people of the gentiles had long been remote from the religion of the . . . temple'.[110] Yet from these locations Bede drew proof of his people's pre-ordained place in heaven.

The universal significance of the temple image also held meaning in light of the Insular world's fierce debates arising from the Easter Controversy during the seventh and eighth centuries, which addressed the nature of the universal Church and heavily utilized the rhetoric of centre and periphery. From early days Christians had emphasized the universal nature of the Church as proof of its orthodoxy; Christ had clearly given a mandate to the apostles to spread the word (e.g. Matthew 24.14) and localized cults were by their nature in opposition to this. Thus a rhetoric of orthodoxy developed, especially in polemic against the Donatists, which condemned heretics as peripheral, vainly believing that holiness existed only in their own rites or the Church only in that corner of the world they inhabited. The temple image often played a part in this rhetoric of the united Church—split by heretics.[111] Church Fathers also associated heresy with Judaism, represented as an exclusive religion, narrowly focused on the temple and Jerusalem, unlike the truly open and universal Christianity. This patristic discourse on unity and universality, centred on Rome, came to be used in the Insular world in relation to the Easter Question.[112]

The Irish monk Cummian attacked the adherents of the Columban dating of Easter on the grounds that the entire world practised the Roman dating, bar a few people in two islands at the end of the earth; God had ordered one temple and one tabernacle to be built to symbolize the desired unity of his Church.[113] An opponent was a 'whited-wall . . . who did not make both one, but divided'—an implicit contrast with the unifying cornerstone.[114] Bede used

---

[109] *HE*, V.16–17 pp. 508–13; Adomnán, *De Locis Sanctis*, ed. L. Bieler, CCSL 175, pp. 175–234; Bede, *De Locis Sanctis*, ed. J. Fraipont, CCSL 175, pp. 249–80.

[110] *Act.*, p. 64 'populum gentium longe a . . . templique religione remotum'.

[111] Optatus of Milevis, *Libri Septem*, ed. C. Ziwsa, CSEL 26, II.1 pp. 32–6, III.10 p. 95; for Augustine's use of the temple image against the Donatists: Dominique Sanchis, 'Le symbolisme communautaire du temple chez Saint Augustin', *Revue d'Ascétique et de Mystique* 37 (1961), pp. 137–47.

[112] Damian Bracken, 'Rome and the Isles: Ireland, England and the Rhetoric of Orthodoxy', *Proceedings of the British Academy* 157 (2009), pp. 75–97.

[113] Cummian, *De Controversia Paschali*, eds and trans. Maura Walsh and Dáibhí Ó Cróinín (Toronto, 1988), pp. 72–5, 78–81.

[114] Cummian, *De Controversia*, p. 92 'quidam paries dealbatus . . . qui utraque non fecit unum, sed diuisit', my translation as Walsh and Ó Cróinín have interpreted the text differently: Conor O'Brien, 'Exegesis as Argument: The Use of Ephesians 2, 14 in Cummian's *De Controversia Paschali*', *Cambrian Medieval Celtic Quarterly* 67 (2014), pp. 73–81.

the same type of arguments: he put a speech detailing the universality of the Church and the liminality of the Insular element within it into the mouth of Wilfrid at the Synod of Whitby.[115] Peripherality could, dangerously, lead to unintended schism: Bede emphasized that the monks of Iona fell into wrong practices not from bad will but because, being set apart from the rest of the world, they had no one to set them right.[116] Nonetheless, he did identify the insularity of heterodox Britons and Ionans as being a mark of 'Jewishness'—an attempt to reject the cornerstone which united them with the gentile Anglo-Saxons.[117] We have previously seen the clear similarity between Bede's approach to ancient Jewish history and that of his own recent time—an unsurprising similarity, perhaps, since he probably worked on the *Ecclesiastical History* simultaneously with *On the Temple*.[118] Scholars have long recognized the thematic connections between these two works: the *History* tells the story of how the Anglo-Saxons were built up into part of that universal temple Church which the commentary describes.[119] Here we see how the temple commentaries' engagement with the Jewish holy sites could have helped serve Bede's purposes in the wake of the Easter Controversy. The spatial contrast between the local and the universal clearly served a similar role to the historical one between the old and new dispensations.

One might expect, therefore, Jerome's contrast of the narrowness of the material temple with the expansiveness of the universal Church to have greatly influenced Bede.[120] Certainly, early in his career, he celebrated the fact that the physically limited temple had been replaced by the universal Church.[121] The cosmic effect of the incarnation, highlighted in the last section, meant that Christian universalism could replace Jewish localism—as a comment in the *Retraction on Acts* makes clear. Bede declared that:

> the entire globe has been cleansed by the Lord's blood . . . just as once the tabernacle or temple was consecrated to the Lord by the blood of victims. Therefore, now throughout the entire world the faithful people has been dedicated by his blood into a house holy to him; nor is the place of prayer only in Jerusalem, but in every place of his rule the elect raise up their pure hands in prayer to the Lord.[122]

---

[115] *HE*, III.25 pp. 300–7. See also *VW*, X pp. 20–23. [116] *HE*, III.4 pp. 224–5.

[117] W. Trent Foley and Nicholas J. Higham, 'Bede on the Britons', *EME* 17 (2009), pp. 154–85. Bede condemned the Jews for trying to keep salvation for themselves: *Act.*, p. 26; compare Arnobius Junior, *Commentarii in Psalmos*, ed. K.-D. Daur, CCSL 25, CXVII p. 186.

[118] Bede, *Epistola ad Albinum*, ed. and trans. Joshua A. Westgard, 'New Manuscripts of Bede's Letter to Albinus', *RB* 120 (2010), pp. 208–15, at 213–15; an earlier edition was printed in Charles Plummer, *Venerabilis Baedae Opera Historica*, 2 vols (Oxford, 1896), I, p. 3.

[119] Henry Mayr-Harting, *The Venerable Bede, The Rule of St Benedict, and Social Class*, Jarrow Lecture (Jarrow, 1976), pp. 12–13, 20–22; O'Reilly, 'Multitude of Isles', pp. 213–16.

[120] Jerome, *In Esaiam*, pp. 86, 585, 634, 694. [121] *Apoc.*, pp. 385, 443.

[122] *Ret.*, p. 112 'uniuersum orbem sanguine domini esse abluendum, ut, sicut aliquando tabernaculum siue templum sanguine uictimarum erat domino consecratum, ita nunc per

However, Bede did not denigrate the temple too much, for Christ, 'appearing in the flesh', had 'scattered the first seeds of the gospel in that temple, and from there he filled the whole world with the shoots of his faith and truth'.[123] Overall, as we have seen, Bede seems to have preferred to read the Church's universalism into, rather than as opposed to, the temple image.

I have located the emphasis on universality and unity which we see in Bede's writings within an Insular Christian discourse, shaped by classical geography and the Easter Controversy. The same emphasis appears in the dedications of the churches at Wearmouth-Jarrow: Saints Peter and Paul, apostles to the Jews and gentiles respectively, patrons of Rome, linked both communities with each other and with the universal Church. Bede's own monastery certainly most directly influenced how Bede used the wider discourse. Wearmouth-Jarrow stood at the forefront when it came to connecting Northumbria with Rome, from its founding by Benedict Biscop onwards. Biscop's ceaseless travels to and from Rome and efforts to create a distinctly Catholic monastery were seen by Bede as building a truly universal network of Christian love which encompassed the entire world and linked Wearmouth-Jarrow to the Roman Church through the daily liturgy and the stone churches in which it took place.[124]

At a time when many educated Christian Anglo-Saxons would have looked to Rome as the centre of their world, Bede and his brothers at Wearmouth-Jarrow must have been more likely to do so than most.[125] In the words of Jennifer O'Reilly: 'Through the sign of the studied *romanitas* of its buildings and art, liturgy and relics, library and script, the monastery of Wearmouth-Jarrow made petrine Rome present at the ends of the earth; by implication the universal church of Christ was being built up in that place'.[126] We might expect Bede's approach to unity via the temple image to share this Roman focus. In the *Ecclesiastical History* the papal and Roman nature of the initial mission to the Anglo-Saxons guaranteed the subsequent place of their national Church within the universal Church.[127] Although Bede mentioned a pope and Roman missionaries as the only named figures from modern times in *On the Temple*, Bede never explicitly discussed Roman centrality through his use of

---

omnem mundum populus fidelium illi in domum sanctam ipsius sanguine dedicaretur, nec solum Hierosolymis esset locus orandi, uerum in omni loco dominationis eius leuarent electi manus suas per orationes puras ad dominum'.

[123] *Abac.*, p. 385 'dominus in carne apparens, in ipso templo prima euangelii semina sparsit, atque exinde orbem totum germine suae fidei et ueritatis impleuit'.

[124] *Hom.*, I.13 p. 92; *HA*, 6 pp. 34–5; *Hom.*, I.13 p. 92; Éamonn Ó Carragáin, *The City of Rome and the World of Bede*, Jarrow Lecture (Jarrow, 1994), esp. pp. 9–14.

[125] Nicholas Howe, *Writing the Map in Anglo-Saxon England: Essays in Cultural Geography* (New Haven CT, 2008), pp. 101–48.

[126] Jennifer O'Reilly, '"All that Peter Stands For": The *Romanitas* of the *Codex Amiatinus* Reconsidered', *Proceedings of the British Academy* 157 (2009), pp. 367–95, at 395.

[127] Tugène, 'Le particularisme et l'universalisme', pp. 132–40.

the temple image.[128] Nonetheless, a link still exists between Bede's temple and papal Rome for, during Bede's own lifetime, the pope received the Codex Amiatinus, with its great diagram of the Jewish tabernacle.

THE CODEX AMIATINUS

Had Bede's family never sent him to learn at the feet of Benedict Biscop and Ceolfrith, or had he been carried off when plague rampaged through the monastery, Wearmouth-Jarrow would still have a place in history as the location where the Codex Amiatinus was produced.[129] The codex is a major book in European history: the oldest surviving complete copy of the Vulgate Bible (and as such an important aid to determining the modern text) and one of the most splendid achievements of Insular artisans and scribes.[130] Hundreds of calf skins went into its production, as well as uncountable man hours; the fact that Ceolfrith had three such pandects (i.e. single-volume copies of the Bible) created proves the wealth and efficiency of the monastery he ruled.[131] One went to the Church of St Peter at Wearmouth and one to St Paul's at Jarrow; both of these volumes are now lost, barring a few folios.[132] In June 716 Ceolfrith announced that he himself would take the third pandect to Rome, suddenly resigning the leadership of Wearmouth-Jarrow, and setting off on a final pilgrimage to the relics of St Peter.[133] Ceolfrith never made it to Rome, dying en route at Langres, although the codex did reach Italy where his name was removed from the dedication text and the volume's origins obscured for centuries.[134] Only long after the codex arrived in Florence was the connection with Ceolfrith rediscovered, for centuries the Mediterranean aspects of the art and the *Romanitas* of the uncial script having been taken as proof of the manuscript's Italian origins.[135]

---

[128] John Moorhead has suggested that Bede was less supportive of papal authority than some of his countrymen: 'Bede on the Papacy', *JEH* 60 (2009), pp. 217–32.

[129] The plague at Wearmouth-Jarrow: *VCeol.*, 13–14 pp. 92–5.

[130] Florence, Biblioteca Medicea Laurenziana, MS Amiatino 1.

[131] Richard Gameson, 'The Cost of the Codex Amiatinus', *Notes and Queries* 39 (1992), pp. 2–9.

[132] *VCeol.*, 20 pp. 98–9; Richard Marsden, *The Text of the Old Testament in Anglo-Saxon England* (Cambridge, 1995), pp. 90–98.

[133] *HA*, 16–21 pp. 60–73; *VCeol.*, 20–32 pp. 98–113; *DTR*, LXVI p. 534.

[134] Richard Marsden, 'Amiatinus in Italy: The Afterlife of an Anglo-Saxon Book', in *Anglo-Saxon England and the Continent*, eds Hans Sauer and Joanna Storey, with Gaby Waxenberger (Tempe AZ, 2011), pp. 217–39.

[135] H. J. White, 'The Codex Amiatinus and its Birthplace', *Studia Biblica et Ecclesiastica* 3 (1890), pp. 273–308.

The dedication verses as recorded in the *Life of Ceolfrith* allow us to see what Ceolfrith originally intended to be read at Rome; the text reveals a definite sense of Anglo-Saxon peripherality and the desire of the community at Wearmouth-Jarrow to be united with the core of the Church at Rome:[136]

> To the body of the excellent Peter, worthy of memory, / Whom the depths of the faith enshrined as head of the Church, / I Ceolfrith, an abbot from the far-off lands of the Angles, / Send the tokens of my sure devotion, / Praying that I and mine, sharing the joys of so great a Father, / May always have a place of remembrance in heaven.[137]

The details of the manuscript's production display this overwhelming longing for unity with the head of the Church, especially the uncial script, of a type clearly much admired at Wearmouth-Jarrow, which seems to have been based closely on that of the Rome of Gregory the Great.[138] Decoration is limited but striking in appearance. Between the Old and New Testaments lies an image of Christ in Majesty, with angels on either side, surrounded by the four evangelists and their symbolic beasts. Most of the decoration and that which concerns us the most, appears in the opening quire of the codex: the dedication verses; the prologue and table of contents (on recto and verso of a purple folio); three sets of diagrams explaining different systems for dividing scripture according to different Fathers; the verso of the folio dedicated to the division according to 'Pope Hilarus' has a large cross made up of five interlinking circles, each of which contains text by Jerome relating to the books of the Pentateuch; an image of Ezra writing in the vestments of a Jewish high priest; and, the largest drawing in the entire pandect, an image of the tabernacle in the desert, spread across an entire bifolium.[139]

Bede indicated that the three pandects derived from an earlier non-Vulgate pandect that Ceolfrith had obtained from Rome.[140] This is likely to be the volume in which Bede had seen images of the temple and tabernacle, placed there by Cassiodorus.[141] Cassiodorus himself described including in his so-called Codex Grandior (a pandect containing Jerome's hexaplaric revision of the Septuagint) images of the temple and tabernacle, as described to him by

---

[136] But see O'Reilly, '*Romanitas* of the *Codex Amiatinus*', pp. 368–73.

[137] *VCeol.*, 37 pp. 118–19 'Corpus ad eximii merito memorabile Petri, / Dedicat aecclesiae quem caput alta fides, [the manuscript (fol. Iv) here has a different word order to that of the *Life*: "quem caput ecclesiae dedicat alta fides"] / Ceolfridus, Anglorum extremis de finibus abbas, / Deuoti affectus pignora mitto mei, / Meque meosque optans tanti inter gaudia patris / In caelis memorem semper habere locum'.

[138] Malcolm Parkes, *The Scriptorium of Wearmouth-Jarrow*, Jarrow Lecture (Jarrow, 1982), p. 3.

[139] For the current order of the folios of the opening quire (in which they were kept for most of the codex's life according to scientific analysis): Paul Meyvaert, 'The Date of Bede's *In Ezram* and his Image of Ezra in the Codex Amiatinus', *Speculum* 80 (2005), pp. 1087–133, at 1104.

[140] *HA*, 15 pp. 56–9.   [141] *Tab.*, p. 81; *Temp.*, p. 192.

a blind Greek monk called Eusebius.[142] He also added diagrams of the divisions of scripture according to Jerome, Augustine, and, amongst others, Hilary of Poitiers (Pope Hilarus in the Codex Amiatinus)—which diagrams, of course, appear in the Northumbrian codex.[143] It thus appears that Ceolfrith had brought the Codex Grandior to Northumbria and used it as the exemplar for much of the Codex Amiatinus imagery. While the earlier Mediterranean volume undoubtedly was a major influence on the Wearmouth-Jarrow manuscript, the decoration in the latter is clearly Northumbrian work and recent scholarship has emphasized how it probably diverged in significant ways from the Codex Grandior.[144] This suggests that the Codex Amiatinus provides us with evidence concerning the ideas and outlook of the Wearmouth-Jarrow community.

Cassiodorus implied that he added two images to the Grandior, one each of the tabernacle and the temple, following the advice of the blind Eusebius (described in the *Institutiones*) that the tabernacle and the temple had been made 'ad instar caeli' ('according to the likeness of heaven'). It seems that Cassiodorus had the cosmic interpretation of the temple explained to him as it may then have circulated in Greek Christendom.[145] This probably explains the similarities between the image that appears in the Codex Amiatinus and other diagrams of the tabernacle in Greek Octateuchs and copies of Cosmas' *Christian Topography*. The depiction of the barrier and its individual columns around the tabernacle is common to these images.[146] The distinctively angled bird's-eye view of the enclosure where the near sides of the barrier are seen from the outside (the east and south sides in the Amiatinus image) while the far sides are seen from the inside (the north and the west in the Amiatinus image) clearly develops the approach taken by the Greek tradition.[147] The

---

[142] Cassiodorus, *Institutiones*, ed. R. A. B. Mynors (Oxford, 1963), I.V.2 pp. 22–3. See Marsden, *Text of the Old Testament*, pp. 131–2.

[143] For possible reasons that Pope Hilarus replaced Hilary of Poitiers: Paul Meyvaert, 'Bede, Cassiodorus and the Codex Amiatinus', *Speculum* 71 (1996), pp. 827–83, at 841–4; Celia Chazelle, 'Ceolfrid's Gift to St Peter: the First Quire of the Codex Amiatinus and the Evidence of its Roman Destination', *EME* 12 (2004), pp. 129–57, at 147.

[144] R. L. S. Bruce-Mitford, *The Art of the Codex Amiatinus*, Jarrow Lecture (Jarrow, 1967) remains the classic work. Celia Chazelle, '"Romanness" in Early Medieval Culture', in *Paradigms and Methods in Early Medieval Studies*, eds Celia Chazelle and Felice Lifshitz (New York, 2007), pp. 81–98; Lawrence Nees, 'Problems of Form and Function in Early Medieval Illustrated Bibles from Northwest Europe', in *Imaging the Early Medieval Bible*, ed. John Williams (University Park PA, 1999), pp. 121–77.

[145] Cassiodorus, *Institutiones*, I.V.2 p. 23. Celia Chazelle, 'Painting the Voice of God: Wearmouth-Jarrow, Rome and the Tabernacle Miniature in the Codex Amiatinus', *Quintana* 8 (2009), pp. 15–59, at 46, suggests that this phrase describes the bird's-eye view from which the tabernacle is depicted, but such a reading does not seem the most obvious.

[146] See Elisabeth Revel-Neher, 'La page double du Codex Amiatinus et ses rapports avec les plans du tabernacle dans l'art juif et dans l'art byzantin', *Journal of Jewish Art* 9 (1982), pp. 6–17, at 12–13.

[147] Meyvaert, 'Bede, Cassiodorus', pp. 847–53. See Fig. 1 within this volume at p. xv.

inclusion of the cardinal points in Greek derives from that tradition.[148] While all the surviving Greek images postdate the pandect, they seem clearly to be reaching back to a tradition that provided it with its exemplar. After all, the images of the Octateuch tradition derived from earlier editions of Cosmas' work and Cassiodorus almost certainly had such a manuscript of Cosmas.[149] Thus, behind the Codex Grandior lies the cosmic interpretation of the temple image; the question remains whether the monks of Wearmouth-Jarrow were aware of the cosmological significance of their diagram of the tabernacle.

Some scholars have suggested that a copy of the *Institutiones* at Wearmouth-Jarrow provided the source for the Codex Amiatinus (which contains depictions of three divisions of scripture very similar to diagrams circulating in copies of the *Institutiones*) and that the Grandior never reached Northumbria.[150] Therefore, Bede and his brothers would have been very aware of Cassiodorus' use of the cosmic interpretation. Unfortunately for that line of argument, little evidence exists that Bede, or anybody else at his monastery, knew the *Institutiones*. Most of the studies of the library at Wearmouth-Jarrow have expressed doubt about the presence of Cassiodorus' book there.[151] Bede himself explicitly stated that his knowledge of Cassiodorus' link to the images of the tabernacle and temple came from the *Exposition on the Psalms*; he never mentioned any other work of Cassiodorus from which he might have learned about this.[152] It has been suggested that Bede's florilegium of extracts from Augustine on the Pauline epistles was prompted by the *Institutiones*, but explicit cases of Bedan reliance on this work of Cassiodorus have not so far been discovered.[153] Wearmouth-Jarrow's extraordinary library contained more than we know but for the moment Ockham's razor must apply: the Codex Grandior was almost certainly there; the presence of the *Institutiones* remains unproved.

Thus the monks at Wearmouth-Jarrow created the Codex Amiatinus and its image of the tabernacle, adapting and changing details from their exemplar. The *Institutiones* would have revealed to them that they were dealing with a cosmic use of the temple image, but without it they would have been forced to

---

[148] Jennifer O'Reilly, 'The Library of Scripture: Views from Vivarium and Wearmouth-Jarrow', in *New Offerings, Ancient Treasures: Studies in Medieval Art for George Henderson*, eds Paul Binski and William Noel (Stroud, 2001), pp. 3–39, at 33.

[149] John Lowden, *The Octateuchs: A Study in Byzantine Manuscript Illustration* (University Park PA, 1992), pp. 86–93; Meyvaert, 'Bede, Cassiodorus', p. 883.

[150] Karen Corsano, 'The First Quire of the Codex Amiatinus and the *Institutiones* of Cassiodorus', *Scriptorium* 41 (1987), pp. 3–34; Michael Gorman, 'The Codex Amiatinus: A Guide to the Legends and Bibliography', *Studi Medievali* 44 (2003), pp. 863–910, at 869–72.

[151] E.g. Michael Lapidge, *The Anglo-Saxon Library* (Oxford, 2006), p. 29.

[152] *Temp.*, p. 192; see Cassiodorus, *Expositio Psalmorum*, ed. M. Adriaen, CCSL 97–8, LXXXVI.1 pp. 789–90.

[153] Alan Thacker, *Bede and Augustine of Hippo: History and Figure in Sacred Text*, Jarrow Lecture (Jarrow, 2005), pp. 7–8; Meyvaert, 'Bede, Cassiodorus', pp. 829–30.

rely on their own interpretation. The pandect may, therefore, provide important evidence of the Northumbrian community's attitude towards the temple
image. The question remains of Bede's relationship with the Codex Amiatinus.
Often scholars tend to assume that Wearmouth-Jarrow's greatest son must
have played a significant role in the production of the monastery's most
famous manuscript.[154] The image of Bede the individual, the great genius,
has obviously proved more compelling than a faceless mass of monks. Hardly
anything has survived from Wearmouth-Jarrow that someone has not laid
claim to on Bede's behalf: both the anonymous *Life of Ceolfrith* and, as we have
seen, Ceolfrith's letter to Nechtan have been ascribed to Bede.[155] With regard
to the Codex Amiatinus an understandable desire exists to see the hand of
Bede in that of one of the scribes who worked on the text: Meyvaert suggested
that Bede may have been responsible for the entire arrangement of the
opening quire or that he drew its images himself.[156] While constantly praising
Bede's modesty, scholars have not tended to be modest on his behalf.

But caution seems necessary. An establishment as large as Wearmouth-
Jarrow and capable of creating a Bede could easily nurture a dozen monks of
lesser but still considerable intellectual ability. The astounding degree
of conformity in the hands of different scribes suggests a body of monks at
Wearmouth-Jarrow solidly and consistently educated in the skills which the
creation of these pandects required.[157] One cannot suppose that the monastery 'only [had] one intellectual amongst its brethren'.[158] Evidence linking
Bede's work with the Codex Amiatinus does not automatically prove Bede's
responsibility for the ideas or programme of the pandect. The influence of
ideas may have gone in the other direction also. As the dedication verses
suggest, Ceolfrith as abbot bore at the least nominal responsibility for the
codex; as the palaeographical evidence makes clear, it was the product of a
team of scribes working together. All this suggests that we will read it most
fruitfully as the product of a religious *community*, which makes a statement
about the (official) shared outlook of its members.

Certainly no reasons exist to suggest that Bede could not have worked on
the Codex Amiatinus. A scribe amended the text of the codex and the sister

---

[154] Michelle P. Brown, *The Lindisfarne Gospels: Society, Spirituality and the Scribe* (London,
2003), pp. 156, 399; Chazelle, '"Romanness"', p. 87.

[155] Judith McClure, 'Bede and the Life of Ceolfrid', *Peritia* 3 (1984), pp. 71–84; that Bede did
not write the *Life of Ceolfrith* seems now established: Christopher Grocock and I. N. Wood,
Abbots of Wearmouth and Jarrow (Oxford, 2013), pp. lxii–lxxxvii. On the letter to Nechtan: see
Ch. 3 within this volume, 'The house made by human hands', p. 61.

[156] Paul Meyvaert, 'Dissension in Bede's Community Shown by a Quire of the Codex
Amiatinus', *RB* 116 (2006), pp. 295–309, esp. 304–8; Meyvaert, 'The Date of Bede's *In Ezram*',
pp. 1115–26.

[157] Parkes, *Scriptorium of Wearmouth-Jarrow*, pp. 20–22.

[158] Simon Coates, 'Ceolfrid: History, Hagiography and Memory in seventh- and eighth-
century Wearmouth-Jarrow', *Journal of Medieval History* 25 (1999), pp. 69–86, at 86.

pandects over time, suggesting an interest in finding new textual variants and improving earlier readings where possible; it seems reasonable to connect these adjustments of the text in Ceolfrith's pandects with the same readings as noted in Bede's exegesis.[159] The Amiatinus has one clear verbal parallel with the work of Bede in the couplet that appears above the portrait of Ezra. The phrase 'burned by the enemy's devestation' appears both here and in *On Ezra and Nehemiah* in the context of the destruction of the sacred scriptures and consequent need to have them replaced by Ezra.[160] At most this suggests that Bede himself authored the couplet and added it to the pandect, but it could as easily indicate his familiarity with and dependence on the wording used in the codex.[161]

Some evidence does indeed suggest that the Codex Amiatinus influenced Bede to write about Ezra. Meyvaert has suggested that Bede was actually writing *On Ezra and Nehemiah* during the years immediately before Ceolfrith's departure with the codex to Rome (*c*.711–15), though the majority of critical opinion favours a later date for that work.[162] Bede wrote about Ezra and his restoration of the scriptures in his commentary on 1 Samuel (three-quarters finished when Ceolfrith left for Rome in 716) and in *Thirty Questions on the Book of Kings*, a work which should probably be dated to *c*.715.[163] In the latter work he also referred to the ancient picture of the layout of the temple, which he would later identify as that of Cassiodorus.[164] If we accept the later dating for *On Ezra and Nehemiah* then these may be the earliest occasions when Bede wrote about Ezra. The only other such candidate is his early version of *On Genesis*, where Bede broke off his work, hoping to continue on at a subsequent date, in order to 'investigate, however inadequately, the book of the holy prophet and priest Ezra'.[165] As previously discussed, this interlude came

---

[159] Richard Marsden, '*Manus Bedae*: Bede's Contribution to Ceolfrith's Bibles', *ASE* 27 (1998), pp. 65–85.

[160] MS Amiatino 1, fol. Vr (Fig. 2) 'Codicibus sacris *hostili clade perustis* / Esdra Deo feruens reparuit opus'; *Ezra.*, p. 307 'Verum quia templo incenso atque urbe Hierosolima subuersa scripturae quoque sanctae quae ibidem seruabantur simul fuerant *hostili clade perustae* . . .'. My emphasis.

[161] The couplet also appears in Alcuin, *Carmina*, ed. E. Dümmler, MGH Poetae Latini Medii Aevi I, LXIX p. 292. For a number of reasons, it seems most likely that Alcuin took the couplet from the pandect rather than the reverse happening: Meyvaert, 'Bede, Cassiodorus', pp. 877–80; Meyvaert, 'The Date of Bede's *In Ezram*', p. 1127; Corsano, 'First Quire', pp. 20–22.

[162] Meyvaert, 'The Date of Bede's *In Ezram*', pp. 1089–97; Scott DeGregorio, *Bede: On Ezra and Nehemiah* (Liverpool, 2006), pp. xxxvii–xlii; Chazelle, '"Romanness"', p. 90.

[163] *Sam.*, p. 80; *Reg.*, VII pp. 301–2. Bede mentioned Ceolfrith's departure at *Sam.*, p. 212. For the date of *Thirty Questions*: Paul Meyvaert, '"In the Footsteps of the Fathers": The Date of Bede's *Thirty Questions on the Book of Kings* to Nothelm', in *The Limits of Ancient Christianity: Essays on Late Antique Thought and Culture in Honour of R. A. Markus*, eds William E. Klingshirn and Mark Vessey (Ann Arbor MI, 1999), pp. 267–86, at 267–77.

[164] *Reg.*, XVIII p. 312; *Temp.*, pp. 192–3.

[165] *Gen.*, p. 2 'librum sancti Esrae prophetae ac sacerdotis . . . parum perscrutatus fuero'; trans. Kendall p. 66.

sometime between 710 and 720.[166] The evidence is complicated at times and many questions remain about the dating of Bede's works. However, it seems clear that at some point in the years around the Codex Amiatinus' departure, Bede became interested in the figure of Ezra and his work. Something inspired him to think more about Ezra, and the inclusion of an image of Ezra in the codex seems the most likely 'something'.[167]

It should thus be clear that bringing the Codex Amiatinus into an investigation of Bede's thought may prove fruitful. I do not think Bede was responsible for the ideas expressed in the pandect (not, at least, as an individual); rather the codex shows us something of the communal ideology and spirituality of Wearmouth-Jarrow that would have influenced Bede's writings (an idea to which I will return). For the remainder of this chapter I wish to explore this idea with reference to the tabernacle diagram in the codex. A cosmic tabernacle, borrowed (probably initially unwittingly) from Cassiodorus, found its way into the Wearmouth-Jarrow pandect and, I argue, very probably helped shape Bede's own interpretation of scripture. While Cassiodorus thought of the tabernacle as being an image of heaven, the Amiatinus tabernacle seems distinctly earthbound.

The image's fidelity to the biblical description of the tabernacle has been noted, although a few key details remind the reader not to fix solely on its historical meaning.[168] A small cross, anachronistically for a Jewish holy site, appears above the entrance to the tabernacle proper. The laver or basin of water sits in the wrong location in the enclosure—not where it should be in the tabernacle but closer to its location in the temple.[169] On the other hand, the names of the twelve tribes of Israel have been added around the edges of the enclosure wall, exactly as they would have been encamped during the forty years in the desert (Bede later interpreted this encampment in relation to the Church's mission to all peoples[170]), and the names of Moses and Aaron appear within the tabernacle precincts. This mixture of the literal and the spiritual is entirely in keeping with the medieval monastic fondness for pictures which provide an opportunity to engage in prolonged meditation.[171] The cross reminds one that the historic tabernacle, in its material reality, also referred to the Christian Church and the heavenly Jerusalem

---

[166] See Ch. 3 within this volume, 'The house made by human hands', p. 57.

[167] See Chazelle, '"Romanness"', pp. 89–91.

[168] MS Amiatino 1, fols IIv–IIIr (Fig. 1). Revel-Neher, 'La page double', pp. 8–9; Chazelle, 'Painting the Voice of God', pp. 44–5.

[169] Jennifer O'Reilly, 'Introduction', in *Bede: On the Temple*, trans. Seán Connolly (Liverpool, 1995), p. liii.

[170] *Marc.*, p. 470.

[171] Mary Carruthers, *The Craft of Thought: Meditation, Rhetoric, and the Making of Images, 400–1200* (Cambridge, 1998), pp. 168–70.

which waits outside history.[172] In other words, the diagram is itself a work of spiritual exegesis.

As mentioned, the four cardinal points add a clear cosmic element to the diagram: all the earth is summed up within those four directions. It should be noted that often in the Cosmas/Octateuch tradition the cardinal points are outside the tabernacle enclosure, whereas here they appear within it.[173] Taking the commonplace interpretation of the temple image as the Church as read, the meaning that the Church has spread out to enclose all the four corners of the world seems obvious; if the tabernacle represents the earth here, it is because the Church fills the earth through evangelization. The cardinal directions emphasize this twice over. Including the directions in Latin would have made the basic point, but by adding them in Greek the monks of Wearmouth-Jarrow included a further mystical significance. The first letters of the Greek names for the cardinal points (Arctos, Dysis, Anatol, and Mesembria) spell out Adam, a point common in Irish exegesis; the Amiatinus tabernacle Church contains all of Adam, i.e. the entire human race descended from him.[174] This Christianization of the world derives from the incarnation since *Adam* had a numerical value of forty-six, the number of years which it took to rebuild the temple, and the number of days it took to form the body of Christ in Mary's womb.[175]

The Amiatinus diagram of the tabernacle cannot be seen solely as the depiction of a specific location; rather the image used the common figural interpretation of the Old Testament details to depict a spiritual truth about the world. The tabernacle makes a grand statement about the universal spread of the Church, Christ's body, to all peoples and all places, which in common with the rest of the pandect, declares Northumbria to be part of the Catholic Church, which has its head in Rome.[176] Cassiodorus' mention of his image of the tabernacle in his Psalm commentary appears just after he discussed how the tabernacle symbolized the universal spread of the Catholic faith; if his work was an important influence on the monks of Wearmouth-Jarrow, they may similarly have seen the image as a comment on the Church's spread throughout the world.[177] Recent scholarship has argued persuasively that Ceolfrith intended the pandect from the beginning as a present for the pope.[178] Like the monastery that Benedict Biscop built, the Codex Amiatinus

---

[172] See Bianca Kühnel, 'Jewish Symbolism of the Temple and the Tabernacle and Christian Symbolism of the Holy Sepulchre and the Heavenly Jerusalem', *Jewish Art* 12/13 (1986–87), pp. 147–68, at 166. For the importance of the figural meaning: Thacker, *Bede and Augustine*, pp. 28–9.

[173] O'Reilly, 'Library of Scripture', p. 33.

[174] *Gen.*, p. 93; O'Reilly, 'Traditions of the Evangelists', p. 67; Corsano, 'First Quire', p. 10.

[175] Augustine, *In Iohannis Evangelium Tractatus*, ed. R. Willems, CCSL 36, X.12 p. 108. See Ch. 5 within this volume, 'The temple as Christ', p. 102.

[176] Brown, *Lindisfarne Gospels*, p. 63.

[177] Cassiodorus, *Expositio Psalmorum*, XIV.1 p. 133.

[178] Esp. Chazelle, 'Ceolfrid's Gift'.

is a deliberate recreation of Roman art and imagery, designed presumably as a deliberate assumption of Roman authority and orthodoxy.[179] In such a context a reading of the diagram of the tabernacle as the universal Church convinces all the more. Just as the 'three Bibles joined together three sites of the one Church of Rome', the Amiatinus diagram argues that the four corners of the world are now united within the one Church, an event seen as, implicitly, the fulfilment of biblical prophecy.[180]

The concerns in Bede's work regarding the Anglo-Saxons' peripheral place in the world and the consequences that could have on their orthodoxy, mirror those of Ceolfrith expressed in the codex's dedication. The Amiatinus diagram places the points of the compass right beside the enclosure walls, inviting the two to be connected; Bede read the tabernacle walls in just this way in *On the Tabernacle*—as linked to the universalizing message of the cardinal points.[181] It seems likely that when writing his commentary he visualized the enclosure as he had seen it drawn in the codex. Any discussions surrounding the meaning of the image during its production in the scriptorium would, no doubt, have influenced Bede's exegesis. We should note then that Bede did not introduce the universal interpretation when the biblical text mentioned the first cardinal point (south representing the Jews), but rather when the focus shifted to the north and gentile (and, therefore Anglo-Saxon) conversion.[182] That was almost certainly the important issue for the creators of the diagram in the Codex Amiatinus. It seems clear that years after the pandect left for Rome, Bede continued to elaborate on its exegetical imagery in his commentaries.

The universal Church depicted in the Codex Amiatinus is also the earthly Church; universal mission obviously relates to the Church still preaching in this world. As previously discussed, the exegetical shorthand for that mission in Bede's writings is the four-fold world, and this rectangular tabernacle maps out just such a world. This image of the earthly tabernacle comes before the Old Testament and may be contrasted with the image before the New Testament that depicts Christ enthroned between seraphim and surrounded by the evangelists with their beasts—a clear depiction of heavenly and apocalyptic revelation.[183] I would, therefore, argue that the Amiatinus tabernacle presents a this-worldly image of the pilgrim Church, contrasted with the heavenly Church in Christ's presence. Interestingly, while Cassiodorus chose to draw both the temple and the tabernacle, Ceolfrith's pandect seems to have only ever contained the tabernacle; this must have required an active decision to

---

[179] See O'Reilly, '*Romanitas* of the *Codex Amiatinus*'.
[180] Chazelle, 'Painting the Voice of God', p. 48.
[181] See within this chapter, 'The Anglo-Saxons' place in the world', pp. 85–6.
[182] *Tab.*, p. 64.
[183] MS Amiatino 1, fol. 796v (Fig. 3). O'Reilly, 'Library of Scripture', pp. 11–13.

deliberately discard the diagram of the temple.[184] We have seen how Bede's exegesis developed the patristic distinction between the temple and the tabernacle, seeing the temple as the Church triumphant in heaven, the tabernacle as the Church militant struggling on earth.[185] The drawing of the Amiatinus tabernacle as the four-fold world, with the image of the temple from the Codex Grandior deliberately left uncopied, may be just the sort of occasion that would have given rise to this development of a patristic commonplace.[186]

A depiction of the universal Church reaching the ends of the earth makes sense in a Northumbrian Bible; but a depiction of the tabernacle as four-fold world as a frontispiece to scripture is appropriate even outside this Anglo-Saxon context. O'Reilly and Carruthers have shown how the tabernacle image functioned as a meditational locus that provided the stimulus to compunction, thus aiding the *lectio divina*.[187] '*Lectio divina* ... requires repentance' and suffering, and hence the tabernacle, with its reminders of the wanderings through the desert, seems highly appropriate in this context.[188] These are the same factors (repentance, suffering, the journey towards the heavenly) which were highlighted in Bede's use of the four-fold world.[189] Autodidact or not, Bede must have been influenced by the community in which he lived. That his interpretation of the temple image emphasized the earthly Church, journeying to heaven through a desert of repentance and compunction seems best explained by the fact that the Amiatinus tabernacle was produced in his monastery with just such an exegesis in mind.

Of course, multivalency always marks Bede's exegesis: he remained willing to interpret aspects of the tabernacle in a heavenly light. In particular we have seen his fondness for interpretations of the temple image that represent Christ's role in moving humanity from earth to heaven. It has been argued that the cross above the doorway to the tabernacle suggests Christ's sacrifice and the movement from earth to heaven through the veil, as described in Hebrews—although the Amiatinus cross does not appear on the veil.[190] It seems to me that this cross, and the cross formed deliberately by the cardinal points, emphasize rather the figural interpretation of the temple image, in which the Christian mysteries of both the Church and heaven are understood

---

[184] See Meyvaert, 'Bede, Cassiodorus', pp. 854–60.

[185] *Tab.*, p. 42; *Temp.*, pp. 147–8. See Ch. 2 within this volume, 'The temple in the Christian tradition before Bede', pp. 44–5.

[186] Thacker, *Bede and Augustine*, pp. 28–30, argues that the Amiatinus diagram represents both the temple and the tabernacle simultaneously, but the lack of the temple's distinctive three colonnades suggests otherwise: *Temp.*, pp. 192–3; *Reg.*, XVIII pp. 311–12.

[187] O'Reilly, 'Library of Scripture'; Carruthers, *The Craft of Thought*, pp. 231–7.

[188] Chazelle, 'Painting the Voice of God', p. 49.

[189] See within this chapter, 'The Anglo-Saxons' place in the world'.

[190] Revel-Neher, 'La page double', p. 17; Herbert L. Kessler, 'Through the Temple Veil: The Holy Image in Judaism and Christianity', *Kairos* 32/33 (1990–91), pp. 53–77, at 71, is mistaken on this point.

as hidden within the old Jewish structures. The monks of Wearmouth-Jarrow might not have considered a cross appearing on the desert tabernacle inappropriate since Bede believed that Moses actually possessed knowledge of Christ and the Church.[191] Christ had always been present in the earthly Church, as we have already seen, but it is clear that Bede thought that Christ's coming in the flesh had worked a dramatic change on both time and the relationship between heaven and earth. It therefore seems appropriate that we turn now to Christ, the one who was 'greater than the temple' but at the same time also himself the true temple.[192]

---

[191] *Tab.*, p. 40.   [192] Matthew 12.6.

5

Bede's Temple as the Body of Christ

The magnificent Insular gospel book, the Book of Kells, illustrates the story of how Satan tempted Christ on the pinnacle of the temple with a striking, almost bizarre image.[1] The Lord's head, shoulders, and arms rise out of the gable of the temple building—the elaborate architectural structure actually functioning as his lower body. Serried ranks of human figures fill the lowest level of the temple, standing therefore literally within the body of Christ. The image probably post-dates the life of Bede by a number of decades but it amply reflects the complexity of interpretation in his temple commentaries: Christ's body is the temple, but also the Church (the most popular ecclesiological image of the early Middle Ages) which therefore shares his temple nature.[2] I begin this chapter by looking at the Christological interpretations of the temple, showing how they supported Bede's concept of the orthodox importance of the incarnation by revealing the saviour to be both priest and sacrifice. Thereafter, I move on to explore how the members of Christ's body participated in his priestly nature, and thus shed some important light on recent debates about how Bede conceived of Church reform.

THE TEMPLE AS CHRIST

One of the most common Christian interpretations of the temple is derived from the gospel of John. There, when Jesus declares 'Destroy this temple; and in three days I will raise it up', the assembled Jews scoff that it took forty-six years to build the temple. 'But', says the evangelist in an explanatory aside,

---

[1] Dublin, Trinity College Library, MS A.I. (58), fol. 202v; for a reproduction of the image: Carol Farr, *The Book of Kells: Its Function and Audience* (London, 1997), p. 33.

[2] For analysis of the image: Farr, *Book of Kells*, ch. 2; Jennifer O'Reilly, 'Exegesis and the Book of Kells: The Lucan Genealogy', in *The Book of Kells: Proceedings of a Conference at Trinity College Dublin, 6–9 September 1992*, ed. Felicity O'Mahony (Aldershot, 1994), pp. 344–97, at 359–61, 366–8, 378–89.

'he spoke of the temple of his body'.[3] This gave Bede a clear mandate to argue that Christ 'became the temple of God by assuming human nature', and to call Christ's physical as well as his spiritual body the temple.[4] He read the temple as the incarnate Christ using a number of diverse interpretations, none dominant in itself. However, when we examine these interpretations throughout Bede's writings together, we can begin to see the importance of the incarnation in his thought.

Grounding himself in the text of John 2.19–21, Bede interpreted the forty-six years of the temple's construction as referring to the number of days which it took for the embryonic Jesus to grow. Forty-six was, Bede claimed, 'the number of days the human body grows in the womb from the time of conception into the developed features of its members'.[5] This reading of the temple came from Augustine who seems to have developed the idea.[6] A recent attempt to suggest that Bede drew principally on ideas from the *Laterculus Malalianus* ascribed to Theodore of Tarsus for this notion is not convincing—Bede's *Homily* II.1 quotes Augustine directly on this interpretation.[7] While Bede and the *Laterculus* do agree in identifying the forty-six years with the building of the second temple, the Northumbrian seems to have taken this idea from Jerome.[8] John 2.19–21 was not the only scriptural text which could be used to support the idea that Christ's humanity provided a dwelling place built for him, as this also appears in Bede's interpretation of Proverbs 9.1: 'Wisdom hath built herself a house'.[9] This embryological interpretation seems clearly intended to highlight the physical humanity of Christ. The 'Lord's most sacred body, which he took from the Virgin' constituted the temple of God, a real human body that went through the normal process of development in the mother's womb.[10]

---

[3] John 2.19–21.

[4] *Temp.*, p. 147 'ille templum Dei per assumptam humanitatem factus est'; trans. Connolly, p. 5. Also *Gen.*, p. 107.

[5] *Ezra.*, p. 300 'dierum numero corpus humanum in utero a tempore conceptionis usque ad perfecta membrorum liniamenta crescendo perueniat'; trans. DeGregorio, p. 97. Also *Hom.*, II.1 p. 189, II.24 p. 365.

[6] Augustine, *De Diversis Quaestionibus Octoginta Tribus*, ed. A. Mutzenbecher, CCSL 44A, LVI pp. 95–6.

[7] James Siemens, 'Another Book for Jarrow's Library? Coincidences in Exegesis between Bede and the *Laterculus Malalianus*', *Downside Review* 132 (2013), pp. 15–34, at 16–23; see Jane Stevenson, *The 'Laterculus Malalianus' and the School of Archbishop Theodore* (Cambridge, 1995), pp. 136–9.

[8] *Ezra.*, p. 300; compare Jerome, *In Danielem*, ed. F. Glorie, CCSL 75A, p. 871. The other points identified by Siemens as not coming from Augustine actually appear in his *In Iohannis Evangelium Tractatus*, ed. R. Willems, CCSL 36, X.10 pp. 106–7, a work well known to Bede.

[9] *Sam.*, p. 83; *Prov.*, p. 62; see also Gregory, *Moralia in Iob*, ed. M. Adriaen, CCSL 143+A+B, XXXIII.XVI.32 p. 1701.

[10] *Hom.*, II.1 p. 189 'templum illud manu factum sacrosanctam domini carnem quam ex uirgine sumpsit . . . figurabat'; trans. Martin and Hurst, II, pp. 8–9.

Leading on from this link between the temple building and Christ's physical body, Bede associated a door on the right-hand side of the temple (3 Kings 6.8) with the wound in Christ's side: 'For *the door to the middle section was on the right of the house* because when the Lord died on the cross *one of the soldiers opened his side with a spear*.'[11] While this interpretation derived from Augustine's ideas about the wound and its connection with the door in Noah's Ark, the link with the temple appears original to Bede.[12] The door of the temple led up initially to the second storey, and then eventually to the third (and highest) storey. Similarly, Bede stated, through the 'door' in Christ's side 'after the very blessed rest of our souls, we arrive at the recovery of our spiritual bodies, climbing as it were from the middle storey up to the third'.[13] He followed Augustine in pointing out that the sacraments that made this possible (the blood of the eucharist and the water of baptism) flowed from Christ's side during the passion.[14] Hence, Bede here represented salvation as coming about through the physical body of the incarnation. The sacramental life of the Church and thus the salvation and resurrection of the individual Christian, had their origin in the reality of Christ's human body. Christ had retained his wounds in his resurrected body in order to prove the tangible physicality of his humanity.[15]

Another interpretation of Bede's, which associated the image of the temple with Christ's incarnation, saw the womb of the Virgin Mary as 'the most sacred temple of God', uncontaminated by the corruption of human seed.[16] The closed temple gate of Ezekiel 44.1–2 also called to mind 'the temple of the virginal womb', which had maintained its enclosed purity even after Christ's birth.[17] A comparatively rare interpretation in the West, this plays a minor role in Bede, who mostly used it in his homilies, possibly drawing on Ambrose who had championed the idea as part of his celebration of virginity and the need for bodily purity.[18] There is some evidence, however, for the particular popularity of this interpretation in the Insular world: Aldhelm (d. 709/710)

---

[11] *Temp.*, p. 166 '*Ostium* namque *lateris medii in parte erat domus dextrae* quia defuncto in cruce domino *unus militum lancea latus eius aperuit* [John 19.34]'; trans. Connolly, p. 29. Also *Reg.*, XII p. 304; *Hom.*, II.1 pp. 190–91; *Ezra.*, pp. 300–301.

[12] Augustine, *DCD*, XV.26 p. 494.

[13] *Gen.*, pp. 109–10 'post animarum beatissimam requiem ad receptionem corporum spiritalium, quasi de medio cenaculo ad tertium usque scandentes'; trans. Kendall, p. 180.

[14] Augustine, *In Iohannis Evangelium*, CXX.2 p. 661.

[15] *Hom.*, II.9 p. 242.

[16] *Hom.*, I.5 p. 35 'nullatenus . . . templum Dei sacrosanctum suae semine corruptionis attaminare potuerint'; trans. Martin and Hurst, I, p. 48.

[17] *Luc.*, pp. 62–3; compare Jerome, *Commentarii in Hiezechielem*, ed. F. Glorie, CCSL 75, pp. 646–7; *Hom.*, I.4 p. 23 'uirginalis uteri templum'; trans. Martin and Hurst, I, p. 33. Natacha Piano, 'De la porte close du temple de Salomon à la porte ouverte du Paradis', *Studi Medievali* 50 (2009), pp. 133–57, at 134–9.

[18] Ambrose, *Expositio Evangelii Secundum Lucam*, ed. M. Adriaen, CCSL 14, II.6 p. 33; Ambrose, *De Spiritu Sancto*, ed. O. Faller, CSEL 79, III.XI.80 p. 183.

seems to have known it;[19] a (probably Irish) gospel commentary links Zacharias entering the temple with Christ entering Mary;[20] most strikingly, the ivory Franks Casket, probably produced in early eighth-century Northumbria, juxtaposes the empty temple on one side with the Christ child in Mary's womb on the other—implying an understanding of the incarnation as superseding the temple.[21] These Insular uses may represent more than a simple celebration of Mary's virginity. Seeing Mary as the temple makes clear her status as 'Mother of God' (*theotokos*—a term Bede knew) and served a doctrinal, anti-Nestorian point in the Eastern Church.[22] In that regard it stood in opposition to the idea of the temple as Christ's humanity assumed or inhabited by his divinity—imagery common to the so-called Antiochene Christology, which underlay Nestorius' thought.[23]

Such imagery tended to stress the separation rather than the unity between Christ's two natures and thus became theologically suspect in the case of Nestorius. Bede's clear preference for speaking of Christ's rather than Mary's body as the temple suggests an interest in emphasizing the two aspects of Christ's identity. Of course, Bede may not have been sufficiently aware of the details of the Nestorian controversy to have had many concerns about his own use of the temple image, although he probably knew Cassian's *De Incarnatione contra Nestorium*, which attacked the Nestorian use of the Christ-as-temple image. Cassian, however, did not so much condemn all such imagery as the implication that Christ only became the temple at his baptism or that God dwelt within him in the same way as within the saints, so his polemic may not have changed Bede's ideas about the temple image.[24] In general Bede consistently celebrated the orthodox unity of human and divine natures in Christ's person: 'our Redeemer, who from his conception and birth existed as perfect

---

[19] Aldhelm, *Carmen de Virginitate*, ed. R. Ehwald, MGH Auctores Antiquissimi 15, p. 423—Aldhelm used *delubrum* rather than *templum*, but he may have still considered this a reference to the Jewish temple judging on his use of the word at *Prosa de Virginitate* (in the same volume), XV p. 244.

[20] *Expositio Quatuor Evangeliorum*, PL 30, col. 567.

[21] James Lang, 'The Imagery of the Franks Casket', in *Northumbria's Golden Age*, eds Jane Hawkes and Susan Mills (Stroud, 1999), pp. 247–55, at 253–4; Herbert L. Kessler, 'Through the Temple Veil: The Holy Image in Judaism and Christianity', *Kairos* 32/33 (1990–91), pp. 53–77, at 71. Ian Wood, 'Ripon, Francia and the Franks Casket in the Early Middle Ages', *Northern History* 26 (1990), pp. 1–19, suggests a Wilfridian origin for the casket; Richard Abels, 'What has Weland to do with Christ? The Franks Casket and the Acculturation of Christianity in Early Anglo-Saxon England', *Speculum* 84 (2009), pp. 549–81, at 563, argues for Wearmouth-Jarrow as a possible place of manufacture.

[22] C. Clarke Carlton, '"The Temple that Held God": Byzantine Marian Hymnography and the Christ of Nestorius', *St Vladimir's Theological Quarterly* 50 (2006), pp. 99–125. *Luc.*, p. 34.

[23] See Ch. 2 within this volume, 'The temple in the Christian tradition before Bede', p. 38.

[24] Cassian, *De Incarnatione contra Nestorium*, ed. M. Petschenig, CSEL 17, V.3 p. 304, VII.21 pp. 378–9; Stephen Lake, 'Knowledge of the Writings of John Cassian in early Anglo-Saxon England', *ASE* 32 (2003), pp. 27–41, at 39–40.

God and perfect man'.[25] One modern commentator has called his Christology 'a rudimentary Chalcedonianism, emphasizing one thing and one thing alone: Christ's dual nature as fully human and fully divine'.[26] Nonetheless, the Bedan variations on the theme of the temple as Christ's body reveal a specific emphasis on his humanity, I would argue. This may have come about because Bede had cause to feel that Christ's humanity needed to be defended against those who, in a desire to stress the unity of the Saviour, ran the risk of denigrating his human nature.

In the seventh century the authorities in Constantinople promulgated the Monothelete doctrine (that Christ had two natures, but only one (divine) will or energy) in an attempt to bridge the gap between Chalcedonians and Monophysites (who denied that Christ's flesh formed a second nature).[27] The compromise failed to win over adherents in the West. The Lateran Council of 649 condemned the doctrine, an action seen as treasonous in Constantinople, and the emperor's response led to the arrest, torture, and death in exile of Pope Martin I in 655.[28] During these events and their aftermath the first Northumbrian pilgrims (Wilfrid and Benedict Biscop) reached Rome, a Rome where anti-Byzantine and anti-Monothelete feeling no doubt ran high.[29] Both men formed a close attachment to Roman orthodoxy in such circumstances and returned to England intent on fostering loyalty to Rome at home.

The Greek monk Theodore of Tarsus, appointed archbishop of Canterbury in 668, may well have helped draw up the initial acts of the 649 Lateran Council; certainly by 680 the papacy considered him the leading expert on Monotheletism in the West.[30] In 679 Theodore presided over a synod of Anglo-Saxon bishops at *Hæthfeld* that condemned Monotheletism as part of a strategy of gathering support for the papacy in its attempts to achieve a rapprochement with Constantinople in the years ahead.[31] John, the precentor of St Peter's in Rome, attended in order to monitor the proceedings. Both

[25] *Tab.*, p. 36 'redemptor noster qui ex conceptione et natiuitate perfectus Deus et homo extitit'; trans. Holder, p. 38. Also *Temp.*, p. 211; *Cant.*, pp. 242, 292; *Hom.*, I.19 p. 136.

[26] W. Trent Foley, 'Bede's Exegesis of Passages Unique to the Gospel of Mark', in *Biblical Studies in the Early Middle Ages*, eds Claudio Leonardi and Giovanni Orlandi (Florence, 2005), pp. 105–24, at 115.

[27] Scholars now often use 'miaphysite' for 'monophysite'—a term coined by Chalcedonians.

[28] See Judith Herrin, *The Formation of Christendom* (London, 1989), pp. 250–59.

[29] For Wilfrid: W. Trent Foley, *Images of Sanctity in Eddius Stephanus' Life* of Bishop Wilfrid, *An Early English Saint's Life* (Lampeter, 1992), pp. 80–84. For Biscop: Celia Chazelle, 'Christ and the Vision of God: The Biblical Diagrams of the Codex Amiatinus', in *The Mind's Eye: Art and Theological Argument in the Middle Ages*, eds Jeffrey F. Hamburger and Anne-Marie Bouché (Princeton NJ, 2006), pp. 84–111, at 98–100.

[30] Bernhard Bischoff and Michael Lapidge, *Biblical Commentaries from the Canterbury School of Theodore and Hadrian* (Cambridge, 1994), pp. 70–81.

[31] Bischoff and Lapidge, *Biblical Commentaries*, pp. 139–46; Henry Chadwick, 'Theodore, the English Church and the Monothelete Controversy', in *Archbishop Theodore: Commemorative*

Theodore and John had come to Britain with Benedict Biscop as a guide; John stayed at Wearmouth during his time in Britain and Biscop took the opportunity to add a copy of the acts of the Lateran Council of 649 to his library.[32] Wearmouth thus constituted the 'Northumbrian outpost of Rome's offensive against Monothelete doctrine'.[33] Scholars in recent years have emphasized the importance of the Monothelete crisis as the backdrop to the foundation of Biscop's monastery and its Roman ideology.[34]

These events, of course, took place decades before Bede wrote his temple commentaries; we should not overemphasize the power of institutional memory or Bede's knowledge of all these factors. Nonetheless, claims that Bede failed to understand the questions at stake at the Synod of *Hæthfeld* because he described it as a response to the heresy of Eutyches (technically Monophysitism) overstate the issue—such terminology was flexible.[35] Recently Marilyn Dunn has suggested that the problem of native polytheism, rather than distant theological disputes, may explain some of the synod's Christology.[36] Considering how little we genuinely know about Anglo-Saxon pre-Christian religion, we can hardly verify this argument either way. Whatever the likelihood that a Church council in the 670s shaped its Christology in response to polytheism, I see little cause for believing that Bede did so fifty years later. Bede rarely mentioned paganism in any meaningful fashion when defending orthodox Christology, while in his commentary on Mark, broadly contemporaneous with his major temple commentaries, he clearly refuted Monotheletism, attacking 'the Eutychians who say that there was one . . . operation and one will in our Lord and Saviour'.[37]

Monotheletism revived briefly in Constantinople in the early eighth century, as Bede knew.[38] He seems to have made use of the copy of the acts of the

---

Studies on his Life and Influence, ed. Michael Lapidge (Cambridge, 1995), pp. 88–95; Catherine Cubitt, *Anglo-Saxon Church Councils c.650–c.850* (London, 1995), pp. 252–8.

[32] *HE*, IV.18 pp. 388–91; *HA*, 3 pp. 28–9, 6 pp. 34–7.

[33] Celia Chazelle, 'Art and Reverence in Bede's Churches at Wearmouth and Jarrow', in *Intellektualisierung und Mystifizierung mittelalterlicher Kunst*, eds Martin Büchsel and Rebecca Müller (Berlin, 2010), pp. 79–98, at 89.

[34] Chazelle, 'Vision of God'; Chazelle, 'Art and Reverence'; Jennifer O'Reilly, ' "All that Peter Stands For": The *Romanitas* of the *Codex Amiatinus* Reconsidered', *Proceedings of the British Academy* 157 (2009), pp. 367–95, at 391–4; Éamonn Ó Carragáin, 'The Wearmouth Icon of the Virgin (A.D. 679): Christological, Liturgical, and Iconographic Contexts', in *Poetry, Place, and Gender: Studies in Medieval Culture in Honour of Helen Damico*, ed. Catherine E. Karkov (Kalamazoo MI, 2009), pp. 13–37.

[35] Bischoff and Lapidge, *Biblical Commentaries*, p. 141; *HE*, IV.17 pp. 384–5.

[36] Marilyn Dunn, *The Christianization of the Anglo-Saxons c.597–c.700: Discourses of Life, Death and Afterlife* (London, 2009), pp. 144–6.

[37] *Marc.*, p. 617 'Eutichianos qui dicunt unam in . . . domino et saluatore nostro operationem unam fuisse uoluntatem'.

[38] Herrin, *Formation of Christendom*, p. 312; *DTR*, LXVI pp. 531–2.

Lateran Council available to him at Wearmouth-Jarrow.[39] And while he certainly had little expertise on the intricacies of Eastern theology, there can be no doubt concerning his conviction that heresies from the East posed a significant attack on Christ's human nature and that orthodox loyalty to Rome required the rejection of such beliefs. Bede's defence of Christian images which appears in *On the Temple* certainly provides a response to the contemporary iconoclast movement in the Byzantine empire of the late 720s.[40] The community at Wearmouth-Jarrow clearly remained informed of developments in Eastern Christianity, though the information that reached Northumbria no doubt came heavily filtered through a Roman lens. If Bede's interpretation of the temple received its intellectual impetus from the making of the Codex Amiatinus, which celebrates Pope Hilarus who had condemned Eutyches and defended Chalcedonian orthodoxy, then this pro-Roman emphasis on Christ's humanity makes even more sense.[41] The orthodox position on Christ may have seemed in constant need of reiteration when 'Bede and his contemporaries could never rule out the possibility that in the future the heresy might again find an emperor to support it'.[42]

Another image associated with Christ's human nature plays a large role in Bede's temple commentaries: the Ark of the Covenant, which Bede understood as 'the humanity assumed by Christ'.[43] In *On the Tabernacle* he interpreted the incorruptible wood of the ark covered with gold inside and out as the spotless humanity of Christ entirely filled with his divinity.[44] Most importantly, the ark rests inside the Holy of Holies 'because after his passion and resurrection from the dead' Christ's human body 'has ascended above the highest heaven and sits at the right hand of the Father'.[45] In carrying his own humanity into heaven, Christ opened the path for all mortals to enter eternal life: 'We see heaven opened, because after the God-man gained entrance into heaven, we recognize that in his name an entry into our heavenly home was

---

[39] Éamonn Ó Carragáin, *Ritual and the Rood: Liturgical Images and the Old English Poems of the Dream of the Rood Tradition* (London, 2005), p. 268, notes verbal parallels between Bede's work and the acts.

[40] *Temp.*, pp. 212–13; Peter Darby, 'Bede, Iconoclasm, and the Temple of Solomon', *EME* 21 (2013), pp. 390–421; but see Chazelle, 'Art and Reverence', pp. 91–2.

[41] Chazelle, 'Vision of God', p. 103.

[42] Ó Carragáin, *Ritual and the Rood*, p. 229.

[43] *Reg.*, XIV p. 306 'designat . . . in sancta sanctorum arca assumptam Christi humanitatem'; trans. Foley, p. 111. Also *Apoc.*, p. 385; *Tab.*, p. 13; *Hom.*, II.25 p. 376; for more on this common interpretation: Ch. 4 within this volume, 'Bede's use of the cosmic interpretation', p. 81.

[44] *Tab.*, p. 15.

[45] *Tab.*, p. 72 'Intra hoc autem uelum templi posita est archa testamenti quia mediator Dei et hominum homo Christus Iesus . . . post passionem suam resurrectionemque a mortuis super caelos caelorum ascendens sedet ad dexteram patris [Colossians 3.1]'; trans. Holder, p. 81. Also *Sam.*, p. 67; *Tab.*, p. 133; *Temp.*, p. 176.

opened up for us believers too'.[46] The presence of the ark in the Holy of Holies seems to be a guarantee that mankind can gain entrance to God's presence—for it has already done so in the person of Christ himself. The ark reminds us that, for Bede, the incarnation, the process of joining God and man, led in some way to the deification of humanity.[47]

The Codex Amiatinus opens its New Testament with an image of Christ in Majesty, a *maiestas domini* probably meant to represent the Lord in Judgement.[48] Set against a heavenly background, Christ appears between two winged angels in what is probably a reference to the ark with its overhanging cherubim.[49] The image thus shows Christ, whose incarnation the New Testament revealed, as the true ark of God present in heaven. The four evangelists and their beasts surround the sphere in which Christ appears; Bede interpreted the beasts as signifying how the gospels displayed Christ's sacrificial humanity (the man and the ox) and his divine victory over death (the lion and the eagle).[50] Interestingly, the discussion of the ark in *On the Tabernacle* inspired Bede to talk about the evangelists' beasts, suggesting that he may have had the codex's image of Christ as ark in mind; the 'two rings on one side and two on the other' made Bede think of the beasts, and indeed in the Codex Amiatinus the animals appear two on either side of Christ.[51] Once again it appears that the themes of Bede's interpretation arose not from solely private interest, but from the shared spirituality of Wearmouth-Jarrow.

Bede often linked Christ's presence as ark in the heavenly Holy of Holies with one of his favourite titles for him: the 'mediator of God and men, the man Christ Jesus' (1 Timothy 2.5).[52] The appellation appears more often in Bede's work than that of any of the major Latin Church Fathers, excluding Augustine's truly giant corpus; it focuses on Christ's humanity, of course, but sees that humanity as linking the divine and the human through itself. Hence the significance of the image of the ark in Bede's writings: the God-man stands continually in the presence of God the Father, interceding for man.[53] We have already seen the importance of Christ's mediation to Bede's use of the temple

---

[46] *Hom.*, I.17 p. 125 'Videmus etenim caelum apertum quia postquam caelum Deus homo penetrauit etiam nobis in nomine eius credentibus supernae patriae patefactum cognoscimus ingressum'; trans. Martin and Hurst, I, p. 174.

[47] See Ch. 4 within this volume, 'Bede's use of the cosmic interpretation', p. 80–81.

[48] Florence, Biblioteca Medicea Laurenziana, MS Amiatino 1, fol. 796v (Fig. 3).

[49] Jennifer O'Reilly, 'The Library of Scripture: Views from Vivarium and Wearmouth-Jarrow', in *New Offerings, Ancient Treasures: Studies in Medieval Art for George Henderson*, eds Paul Binski and William Noel (Stroud, 2001), pp. 3–39, at 13; Janina Ramirez, '*Sub culmine gazas*: The Iconography of the *Armarium* on the Ezra Page of the Codex Amiatinus', *Gesta* 48 (2009), pp. 1–18, at 12.

[50] *Tab.*, p. 16.

[51] *Tab.*, p. 16 'Duo autem circuli in latere uno et duo sunt in altero'; trans. Holder, p. 14; Exodus 25.12. Gregory, *Homiliae in Hiezechihelem Prophetam*, ed. M. Adriaen, CCSL 142, I.IV.3 pp. 48–9, while in part no doubt Bede's source here, differs on this point.

[52] E.g. *Temp.*, p. 178; *Tab.*, p. 72.   [53] E.g. *Tab.*, p. 132.

image: Christ as cornerstone, for example, linked the Jewish and the gentile peoples through his own person;[54] Christ 'as a benevolent mediator and reconciler has made one house of God of angels and men'.[55] Christ intercedes for humanity before the Father, not just as ark, but also as priest and Bede saw Christ's priestly function as an important part of his status as mediator.[56] In the Old Testament only the high priest could enter into the presence of God and he performed intercessory sacrifices on behalf of all the people. Bede closely linked the assumption of humanity in the incarnation to Christ's priesthood—he interpreted Samuel performing his priestly duties in a linen ephod as Christ humbly ministering to Christians in his sinless humanity.[57] An important role of the old Jewish priesthood had been sacrifice as part of the mediation between God and humans and Bede followed the Letter to the Hebrews and the Church Fathers in declaring Christ 'the true high priest' because he 'offered his very self for us as a sweet-smelling oblation and sacrifice to God'.[58] Bede recognized Christ as both king and priest—but whereas the first title related to the eschatological kingdom, Christ's priesthood arose from his passion and constant heavenly intercession for humanity.[59]

Christ's passion, therefore, provided a cleansing sacrifice for human sins and the Lord's risen body constantly performed a priestly intercession with the Father. Bede repeatedly spoke of Christ as a victim or a sacrifice and linked him with the animal victims sacrificed on the altars of the tabernacle and the temple.[60] The Lord offered himself 'on the altar of the cross' (a phrase, rare in earlier patristic writings though appearing in Origen, of which Bede was strikingly fond) as the 'true sacrifice of the Father'.[61] In Bede's exegesis, therefore, the image of the temple inspired a constant remembrance of the priesthood of the incarnate Christ and the sacrifice of his passion. Solomon built the temple on the mountain where Abraham had offered Isaac as a

---

[54] *Tab.*, p. 76; *Act.*, p. 26; *EpCath.*, p. 236; *Sam.*, p. 167. Ephesians 2.20.

[55] *Hom.*, I.6 p. 37 'qui de angelis et hominibus unam Dei domum pius mediator et reconciliator instituit'; trans. Martin and Hurst, I, p. 53. Also *EpCath.*, p. 235; *Temp.*, p. 147; *Ezra.*, pp. 371, 384; see Ch. 7 within this volume, 'Imitation', pp. 171–4.

[56] *Luc.*, p. 402; *Tab.*, p. 132; *Apoc.*, p. 559; *DTR*, VIII p. 303.

[57] *Sam.*, p. 27; see also *VIII Q.*, VIII p. 73.

[58] *Tab.*, p. 96 'ueri pontificis Iesu Christi qui semet ipsum obtulit oblationem et hostiam Deo pro nobis in odorem suauitatis'; trans. Holder, p. 110; *Luc.*, p. 24; Ephesians 5.2; Hebrews 9.11–14. Giovanni Caputa, *Il Sacerdozio dei Fedeli secondo San Beda: un itinerario di maturità cristiana* (Vatican City, 2002), pp. 195–203; for patristic uses of this imagery: Ch. 2 within this volume, 'The temple in the Christian tradition before Bede', pp. 37, 39, 40–41.

[59] *Ret.*, p. 117; *Ezra.*, p. 264; *Hom.*, I.3 pp. 19–20, II.10 p. 249.

[60] *Ret.*, p. 112; *Tab.*, p. 71; *Ezra.*, pp. 306, 329; *Luc.*, pp. 350, 378 (= *Marc.*, p. 611).

[61] *Tab.*, pp. 16 'in altari crucis', 138; *Apoc.*, p. 245; *Luc.*, p. 404 (= *Marc.*, p. 632); *Sam.*, p. 62. *Luc.*, p. 354 'uera patris hostia Christus'. Compare Origen/Rufinus, *In Genesim Homiliae*, ed. W. A. Baehrens, *Origenes Werke* 6 (Leipzig, 1920), VIII.9 pp. 84–5.

prefiguration of Christ's sacrifice;[62] in *On Luke* Bede linked the place of the altar of holocausts outside the tabernacle with the crucifixion outside Jerusalem.[63] He argued that Luke's gospel began and ended in the temple precincts because it focused especially on Christ as priest and victim.[64] The one true sacrifice of the passion underlay all history;[65] the Jews had celebrated it through animal sacrifices but Christ transferred his priesthood to the Church, which offered up the sacrifice of the eucharist.[66]

Scholars have recognized the importance of this view of salvation as sacrifice in the medieval Western Church, where it eventually fed into the twelfth-century consolidation of a doctrine of redemption by Anselm.[67] In that light, Bede's wholehearted support for the image becomes potentially significant. One must question the assumption that in the early Middle Ages the image of Christ as a divine king dominated, especially in the 'Germanic' society that produced poems such as *The Dream of the Rood*.[68] Even when Bede thought of the passion as a victory, sacrificial imagery remained central to his understanding of redemption because the victory Christ won on the cross came about through his self-oblation: 'to vanquish the powers of the air he offered himself for the world as a sacrifice to the Father'.[69] As king, Christ will bring the elect into the kingdom of heaven, but as priest and sacrifice he has cleansed humanity of its sins and continuously works for their salvation; even the title 'King of the Jews' on the cross caused Bede to discuss Christ's priestly sacrifice on the altar of the cross—a focus on the Lord's divinity never eclipsing an appreciation of his humanity.[70]

Herren and Brown have noted many of the issues here highlighted as common in 'Celtic' rather than 'Germanic' Christianity. They see the emphasis on Christ's humanity as a common Pelagian feature in Insular texts, and they

---

[62] *Temp.*, p. 159; *Ezra.*, p. 271.   [63] *Luc.*, p. 354.

[64] *Luc.*, pp. 71, 402, 424–5.   [65] *Gen.*, pp. 127–8; *Ezra.*, pp. 271–2.

[66] *Tab.*, p. 48; *Ezra.*, p. 329; *Hom.*, I.15 p. 106; *Sam.*, p. 31; *Reg.*, I pp. 296–7. On Jewish sacrifice and the eucharist: Mary Thomas Aquinas Carroll, *The Venerable Bede: His Spiritual Teachings* (Washington DC, 1946), pp. 124–5.

[67] H. E. W. Turner, *The Patristic Doctrine of Redemption: A Study of the Development of Doctrine during the First Five Centuries* (London, 1952), pp. 96–111; Rowan A. Greer, 'Christ the Victor and the Victim', *Concordia Theological Quarterly* 59 (1995), pp. 1–30.

[68] Giles Constable, *Three Studies in Medieval Religious and Social Thought* (Cambridge, 1995), pp. 157–8; Michael W. Herren and Shirley Ann Brown, *Christ in Celtic Christianity: Britain and Ireland from the Fifth to the Tenth Century* (Woodbridge, 2002), p. 160; *The Dream of the Rood*, ed. and trans. Richard Hamer, *A Choice of Anglo-Saxon Verse* (London, 1970), pp. 159–71. See Rosemary Woolf, 'Doctrinal Influences on *The Dream of the Rood*', *Medium Aevum* 27 (1958), pp. 137–53.

[69] *Sam.*, pp. 13, 106 'ad debellandas aerias potestates se ipsum pro mundo offerret hostiam patri'. The classic study of redemption as Christ's victory is Gustaf Aulén, *Christus Victor*, trans. A. G. Herbert (London, 1931).

[70] *Luc.*, p. 404 (= *Marc.*, p. 632). See also Claudio Leonardi, 'Il Venerabile Beda e la Cultura del Secolo VIII', *Settimane di studio del Centro italiano di studi sull'alto medioevo* 20 (1973), pp. 603–58, at 630.

also note a focus on the passion rather than the resurrection.[71] It seems to me that the utility of terms such as 'Germanic' or 'Celtic' is limited: they run the risk of being misinterpreted (especially when, like 'Celtic', they have a long historiography) and encourage explanations based, not on the specifics of time and place, but on generalizations. Nonetheless some of these points, such as the importance of Christ's humanity for a monastic ideology of imitation, prove relevant to Bede's situation as we shall see in Chapter 7 within this volume. But we ought to emphasize that Bede always highlighted the perfection of the humanity of the incarnate Christ, superior to that of mortal men, and linked with a divinity that had pre-existed it.[72] The resurrection also remained central to Bede's soteriology—by raising his own human body Christ guaranteed the resurrection of mortal human bodies. The resurrection brought the body of the incarnation into heaven after all and thus 'revealed the pathway of ascent to his faithful ones who humbly follow him'.[73]

The temple provided a way for Bede to talk and think about Christ; its imagery of priesthood and sacrifice proved fundamental to his understanding of the saving work of the incarnate God. Bede constantly emphasized through his use of the temple image that God had saved humanity through a real, physical human body. But Christ's body was much more than just that; its *membra* were not just the limbs of the incarnation—they were every member of the Christian Church of which Christ was head.[74] Thus in some way every Christian participated in the temple image as it applied to the Lord. As a result, Christ's sacrificial and priestly actions had the potential to turn every Christian into a priest and sacrifice through their participation in him. If the Church truly functioned as Christ's body then the consequences for its members could be quite dramatic.

THE PRIESTHOOD OF ALL BELIEVERS

For Bede, all members of the Church deserved the title 'priest' because all belonged to the body of Christ, the true high priest.[75] The entire Church as an institution possessed a spiritual priesthood that had once belonged only to the house of Aaron within Israel.[76] Bede followed the footsteps of his predecessors

---

[71] Herren and Brown, *Celtic Christianity*, pp. 64–5, 138–9, 281.

[72] *Temp.*, pp. 158, 211; *Ezra.*, p. 311; *Tab.*, p. 13.

[73] *Ezra.*, p. 311 'fidelibus suis se humiliter sequentibus ascensionis iter ostendit'; trans. DeGregorio, p. 116.

[74] *Sam.*, p. 139; *Luc.*, p. 417; *Hom.*, II.1 p. 189, II.18 p. 315.

[75] *EpCath.*, pp. 235, 237; *Apoc.*, pp. 239, 247–9, 509; *Temp.*, p. 214; compare Augustine, *DCD*, XX.10 pp. 719–20.

[76] *Luc.*, p. 312; *Sam.*, p. 137; *Reg.*, I p. 297. Bede's point at *Temp.*, p. 150 seems to be that any Christian can become a priest/teacher, rather than that all Christians are priests.

in this for he had inherited a tradition from the Fathers which emphasized that the entire Church formed a 'kingly priesthood'.[77] Hence he interpreted the *sacerdotes* of the Old Testament as on occasion referring to all Christians or all the perfect.[78] Recent scholarship has noted Bede's clear interest in the priesthood of all believers; he seems, indeed, to have used this non-clerical interpretation of biblical *sacerdotes* far more often than many of his patristic predecessors.[79] This theme in the monk's work deserves careful consideration because it has important links with one of the most important approaches to the Bedan corpus of recent years: that is, reading it in the light of Bede's agenda to reform the Northumbrian Church through the use of preachers and teachers.

Bede's temple commentaries display an unfavourable opinion of his own times. Just as the sons of Aaron suffered death for offering illicit fire on the altar to God, Bede wrote, many priests and teachers of 'our unhappy time... are consumed by the fire of heavenly vengeance' for their greed.[80] The two pillars at the entrance to the temple displayed the characteristics expected of teachers of the Church and 'note tacitly the sluggishness of our time'.[81] The present times contrasted negatively with the zealous activity of the Jews returned from Babylon; Bede even called out for a Nehemiah to come in his age to reform the Church.[82] *On Ezra and Nehemiah* contrasted the Jewish people who, having rebuilt the temple, supplied it with priests and Levites for its service with contemporaries who built magnificent monasteries and failed to provide 'teachers to exhort the people to God's works'.[83]

Scholars (especially Thacker, and subsequently DeGregrio in work concerning *On Ezra and Nehemiah*) have long recognized such statements as part of an agenda to reform the Northumbrian Church which permeates Bede's exegesis.[84] Historians now agree that Bede's sense, that contemporary

---

[77] 1 Peter 2.9; Yves Congar, *L'Ecclésiologie du Haut Moyen Age: De saint Grégoire le Grand à la désunion entre Byzance et Rome* (Paris, 1968), p. 109, esp. n. 216. The idea appears in Irish exegesis known to Bede: *Commentarius in Epistolas Catholicas Scotti Anonymi*, ed. R. E. McNally, CCSL 108B, p. 31; compare *Apoc.*, p. 239.

[78] *Tab.*, p. 138; *Temp.*, pp. 194, 207, 214; *Ezra.*, pp. 242, 264.

[79] Caputa, *Sacerdozio dei Fedeli*, throughout but esp. pp. 84–143 on the temple commentaries; Georges Tugène, *L'idée de nation chez Bède le Vénérable* (Paris, 2001), pp. 252–8.

[80] *Tab.*, p. 96 'miserabilis nostri temporis... igne supernae ultionis absumuntur'; trans. Holder, p. 110. Also *Tab.*, p. 115.

[81] *Temp.*, p. 207 'nostrique temporis inertia tacite notaretur'; trans. Connolly, p. 84. Also *Reg.*, XXX pp. 320–1.

[82] *Ezra.*, pp. 277–8, 360. Scott DeGregorio, *Bede: On Ezra and Nehemiah* (Liverpool, 2006), p. xxxii.

[83] *Ezra.*, p. 303 'doctores qui ad opera Dei populum cohortentur'; trans. DeGregorio, p. 102.

[84] Alan Thacker, 'Bede's Ideal of Reform', in *Ideal and Reality in Frankish and Anglo-Saxon Society: Studies presented to J. M. Wallace-Hadrill*, eds Patrick Wormald et al. (Oxford, 1983), pp. 130–53, esp. 130–33; Scott DeGregorio, '"Nostrorum socordiam temporum": the Reforming Impulse of Bede's Later Exegesis', *EME* 11 (2002), pp. 107–22; DeGregorio, 'Bede's *In Ezram et Neemiam* and the Reform of the Northumbrian Church', *Speculum* 79 (2004),

ecclesiastical and monastic affairs had suffered a great falling off from the 'golden age' of the seventh century, shaped his vision of the Church as an institution in need of the reform which his works encouraged. His writings consistently outline a vision of the Church focused heavily on the pastoral and missionary obligations of its leadership. Church rulers should provide preaching and sacramental care to the laity in the way in which the saintly missionaries of seventh-century Northumbria had once done. This vision relates to a Gregorian conception of the preacher, the ascetic *pastor* who carefully mixed the contemplative and active lives in order to bring both themselves and their flock to salvation.[85]

Bede's letter to Bishop Ecgberht of York provides the key that unlocks the reform agenda in his exegesis.[86] In one substantial strand of the letter Bede argued that bishops failed to provide adequate pastoral care to their dispersed flocks, highlighting especially the lack of preaching, baptism, and the laying on of hands.[87] He demanded, consequently, that Ecgberht should appoint more priests and teachers (*doctores*) to assist in providing pastoral care and preaching.[88] Bede suggested Gregory the Great's *Regula Pastoralis* to Ecgberht as vital reading for a bishop.[89] Some argue that the pope had opened the role of *rector* (ruler) or *praedicator* (preacher) not just to the clergy, but to any suitably moral Christian;[90] the question arises therefore whether this was also the case for Bede. Thacker suggests that while Bede's order of teachers overlapped with the clerical hierarchy, on occasion it went beyond it.[91]

Bede certainly applied the term *pastor* not exclusively to bishops, priests, deacons, and abbots but also it seems to lay heads of household.[92] At one point

---

pp. 1–25; DeGregorio, 'Footsteps of His Own: Bede's Commentary on Ezra-Nehemiah', in *Innovation and Tradition in the Writings of the Venerable Bede*, ed. Scott DeGregorio (Morgantown WV, 2006), pp. 143–68.

[85] Thacker, 'Ideal of Reform', pp. 133–5. For the contemplative and active lives in Bede's representation of Cuthbert and bishops in general: Clare Stancliffe, 'Cuthbert and the Polarity between Pastor and Solitary', in *St Cuthbert, His Cult and His Community until AD 1200*, eds Gerald Bonner et al. (Woodbridge, 1989), pp. 21–44; Simon Coates, 'The Bishop as Pastor and Solitary: Bede and the Spiritual Authority of the Monk-Bishop', *JEH* 47 (1996), pp. 601–19.

[86] The letter presents Bede's viewpoint, rather than an objective one: Patrick Sims-Williams, *Religion and Literature in Western England, 600–800* (Cambridge, 1990), pp. 126–9; John Blair, *The Church in Anglo-Saxon Society* (Oxford, 2005), pp. 100–8.

[87] *EpEcg.*, 5 pp. 130–31, 7 pp. 134–7.   [88] *EpEcg.*, 5 pp. 130–33, 9 pp. 138–41.

[89] *EpEcg.*, 3 pp. 126–7.

[90] Conrad Leyser, *Authority and Asceticism from Augustine to Gregory the Great* (Oxford, 2000), p. 157; R. A. Markus, 'Gregory the Great's *Rector* and His Genesis', in *Grégoire Le Grand*, eds Jacques Fontaine et al. (Paris, 1986), pp. 137–46.

[91] Thacker, 'Ideal of Reform', p. 131; Thacker, 'Bede and the Ordering of Understanding', in *Innovation and Tradition*, ed. DeGregorio, pp. 37–63, at 43; Thacker, 'Priests and Pastoral Care in Early Anglo-Saxon England', in *The Study of Medieval Manuscripts of England: Festschrift in Honor of Richard W. Pfaff*, eds George Hardin Brown and Linda Ehrsam Voigts (Tempe AZ, 2010), pp. 187–208, at 203.

[92] *Hom.*, I.7 p. 49.

in *On Ezra and Nehemiah* Bede seems to have supported female preachers.[93] If such a comment stands up then it would seem difficult to maintain, as some have, that Bede conceived of missionary work and pastoral care as provided entirely by ordained 'priest-preachers'.[94] The issue has attracted much attention because Bede's outlook may help to expand our understanding of the provision of pastoral care in early Anglo-Saxon England.[95] The 1990s saw a major scholarly debate about the importance of monastic communities to the development of parochial structures, which fuelled this interest in pastoral care.[96] In this light the relationship between Bede's belief that Christians shared in the priesthood of Christ, to whose body they belonged, and his reform agenda has a clear importance. Belief in a priesthood of all believers could lie behind a Bedan conviction that his own contemporary Church might be reformed by the active preaching of men and women, clergy and laity, religious and secular.

Who then were to be the foot soldiers of reform? Bede used a number of words to describe people whose function he conceived of as broadly the same: *doctores, praedicatores*, and *magistri* seem the most common, but also related are *rectores, ministri verbi/sermonis*, and (albeit in a complicated fashion) *sacerdotes*.[97] While the choice of title may imply some differences of emphasis, in practice Bede used these words interchangeably, suggesting that usually in his exegesis he considered them to describe the same group of people.[98] Preachers were the successors of the apostles (Bede spoke of apostles and 'apostolic men' together), but they consisted not just of missionaries to non-Christians: some also built up the Church within existing Christian societies.[99] As the heirs to the apostolic mission these individuals seem to have shared in the power of binding and loosening (which Bede understood as having been

---

[93] *Ezra.*, p. 257.

[94] Carroll, *Spiritual Teachings*, pp. 242–6; Catherine Cubitt, 'Pastoral Care and Conciliar Canons: the Provisions of the 747 Council of *Clofesho*' in *Pastoral Care before the Parish*, eds John Blair and Richard Sharpe (Leicester, 1992), pp. 193–211.

[95] E.g. Alan Thacker, 'Monks, Preaching and Pastoral Care in early Anglo-Saxon England', in *Pastoral Care*, eds Blair and Sharpe, pp. 137–70.

[96] Eric Cambridge and David Rollason, 'Debate: The Pastoral Organization of the Anglo-Saxon Church: a Review of the "Minster Hypothesis"' and John Blair, 'Debate: Ecclesiastical Organization and Pastoral Care in Anglo-Saxon England', *EME* 4 (1995), pp. 87–104 and pp. 193–212, respectively. Also Ch. 1 within this volume, 'Bede's world', p. 18.

[97] Thacker, 'Ideal of Reform', p. 130, agrees that these terms mean the one thing, but in 'Ordering of Understanding', p. 43, suggests a differentiation between the scholarly *doctor* and the more active *praedicator*.

[98] Examples of *praedicatores* and *doctores* being equivalent: *Reg.*, XIV p. 306; *Tab.*, p. 57; *Ezra.*, pp. 274–5; *Temp.*, pp. 200–206. *Doctores* and *magistri*: *Sam.*, p. 102; *Tab.*, pp. 52–3. *Rectores* and *doctores* or *praedicatores*: *Sam.*, p. 122; *Tab.*, p. 51. *Doctores* are associated with *pastores* (*Luc.*, p. 234), *praesules* (*Ezra.*, p. 379), *sacerdotes* (*Temp.* p. 232), and *interpretes* (*Tab.*, p. 65). See also Markus, 'Gregory the Great's *Rector*', p. 142.

[99] *Tab.*, pp. 27, 58, 97; *Temp.*, pp. 210, 227; *Ezra.*, p. 321. For two concepts of mission, i.e. evangelizing non-Christians and strengthening the faith of existing Christians: *Temp.* p. 218.

given to all the apostles and thence to the entire Church hierarchy), identified with their control over membership of the Church.[100]

Examining Bede's use of the temple image may illuminate some of the issues here—his interest in the contemporary Anglo-Saxon Church probably influenced more of his exegesis than just the explicitly reformist statements.[101] Certainly his presentation of the priests of the temple cult seems infused with his reforming interest in teachers. Zacharias sacrificing at the altar inside the temple while the people prayed outside, represented the contrast between the teacher enkindled with divine wisdom and the less-learned who wait humbly for his teaching.[102] The link did not only carry positive association: Heli's sons seduced women at the door of the tabernacle just as wicked preachers prevent weak souls entering through the door of life.[103] This link between the Old Testament priesthood and the *doctores* and *praedicatores* of the Church, therefore, seems worth investigation. Bede provided, in *On the Tabernacle*, an exhaustive commentary on the vestments of the Jewish priests. In these garments he saw the model for his own reformed pastorate displayed; they reveal 'the works of righteousness and holiness which the Scripture of the sacred law recommends [the Church's] rulers to possess'.[104] Any summary runs the risk of being selective, but taken together the vestments display the purity of word, thought, and deed necessary for a *pastor*. The preacher actualizes in deed the care for his flock, the models of the saints, and the heavenly virtues which they hold in the mind. The message of the robes of the Aaronic priests matches that of Bede's other reforming texts: 'the faith of faithful teachers is joined together with action'.[105]

Here again the creation of the Codex Amiatinus may have provided the inspiration for Bede's ideas. We have already discussed the image of Ezra in the codex and shown that sufficient grounds exist for connecting Bede's writings with this image.[106] In this portrait Ezra appears as a Jewish high priest; although some have argued that the image does not contain all eight priestly vestments, which Bede went on to interpret in such detail in *On the Tabernacle*, at least four seem to be clearly present and it seems unlikely that

---

[100] *Temp.*, pp. 186, 217; *Ezra.*, p. 364. On the power to bind and loosen: *Hom.*, I.20 pp. 145–6; John Moorhead, 'Bede on the Papacy', *JEH* 60 (2009), pp. 217–32, at 224–5.

[101] Scott DeGregorio, 'Monasticism and Reform in Book IV of Bede's "Ecclesiastical History of the English People"', *JEH* 61 (2010), pp. 673–87, at 674–5; but see N. J. Higham, 'Bede's Agenda in Book IV of the "Ecclesiastical History of the English People": A Tricky Matter of Advising the King', *JEH* 64 (2013), pp. 476–93, at 478.

[102] *Luc.*, p. 29.   [103] *Sam.*, p. 30.

[104] *Tab.*, p. 97 'opera sunt iustitiae et sanctitatis quae scriptura sacrae legis rectoribus habenda commendat'; trans. Holder, p. 111.

[105] *Tab.*, p. 106 'doctorum fidelium . . . fides cum operatione coniungitur'; trans. Holder p. 122. For the entire commentary on the sacerdotal vestments: *Tab.*, pp. 97–123.

[106] See Ch. 4 within this volume, 'The Codex Amiatinus', pp. 95–6; MS Amiatino 1, fol. Vr (Fig. 2).

any artist could have depicted the priest's linen undergarments and tunic with much ease.[107] Traditionally art historians have denied that this image casts any light on Wearmouth-Jarrow, arguing 'that the figure represented in this miniature is not primarily Ezra, but essentially Cassiodorus in the guise of Ezra'.[108] This arises from the probable connection between nine volumes in the bookcase of the image and Cassiodorus' *novem codices*, a nine-part division of the Bible he produced at Vivarium.[109] However, we have no reason for believing that Cassiodorus would ever have depicted himself as Ezra other than the Amiatinus diagram; the evidence increasingly suggests that the iconography of the image was designed for the first time at Wearmouth-Jarrow.[110] Even if Cassiodorus had created the image, we would still need to investigate what it meant to the community at Wearmouth-Jarrow.

Scholars have suggested numerous interpretations: that Ezra here represents Christ in his role as author of both testaments;[111] that the Jewish high priest's vestments link the image with the codex's papal audience.[112] O'Reilly has suggested that the depiction of the priestly scribe calls the reader to undertake the work of studying, interpreting, and internalizing scripture.[113] For DeGregorio, Ezra symbolizes the Wearmouth-Jarrow community's commitment to the reform of the Northumbrian Church.[114] Bede wrote *On the Tabernacle* years after the Codex Amiatinus had left Northumbria and we might question, therefore, whether Bede's statements reflect the manuscript's intellectual programme. However, he mentioned the priestly vestments a number of times in passing in the commentary he was writing on the book of Samuel at the time of the codex's departure from Wearmouth-Jarrow. There they symbolized the grace of different virtues in the holy man, the examples of good works, and the preaching by word and example of the teachings of the Fathers.[115] David putting the 'priestly dress [i.e. the ephod]

---

[107] O'Reilly, 'Library of Scripture', p. 20; DeGregorio, *Bede: On Ezra and Nehemiah*, p. 232. The garments that do appear are: the rational/breastplate, the headdress (Paul Meyvaert, 'Bede, Cassiodorus and the Codex Amiatinus', *Speculum* 71 (1996), pp. 827–83, at 876–7), and the superhumeral and blue tunic (Paul Meyvaert, 'The Date of Bede's *In Ezram* and his Image of Ezra in the Codex Amiatinus', *Speculum* 80 (2005), pp. 1087–133, at 1120–22).

[108] R. L. S. Bruce-Mitford, *The Art of the Codex Amiatinus*, Jarrow Lecture (Jarrow, 1967), p. 14; questioned most extensively in the work of Celia Chazelle.

[109] Richard Marsden, 'Job in his Place: The Ezra Miniature in the Codex Amiatinus', *Scriptorium* 49 (1995), pp. 3–15.

[110] Karen Corsano, 'The First Quire of the Codex Amiatinus and the *Institutiones* of Cassiodorus', *Scriptorium* 41 (1987), pp. 3–34, at 15–20; Celia Chazelle, '"Romanness" in Early Medieval Culture', in *Paradigms and Methods in Early Medieval Studies*, eds Celia Chazelle and Felice Lifshitz (New York, 2007), pp. 81–98, at 87.

[111] Meyvaert, 'Bede, Cassiodorus', pp. 881–2.

[112] Celia Chazelle, 'Ceolfrid's Gift to St Peter: the First Quire of the Codex Amiatinus and the Evidence of its Roman Destination', *EME* 12 (2004), pp. 129–57, at 155.

[113] O'Reilly, '*Romanitas* of the *Codex Amiatinus*', pp. 379–84.

[114] DeGregorio, *Bede: On Ezra and Nehemiah*, pp. 231–3.

[115] *Sam.*, pp. 27, 118, 209, 214–15.

upon himself' signifies 'when pastors of the Church have been taught within by the grace of their creator through the reading of sacred scripture in which the teachers engaged in the ministry of the word ought always to be clothed'.[116] In other words, in the years when the Codex Amiatinus likely dominated much discussion and thought at Wearmouth-Jarrow, Bede interpreted the vestments of the Aaronic priesthood as emblematic of the kind of preachers he wanted in the Church.[117]

Of course, Bede could have commented on the priestly vestments even if none of his colleagues had ever thought about the matter. His detailed exegesis owes much to Gregory the Great's previous interpretation of the same garments.[118] But Bede cannot have been alone at Wearmouth-Jarrow in reading Gregory's advice for pastors. No doubt the brothers working on the Codex Amiatinus would have discussed Gregory's interpretation of the priestly robes and other influences at the time. We should not imagine the major work in the scriptorium as removed from the communal life of the monastery, nor should we see Bede's writings as distant from such activity. The link between the priestly vestments and preachers appears in Bede's earliest exegesis, alongside a Christological interpretation, the significance of which appears much reduced in later work.[119] The Ezra image did not make available to Bede otherwise unknown interpretations of the priestly garb, but does seem to have inspired a particular interest in interpretations focused on preachers.

The role of the wider Wearmouth-Jarrow community may help us to understand why Bede thought that he had the right and authority to lecture a bishop as he did in the *Letter to Ecgberht*.[120] A simple priest and choir monk, he possessed no official authority over anyone other than perhaps his students. Ecgberht may once have been one of those, but even assuming such a master-pupil relationship does not explain a reform agenda reaching back long before Ecgberht's accession to the episcopate.[121] Seeing Bede not simply as an individual author speaking with personal authority, but as a monk within a wealthy and powerful community where his ideas had arisen from a collective discussion, goes some way towards explaining this situation. The call for more

---

[116] *Sam.*, pp. 261–2 'Dauid igitur applicata ad se stola pontificali . . . cum pastores ecclesiae gratia sui auctoris intus edocti per scripturae sacrae lectionem qua doctores in ministerio uerbi semper oportet indui'.

[117] Thacker, 'Ordering of Understanding', p. 54, sees *On 1 Samuel* as the turning point in Bede's exegesis, which introduced his distinctive later themes.

[118] Gregory, *Regula Pastoralis*, PL 77, II.2–4 col. 23–32; Arthur G. Holder, 'New Treasures and Old in Bede's "De Tabernaculo" and "De Templo"', *RB* 99 (1989), pp. 237–49, at 243; Thacker, 'Ideal of Reform', p. 134.

[119] *Apoc.*, pp. 527, 559; *Sam.*, p. 27; *Tab.*, pp. 96–7.

[120] See George Hardin Brown, 'Bede Both Subject and Superior to the Episcopacy', in *Envisioning the Bishop: Images and the Episcopacy in the Middle Ages*, eds Sigrid Danielson and Evan A. Gatti (Turnhout, 2014), pp. 91–102.

[121] *Vita Alcuini*, ed. W. Arndt, MGH Scriptores 15, 4 p. 186.

monasteries to become episcopal seats may represent an attempt by Wearmouth-Jarrow to improve its own status.[122] In Bede's texts we may hear not just the voice of one monk, but that of a vocal element in the community at Wearmouth-Jarrow.

A recent suggestion that the Ezra image could itself have invoked the idea of the priesthood of all believers raises the question whether the monastery wished to present an image of teachers sharing the spiritual priesthood of the Church, rather than the institutional priesthood of ordination.[123] But considering the papal audience of the codex, the image may equally have been intended to have a clerical reference and the writings from Wearmouth-Jarrow suggest this as the more probable interpretation. We should note the anonymous *Life of Ceolfrith*'s association of Biscop with Moses and Ceolfrith with Aaron—the latter because Ceolfrith was an ordained priest who could perform the sacraments of the altar.[124] This association of the Old Testament priesthood with the institutional priesthood also appears in Bede who opened his discussion of the Aaronic priesthood's vestments with the declaration that their details provided precepts for the 'priests of the Church'.[125]

The Codex Amiatinus shows Ezra robed as an Old Testament high priest (*pontifex*) and DeGregorio has discussed in detail the word *pontifex* in the context of Bede's account of Ezra.[126] He claims that Bede deliberately embraced the anachronism of making Ezra high priest to heighten his relevance to the contemporary Northumbrian Church. Discussing Ezra's role in correcting the leaders of the community, Bede explained the word *pontifex* with 'i.e. an archbishop': one need hardly point out the relevance to the *Letter to Ecgberht*. The Jewish hierarchy thus became directly analogous to the ecclesiastical hierarchy and Ezra's behaviour formed the model for how an archbishop should correct his erring clergy.[127] Interestingly Bede seems to have used *pontifex* in a similar way previously, when he spoke in *On the Tabernacle* of how 'the *pontifex* of our time' ought to pray for the entire human race.[128] He clearly did not mean the Aaronic high priest here, nor Christ; rather Bede seems to have referred to the duties of contemporary bishops to offer up prayers not simply for themselves.

[122] *EpEcg.*, 10 pp. 140–43; Vicky Gunn, *Bede's Historiae: Genre, Rhetoric and the Construction of Anglo-Saxon Church History* (Woodbridge, 2009), pp. 92–3.

[123] Ramirez, 'Iconography of the *Armarium*', p. 11.   [124] *VCeol.*, 6 pp. 84–5.

[125] *Tab.*, p. 95 'habitus recte ecclesiae sacerdotibus congruit'; trans. Holder, p. 109.

[126] DeGregorio, 'Reform of the Northumbrian Church', pp. 19–20; DeGregorio, 'Footsteps of His Own', pp. 164–5.

[127] *Ezra.*, p. 327 'id est archiepiscopum'; see Charles Plummer, *Venerabilis Baedae Opera Historica*, 2 vols (Oxford, 1896), II, p. 384. For other examples of Bede connecting ranks in the Jewish hierarchy to those in the Church: *Ezra.*, pp. 255, 262, 279–80.

[128] *Tab.*, p. 123 'nostri temporis pontifex'.

All this strengthens any link we might want to make in Bede's work between the Jewish priesthood and the ordained clergy. Christian thinkers established this link long before the eighth century and the liturgy for the ordination of bishops explicitly drew on spiritual interpretations of the Aaronic vestments.[129] The Irish clerical elite saw themselves as heirs to the ancient Jewish priesthood—such ideas clearly circulated in an Insular context.[130] This tradition must be set beside that of the priesthood of all believers when considering the links between the priesthood of the temple cult and the *praedicatores* who would reform and lead the contemporary Church in Bede's exegesis. God certainly called all Christians, lay and ordained, to fulfil a spiritual ministry; all the living stones of the temple built up the Church through teaching or at least showing patience to their neighbours.[131] The question is whether all Christians, therefore, were also called to act as pillars of the temple, those *doctores* who would spearhead Bede's envisioned reform.[132] The exact term *presbiter* (referring to the clerical grade of priest) appears rarely in Bede's writings, while *sacerdos* has a wide range of meaning, sometimes applying to priests, sometimes also to bishops: it includes anyone who possesses sacerdotal authority in a general sense.[133] The implication of his references to both the 'ministry of the altar' and 'ministry of the word' is that the exegete sometimes differentiated the ordained from preachers.[134] Evidence therefore exists for reading the conflation of 'priests' with those who preach as potentially referring to either the spiritual priesthood of the body of Christ or the institutional priesthood of the ordained.

Nonetheless, I believe that careful examination of Bede's writings suggests that while the theme of the priesthood of all believers is ecclesiological insofar as it describes the Church's true nature as one with its saviour, it has almost no reformist significance. Bede interpreted the laver in which the priests of the temple washed as a reference to baptism in which all Christians become one with Christ.[135] The theme of spiritual priesthood appeared in his

---

[129] Arthur G. Holder, *Bede: On the Tabernacle* (Liverpool, 1994), p. 109, n. 2; Isidore, *Etymologiae sive Origines*, ed. W. M. Lindsay, 2 vols (Oxford, 1911), VII.XII.13–33; *Liber Sacramentorum Romanae Aeclesiae Ordinis Anni Circuli*, eds Leo Cunibert Mohlberg et al. (Rome, 1960), XCVIV.769 pp. 120–21.

[130] Donnchadh Ó Corráin et al., 'The Laws of the Irish', *Peritia* 3 (1984), pp. 382–438, at 394–400.

[131] *EpCath.*, p. 234; *Temp.*, pp. 156, 169–70; compare Gregory, *In Hiezechihelem*, II.I.5 p. 211.

[132] *Hom.*, II.25 p. 377; *Temp.*, pp. 198–207; *Tab.*, pp. 74–5, 88–90; *Cant.*, p. 240.

[133] *Luc.*, pp. 213–14; Putnam Fennell Jones, *A Concordance to the Historia Ecclesiastica of Bede* (Cambridge MA, 1929), pp. 417–18, 472–3; Benjamin Thomas, 'Priests and Bishops in Bede's Ecclesiology: the use of sacerdos in the *Historia Ecclesiastica Gentis Anglorum*', *Ecclesiology* 6 (2010), pp. 68–93.

[134] *Tab.*, pp. 26, 97; *Temp.*, pp. 194, 209. But *Ezra.*, p. 256, states that preaching, in addition to administering the sacraments, is the role of the minister of the altar.

[135] *Temp.*, pp. 207, 214; *Tab.*, p. 138 is very similar but refers to the compunction of tears, not baptism.

interpretation of David and his men eating the loaves usually reserved for the priests; once again we see the focus on sacramental union with Christ (in the eucharist this time) influencing Bede here.[136] Participation in Christ means that all the faithful become 'kings' and 'christs' as well; 'We rightly', Bede said, 'call all the anointed christs on account of their chrismation', but this hardly means that he believed that all the baptized laity possessed royal power or practical messiahship in any earthly sense.[137] In other words, the reality of the spiritual priesthood in no way undermined or replaced the institutional reality of the clerical hierarchy.[138] Bede also knew, of course, that when Peter called the entire Church 'a kingly priesthood' he had quoted the words of Exodus 19.6 addressed to Israel. Thus Bede interpreted the Jewish priesthood as a figure of the new priesthood in the Church; the image signified the transference of election from Israel exclusively to all the gentile nations.[139]

In other words, if Bede interpreted the Jewish priesthood as symbolizing all Christians in specific cases, he also generally saw it as representing the ordained only. Indeed, the very structure of the temple's priesthood served as a forerunner for the institutional Church of Bede's own day.[140] The Jewish *sacerdos* symbolized Christians who possess the ministry of the altar.[141] Hence, we should take the association of the Aaronic priesthood with the 'priests of the church' at face value: Bede intended the image of the teacher pure in mind and action for the clergy.[142] We can follow Bede's train of thought in one section of *On Ezra and Nehemiah* to see how he connected the ordained with the *doctores* through the image of the Jewish priesthood:

> it is fitting that Ezra entrusts [the gold and silver vessels of the temple] to priests to convey them to Jerusalem, because all who desire to join the community of the Holy Church must be washed in baptism and consecrated to the Lord through the hands of priests . . . And it is well that there are twelve priests to whom this charge was assigned because there are twelve apostles by whose teaching the Church was first established throughout the world and by whose successors it does not cease to be built until the end of the world.[143]

---

[136] 1 Kings 21.4–6; *Luc.*, p. 129 (= *Marc.*, p. 464); *Sam.*, p. 196; compare Ambrose, *Expositio Evangelii*, V.33 p. 147.

[137] *Hom.*, I.16 p. 114; *Apoc.*, p. 509; *Sam.*, p. 25 'Omnes quippe unctos eius chrismate recte christos appellamus'. Caputa, *Sacerdozio dei Fedeli*, pp. 148–51.

[138] Caputa, *Sacerdozio dei Fedeli*, pp. 92–5, 111–13.

[139] *EpCath.*, pp. 237–8; *Sam.*, p. 197; *Luc.*, p. 312; *Reg.*, I p. 297.

[140] *Hom.*, II.19 p. 320.   [141] *Luc.*, p. 245 (see also *Apoc.*, p. 487).

[142] *Tab.*, p. 95.

[143] *Ezra.*, p. 321 'apte . . . uasa sacerdotibus commendat Ezras . . . quia per sacerdotum necesse est manus diluantur in baptismo et consecrentur domino quicumque ad consortium sanctae ecclesiae pertingere desiderant . . . bene duodecim sunt sacerdotes quibus haec cura delegata est propter duodecim apostolos per quorum doctrinam ecclesia et per orbem primo fundata est et usque ad finem saeculi per successores eorum aedificari non desinit'; trans. DeGregorio, p. 130.

Bede easily united the the sacramental ministry of the ordained with the apostolic mission of evangelization and preaching through the Jewish priesthood—the priests are undoubtedly *doctores* of the Church (explicitly stated in the next line).

Bede further linked the priest and the teacher through the image of sacrifice, the supreme duty of the Jewish hierarchy. Preachers aimed to turn Christians into 'living sacrifices' and Bede saw the act of converting someone as offering a sacrifice to God.[144] This imagery makes the most sense when read in connection with Bede's analysis of how Christian priests offered sacrifice through the sacraments. Baptism itself was a sacrifice;[145] or, more correctly explained, baptism proved analogous to the washing of victims in preparation for sacrifice. The Christian only became a burnt offering for the Lord when the fire of the Spirit descended in confirmation through the mediating hands of the bishop.[146] For Bede, conversion required sacramental initiation, thus preachers probably 'sacrificed' through the performance of the sacraments. Hence, he even spoke of *doctores* administering baptism—a statement which makes perfect sense in the light of this analysis and which reveals that usually when Bede spoke of *doctores*, he thought of ordained clergy.[147] Bede's focus on the sacramental aspects of pastoral care in the *Letter to Ecgberht* proves understandable in this light.

THE HIERARCHICAL BODY OF CHRIST

We therefore must take the theology of Christ's body into account when considering Bede's reform agenda—but to do so does not result in the impression that Wearmouth-Jarrow encouraged any radical lay spirituality based on evangelization. But this does not amount to saying that participation in the body of Christ had no practical consequences. Many of the faithful could clearly perform some pastoral and even priestly functions, preaching not least. Bede felt that simply by living an exemplary Christian life, one effectively preached: 'For it is not only one who instructs a brother by word who carries on the ministry of a teacher, but also one who by his example turns him to better things'.[148] Bede stressed the importance of good works and setting a

---

[144] *Ret.*, pp. 140–41; *Luc.*, p. 128 (= *Marc.*, p. 463); compare Jerome, *In Matheum*, eds D. Hurst and M. Adriaen, CCSL 77, p. 88. Giovanni Caputa, 'Aspects of the Priestly Ministry according to Saint Bede', in *Priests of Christ: In the Church for the World*, eds Giovanni Caputa and Julian Fox (Jerusalem, 2010), pp. 70–95, at 82–3.

[145] *Hom.*, II.17 p. 308; *Sam.*, p. 81.

[146] *Temp.*, p. 214; *Cant.*, p. 322. Caputa, 'Priestly Ministry', pp. 83–6.

[147] *Temp.*, pp. 218, 220; Thacker, 'Priests and Pastoral Care', p. 203.

[148] *Hom.*, I.21 pp. 150–51 'Neque enim solum qui uerbo fratrem erudit sed etiam qui exemplo ad meliora conuertit ministerium gerit doctoris'; trans. Martin and Hurst, I, p. 208. Also *EpCath.*, pp. 223–4.

good example to others so frequently that it certainly had a general application to every believer, not just to ecclesiastical *rectores*. But the very fact that he described individuals as 'ordained' to the specific role of *doctor* implies that he did not see it as the automatic state of all Christians, although ordination in the early Middle Ages may not have had a sacramental meaning but rather a broader implication of someone being appointed to a specific office.[149] One could preach without being a *praedicator*—a distinction existed between role and office.[150] This allows us to understand the contradictions that might otherwise arise when looking at the role of women in Bede's theology of the body of Christ.

Two very distinct interpretations of Bede's attitudes to women coexist. The early Anglo-Saxon Church included female religious who possessed extensive wealth, learning, and influence, and Bede openly wrote his commentary on the *Canticle of Habbakuk* to a nun, most likely from just such a background.[151] Some scholars consequently have argued that he believed that female religious could involve themselves in teaching and preaching—for they too were members of the body of Christ, sharers of its spiritual priesthood.[152] Certainly Bede recognized Abbess Ælfflæd of Whitby (654–714) as *magistra* and *doctrix*—at least in a monastic context.[153] But other studies of his attitudes to women suggest that Bede tried to downgrade women's role in the public life of the Church and society in general.[154] On close examination of *On Ezra and Nehemiah* we find that his female 'preachers' (only mentioned because of the specific wording of the biblical text) are not themselves directly building the temple: 'there are many women found who not only by the way they live but also by preaching enkindle the hearts of their neighbours to the praise of their Creator and . . . *assist the labour of those who build the Lord's temple*'.[155] Such women may be able to preach but, denied participation in the

---

[149] *Tab.*, p. 29; *Temp.*, p. 151; *Ezra.*, p. 277; *Hom.*, I.7 p. 49. Gary Macy, *The Hidden History of Women's Ordination: Female Clergy in the Medieval West* (Oxford, 2008), pp. 23–48.

[150] I am indebted to Thomas Charles-Edwards for suggesting this formulation.

[151] *Abac.*, pp. 381, 409.

[152] Sarah Foot, 'Women, Prayer and Preaching in the Early English Church', in *Prayer and Thought in Monastic Tradition: Essays in Honour of Benedicta Ward SLG*, eds Santha Bhattacharji et al. (London, 2014), pp. 59–75; Caputa, *Sacerdozio dei Fedeli*, pp. 268–70.

[153] *HE*, III.24 pp. 292–3, IV.26 pp. 430–31.

[154] Stephanie Hollis, *Anglo-Saxon Women and the Church: Sharing a Common Fate* (Woodbridge, 1992), esp. pp. 269–70, n. 136; Clare A. Lees and Gillian R. Overing, 'Birthing Bishops and Fathering Poets: Bede, Hild, and the Relations of Cultural Production', *Exemplaria* 6 (1994), pp. 35–65; David Pelteret, 'Bede's Women', in *Women, Marriage, and Family in Medieval Christendom: Essays in Memory of Michael M. Sheehan, C.S.B.*, eds Constance M. Rousseau and Joel T. Rosenthal (Kalamazoo MI, 1998), pp. 19–46.

[155] *Ezra.*, p. 257 'plurimae . . . personae quae non solum uiuendo uerum etiam praedicando corda proximorum ad laudem sui creatoris accendant et . . . *aedificantium templum domini adiuuent laborem*'; adapted from trans. DeGregorio, p. 32 (my emphasis).

sacramental priesthood, they could never hold the office of preacher, could never be builders of the temple.

Bede did not consider all members of the body of Christ as equal and when we look at his temple commentaries we see that his ideal reformed Church retains important hierarchical distinctions. Bede made a frequent simple distinction between the perfect (*perfecti*) and the majority of Christians, the carnal (*carnales*). All Christians must obey the ten commandments but those who go further and do things not strictly required for salvation are counted perfect; in particular Bede emphasized the rejection of private property and celibacy as optional routes leading to perfection.[156] Such a focus makes it very probable that he considered perfection as a reward for the monastic state, separated from the rest of society by vows of chastity and poverty—certainly Bede's homily on Benedict Biscop links very clearly the perfection of renouncing wealth and marriage with the monasticism of Wearmouth-Jarrow.[157] The contrast between the (bronze) altar of holocausts and the (gold) altar of incense also helps explain the difference between the perfect and the carnal. The altar of holocausts represents those who offer up their own fleshly desires to God by struggling against them; the altar of incense symbolizes those who have escaped all such desires and thus constantly offer prayers of love and longing to God.[158] Bede understood this contrast in relation to ideas about compunction arising from a deeply Gregorian background. The perfect of the altar of incense possess the compunction of love, the end state to which the monastic life leads.[159] Sometimes Bede did differentiate between the perfect and beginners (*incipientes*), implying room for development, but usually he insisted that the perfect, an elite minority, would always be much fewer in number than the carnal.[160]

Alongside this twofold division appear a number of threefold divisions deriving from the patristic hierarchy of the married, continent, and the rulers/preachers of the Church.[161] Initially Bede seems to have followed this traditional approach with some variations in vocabulary.[162] In *On the*

---

[156] *Temp.*, pp. 175, 194–6; *Ezra.*, pp. 259, 269; *Tab.*, p. 24.

[157] *Hom.*, I.13 pp. 88–94.   [158] *Temp.*, pp. 176, 224–5; *Tab.*, pp. 125–6, 131–2.

[159] *Tab.*, pp. 132, 136–7; compare Gregory, *In Hiezechihelem*, II.X.21 pp. 395–6. Carole Straw, *Gregory the Great: Perfection in Imperfection* (Berkeley CA, 1988), pp. 223–5; Jean Leclercq, *The Love of Learning and the Desire for God: A Study of Monastic Culture*, trans. Catherine Misrahi, 3rd ed. (New York, 1982), pp. 29–32.

[160] *Sam.*, p. 20; *Luc.*, p. 200; *Temp.*, pp. 194, 225–6. Caputa, *Sacerdozio dei Fideli*, pp. 123–4; Arthur G. Holder, 'The Venerable Bede on the Mysteries of Our Salvation', *American Benedictine Review* 421 (1991), pp. 140–62, at 151–2.

[161] Leyser, *Authority and Asceticism*, pp. 12, 156; Gregory, *In Hiezechihelem*, II.IV.5 pp. 261–2; Augustine, *Enarrationes in Psalmos*, eds E. Dekkers and J. Fraipont, CCSL 38–40, CXXXII.4–5 pp. 1928–30.

[162] E.g. *Sam.*, p. 97; *Luc.*, p. 321. Bede followed tradition in making Noah, Daniel, and Job represent the different ranks: Georges Folliet, 'Les trois categories de chrétiens: Survie d'un thème augustinien', *L'Année Théologique Augustinienne* 49–50 (1954), pp. 81–96.

Tabernacle, however, a slippage occurs between the continent and the *rectores*, as the virginity that marks the one group passes to the other. Preaching *and* virginity mark out *rectores*: 'the merit of those who preach is more sublime than that of those who are zealous to devote themselves to continence only, and not to the work of teaching as well'.[163] Indeed when Bede came to sum up on his discussion, virgins had completely replaced *rectores*. Having first stated that 'both before and after the Lord's incarnation there were in the Church three states of those who served the Lord faithfully, namely: the married, the continent, and the rulers', he finished up referring to 'the three grades of the faithful of which we have spoken more than once (namely, the married, the continent, and the virgins)'.[164] A few years later in *On the Temple* Bede had completed the transformation of this trinity; virgins had become the top level of the hierarchy with the continent reduced to those practising conjugal abstinence.[165] Aldhelm set out a very similar threefold hierarchy of chastity and both writers shared an interest in those who had abandoned the married life, a practice not uncommon in Anglo-Saxon monasticism at the time.[166] But whereas Aldhelm had concerned himself with sexual purity, Bede's hierarchy had a wider significance as virgins clearly performed leadership duties within the Church. One could not consider the paterfamilias of a secular household a *rector* under such a scheme that significantly combined preaching, virginity, and leadership.

This seems to indicate a monastic ideal for preaching. Many early Anglo-Saxon monastic foundations did engage regularly with the surrounding laity, and members would have provided essential pastoral care either in the monastery itself or while travelling.[167] On one occasion Bede stated that the less 'perfect', i.e. those represented by the altar of bronze, must provide preachers since the gold altar represents those who find it almost impossible to express their contemplative experiences.[168] However, often elsewhere he indicated that the *perfecti* must supply *doctores* and *praedicatores*.[169] This seems consistent with the divergence noted between Bede and Gregory the Great's attitudes to contemplation;[170] for Bede, while the possibility of limited

---

[163] *Tab.*, p. 32 'sublimius est meritum praedicantium quam eorum qui solummodo continentiae et non etiam operi doctrinae student'; trans. Holder, p. 34.

[164] *Tab.*, pp. 31 'et ante et post incarnationem dominicam terni fuere gradus eorum qui fideliter in ecclesia domino seruirent coniugatorum uidelicet continentium et rectorum', pp. 34–5 'tribus fidelium gradibus de quibus saepius diximus coniugatorum uidelicet continentium et uirginum'; trans. Holder, pp. 33–4, 37.

[165] *Temp.*, p. 163 (linked with the twofold distinction between perfect and carnal).

[166] Michael Lapidge and Michael Herren, *Aldhelm: The Prose Works* (Cambridge, 1979), pp. 53–6. See also Augustine, *DCD*, XV.26 p. 494.

[167] Sarah Foot, *Monastic Life in Anglo-Saxon England, c.600–900* (Cambridge, 2006), pp. 285–321.

[168] *Tab.*, p. 125.   [169] *Temp.*, p. 196; *Ezra.*, pp. 248, 272, 380; *Tab.*, pp. 5, 9–10, 52.

[170] Scott DeGregorio, 'The Venerable Bede on Prayer and Contemplation', *Traditio* 54 (1999), pp. 1–39, at 26–32.

contemplation existed, one could never escape the active life of ministering to others.[171] However, some *perfecti* can enjoy the delights of contemplation in this world and for Bede, as for Gregory, the preacher must turn inwards on occasion, recharging their spiritual batteries with meditation.[172]

References that seem to suggest that preachers both must and cannot come from amongst the perfect, that Old Testament priests can refer to either all Christians or just to the clergy, remind us that Bede did not seek to create a systematic vision of the Church through his exegesis. A methodological risk exists in taking the thematic approach that underlies the present study, as it can impose on Bede's works a coherence and harmony never intended when he wrote them. Constant references to *doctores* and *perfecti* across many different works (the effort of many years) may create an illusion of consistency of thought behind the mere consistency of vocabulary. I feel then that we should not see inconsistencies within the commentaries as fatal blows to a Bedan 'system' since Bede never consciously intended to create such a system. Getting a sense for the overall tenor of Bede's work or the general world view that emerges from it will probably prove more fruitful than searching for any system. The exact boundaries between the preaching of the laity and that of ordained ministers remain rather fuzzy for us, because they probably were unclear for Bede also.

Nonetheless the context in (and the audience for) which Bede wrote undoubtedly framed the intended meaning of much of his work. We must remember therefore that that audience was not primarily lay: while he dedicated the *Ecclesiastical History* to a layman, whether King Ceolwulf could read remains an unanswered question.[173] Bede's corpus appears overwhelmingly in intention aimed at and in practice read by clerical figures in monastic communities.[174] This means that frequently when Bede seems to have given general advice on how to behave, he probably had this audience primarily in his mind. Such an audience could include women, of course, but men would have dominated in it although split between those who had been ordained and the lay religious; on the whole the community Bede intended to address would not have been dissimilar to that found at his own monastery. We must keep in mind the underlying context of an environment where mutual religious teaching and support were expected and where many (though not all) of the

---

[171] *Hom.*, I.9 pp. 64–5; *Act.*, p. 52; *Temp.*, pp. 219–20; *Tab.*, p. 22.

[172] *Temp.*, pp. 152, 162, 220; *Tab.*, p. 10; *Luc.*, pp. 310–11. Gregory, *Regula*, IV col. 125–128, II.5 col. 32–34.

[173] N. J. Higham, *(Re-)Reading Bede: The* Ecclesiastical History *in Context* (London, 2006), pp. 41–4.

[174] Much secondary literature has presented Bede's works as designed to train other monks or priests to engage in preaching: Carroll, *Spiritual Teachings*, p. 154; Judith McClure, 'Bede's *Notes on Genesis* and the Training of the Anglo-Saxon Clergy', in *The Bible in the Medieval World: Essays in Memory of Beryl Smalley*, eds Katherine Walsh and Diana Wood (Oxford, 1985), pp. 17–30; Thacker, 'Ordering of Understanding'.

male inmates had received ordination. Of course, such an audience in turn had to engage with the laity, had to teach them, and inculcate a sense of the dignity of being Christian in them. Thus on occasion Bede certainly gave advice for all Christians, and on occasion for religious in particular.[175]

Therefore when he stated that one ought to choose those who teach (equated with priests) only from amongst the 'spiritual servants of God' ('de coetu spiritalium Dei famulorum') should we take this as clear proof that Bede conceived of preachers as being monks?[176] While the title *famulus Dei* could also apply to others (such as the saintly King Oswald), usually *famulus* and *famula* refer to an individual in the monastic life.[177] Clearly then Bede saw a link between monastic perfection and the life of the preacher, but the monastic state and the office of preacher do not overlap simply and straightforwardly. The fact that Bede seems to have seen the monastic state as a model way of life that ought to influence how all Christians lived their lives might complicate the situation.[178] In the debate over the relative virtues of the monastic and clerical ways of life, Bede clearly argued for the value of monasticism as the best spiritual context from which to undertake ordained ministry.[179] Bede believed that all priests should make the essential choices that made one perfect (effectively the rejection of property and sex). His attitudes to sexuality highly conditioned by his monastic state, Bede considered sexual activity inappropriate for priests. Just as for Jewish priests, sex polluted the Christian cleric and rendered the sacraments invalid—but while the Jewish hierarchy worked in shifts, the Christian priest required the unmarried freedom to sacrifice at all times.[180] Bede sat on the extreme (albeit better recorded) edge of opinion for his time.[181] The *Letter to Ecgberht* envisages a plan of extending regular communion to the laity—so long as they maintain sexual purity of course.[182] If ever put into action such a plan would have marginalized the married, although they could receive the sacrament if they restrained their conjugal activity within exceptionally narrow limits.[183] In his commentary on 1 Peter, Bede let slip his ideal for married couples—total abstinence.[184]

---

[175] For the moral advice in *On Ezra and Nehemiah* having a monastic/Benedictine hue: Scott DeGregorio, 'Bede and Benedict of Nursia', in *Early Medieval Studies in Memory of Patrick Wormald*, eds Stephen Baxter et al. (Farnham, 2009), pp. 151–63, at 158–62. For Bede conceiving of a wider audience than just his fellow clerics: Gerald Bonner, 'The Christian Life in the Thought of the Venerable Bede', *Durham University Journal* 63 (1970), pp. 39–55, at 44–6.

[176] *Tab.*, p. 29. See Thacker, 'Monks', p. 153.   [177] Jones, *Concordance*, p. 202.

[178] Tugène, *L'idée de nation*, pp. 244–5; Thacker, 'Monks', p. 159.

[179] Clare Stancliffe, 'Disputed episcopacy: Bede, Acca and the relationship between Stephen's *Life of Wilfrid* and the early prose Lives of St Cuthbert', *ASE* 41 (2012), pp. 7–39.

[180] *Tab.*, pp. 116, 121; *Luc.*, pp. 27–8; *Sam.*, p. 30.

[181] Thacker, 'Priests and Pastoral Care', pp. 190–91.   [182] *EpEcg.*, 15 pp. 154–5.

[183] Thacker, 'Monks', pp. 154–5.

[184] *EpCath.*, pp. 243–4. Carroll, *Spiritual Teachings*, pp. 241–2, interprets this text as only referring to priests since Bede elsewhere supported marriage—thus engaging in the kind of

Many ordained clergy in Bede's Northumbria probably had wives and active sex lives.[185] Bede probably disapproved of 'false monasteries' in part because their leaders generally were married and thus, in his eyes, could not provide the priestly pastoral care that mattered so much.[186] Hence the link between preachers and virginity in the commentaries, and the demands for sacerdotal purity; these form not separate interests but a linked vision of a reformed clergy, carrying out their active ministry while following a rigorously monastic way of life. Monastic communities at the time probably did engage in pastoral care primarily through their ordained brethren.[187] A community of 'perfect' contained ordained priests who could provide the laity with the sacramental care Bede demanded, while also giving a home to those other *perfecti* whose contemplative way of life lay above communicating with the wider world. Bede's great respect for the clerical life depended on it having blurred into the monastic, reflecting the circumstances of religious communities in his own age and seen in his own sense of pride at being both *presbiter* and *famulus Christi*.[188]

This essential mixture of the clerical and the monastic lifestyles probably explains the mixing of humility and authority within Bede's reform agenda. Bede, on occasion, identified himself with preachers and those who have to teach others; but he also identified himself with those lesser, imperfect individuals, who require guidance.[189] The willingness to humble oneself and learn proved the necessary preparation to exercising authority and teaching others. Christ had asked questions of the elders in the temple in order to set an example for teachers who themselves need to be taught first.[190] We must remember that for Bede, as for Gregory, the issue of preaching essentially consisted of moral authority.[191] *Doctores* did not merely perform the necessary function of evangelizing or instructing others; they led the Church and did so wielding great spiritual power. Their moral purity partly presented a necessary limitation on abuse of that power, but also a justification for its use. To simply claim possession of such authority without humility would, in

---

harmonizing approach which irons out contradictions; Bede's defence of marriage at *Gen.*, pp. 28–9, fast becomes a celebration of the superiority of virginity.

[185] Catherine Cubitt, 'The Clergy in early Anglo-Saxon England', *Historical Research* 78 (2005), pp. 273–87.

[186] *EpEcg.*, 13 pp. 148–9; Thacker, 'Priests and Pastoral Care', p. 202.

[187] Foot, *Monastic Life*, pp. 332–3.

[188] Henry Mayr-Harting, *The Venerable Bede, The Rule of St Benedict, and Social Class*, Jarrow Lecture (Jarrow, 1976), pp. 14–15, 17; Thacker, 'Priests and Pastoral Care', pp. 203–7; Carroll, *Spiritual Teachings*, pp. 239–40. Contemporaries described different types of community, clerical and monastic, using the same language: Foot, *Monastic Life*, p. 4.

[189] *Ezra.*, pp. 264, 303; *Temp.*, pp. 153, 155. Association with less perfect: *Ezra.*, p. 375; *Tab.*, p. 7, 80; *Temp.*, p. 232.

[190] *Hom.*, I.19 pp. 135–6.

[191] This paragraph is influenced by Leyser, *Authority and Asceticism*.

essence, undermine that claim. Notice the painstaking protestations of humility beside strident demands in the *Letter to Ecgberht*: perhaps the clearest expression of Bede's claim to authority.

That humility is a monastic attribute, of course, for monks lived their lives in imitation of Christ who humbly stooped down to earth, took on a real human body, and then offered that up to the Father in sacrifice. That incarnation and sacrifice made Christ a priest and he passed on his priesthood to all his body, the entire community of believers that formed the Church. We have seen the complexity of the priesthood of the Church for Bede: spiritually it referred to the very real union between Christians and their saviour, but when it came to the practical business of reforming the Northumbrian Church, Bede believed that only the monastic clergy could take the lead. This reminds us that the temple Church did not just exist on a cosmic scale stretching across space and time, nor simply as the metaphoric body of Christ; Bede was very much concerned with the institution that had to grapple with corruption and impiety in a less-than-perfect world. We turn to that aspect of the temple as Church in the next chapter.

6

Bede's Temple as Church

'The house of God ... was made as a figure of the holy universal Church': thus Bede began his exegesis of Solomon's temple.[1] The building up of the temple represented the great development of the Church through time; the richness of the temple's decoration signified the diversity of different people within the community of the elect. In the previous three chapters we have seen how Bede understood much about the Church's spiritual nature through reference to the temple image: its historical development, its universal reach, and its identity with the body of Christ, in particular. The last chapter raised the question of how the spiritual nature of the Church, as it appears in Bede's exegesis of the temple, related to the quotidian reality of the institutional Church within which Bede lived. Here I want to look at how Bede used the temple to understand that institution, its members, and its relationship with rival religious groupings, all the while keeping an eye on the Church in contemporary Northumbria. Taking up from the importance of reform (raised in the last chapter) I study the little-discussed excursus on the temple in *On Genesis* to explore how Bede understood the relationship between true and false ecclesiastical institutions. This analysis raises the question as to the relationship between the sacramental institution of the Church and the cosmic community of the elect, the body of Christ—a question to which I turn at the end of this chapter.

While Bede feared that there were areas of Northumbria into which institutional Christianity had yet to reach, it seems unlikely that any visitor to that or any other Anglo-Saxon kingdom in the early eighth century could have failed to be struck by the Church's dramatic impact on society. Journeying through the kingdom the visitor would have come across dozens of religious houses dotted throughout the landscape—not all perhaps as visually dramatic as Wilfrid's monastery at Hexham, but all reflecting a genuine social revolution.[2] Across Europe the early Middle Ages saw an unprecedented transfer of

---

[1] *Temp.*, p. 147 'Domus Dei ... in figuram facta est sanctae uniuersalis ecclesiae'; trans. Connolly, p. 5. Also *Ezra.*, p. 241; *Tab.*, pp. 42–3.

[2] *VW*, XXII pp. 44–7.

landed wealth into the hands of the Church.[3] In Northumbria this transfer mainly came not in the form of vast donations to bishoprics but of large numbers of aristocrats turning their own properties into monasteries, established by charter. The economic advantages of doing this (whether exemption from military obligations or the opportunity to avail oneself of a particularly secure and alienable form of landholding, with the chance to make land directly inheritable by one's descendants rather than returned to the king or the wider kin group on death[4]) provided a clear incentive for this behaviour. Bede bemoaned, in his *Letter to Ecgberht*, aristocrats who set up false monasteries under royal charter, which they ruled despite remaining married and knowing nothing of the monastic life.[5] Such foundations proved 'neither of use to God nor men'; with regard to their use for men, Bede warned that 'false' monasteries were misusing land that could have been used to support Northumbria's military needs.[6] Ecgberht, Bede suggested, should tear up the charters for false monasteries and seize their land. Monasteries would become the seats for new bishops whom these communities would elect, thus helping to address Northumbria's pastoral care deficit.[7] Bede hoped that King Ceolwulf, Ecgberht's kinsman, would assist the bishop in these reforms.[8]

Bede probably responded to a growing debate about the possible dangers of so much land being redesignated as monastic (and the consequences especially for the kingdom's military health) rather than functioned as a solitary voice crying in the wilderness.[9] While the major institutional response to the crisis came shortly after Bede's death (both in synods seeking to respond to criticism of religious communities and kings trying to claw back monastic land), the *Letter to Ecgberht* attempts to set decisively the moral framework for the debate that clearly had to come.[10] By identifying a distinctive group of wicked 'false' monasteries and by arguing that their land should be repurposed to support an alliance of good monasteries and the episcopacy, Bede tried to neutralize the toxic effects which the growth in (corruptly gained) religious lands could have on the entire ecclesiastical establishment. As John Blair has

---

[3] Ian Wood, 'Entrusting Western Europe to the Church, 400–750', *Transactions of the Royal Historical Society* 6th Series 23 (2013), pp. 37–73.

[4] Patrick Wormald, 'Bede and the Conversion of England: The Charter Evidence', repr. in *The Times of Bede*, ed. Stephen Baxter (Oxford, 2006), pp. 135–66; Richard Abels, *Lordship and Military Obligation in Anglo-Saxon England* (London, 1988), pp. 28–30.

[5] *EpEcg.*, 9–13 pp. 140–51.

[6] *EpEcg.*, 11 pp. 142–3 'neque Deo neque hominibus utilia sunt', 144–5.

[7] *EpEcg.*, 9–10 pp. 138–43.   [8] *EpEcg.*, 9 pp. 138–9, 11 pp. 144–5.

[9] I am indebted to John Blair for sharing, some years ago now, many of his insights into this question.

[10] Catherine Cubitt, *Anglo-Saxon Church Councils c.650–c.850* (London, 1995), pp. 100–101, 112–13; John Blair, *The Church in Anglo-Saxon Society* (Oxford, 2005), pp. 121–34; Christopher Grocock and I. N. Wood, *Abbots of Wearmouth and Jarrow* (Oxford, 2013), pp. lvi–lviii. For the importance of Bede in developing the idea of the 'false' monastery: Blair, *Anglo-Saxon Society*, pp. 106–7.

stated, 'there clearly was a principled drive for reform, but it could all too easily become a cloak for asset-stripping'—it was to avoid such a danger that Bede acted.[11] Wearmouth-Jarrow's own attempts to prove itself something other than just another aristocratic monastery, underpinned by an apparent fear that its ownership of some lands might be challenged (Wilfrid's career having made it clear that ecclesiastical land was by no means entirely secure), suggests that this was an issue which might have mattered close to home.[12]

The identification of good and bad, true and false religious communities partly served, therefore, as a means of vigorously defending the Church's status in Anglo-Saxon society. Such a purpose linked quite closely with Bede's spiritual and reform agenda. We have seen that he had a vision of an ideal Church, which imbued all people with Christian charity, but especially a clerical elite of preachers and teachers who, while ordained to the higher orders, continued to lead the regular life. Monasteries were to provide the spiritual as well as the economic material necessary for the reform of the Northumbrian Church, as was clear from Bede's suggestion that monastic communities would elect the new bishops.[13] Bede felt that the greed which led aristocrats to play at the religious life also infected the bishops who failed to appoint sufficient *doctores* to meet the needs of the laity. Bede's letter to the bishop of York attacked a corrupt and false type of Christianity that prevented the Church fulfilling its true goal in Northumbria and (by implication) risked dragging it into disrepute and ruin.

Turning back to Bede's exegesis of the temple image, we will find that he addressed many of these concerns years before writing to Ecgberht. While the temple could represent the Church as it ought to be, and its priesthood the Christian clergy as they should behave, the image could also be manipulated to reveal that there were sinister forces at work in the world, opposed but suspiciously similar to the one true Church. Bede's preachers and teachers did not just spread the true faith, they also had to defend it from its opponents: they acted as doors bringing in new souls or walls excluding all sorts of undesirables.[14] Just like Wearmouth-Jarrow, the temple Church faced threats and Bede's writings display a real sense of the Church as locked in constant struggle with external forces. *On Ezra and Nehemiah* contains much condemnation of episcopal greed, but has almost as much to say about the importance of defending against heresy—a topic barely mentioned in the *Letter to Ecgberht*. But Bede's assault on heresy may still prove relevant to the letter as we shall see.

---

[11] Blair, *Anglo-Saxon Society*, p. 107.
[12] Ian Wood, 'The Foundation of Bede's Wearmouth-Jarrow', in *The Cambridge Companion to Bede*, ed. Scott DeGregorio (Cambridge, 2010), pp. 84–96, at 87.
[13] *EpEcg.*, 10 pp. 140–43. For contemporary practice: Catherine Cubitt, 'Wilfrid's "Usurping Bishops": Episcopal Elections in Anglo-Saxon England, *c.*600–*c.*800', *Northern History* 25 (1989), pp. 18–38.
[14] *Cant.*, p. 350.

THE TEMPLE VERSUS THE TOWER

Towards the end of his interpretation of the tower of Babel in *On Genesis*, Bede deployed an elaborate contrast between the tower and its city, Babylon, and the temple and its city, Jerusalem.[15] The contrast extended to the materials from which both buildings were constructed and made use of the kind of architectural allegory so common in his interpretation of the temple. Bede, deriving the popular basic contrast between Jerusalem and Babylon from tradition, seems to have had no predecessors for the comparison of the architectural details of the tower and temple.[16] The Bible gives details concerning the construction of both buildings and, in stating that the builders of the tower 'had bricks instead of stones and pitch instead of mortar', suggests some significant contrast.[17] So Bede applied the manner of interpretation he used in his temple commentaries to the tower. The comparison highlighted points of both similarity and difference. The temple represented the Church and the tower represented those religious groups ranged against it: the Jews, pagans (conceived, here at least, in terms of classical philosophy), heretics, and false Catholics—all part of a diabolic community, the City of the Devil which mimicked the City of God.[18]

The contrast between the tower and temple allows us to examine how Bede set up these two communities in contrast to each other, two societies in constant conflict—the one good and the other evil. The unified society of good, the Church, focused on the divine, whereas the discordant society of evil had purely earthly interests.[19] Throughout Bede's mature work this theme of the cosmic battle between the body of Christ and that of Satan appears, as noted by Hilliard who has drawn attention to the importance of the language of spiritual warfare in the exegesis.[20] Nonetheless, the comparison of the tower and the temple highlights the fact that Bede saw many points of valid comparison as well as contrast between these two communities, the Church on the one hand and its rivals on the other. This sense of the similarity between rival institutions, and Bede's fierce emphasis on the essential difference, seems to relate, I argue, to the Northumbrian context as presented in the

---

[15] *Gen.*, pp. 157–62.

[16] *Reg.*, XXX pp. 320–1; *Ezra.*, p. 253; Johannes van Oort, *Jerusalem and Babylon: A Study of Augustine's* City of God *and the Sources of his Doctrine of the Two Cities* (Leiden, 1991), pp. 118–23. Jerome, *In Esaiam*, ed. M. Adriaen, CCSL 73+A, p. 771, contrasted inhabitants of the temple with the builders of the tower, but made no comparison of the structures.

[17] Genesis 11.3, as per trans. Kendall, p. 228—Douay-Rheims translates *bitumen* as 'slime'.

[18] *Gen.*, p. 161.

[19] Jan Davidse, 'The Sense of History in the Works of the Venerable Bede', *Studi Medievali* 23 (1982), pp. 647–95, at 678–9.

[20] Paul Hilliard, 'Sacred and Secular History in the Writings of Bede (†735)', (PhD thesis, University of Cambridge, 2007), pp. 67–8, 80–81, 85, 101–2, 112–13, 121–3, 172–5, 188–90, 219–23.

Letter to Ecgberht. The close proximity of varying responses to the same religious ethos primed Bede's imagination to understand that heretics, pagans, and contemporary Jews sought to fulfil a similar purpose to that of the Church.

Bede recognized that these groups 'are attempting to build the whiteness of innocence, the strength of faith, and the harmony of brotherhood', just like the Church.[21] But, however much heretics or schismatics may seem to rise up they inevitably fall because they are acting outside the Church.[22] While the tower sought to rise up to heaven though built on an earthly plain, the temple rested atop the heavenly mountain which is Christ; the bricks of the tower represented souls hardened in pride against God and the stones of the temple symbolized those broken in humility so as to be turned into unifying mortar.[23] Elsewhere Bede acknowledged that non-Christians may seem superficially to lead good lives. Greek philosophers such as Diogenes mastered the ascetic lifestyle, but that helped them not in the least since they did not follow the Lord.[24] Heretics occasionally performed good works or miracles, they believed they offered sacrifices of prayer and work, but their incorrect beliefs corrupted everything.[25] False Catholics also contaminate their sacrifices with alien fire because they do good works only for the wrong reasons.[26] For Bede no single part of the good life proved sufficient for salvation, which required the possession of it all. The builders of the tower may have had the same aims as those of the temple, but they would never achieve them.

Bede understood the world through a Tyconian and Augustinian lens: the City of God had its shadow double, the City of the Devil.[27] As all true orthodox Christians formed one temple, one house of God, one body of Christ, the heretics, pagans, Jews, and schismatics formed the tower of Babel, the house the Devil built up throughout the world, the body of which Satan was head.[28]

---

[21] *Gen.*, pp. 160–61 'candorem innocentiae, robur fidei, concordiam fraternitatis . . . munire conantur'; trans. Kendall, p. 237. Compare Augustine's argument that all humans (both good and bad) desire and work towards peace: Augustine, *DCD*, XIX.12 pp. 675–8.

[22] *Temp.*, p. 164.   [23] *Gen.*, pp. 158–60.

[24] *Ezra.*, p. 265; *Hom.*, I.13 p. 88. For Bede's attitude to philosophers: Arthur G. Holder, 'Using Philosophers to Think With: The Venerable Bede on Christian Life and Practice', in *The Subjective Eye: Essays in Culture, Religion, and Gender in Honor of Margaret R. Miles*, ed. Richard Valantasis (Eugene OR, 2006), pp. 48–58.

[25] *Tab.*, p. 105; *Ezra.*, p. 295; *Prov.*, pp. 58, 87.

[26] *Tab.*, p. 78. Also *Hom.*, II.1 pp. 186–7; *EpCath.*, pp. 185, 310–11. For a neat summation of the difference between heretics and false Catholics: Augustine, *Quaestiones XVI in Matthaeum*, ed. A. Mutzenbecher, CCSL 44B, XI p. 125.

[27] Augustine, *Enarrationes in Psalmos*, eds E. Dekkers and J. Fraipont, CCSL 38–40, LXIV.1–4 pp. 822–7; Augustine, *DCD*, XV.1 pp. 453–4. Tyconius' 'two-cities' analysis forms a major theme in Bede's commentary on the Apocalypse: *Apoc.*, pp. 379, 475, 487; see Gerald Bonner, *Saint Bede in the Tradition of Western Apocalyptic Commentary*, Jarrow Lecture (Jarrow, 1966); van Oort, *Jerusalem and Babylon*, pp. 267–74.

[28] *Ezra.*, p. 251; *Luc.*, p. 151; *Sam.*, p. 169. The tower as the Devil's city: *Ret.*, p. 127; *Gen.*, pp. 158–9.

This tendency to group all types of non-Catholics together appears throughout Bede's work:[29] pagan philosophers taught the heretics;[30] false Catholics and heretics choose to attack the Church together;[31] while calling themselves Christians such people remain heathen in nature.[32] Augustine understood this basic two-city dichotomy as arising from two different loves, the love of God versus the love of the world, and constructed an elaborate theory to support it.[33] Bede followed this analysis, albeit on somewhat simpler lines: the community of the wicked defined itself by its earthly nature and worldly purposes.[34]

Hence the tower built of bricks made from clay and bound together by pitch drawn up from the pits of the earth highlighted, through allegory, the earthly focus of the builders.[35] The Jews who rejected Christ failed to understand that the Messiah came as God and not simply as an earthly king.[36] Heretics and false Catholics followed their own earthly ideas and desires, in a manner akin to the idolatry to which the true temple of the Lord had historically been opposed.[37] O'Reilly has pointed out that Bede always represented Anglo-Saxon paganism as biblical idolatry—the worship of earthly creations rather than the divine Creator.[38] Bede used the model of idolatry, prioritizing earth over the divine, to define any form of behaviour of which he disapproved. He framed the 'false Catholics' attacked in the *Letter to Ecgberht* as idolaters who had set up their charters as a form of diabolic scripture, just as pagans worshipped things made by human hands and the Pharisees preferred their own traditions to the Law of God.[39] Contemporary Northumbrians in less strict monasteries than Wearmouth-Jarrow belonged to the Devil's city;

---

[29] *Sam.*, p. 270; *Marc.*, p. 623; *Apoc.*, p. 461 lists the same four types of non-Catholics as *On Genesis* but in three groups following Primasius, *Commentarius in Apocalypsin*, ed. A. W. Adams, CCSL 92, IV.16 p. 235. Also *Act.*, p. 78; *EpCath.*, p. 297.

[30] *Ezra.*, pp. 285–6, 391; *Sam.*, p. 267. Holder, 'Philosophers', pp. 54–5.

[31] *Ezra.*, p. 282; *Tab.*, p. 51; *Hom.*, II.25 p. 373.

[32] *Ezra.*, p. 356. For the narrow boundary between bad Christians and heathens: R. A. Markus, 'Gregory the Great's Pagans', in *Belief and Culture in the Middle Ages: Studies Presented to Henry Mayr-Harting*, eds Richard Gameson and Henrietta Leyser (Oxford, 2001), pp. 23–34.

[33] Augustine, *De Doctrina Christiana*, ed. and trans. R. P. H. Green (Oxford, 1995), Book I; van Oort, *Jerusalem and Babylon*, pp. 142–5.

[34] See Hilliard, 'Sacred and Secular History', pp. 123, 170–75, 219–23.

[35] *Gen.*, pp. 159–60.   [36] *Ezra.*, p. 262; *Hom.*, II.24 p. 359.

[37] *Ezra.*, pp. 313, 356; see also *Tab.*, p. 94, on the preacher's duty to preach God's word and not their own. *Act.*, p. 36; *Reg.*, XXXIV p. 319; *Temp.*, p. 160—the word *simulacra* for idols emphasizes their artificial and constructed nature.

[38] Jennifer O'Reilly, 'Islands and Idols at the Ends of the Earth: Exegesis and Conversion in Bede's *Historia Ecclesiastica*', in *Bède le Vénérable entre tradition et postérité: The Venerable Bede. Tradition and Posterity*, eds Stéphane Lebecq et al. (Lille, 2005), pp. 119–45, at 135–8; *HE*, III.22 pp. 280–83; *Ezra.*, p. 356. See also Augustine, *DCD*, XIV.28 p. 452.

[39] *EpEcg.*, 17 pp. 156–9.

explicitly guilty of the very sin that lead to the angelic fall, they implicitly became builders of the tower and not of the temple.[40]

Bede believed, therefore, that the earthly and self-interested aims of the Church's rivals undermined their religious ideals and apparently valid goals. In the same way the sellers in the temple had sold things necessary for the temple cult but Christ still drove them out; Bede understood them as individuals who provided ecclesiastical services for earthly profit.[41] Since the Hebrews had given their goods freely to build the tabernacle, so too one ought to build the Church without consideration of material reward.[42] A long tradition existed associating the traders in the temple with corrupt greed amongst the Christian clergy,[43] but this may have had resonances in Anglo-Saxon England which Bede connected to the behaviour condemned in the *Letter to Ecgberht*. A contemporary charter for the foundation of Crediton monastery actually speaks of 'buying' eternal goods with material wealth.[44] Bede did not just condemn the search for monetary riches, but also the desire for earthly favour rather than a heavenly reward.[45] He drew, once again, on patristic tradition here, but in the early eighth century Northumbrian monastic leaders knew how important it was to maintain good relations with lay elites, and thus could easily get sucked into aristocratic gift-giving and wealth exchange.[46] Ceolfrith's desire to avoid receiving any gifts from local grandees implies that such issues affected Wearmouth-Jarrow as much as elsewhere.[47]

Following Gregory the Great, Bede read the corruption of the temple ('the life of the religious in the faithful people') as the secularization of the religious and clerical way of life when those who 'receive the religious habit . . . assign the duty of religion according to the commerce of earthly business'; his condemnation of those 'perverse men' who hold a 'place of religion' but use it to cause spiritual harm rather than engaging in life-giving intercession

---

[40] *EpEcg.*, 17 pp. 158–61. [41] *Hom.*, II.1 pp. 186–7; *Marc.*, p. 579; *Luc.*, p. 349.

[42] *EpCath.*, pp. 256–7.

[43] Jerome, *In Matheum*, eds D. Hurst and M. Adriaen, CCSL 77, p. 188; Gregory, *Homiliae in Evangelia*, ed. R. Étaix, CCSL 141, XVII.13 p. 127; Augustine, *In Iohannis Evangelium Tractatus*, ed. R. Willems, CCSL 36, X.6 p. 104.

[44] *The Electronic Sawyer*, eds Susan Kelly et al., S255 (A Charter of King Æthelheard to Bishop Forthere, 10 April 739), <http://www.esawyer.org.uk/charter/255.html#> [accessed 14 October 2014]. I owe this reference to Richard Abels, 'What has Weland to do with Christ? The Franks Casket and the Acculturation of Christianity in Early Anglo-Saxon England', *Speculum* 84 (2009), pp. 549–81, at 569.

[45] *Ezra.*, p. 347; *Temp.*, p. 151; *Gen.*, p. 159; *Tab.*, pp. 78, 100; *Hom.*, II.1 p. 187; compare Gregory, *Homiliae in Hiezechihelem Prophetam*, ed. M. Adriaen, CCSL 142, II.IX.16 p. 370.

[46] *VW*, LXIII pp. 136–7; Abels, 'Franks Casket', pp. 564, 570–71. For Bede's opposition to aristocratic culture penetrating monastic life: Patrick Wormald, 'Bede, *Beowulf* and the Conversion of the Anglo-Saxon Aristocracy', repr. in *Times of Bede*, ed. Baxter, pp. 30–105.

[47] *VCeol.*, 22 pp. 100–101. Ian Wood, 'The Gifts of Wearmouth and Jarrow', in *The Languages of Gift in the Early Middle Ages*, eds Wendy Davies and Paul Fouracre (Cambridge, 2010), pp. 89–115; Simon Coates, 'Ceolfrid: History, Hagiography and Memory in seventh- and eighth-century Wearmouth-Jarrow', *Journal of Medieval History* 25 (1999), pp. 69–86, esp. 80, 83.

sounds like it could come from the *Letter to Ecgberht*.[48] While Gregory probably worried about clerical corruption, his words took on a monastic flavour in Bede's corpus: elsewhere Bede made clear that the *religionis habitus* was the monastic garment that symbolized the difference between the secular and religious ways of life.[49] The implication that ecclesiastical 'traders' should justify their place in the temple by interceding for the rest of society through prayer, finds an echo in Bede's reminders that the Church has to pray for all people (especially kings)—a probable attempt to respond to negative impressions the laity held concerning religious communities.[50] Bede could never forget that throughout Northumbria there lived many earthly individuals, wrong-headedly seeking to follow the monastic life, mixing it with their ongoing earthly business, and in the process (as he saw it) debasing it.[51] I think this explains why he understood that the tower of Babel sought similar religious ends to the temple—Bede's exegesis could provide a way of commenting on the misguided aims of those founding 'false' monasteries. The 'lofty buildings' of Coldingham, the monastery where worldly misdemeanours led to destruction, may have reminded readers of the disastrously high tower of Babel.[52]

In real terms a pure Church unsullied by any earthly contacts and holding to a communistic purity proved a fantasy in eighth-century Northumbria and certainly did not even match Bede's own lifestyle, which included the ownership of private property of which he could dispose at will.[53] The temple commentaries, consequently, do not present the Church as an institution that could have no contact with the realities of the world—Bede happily admitted the helpful role of royal power and wealth in establishing the Church.[54] He reflected here, no doubt, Wearmouth-Jarrow's own belief that the monastery's focus on spiritual wealth and rejection of the world in fact

---

[48] *Luc.*, p. 349 'Sicut templum Dei in ciuitate est ita in plebe fideli uita religiosorum. Et saepe non nulli religionis habitum sumunt sed dum sacrorum ordinum locum percipiunt sanctae religionis officium in commercium terrenae negotiationis tribuunt...dum non numquam peruersi homines locum religionis tenent ibi malitiae suae gladiis occidunt ubi uiuificare proximos orationis suae intercessione debuerunt'; compare Gregory, *In Evangelia*, XXXIX.6 p. 386.

[49] *Ezra.*, p. 353; Hurst, in *Gregory the Great: Forty Gospel Homilies*, trans. David Hurst (Kalamazoo MI, 1990), pp. 362–3, translates it as 'the appearance of religion'.

[50] *Tab.*, p. 123; *Ezra.*, p. 295; 1 Timothy 2.1–2. Cubitt, *Anglo-Saxon Church Councils*, pp. 110–13.

[51] Blair, *Anglo-Saxon Society*, pp. 105–7.

[52] *HE*, IV.25 pp. 424–5 'aedificia...sublimiter erecta'; Scott DeGregorio, 'Monasticism and Reform in Book IV of Bede's "Ecclesiastical History of the English People"', *JEH* 61 (2010), pp. 673–87, at 685–6.

[53] Cuthbert, *Epistola de Obitu Bedae*, eds and trans. Bertram Colgrave and R. A. B. Mynors, in *Bede's Ecclesiastical History of the English People* (Oxford, 1969), pp. 579–87, at 584–5.

[54] *Temp.*, pp. 148–9; *Ezra.*, pp. 294–5—and also the citations in footnote 55. For the interaction between secular politics and Christian virtue: Davidse, 'Sense of History', pp. 685–90.

justified its extensive landholdings. Benedict Biscop gave up 'his own homes and lands ... for the sake of Christ, from whom he hoped to receive ... a home not made by hands but eternal in heaven ... He received homes and lands a hundredfold when he secured these places where he would build his monasteries'.[55] Similarly by a careful sleight of hand in the temple commentaries Bede shifted the emphasis from the Church's need for material resources and wealth to the duty of others to provide such things—hinting, for good measure, that the religious should not be taxed.[56] Bede understood enough of Augustine's theory of utility to understand that one could 'use' the world, so long as the emphasis remained on celestial minds and the pilgrimage towards heaven.[57] All this strengthens the likelihood that the argument of the *Letter to Ecgberht* is not that the Church in Northumbria had too much wealth, but that the wrong people controlled the wealth and therefore misused it.

Thus arose the need to distinguish the heavenly focus of the Church from the earthly interests of the Body of Satan, since their means and ways were so similar. The latter could be distinguished from the former by their divided nature. Having grouped all the Church's rivals together as different aspects of the one satanic and earthly city, Bede also went on, in *On Genesis*, to insist on their division and separateness.[58] Just as the builders of the tower of Babel descended into a chaos of different tongues, so too internal divisions racked the body of Satan. This served as a providential safety valve ensuring that these groupings could never gain the upper hand over the Church: 'For there is no heresy which may not be attacked by other heretics, no school of worldly philosophy which may not be refuted by other equally foolish schools of the philosophy of falsehood'.[59] The rhetorical power of this emphasis on division arises from the previous emphasis on connection; the point is that the body of Satan is divided within itself. This marked the limit of Bede's ability imaginatively to sympathize with the goals while condemning the means of the Church's rivals. This diversity of institutions does not serve to harm the Church, which never appears as just one group amongst many.

---

[55] *Hom.*, I.13 pp. 92–3 'Reliquit domos et agros quos habuerat pro Christo a quo ... domum non manu factam sed aeternam in caelis [2 Corinthians 5.1] se accipere sperabat ... Accepit centuplum [Matthew 19.29] domos et agros quando loca haec in quibus monasteria construeret adeptus est'; trans. Martin and Hurst, I, p. 130. Michael Winterbottom, 'Bede's Homily on Benedict Biscop (*Hom.*, i. 13)', *Journal of Medieval Latin* 21 (2011), pp. 35–51, at 42; see also Michael Gleason, 'Bede and his Fathers', *Classica et Mediaevalia* 45 (1994), pp. 223–38, at 229–30.

[56] *Ezra.*, pp. 248, 250; *Temp.*, p. 195; *Ezra.*, p. 318.   [57] *EpCath.*, pp. 293–4.

[58] He was not without precedent here since Isidore of Seville similarly saw the discord of languages at Babel as the discord of heresies: *Quaestiones in Vetus Testamentum*, PL 83, Gen.IX.3 col. 237–238.

[59] *Gen.*, pp. 161–2 'Nulla est enim haeresis quae non ab aliis haereticis impugnetur, nulla philosophiae secularis secta quae ab aliis aeque stultae philosophiae sectis mendacii redarguatur'; trans. Kendall, p. 238. Also *EpCath.*, p. 329; *Act.*, p. 89; *Sam.*, pp. 96–7, 117–18.

Rather the division highlights what Bede believed to be the defining mark of the Church: the unity of its members. Christians are cemented together in the building of the temple Church as a direct result of their humility; on the other hand the earthly tried to build a tower out of pride and so fell into confusion.[60] The apostles who had 'but one heart and one soul' (Acts 4.32), owning all things in common, epitomized the unity of Christians, and this provided the model for monastic communities.[61] Hence Bede frequently contrasted the building of the tower with Pentecost, where the humility of the Church created unity out of diversity, reversing the alienating influence of the tower, and providing a glimpse of the unity of the heavenly temple.[62] Scholars have analysed the use of the stories of Pentecost and Babel for what they can tell us about positive attitudes to linguistic diversity and the vernacular in the Anglo-Saxon Church.[63] However, we should note that Bede (drawing on Gregory Nazianzen) considered the miracle of Pentecost to have been that the speakers of many tongues *understood* the apostles, rather than necessarily that they themselves *spoke* different languages.[64] While an emphasis on linguistic diversity no doubt helps us to understand how Bede felt these issues directly related to his people's place in the universal Church, it may on occasion miss his major point: Christians built a single structure that would end in heaven where 'there is no discord of minds, no disharmony of speech'.[65]

This reminds us of the unity that formed such an important part of Wearmouth-Jarrow's self-definition: 'one monastery based in two places'.[66] Bede's fervent celebrations of Christian unity based on charity may be reflective of the message that his community's leadership felt it necessary to repeat frequently.[67] For Bede, Christians formed the varied materials, diverse in terms of race, gender, background, or talents, built into the one temple because all believed in one God and hoped for the one heaven.[68] Charity transformed

---

[60] *Gen.*, p. 160; *Temp.*, pp. 170, 185. The condemnation of pride was almost always seen as the main message of the tower: Augustine, *DCD*, XVI.4 pp. 504–5; Augustine, *In Iohannis Evangelium*, VI.10 pp. 58–9.

[61] *Temp.*, pp. 163, 173–4; *Ezra.*, pp. 256–7, 304; *Tab.*, p. 74. For the interpretation of this verse as referring to monasticism: Glenn Olsen, 'Bede as Historian: The Evidence from his Observations on the Life of the First Christian Community at Jerusalem', *JEH* 33 (1982), pp. 519–31, at 520–22.

[62] *Ret.*, pp. 126–7; *Act.*, p. 16; *Temp.*, p. 167; *Luc.*, p. 185 (= *Marc.*, p. 493).

[63] Georges Tugène, *L'idée de nation chez Bède le Vénérable* (Paris, 2001), pp. 306–29.

[64] *Act.*, p. 17; *Ret.*, pp. 110–11; Gregory Nazianzen/Rufinus, *Orationes*, ed. A. Engelbrecht, CSEL 46, IV.15 pp. 160–61; William D. McCready, *Miracles and the Venerable Bede* (Toronto, 1994), p. 60.

[65] *Hom.*, II.16 p. 295 'in qua nulla diuersitas mentium nulla est dissonantia linguarum'; trans. Martin and Hurst, II, p. 155.

[66] *HA*, 15 pp. 56–7 'in duobus locis posito uni monasterio'.

[67] E.g. *HA*, 13 pp. 52–3; *VCeol.*, 16 pp. 94–5.

[68] *Temp.*, pp. 175–6, 233–4; *Tab.*, pp. 44–5, 89–90; *Sam.*, pp. 59–60. Arthur G. Holder, 'The Venerable Bede on the Mysteries of Our Salvation', *American Benedictine Review* 421 (1991), pp. 140–62, at 145–50; note the similarities between Bede's thought on this matter and that of

the diversity of the Church community into unity—the reprobate lacked this love that acted as a glue holding the faithful together.[69] In Chapters 3 and 4 we saw how the unity of Old Testament and New, Jews and gentiles, in the Church was essential to Bede's vision.[70] For him the love that Jews and gentiles felt for each other within Christ's body, the love that the angels and saints in heaven felt for mortals on earth, the love that all members of Christ felt for their neighbour, this overcame the cosmic distances of time and space.[71] The worship of the one God and the communal love of all his worshippers for each other formed two sides of the one coin, resulting in the steadfast unity of the Church.[72] The use of the temple as a single structure whose diverse materials represent the many different types of faithful provided a key image in Bede's presentation of the unified Church.

The unity and charity of the Church does have its limits, however. The unclean have no place in the temple, and while heretics and schismatics wish to offer sacrifices alongside the righteous and build the temple with them, the faithful must utterly reject them.[73] When Bede stated that heretics claim the right to preach alongside the orthodox one cannot help but think of the long struggle to impose Catholic unity on the missionary diversity of the Insular churches.[74] Who should and should not be allowed to preach had been a live issue for some time in Northumbria, whose rival missionary traditions saw each other in terms of schism and heresy. In such light we might note that Bede read the struggles of Ezra and Nehemiah to purify Israel racially as the Church's struggle to separate itself from the unorthodox; the fear of miscegenation found itself transposed onto the corrupting power of contact with heretics. Such contact would result in the confusion of Babel again, i.e. the diversity of languages spoken by the mixed-race children contrasted with ecclesiastical unity.[75] Language could have constituted an important marker of ethnic difference in early medieval Britain, which may explain why Bede saw multilingualism in a threatening light here—but the point should not be taken too far since elsewhere he expressed no concerns about Anglo-Saxons speaking other languages and the negative interpretation of the children's multilingualism derives from the biblical text of Esdras rather than anything

Gregory the Great on occasion: Paul Meyvaert, 'Diversity within Unity, a Gregorian Theme', *The Heythrop Journal* 4 (1963), pp. 141–62.

[69] *EpCath.*, p. 341.

[70] See Ch. 3 within this volume, 'The house made by human hands', p. 47 and Ch. 4 within this volume, 'The Anglo-Saxons' place in the world'.

[71] *Tab.*, p. 62; *Temp.*, pp. 179–81.

[72] *Hom.*, II.25 p. 375; *Tab.*, p. 11, 46; *Temp.*, p. 190; Mary Thomas Aquinas Carroll, *The Venerable Bede: His Spiritual Teachings* (Washington DC, 1946), pp. 219–20.

[73] *Ezra.*, pp. 281–2, 388; 2 Corinthians 6.15–17. Heretics want the orthodox to join them on the 'plain' where they live, also the home of the tower's builders: *Ezra.*, p. 362; *Gen.*, p. 158.

[74] *Ezra.*, p. 281; see also *Prov.*, p. 132.   [75] *Ezra.*, pp. 327, 391.

Bede brought to it.[76] Ecclesiastical rather than ethnic pollution seems to have worried the exegete. Bede had to balance protecting the Church's unity with not restricting its openness; he seems to have had great confidence in the power of penance to bring people back into the Church, providing that they return to ecclesiastical unity.[77] Baptism by heretics and schismatics became effective for those who, having received it, later entered the Church.[78] Once again Bede's Northumbria, whose contemporary orthodoxy rested on a diverse ecclesiastical heritage, probably lay in the background here.

While Bede's desire to differentiate the Church from alternative religious institutions may not surprise us, the degree to which he seems to have used the Church to understand these alternatives still remains striking. Just as he interpreted the tower in the light of how he understood the temple, he understood heretics, pagans, and other such diabolic groupings by turning on their head ideas familiar from his ideal of the Church. As the Church has its teachers, the *doctores* and *magistri* so vital to it, so do these alternative structures have wicked teachers and preachers of error.[79] The builders of the tower, like those of the temple, represent *doctores*, though *mali doctores*, and Bede even referred to pagan and schismatic *doctores*;[80] the teachers of the New Testament Jews (*sinagogae magistri*) were those misguided builders of the temple who rejected the cornerstone.[81] The body of Satan precisely mirrored the body of Christ—as God dwells within the heart of the faithful, so too, for Bede, does the Devil inhabit the heart of the wicked.[82] We have seen how Bede almost acknowledged certain philosophers as the monks of the pagans.[83] This tendency seems to recall Bede's sense of the outward similarities of 'true' and 'false' monasteries. His *Letter to Ecgberht* suggested that those outside the City of God constantly tried to create establishments modelled on those of the true Church but their results proved purely noxious: 'wasps may well build combs, but they store up poison in them, not honey'.[84]

---

[76] Alan Thacker, 'Bede, the Britons and the Book of Samuel', in *Early Medieval Studies in Memory of Patrick Wormald*, eds Stephen Baxter et al. (Farnham, 2009), pp. 129–47, at 129; *HE*, III.3 pp. 220–21.

[77] *Ezra.*, pp. 255–6; *Hom.*, I.20 p. 146; *Luc.*, p. 249: the latter reference is the more striking, as Bede here disagreed with Augustine: François Dolbeau, 'Bède, lecteur des Sermons d'Augustin', *Filologia Mediolatina* 3 (1996), pp. 105–33, at 121–2.

[78] *Tab.*, p. 69; *Gen.*, pp. 111, 124; compare Augustine, *Contra Faustum*, ed. J. Zycha, CSEL 25, XII.20 pp. 348–9.

[79] *Gen.*, p. 157; *EpCath.*, p. 265; *Apoc.*, p. 351.

[80] *Gen.*, p. 162; N. J. Higham, 'Bede's Agenda in Book IV of the "Ecclesiastical History of the English People": A Tricky Matter of Advising the King', *JEH* 64 (2013), pp. 476–93, at 482.

[81] *Luc.*, p. 355 (= *Marc.*, p. 586).

[82] *Sam.*, p. 147; see Ch. 7 within this volume, 'Morality', p. 157.

[83] See within this chapter, p. 133.

[84] *EpEcg.*, 12 pp. 148–9 'uespae fauos quidem facere cum possint non tamen in his mella sed potius uenena thesaurizent'.

This application of the image of the temple Church to understand rival structures also, however, ties into strategies Bede used in his history. While traditionally scholars read the little information given in the *Ecclesiastical History* about Anglo-Saxon polytheism as essentially accurate, recent work has led to an increasing awareness that Bede's account of paganism largely derives from biblical and patristic sources.[85] Aspects of the conversion account such as temples containing altars and idols and a structured priestly hierarchy marked off from normal warrior society may have arisen from reading the contemporary Church structures or biblical descriptions of idolatry back into the Anglo-Saxon past.[86] For example, Bede described the high priest Coifi as a *pontifex*, a word that carried associations with the Jewish and Christian hierarchies; he did not use the word *magus* ('wizard'), with its connotations of magic and strangeness, to refer to pagan priests as did other Insular authors.[87] The royal-focused structures of idol-worshipping that Bede presented do not match the information we have on the lingering remains of 'paganism' in his own time. This suggests a more diffuse culture of charms and rituals that individuals could perform for themselves.[88] Such a realization also raises questions about Bede's discussion of heresy, paganism, and Judaism in the commentaries. Does the tower simply act as an abstract anti-temple used by the exegete to throw light on what the Church should and should not be? Or does it suggest genuine concerns about these alternative belief systems or unorthodox versions of Christianity in the contemporary world?

Historians have long recognized that Bede displayed a constant interest in heresy throughout his work.[89] As an ecclesiastical historian and teacher, the

---

[85] Gregory's conversion strategy was probably similarly influenced: Flora Spiegel, 'The *tabernacula* of Gregory the Great and the Conversion of Anglo-Saxon England', *ASE* 36 (2007), pp. 1–13.

[86] S. D. Church, 'Paganism in Conversion-Age Anglo-Saxon England: The Evidence of Bede's *Ecclesiastical History* Reconsidered', *History* 93 (2008), pp. 162–80; R. I. Page, 'Anglo-Saxon Paganism: The Evidence of Bede', in *Pagans and Christians: The Interplay between Christian Latin and Traditional Germanic Cultures in Early Medieval Europe*, eds T. Hofstra et al. (Groningen, 1995), pp. 99–129. But for actual Anglo-Saxon pagan temples and priests: John Blair, 'Anglo-Saxon Pagan Shrines and their Prototypes', *Anglo-Saxon Studies in Archaeology and History* 8 (1995), pp. 1–28; James Campbell, 'Some Considerations on Religion in Early England', in Collectanea Antiqua: *Essays in Memory of Sonia Chadwick Hawkes*, eds Martin Henig and Tyler Jo Smith (Oxford, 2007), pp. 67–73.

[87] *HE*, II.13 pp. 182–7; *VW*, XII pp. 28–9; Adomnán, *Vita S. Columbae*, eds and trans. Alan Orr Anderson and Marjorie Ogilvie Anderson, *Adomnan's Life of Columba* (Oxford, 1991), I.37 pp. 70–71, II.33 pp. 140–43.

[88] Paul Willem Finsterwalder (ed.), *Die Canones Theodori Cantuariensis und ihre Überlieferungsformen* (Weimar, 1929), I.XV pp. 310–11.

[89] Charles Plummer, *Venerabilis Baedae Opera Historica*, 2 vols (Oxford, 1896), I, p. lxii n. 3; Arthur G. Holder, 'Hunting Snakes in the Grass: Bede as Heresiologist', in *Listen, O Isles, unto me: Studies in Medieval Word and Image in Honour of Jennifer O'Reilly*, eds Elizabeth Mullins and Diarmuid Scully (Cork, 2011), pp. 105–14. I discussed the possible importance of Christological heresies in Bede's work at Ch. 5 within this volume, 'The temple as Christ'.

monk may simply have considered it his duty to point out and disprove the heresies that had proven troublesome to the Church.[90] Bede's own earliest computistical writings had occasioned an accusation of heresy: by adopting a chronology from the Hebrew Bible, which located the incarnation much earlier than the traditional Septuagint chronology, he had, the argument ran, put Christ's coming in the wrong age of the world.[91] The criticism, which we should not imagine as presenting any real danger to Bede personally, elicited a sharp response.[92] Some studies have tended to emphasize the traumatic nature of this episode and located Bede's passion for orthodoxy therein; certainly, it may partly explain his later scientific writings but we should not exaggerate the importance of the episode.[93] The debate centred on very specific issues of biblical chronology that hardly explain Bede's continuing wide interest in varied heresies.

There has long existed a tradition of scholarship suggesting that the Pelagian heresy remained particularly active in the British Isles and may have posed a major problem in the early Insular Church.[94] The arguments against any particular British or Insular leanings toward Pelagianism prove by far the more convincing;[95] nevertheless, supporters of the Roman and Dionysian Easter certainly did interpret certain anomalous Easter calculations as implicitly Pelagian.[96] Bede himself argued this and his frequent attacks on Pelagianism may actually have been aimed at Easter calculations with which he disagreed.[97] It would seem unlikely that we should understand every defence of grace in Bede's work entirely as a reference to Easter, but such an issue in the background may have added sharpness to Bede's not infrequent engagement with Pelagianism in the temple commentaries.[98] We can similarly acknowledge that no Donatists existed in the Insular Church, while still

---

[90] Carroll, *Spiritual Teachings*, p. 96.

[91] Peter Darby, *Bede and the End of Time* (Farnham, 2012), pp. 35–64.

[92] Bede, *Epistola ad Pleguinam*, ed. C. W. Jones, CCSL 123C, pp. 613–26.

[93] Charles W. Jones, *Bedae Opera de Temporibus* (Cambridge MA, 1943), pp. 132–5; Faith Wallis, *Bede: On the Reckoning of Time* (Liverpool, 1999), pp. xxx–xxxi.

[94] Michael W. Herren and Shirley Ann Brown, *Christ in Celtic Christianity: Britain and Ireland from the Fifth to the Tenth Century* (Woodbridge, 2002), make the most up-to-date and developed case for Pelagianism's major role in the Insular Church.

[95] Gerald Bonner, 'The Pelagian Controversy in Britain and Ireland', *Peritia* 16 (2002), pp. 144–55; Gilbert Márkus, 'Pelagianism and the "Common Celtic Church"', *Innes Review* 56 (2005), pp. 165–213.

[96] Dáibhí Ó Cróinín, '"New Heresy for Old": Pelagianism in Ireland and the Papal Letter of 640', *Speculum* 60 (1985), pp. 505–16.

[97] *HE*, V.21 pp. 544–5; *DTR*, VI p. 292. Arthur G. Holder, 'The Anti-Pelagian Character of Bede's Commentary on the Song of Songs', in *Biblical Studies in the Early Middle Ages*, eds Claudio Leonardi and Giovanni Orlandi (Florence, 2005), pp. 91–103, at 100–102.

[98] *Ezra.*, pp. 281–2, 302; *Tab.*, pp. 10, 82. The last citation speaks of the Pelagians hardening their hearts against God, similarly to how *On Genesis* speaks of the builders of the tower: *Gen.*, p. 159.

recognizing that the issues of centre and periphery which Donatism raised were ones relevant to the world in which Bede lived.[99]

There were certainly no Jews in Anglo-Saxon England, but Bede believed that some Christians maintained a 'Jewish' or earthly understanding of religion—not in wishing to follow the Law according to the letter, but that their sole interest was in receiving earthly benefits.[100] In addition, the history of the Jews could help one to understand the history of Britain, to condemn the Britons, and to defend the Anglo-Saxon invasion; Bede, of course, drew this application of Jewish history to the Insular world from earlier writings, especially Gildas' *De Excidio Britanniae*.[101] It has recently been argued that around 716, in a time of dynastic upheaval, the threats posed to Northumbria by those willing to engage with 'heretical' threats from without proved of particular concern to Bede., i.e. threats from British polities refusing to accept the Romanist views of the Anglo-Saxon Church.[102] If the formulation of Bede's ideas on Ezra took place around this time (in close proximity to the Codex Amiatinus' departure), then it may go some way to explaining why the theme of protecting the 'chosen people' from corrupting influences appeared so important when Bede finally published the commentary probably many years later.

Continued fear of the threat posed by the Britons, who by refusing the Roman Easter remained outside the unity of the Catholic Church, may have further added to Bede's attack on the 'false Catholics' of his own time in the *Letter to Ecgberht*.[103] Certainly Bede considered that references to the danger of invasion, which 'false' monasteries opened up, were a worthwhile addition to his argument in the letter—it is likely that such talk already circulated in Northumbria.[104] But it only formed one element of his argument; he attacked 'false' monasteries and lazy clergy because their forms of Christianity did not match his vision of right religion. He strove to present the people he disagreed with as earthly idolaters because this tied into an idea he had used throughout his own work whereby all alternatives to perfect and orthodox Christianity formed no more than the limbs of the body of Satan. Such an idea possessed

---

[99] See Ch. 4 within this volume, 'The Anglo-Saxons' place in the world', pp. 87–8.

[100] *Gen.*, p. 242.

[101] W. Trent Foley and Nicholas J. Higham, 'Bede on the Britons', *EME* 17 (2009), pp. 154–85; Alan Thacker, 'Bede and the Ordering of Understanding', in *Innovation and Tradition in the Writings of the Venerable Bede*, ed. Scott DeGregorio (Morgantown WV, 2006), pp. 37–63, at 55–7.

[102] Thacker, 'Britons and the Book of Samuel'.

[103] Clare Stancliffe, *Bede and the Britons*, Whithorn Lecture 2005 (Whithorn, 2007), pp. 19–22, 39–40, argues that the *Letter to Ecgberht* was driven by a fear that moral decline (and the economic consequences of 'false monasteries') would leave Northumbria exposed to the threat of British attack.

[104] Similar points had already been made elsewhere in Western Europe: Patrick Sims-Williams, *Religion and Literature in Western England, 600–800* (Cambridge, 1990), p. 127.

great rhetorical power as the conclusion of the letter shows, where Bede linked the clerics and monks he condemned with a continuous tradition of wicked greed from the Fall to Judas and beyond.[105] It also provided a heuristic which helped him understand and deal with those who disagreed with his vision of Christian life in Northumbria. Issues in eighth-century economic and ecclesiastical life could be seen as part of an eternal struggle between righteousness and evil. By contending that the issues facing Ecgberht had afflicted the Church from its beginning, Bede tried to create an argument that transcended the local context.[106]

Locating the approaching crisis of the Northumbrian elite within the cosmic struggle between the Cities of God and the Devil meant that Bede encouraged his readers to act in solving the problem not as Northumbrian nobles and prelates, but as members of the body of Christ. No doubt what he would have considered support for the true Church would also have proved to be in the interests of Wearmouth-Jarrow. From the perspective of the current study the importance of the contrast between the tower of Babel and the temple of Jerusalem lies in the fact that it indicates just how central the image of the temple had become to Bede's vision of the Church. When Bede thought of the Church, the temple image came to mind and therefore he used that image to help represent all those alternative demonic groups he saw ranged against the Church. The relevant section of *On Genesis* probably dates from the 720s, the period in which the issues that led to the *Letter to Ecgberht* seem to have especially exercised Bede in writing the temple commentaries;[107] we could, therefore, understand the excursus on the tower and the temple as part of Bede's use of the temple image to promote his reform agenda—in particular in the way it attacked those outside the one true Church. But it also allows us to catch a glimpse of Bede's perspective on the cosmic struggle between God and Satan in which he saw himself participating and on a much more local dispute in Northumbrian society, which he wished to be read in similarly stark terms of good and evil.

THE TEMPLE AS WHICH CHURCH?

In these last few chapters I have dealt with rather different images of the Church: on the one hand we have the universal, cosmic Church, which

---

[105] *EpEcg.*, 17 pp. 158–61.
[106] Note the importance of the early Church and Acts to the letter: *EpEcg.*, 4 pp. 128–31, 16 pp. 156–7, 17 pp. 160–61.
[107] Scott DeGregorio, '"Nostrorum socordiam temporum": the Reforming Impulse of Bede's Later Exegesis', *EME* 11 (2002), pp. 107–22, at 113–21.

stretches across all time and space, and on the other we have the Church which must struggle against heretics, devote itself to preaching, and generally behave as an institution in the present world. How are these churches connected? This question relates to a confusion that seems to have plagued medieval theological writings since at least the time of Augustine. The Church existed both as the sacramental institution operating on earth and as the community of all the elect, transcending time and space.[108] In practice theologians clearly often used the word 'Church' to refer to many different possible realities.[109] Markus influentially argued that Augustine saw the institutional Church as a 'secular' institution, a mixed body of elect and reprobate who would only be separated at the end of time; seen in that earthly and institutional light the Church cannot be the same as the City of God, though in a 'true' eschatological perspective, both are one.[110] Augustine's predecessor Tyconius (d. *c*.400) had developed an even stronger theory of the twofold body of Christ, which stressed the fact that both good and bad, the elect and reprobate, existed all unavoidably mixed together in the Church; since Tyconius' work on the Apocalypse was an important source for Bede, the Anglo-Saxon must have been familiar with such ideas from his very first foray into exegesis.[111]

The mixed Church (*ecclesia permixta*), therefore, appears frequently in the *Explanation of the Apocalypse* and on occasion elsewhere in Bede's writings; but from the start it troubled the Anglo-Saxon who felt the need to undercut Tyconian passages in his sources by stating that the unclean and false did not really belong in the Church.[112] Thus, while some have argued that Bede held an Augustinian view that the mixture of wicked and righteous within the Church was unavoidable, Wallis's argument that, in fact, Bede distanced himself from such an outlook, seems to me the more convincing.[113] After all, in his main interpretation of the major proof text for this ecclesiology, the beloved's declaration to be both 'black and beautiful' (Song of Songs 1.4), Bede deliberately dismissed the reading that the Church was black because of

---

[108] Yves Congar, *L'Ecclésiologie du Haut Moyen Age: De saint Grégoire le Grand à la désunion entre Byzance et Rome* (Paris, 1968), pp. 90–92; Glenn W. Olsen, 'From Bede to the Anglo-Saxon Presence in the Carolingian Empire', *Settimane di studio del Centro italiano di studi sull'alto medioevo* 32 (1984), pp. 305–82, at 345–8.

[109] Michael A. Fahey, 'Augustine's Ecclesiology Revisited', in *Augustine: From Rhetor to Theologian*, eds Timothy D. Barnes et al. (Waterloo, 1992), pp. 173–81, at 177–9.

[110] Augustine, *DCD*, I.35 pp. 33–4, XVIII.49 p. 647; Augustine, *Enarrationes*, LXI.8 pp. 778–80. R. A. Markus, *Saeculum: History and Society in the Theology of St Augustine*, rev. ed. (Cambridge, 1988), pp. 58–63, 116–24; van Oort, *Jerusalem and Babylon*, pp. 126–9, 151–3.

[111] Faith Wallis, *Bede: Commentary on Revelation* (Liverpool, 2013), pp. 69–70.

[112] *Apoc.*, pp. 249, 563; compare Primasius, *Commentarius in Apocalypsin*, ed. A. W. Adams, CCSL 92, I.2 p. 23, V.21 p. 299—Tyconius provided Primasius' source.

[113] Hilliard, 'Sacred and Secular History', pp. 26, 36; Wallis, *Bede: Commentary on Revelation*, p. 229, n. 826; J. N. Hillgarth, 'L'influence de la *Cité du Dieu* de saint Augustin au Haut Moyen Age', *Sacris Erudiri* 28 (1985), pp. 5–34, at 21.

sinners (a viewpoint he associated with unnamed exegetes); instead he read it in terms of spiritual warfare, focusing on the purely external sufferings that it must endure: sins and the vice of sins do not darken the Church, temptations and trials do.[114] Constructing an entirely consistent ecclesiology from every comment within the Bedan corpus proves difficult, but I would argue that focusing on the temple image we see Bede thinking primarily of the Church as the universal community of the elect.[115]

We have already touched on this when discussing Bede's ideas concerning the 'present Church', which, we have seen, does not appear to be the mixed Church awaiting an eschatological purification.[116] Certainly the general tenor of Bede's use of the temple image matches such statements: while Tyconius declared that the temple was bipartite (containing both elect and reprobate), Bede clearly stated (at least on occasion) that it represented the Church of the predestined elect.[117] The snowy white walls of Solomon's temple symbolize the elect's purity of thought and action.[118] The wicked may seem to worship at the tabernacle but in reality in their minds they sacrifice at the temple of Moloch.[119] Pagan ascetics may offer a holocaust, but they do not do so on the altar of the God of Israel.[120] Isidore's suggestion that the mixture of various materials in the tabernacle symbolized the mixture of saints and sinners in the Church, echoed in the Irish 'Reference Bible', finds no parallel in Bede.[121]

Bede expressed a definite sense of the mixture of carnal and perfect within the temple Church, which may conjure up the image of the Augustinian mixed Church.[122] Certainly the courtyards of the temple, which separate the carnal members of the Church from those perfect who have managed to leave all desires of the flesh behind and made the transition from earth to heaven in their minds, may seem to recall the contrast between the heavenly temple and earthly tower.[123] Bede even pointed out that the separation existed on the vertical (like that between the temple and tower) as well as horizontal plane, with the inner temple standing above the outer courtyards.[124] But on closer examination a

---

[114] *Cant.*, p. 196. Bede's earlier use of this verse (*Apoc.*, p. 225) follows Augustine's Tyconian interpretation at *Doctrina*, III.101 pp. 176–7.

[115] For Bede's ecclesiology in general, devoting attention to the problem of sinners within the Church in particular: Johannes Beumer, 'Das Kirchenbild in den Schriftkommentaren Bedas des Ehrwürdigen', *Scholastik* 28 (1958), pp. 40–56.

[116] See Ch. 3 within this volume, 'History and the figural interpretation of the temple', pp. 68–70.

[117] Tyconius, *Liber Regularum*, ed. F. C. Burkitt, *The Book of Rules of Tyconius* (Cambridge, 1894), I p. 7; *Gen.*, p. 86; *Tab.*, p. 42; *Ezra.*, pp. 241, 300.

[118] *Gen.*, p. 160; *Temp.*, p. 156; *Hom.*, II.1 p. 190.   [119] *Act.*, p. 36.   [120] *Ezra.*, p. 265.

[121] Isidore, *Quaestiones*, Exodus.L.2 col. 313; *Pauca Problemata de Enigmatibus ex Tomis Canonicis: Praefatio et Libri de Pentateucho Moysi*, ed. G. MacGinty, Corpus Christianorum Continuatio Mediaeualis 173, 407.XXVII p. 180.

[122] Alan Thacker, *Bede and Augustine of Hippo: History and Figure in Sacred Text*, Jarrow Lecture (Jarrow, 2005), pp. 25, 28.

[123] *Temp.*, pp. 194–6.   [124] *Temp.*, p. 193; *Reg.*, XVIII p. 312.

fundamental difference appears: the mixed Church includes both the elect and the reprobate, but Bede's carnal and perfect both end up in heaven, i.e. they are all from the elect: 'all the carnal and weak who are still in the Church have a share in the lot of the elect through the merit of pure faith and of piety which is dedicated to God'.[125] The carnal in the Church simply consists of those who have not utterly lost the desires of the flesh but rather still battle against them. But for Bede even such people could possess 'purity of conduct'.[126]

A reference to the mixture of elect and reprobate occurs in relation to the threefold hierarchy of married, continent, and preachers which I have discussed previously.[127] The candelabrum of the tabernacle inspired Bede to speak of these three orders of faithful, connecting them to Noah, Daniel, and Job;[128] he went on to link them with those in the bed, the mill, and the field described in Luke 17.34–5 of whom 'one shall be taken and the other shall be left': 'because in all of these states some will be chosen, some reprobated'.[129] The connection with the passage from Luke comes from Augustine himself who used it to speak of the mixture of the two cities, while Noah, Daniel, and Job exclusively referred to the elect from each of the three categories of Christian.[130] In *On the Tabernacle* the relationship between these two different uses of the hierarchy seems rather vague. It does, however, seem clear from the overall passage that the candelabrum itself refers to the elect in their many different forms: 'The elect are doubtless imbued with one true faith, even if their merits differ in rank; for they will come to one light of eternal truth in heaven'.[131] Hence the image explored seems primarily one of the Church of the saved, though it does inspire a brief reference to an idea inherited from Augustine concerning the *permixta ecclesia*.

We should not say that members of the temple Church do not sin—for Bede, none of the saints could avoid all sin. Note *Homily* II.24 where he deals with the temple's history:

> That the temple was rebuilt by the mercy of God after it had been burned by [Israel's] enemies, and that it was cleansed again with the help of benevolence

---

[125] *Temp.*, p. 194 'carnales quique atque infirmi adhuc in ecclesia, etsi ob meritum castae fidei ac pietatis Deo deuotae ad electorum sortem pertinent'; trans. Connolly, p. 69.

[126] *Temp.*, p. 196 'operum . . . munditiam'; trans. Connolly, p. 71.

[127] See Ch. 5 within this volume, 'The hierarchical body of Christ', pp. 123–4; Holder, 'Mysteries of Our Salvation', p. 148.

[128] *Tab.*, pp. 31–2.

[129] *Tab.*, p. 32 'quia in omnibus his gradibus quidam eligendi quidam reprobandi sunt'; trans. Holder, p. 34.

[130] Georges Folliet, 'Les trois categories de chrétiens: à partir de Luc (17, 34–36), Matthieu (24, 40–41) et Ézéchiel (14, 14)', in *Augustinus Magister*, vol. 2 (Paris, 1954), pp. 631–44. Bede's exegesis of Luke 17.34–35 at *Luc.*, pp. 320–21 draws on Augustine, *Quaestiones Evangeliorum*, ed. A. Mutzenbecher, CCSL 44B, II.44 pp. 104–6.

[131] *Tab.*, p. 32 'electi, etsi meritorum sunt gradibus discreti, una sunt fide ueritatis imbuti ad unam in caelis lucem ueritatis aeternae peruenturi'; trans. Holder, p. 35.

from on high after it had been polluted with idols suggests the various events
which happen to holy Church: at one time she is overwhelmed by the persecutions of unbelievers; at another she is freed from persecutions and serves her Lord
peacefully; at another she is endangered in certain of her members by the snares
of the ancient enemy; at another because of the meticulous concern of her faithful
teachers, she recovers those whom for a while she seemed to have lost, chastised
by repentance.[132]

At first this seems like a clear statement that some members of the Church
could be followers of Satan. Rather, on closer examination, I think Bede can be
found to have recounted a recurring tale of danger and recovery, sin and
pardon. The Church suffers persecution externally, and then is freed from
persecution; the Devil ensnares members of the Church, but teachers then win
them back. These individuals remained elect, they only 'seemed . . . lost'. The
return from Babylon and rebuilding of the temple symbolized that God builds
his house out of repentant sinners as well as the newly baptized; indeed Bede
deemed it heresy to believe that penance could fail to build burnt stones—
those who had lost the purity of their works through vices but subsequently
improved their morals—back into the wall of the Church.[133]

While sinning did not form an unmovable bar to entry into the Lord's
house, sin itself had no place there. Bede's temple commentaries show perfect
awareness of corruption within the Church and one could understand this as
Bede acknowledging the Church's mixed nature on earth.[134] But we ought to
highlight that when Bede spoke of false Catholics, the emphasis fell on *false*.
The Lord in the Apocalypse instructed John not to measure the atrium of the
temple because those who adhered to the Church in name only would not be
counted as part of God's house.[135] Insofar as the Church is eschatologically
pure, such a statement perfectly agreed with Augustine's understanding of the
mixed Church; similarly Bede warned that sinners ought to correct themselves
'if they wish not to be removed from the Church when the Lord comes'.[136] But
earlier in the same homily Bede stated that Christ visits 'the temple of holy
Church' daily and therefore one must be constantly wary 'lest he come
unexpectedly and find something evil in us, as a result of which we should

---

[132] *Hom.*, II.24 p. 365 'Quod templum ab hostibus incensum rursum domino miserante
construitur quod ab idolatriis coinquinatum denuo supernae pietatis auxilio mundatur uarios
sanctae ecclesiae insinuat euentus quae nunc infidelium persecutione premitur nunc a persecu-
tionibus reddita liberior tranquilla domino seruitute famulatur nunc in quibusdam suis membris
hostis antiqui periclitatur insidiis nunc instante solertia doctorum fidelium quos ad horam
perdere uidebatur per paenitentiam iam castigatos recipit'; trans. Martin and Hurst, II, p. 250.

[133] *Hom.*, I.14 p. 101; *Ezra.*, pp. 242, 356.

[134] E.g. *Tab.*, p. 78; Davidse, 'Sense of History', p. 682.

[135] *Apoc.*, p. 369; *DTR*, LXVIV p. 538. Apocalypse 11.2.

[136] *Hom.*, II.1 p. 188 'si nolunt ueniente domino de ecclesia auferri'; trans. Martin and
Hurst, II, p. 6.

rightly be scourged and cast out of the Church'.[137] Clearly one cannot afford to wait for the Day of Judgement if the wicked are expelled from the Church in the here and now also. As I have discussed above, the use of the tower image surely aimed to show that while heretics, pagans, or even false Catholics may look superficially like the temple Church, they were in fact fundamentally different.[138] Bede's temple always strained towards purity, impatient for the Lord to separate the wheat from the chaff at Judgement; if sinners or heretics would not reform, proving dead rather than living stones, the authorities removed them from the temple.[139] Good patristic examples existed for such an approach: Augustine himself had emphasized that one should not have to put up with heretics within the ecclesiastical community.[140]

In previous chapters I argued that Bede saw little difference between the present Church and the future, the work of Christ having partly collapsed the difference between the pilgrim tabernacle on earth and the triumphant temple in heaven, making both parts of a universal and transcendent Church. He may have interpreted the temple and the tabernacle as separate aspects of the Church, but in practice the separate structures blurred into one image combining heavenly and earthly Church.[141] The discussion on the body of Christ in the previous chapter, highlighting the importance of the institutional hierarchy and the sacraments, suggests that the institutional Church plays an important role in this cosmic Church. Since Bede stressed that devout Jews from before the incarnation belonged to the temple Church, that body cannot simply be equated to the institution of his own time. But his interest in Old Testament Judaism ascribes a great deal of importance to cultic rituals and institutional hierarchies. Bede did not just see the pre-incarnation elect as a scattered few pious souls; rather he thought particularly of the Jewish nation at worship;[142] indeed he seems to have believed in the existence of a 'Jewish Church' operating through sacramental acts just as the New Testament Church did.[143] In other words, he thought that a sacramental institution had always been central to salvation. The community of the elect gathered

---

[137] *Hom.*, II.1 pp. 185–6 'Sed hoc idem eum in templo sanctae ecclesiae examine cotidianae uisitationis agere omnis qui recte sapit intellegit. Vnde multum tremenda sunt haec ... ne ueniens inprouisus peruersum quid in nobis unde merito flagellari ac de ecclesia eici debeamus inueniat'; trans. Martin and Hurst, II, p. 3.

[138] Though heathens may confuse all Christians, heretics and orthodox, with each other: *Ezra.*, p. 292; *EpCath.*, p. 269.

[139] *Ezra.*, pp. 364, 388–9; *EpCath.*, p. 235.

[140] Augustine, *Sermones*, PL 38, III, col. 33; see also Bede, *Excerpts from the Works of Saint Augustine on the Letters of the Blessed Apostle Paul*, trans. David Hurst (Kalamazoo MI, 1999), p. 218.

[141] *Temp.*, p. 148; *Tab.*, p. 43.

[142] Georges Tugène, 'Le thème des deux peuples dans le *De Tabernaculo* de Bède', in *Bède le Vénérable*, eds Lebecq et al., pp. 73–84, at 75–6.

[143] Conor O'Brien, 'Bede on the Jewish Church', in *The Church on its Past*, eds Peter D. Clarke and Charlotte Methuen (Woodbridge, 2013), pp. 63–73, at 64–8.

in some such institution, even though at different times different earthly structures proved appropriate.

Bede constantly identified membership of the temple Church and becoming a temple of God oneself with the sacrament of baptism. In particular he drew attention to the renunciation of Satan, which formed part of the baptismal liturgy.[144] This links with the two-cities rhetoric we have seen above: in baptism one receives membership of the body of Christ rather than the body of Satan. Not just a sacrament performed within the earthly Church, it also constituted a change of cosmic allegiance, as Davidse recognized: 'to Bede, converting to Christianity is the same as leaving the community of the devil and entering the community of God'.[145] As almost always in Bede's vast corpus, one can find exceptions—Simon Magus accepted baptism in order to do the Devil's work.[146] But the overall emphasis reminds us that Bede did not consider the body of Satan as just a rhetorical image; the sacramental Church combated a real diabolic threat in the here and now.[147] Bede did not simply believe that the sacraments (through which one joins the priesthood of Christ) proved ineffective for those outside the true Church, but rather that the morally impure should not participate in them lest the house of prayer become a den of thieves when 'one still abiding in death' presumed 'to receive the holy mysteries of life'.[148] The *Letter to Ecgberht* takes it as given that the sexually impure ought not to receive the sacraments.[149]

This Bedan unity between the cosmic and institutional churches seems to mirror his distinctive celebration of action and contemplation personified in Cuthbert. Bede probably distorted the realities of Cuthbert's own drive to sanctity to downplay the extent to which the otherworldly saint sought to flee the activities of the institutional Church.[150] Cuthbert's hermitage had walls so high that he could not see anything other than the sky above—a reification of the heavenly mind enjoyed by the perfect in the temple commentaries.[151] And like those *perfecti*, Cuthbert did not remain cut off from people but served as an exemplary *doctor*, mediating between heaven and earth, the carnal and the

---

[144] *Reg.*, XVI p. 309; *Temp.*, p. 155; *Ezra.*, pp. 267–8, 275–6, 305; *DTR*, LXIII p. 455; *Sam.*, p. 161. For the renunciation of Satan in baptism: Henry Ansgar Kelly, *The Devil at Baptism: Ritual, Theology, and Drama* (Ithaca NY, 1985), pp. 94–105.

[145] Davidse, 'Sense of History', p. 679.   [146] *Ezra.*, p. 282.

[147] For the problems with Bede's use of such imagery: Beumer, 'Das Kirchenbild', pp. 54–5.

[148] *Hom.*, II.4 p. 208 'Nemo domum orationis conuertat in speluncam latronum... nemo manens adhuc in morte ad accipienda uitae mysteria praesumat accedere'; trans. Martin and Hurst, II, p. 34. Giovanni Caputa, *Il Sacerdozio dei Fedeli secondo San Beda: un itinerario di maturità cristiana* (Vatican City, 2002), pp. 159–67.

[149] *EpEcg.*, 15 pp. 154–5.

[150] Clare Stancliffe, 'Cuthbert and the Polarity between Pastor and Solitary', in *St Cuthbert, His Cult and His Community until AD 1200*, eds Gerald Bonner et al. (Woodbridge, 1989), pp. 21–44, esp. 28, 32–3.

[151] *HE*, IV.28 pp. 436–7; *VCP*, XVII pp. 216–17.

divine.[152] In individuals such as Cuthbert, Bede revealed how the pure Church, which his temple represented, did not stay separate from the institution that taught the rustic laity and rejected all contact with heretics: the saint on his deathbed, while urging his brethren to monastic charity, still felt the need, according to Bede, to forbid them communion 'with those who depart from the unity of the catholic peace, either in not celebrating Easter at the proper time or in evil living'.[153]

This draws our attention to the bitter ecclesiastical disputes of the late seventh and early eighth centuries, reminding us that the issue of communion with 'unorthodox' or at least different Christians remained a live one in the Insular Church well into the earlier half of Bede's life. The attitudes that have been recorded in other sources suggest that the search for a pure institutional Church did go on in the world behind Bede's temple commentaries. British clergy would happily ostracize totally any ecclesiastic whose practice they did not consider correct, including Roman-leaning clergy.[154] A similar type of ostracism befell the Wilfridians when excommunicated in the early eighth century.[155] The fanciful modern idea that only the hard-line followers of the Roman Easter were intolerant of difference does not appear justified by the sources where both sides behaved intolerantly when occasion arose.[156] Clearly the *Romani* were very concerned with keeping their Church pure from those they considered schismatics, heretics, or at the very least fellow travellers of the heterodox. The complex circumstances surrounding the consecrations of Wilfrid and Chad seem related to just such concerns for ecclesiastical purity amongst the Roman-leaning Anglo-Saxon clergy, since Wilfrid expressed concerns not only about having direct contact with schismatics but also with those who consorted with schismatics.[157] Recent work has helped to show just how starkly the dividing lines came to be drawn in late seventh-century Britain. Both Wilfrid and Theodore, at least on his initial arrival in Britain, believed that anyone who rejected the Roman Easter was a heretic and

---

[152] *Temp.*, p. 195; VCP, XVIII pp. 218–21. For Bede's emphasis on Cuthbert as interacting with and teaching people: Carole E. Newlands, 'Bede and Images of Saint Cuthbert', *Traditio* 52 (1997), pp. 73–109, at 95–9, 101.

[153] VCP, XXXIX pp. 282–5 'Cum illis autem qui ab unitate catholicae pacis uel pascha non suo tempore celebrando, uel peruerse uiuendo aberrant, uobis sit nulla communio'.

[154] HE, II.4 pp. 146–7; Aldhelm, *Epistulae*, ed. R. Ehwald, MGH Auctores Antiquissimi 15, IV p. 484; Herren and Brown, *Christ in Celtic Christianity*, pp. 130–33.

[155] VW, XLIX pp. 100–101.

[156] Such a viewpoint may arise from Columbanus' appeal to the papacy that both traditions continue on with their own practices in charitable disagreement: *Epistulae*, ed. and trans. G. S. M. Walker, *Sancti Columbani Opera* (Dublin, 1957), III.2 pp. 24–5. Previously, however, he had explicitly declared that anyone who disagreed with his authorities on Easter ran the risk of being a heretic and reprobate: *Epistulae*, I.5 pp. 8–9.

[157] VW, XII pp. 24–5; HE. III.28 pp. 314–17.

those willing to cooperate with 'heretics' were themselves contaminated by the contact.[158]

After the Synod of Whitby and with Theodore's arrival at Canterbury an attempt to purge the Church of heterodox members got under way, probably quickly becoming associated with a Northumbrian push to extend its influence into British and Irish territory—political expansion being justified by the spread of Catholic Christianity.[159] The Wilfridians clearly saw this purge in terms of removing the reprobate from Christ's body: Thomas Charles-Edwards has shown that Wilfrid's famous reference to the 'weeds' planted by the Columbans is a probable reference to Matthew 13.24–30's parable of the wheat and the tares (weeds), picking up on Pope Vitalian's letter to King Oswiu of Northumbria which announced the need to root out the weeds scattered by the Devil throughout Britain, and possibly also on Jerome's suggestion that the Church begin the process of separating the wheat and the obvious tares in the present.[160] Stephen's life seems to emphasize the institutional Church as the community of saints, outside of which there lies only darkness.[161] Raised in an institution established against this background, Bede may have been influenced by just such attitudes long before he ever came to demand that leprous stones be removed from the temple. Of course, the monk of Jarrow made it very clear that adherence to the Columban Easter did not constitute heresy; Bede's emphasis on charity and ecclesiastical unity may imply a less intolerant attitude.[162] However, the evidence I have discussed as part of this study and the dying speech Bede gave to Cuthbert suggests, in theory at least, a viewpoint not dissimilar to Wilfrid's.[163]

Certainly, even if Bede differed from Theodore and the Wilfridians in specifics, the general attitude they shared with regards to the Church in the world seems to have been common throughout Anglo-Saxon England. A recent study of early Anglo-Saxon writers on guardian angels emphasizes that they 'presumed that those who would eventually number among the saved and the damned could already be easily distinguished from each other during life'.[164] The evidence does not all point in one direction—many

---

[158] Clare Stancliffe, *Bede, Wilfrid, and the Irish*, Jarrow Lecture (Jarrow, 2003), pp. 5–11. See Finsterwalder (ed.), *Canones Theodori*, I.V pp. 205–7.

[159] Thomas Charles-Edwards, *Wales and the Britons 350–1064* (Oxford, 2013), pp. 406–9; Charles-Edwards, 'Wilfrid and the Celts', in *Wilfrid: Abbot, Bishop, Saint; Papers from the 1300th Anniversary Conferences*, ed. N. J. Higham (Donington, 2013), pp. 243–59, at 244–9, 252–9.

[160] *VW*, XLVII pp. 98–9; *HE*, III.29 pp. 320–21; Jerome, *In Matheum*, p. 112; Charles-Edwards, 'Wilfrid and the Celts', pp. 249–50.

[161] Sandra Duncan, 'Prophets Shining in Dark Places: Biblical Themes and Theological Motifs in the *Vita Sancti Wilfridi*', in *Wilfrid*, ed. Higham, pp. 80–92.

[162] Stancliffe, *Bede, Wilfrid, and the Irish*, pp. 22–8.

[163] The speech does not appear in the earlier anonymous *Life of Cuthbert*.

[164] Richard Sowerby, 'Angels in Anglo-Saxon England, 700–1000', (DPhil thesis, University of Oxford, 2013), p. 99; Dr Sowerby's book arising from this thesis is forthcoming.

Anglo-Saxon churchmen made it clear that only God could be sure whether any individual was damned or saved, something humans could not necessarily determine at the point of death.[165] Daniel of Winchester relied on the theory of the mixed Church to assure Boniface that he could deal with the corrupt clergy of the Frankish court without risk of contamination; but the fact that Boniface instinctually wished to separate himself from the wicked strikes one as quite important.[166] Such an attitude to how one ought to behave in the institutional Church bears many resemblances to Bede's perspective on the Northumbrian Church.

Not an awareness of the secular and mixed nature of the earthly Church, but rather a refusal to accept that earthly individuals could have any part in that institution drove Bede to write to Ecgberht. The *Letter to Ecgberht* shares with the commentaries a concern over those who are Catholic in name only: many places, while 'described by the title monastery by a most foolish pen' in charters, did not really count as monasteries.[167] Modern scholars recognize that a clear-cut and monolithic Church never really existed in the Middle Ages and that Bede's firm vision in fact defined itself in opposition to the muddle of different approaches to Christianity which, no doubt, coexisted in Northumbria.[168] But we must remember that Bede's argument arose from the conviction that by rising out of the local muddle one would be able to see the true division between the eternal, pure, and institutional Church and the diabolic City of the World. Christ's incarnation had forced the wicked and the righteous to reveal themselves;[169] hence in Bede's well-known story of the reprobate Bernician monk, the brethren had no doubts concerning his way of life, only tolerating him for purely earthly reasons. The Lord had already divided the light and darkness and, for Bede, in tales such as those concerning Coldingham and the wicked monk that division could already be partly seen in history.[170] If Anglo-Saxon culture particularly fostered this conviction that the pure heavenly Church was already making itself known in the institutions of this world, then, during Bede's own lifetime, churchmen from England would begin to export similarly rigorous views to Frankia where they would resort to tactics similar to those of the *Letter to Ecgberht* when seeking to impose their own vision of correct Christianity.[171]

---

[165] Helen Foxhall Forbes, *Heaven and Earth in Anglo-Saxon England: Theology and Society in an Age of Faith* (Farnham, 2013), pp. 294–300.

[166] M. Tangl (ed.), *Die Briefe des Heiligen Bonifatius und Lullus*, MGH Epistolae Selectae 1, 64 pp. 132–6.

[167] *EpEcg.*, 10 pp. 142–3 'stilo stultissimo, ut nouimus omnes, in monasteriorum ascripta uocabulum'.

[168] Foxhall Forbes, *Heaven and Earth*, p. 17.   [169] *Hom.*, I.18 p. 132.

[170] *HE*, V.14 pp. 502–5, esp. 503.

[171] See Matthew Innes, '"Immune from Heresy": Defining the Boundaries of Carolingian Christianity', in *Frankland: The Franks and the World of the early Middle Ages. Essays in honour of Dame Jinty Nelson*, eds Paul Fouracre and David Ganz (Manchester, 2008), pp. 101–25.

Bede intended the stories of Coldingham and the wicked monk (along with much else in Book Five of the *Ecclesiastical History*) to inspire repentance, and he certainly worried about the temple as the individual soul or Christian, if not as the Church;[172] while, as we have seen in the discussion of Bede's views of the 'present Church', the ecclesiastical community could be assured of its salvation, it remained important to remind the individual that damnation always remained a possibility lying disturbingly just out of sight, held off by grace.[173] Clearly some doubt remained in the present world; Bede's concluding remarks in the *Ecclesiastical History* combine the trite truisim that the result of current actions lies in the future, a hint at the moral opacity of the present, and a warning to the reader not to grow too confident in their own salvation.[174] But this sense of doubt, this tension between election and damnation, seems evident only in the Christian soul and not in the Church itself for Bede had learnt from Augustine that the Church remained pure in itself, if not in its individual members.[175] Augustine, after all, had chosen the phrase *permixta ecclesia* because he was uncomfortable with Tyconius' claim that the reprobate existed in Christ's body; he changed the vocabulary used to make the falsity of such Christians clear, a change of which Bede strongly approved.[176] What differentiated the two writers was the degree to which Bede sought to transfer that purity from the eschatological future to the present, thereby emphasizing the unity of the transcendental and sacramental Church.[177] Paradoxically that unity utterly excluded the unorthodox and impure.

In Chapters 3 and 4 we saw how Bede used the image of the temple to represent the Church as an eternal and cosmic body rooted in Christ; Chapter 5 and the current chapter have detailed how the temple image also presented a model as to how the body of Christ should operate in the world, in particular through its duty to preach and protect Christians from unorthodox dangers. Throughout this discussion the importance of the individual has been obvious. For Bede, a reformed and pure institutional Church had to possess teachers of exemplary morality. Bede's belief in the importance of hierarchy existed alongside his conviction that all Christians shared in Christ's

[172] Ralph Walterspacher, 'Book V of Bede's *Historia ecclesiastica gentis Anglorum*: Perspective on Salvation History and Eschatology', *Archa Verbi: Yearbook for the Study of Medieval Theology* 1 (2004), pp. 11–24.

[173] *Temp.*, p. 168; *Ezra.*, pp. 336, 347, 359. *Tab.*, p. 110. The preacher needs to devote twice as much time to their own soul as they do to others': *Temp.*, p. 151.

[174] *HE*, V.23 pp. 560–61; R. A. Markus, *Bede and the Tradition of Ecclesiastical Historiography*, Jarrow Lecture (Jarrow, 1975), pp. 14–15; Stancliffe, *Bede and the Britons*, pp. 37–40.

[175] Hence the Church could simply be equated with the City of God: e.g. Augustine, *DCD*, XIII.16 p. 396. Markus, *Saeculum*, pp. 118–19; Olsen, 'From Bede', p. 376.

[176] Augustine, *Doctrina*, III.100 p. 176; *Apoc.*, p. 225.

[177] Carroll, *Spiritual Teachings*, p. 69, sees the two aspects of the Church as 'complementary', rather than antagonistic'.

priesthood, because the faithful individual had become one with Christ. The Church, institutional and transcendent at the same time as I have argued, provided a bridge between eternity and the individual Christian soul. We must, therefore, narrow our focus yet again and study the temple as a symbol of the individual.

7

Bede's Temple as Individual

We have already noted many reasons why Bede would have been interested in the individual Christian soul. His reform agenda aimed to create an elite of *doctores* who held themselves to the highest standards and whose lives reflected the best apostolic models; more generally, as a teacher himself, Bede sought to inculcate the essential Christian virtues in his readers in whom he sought to stir up repetence and compunction in preparation for their final judgement. Above all our exploration of various themes has revealed the importance of one particular individual—the incarnate Christ—to Bede's theology. The central mystery of Christian faith, that human and divine united in Jesus Christ, rendered the theological focus on the individual particularly intense. For Bede, the incarnation was important not just because of his 'Christ-centred view of salvation history', but because he believed that as members of the Body of Christ all the faithful to some extent shared in the Saviour's nature.[1] The fact that God had become a human himself opened up wonderful possibilities for every individual human.

Obviously, we should be cautious in suggesting that Bede had an awareness of the individual or self in the modern sense. The appropriateness of talking about a pre-modern sense of the self has stimulated much debate, and scholars of the Middle Ages have struggled with the question of whether the twelfth century in particular saw the growth of a consciousness of the individual that had not previously existed.[2] As we shall see later in this chapter, for Bede the individual Christian was not utterly distinct and independent from other Christians. Nonetheless, he asserted that the temple image referred to 'each one of the elect', as well as 'all the Church together', and it is in this primarily numerical sense that I speak of the individual.[3]

---

[1] Máirín Mac Carron, 'Bede, *Annus Domini* and the *Historia ecclesiastica gentis anglorum*', in *The Mystery of Christ in the Fathers of the Church: Essays in Honour of D. Vincent Twomey SVD*, eds Janet E. Rutherford and David Woods (Dublin, 2012), pp. 116–34, at 134.

[2] Caroline Walker Bynum, 'Did the Twelfth Century Discover the Individual?', *JEH* 31 (1980), pp. 1–17; Colin Morris, *The Discovery of the Individual, 1050–1200* (London, 1972).

[3] *Ezra.*, p. 241 'liquet . . . templum Dei in scripturis sanctis et unumquemque electorum et omnem simul ecclesiam . . . solere appellari'; trans. DeGregorio, p. 6.

Every living stone in God's temple represented an elect soul, something of independent value but nonetheless shaped according to a correct standard that was anything but individual.

MORALITY

On a number of occasions the New Testament Pauline letters describe the faithful as the temple of God. Frequently the letters focus on the collective aspects of this temple; Bede certainly knew that when Paul declared 'the temple of God is holy, which you are', he spoke to all the society of believers, to 'you' plural.[4] But equally he knew that Paul had described the Christian's physical body itself as the temple and thus one could deem all Pauline uses of the temple to refer to the individual.[5] For Paul, the believer became a temple because God dwelt within that person and this image had definite moral implications. A temple, as a sacred space, must be kept unsullied and Paul used the image to demand purity of Christians, both bodily (union with a prostitute polluted the temple) and as a community (the Christian should not defile the temple by associating with unbelievers).[6] The theme of moral purity was also, of course, an important part of Bede's interpretation of the temple, as we will see in what follow; this investigation will bring us back to the importance of Christ's incarnation.

Bede represented the individual as the temple in a similar fashion to Paul: the idea of God dwelling within the Christian person remained central.[7] But while Paul's originality lay in thinking of this inhabitation as bodily in nature, many of the Fathers had preferred to think of it as being interior or spiritual.[8] Bede preserved such interpretations of the temple, which saw it as 'the mind and conscience of the faithful'.[9] Hence, the interior temple of the individual, and especially the heart as the dwelling place of God, appears regularly in his work.[10] The common New Testament trope of the body as a *tabernaculum* (probably meaning tent here, rather than referring to Moses' tabernacle),

---

[4] 1 Corinthians 3.17 'templum enim Dei sanctum est quod estis vos' (also 2 Corinthians 6.16); *DST*, II.12 pp. 168–9.

[5] 1 Corinthians 6.19; *DST*, II.12 p. 169. See *Temp.*, p. 147; *Tab.*, p. 43.

[6] 1 Corinthians 6.13–20; 2 Corinthians 6.14–18.

[7] *Tab.*, p. 11; *Temp.*, p. 147; *Ezra*, pp. 241, 300; *Sam.*, p. 58.

[8] See Ch. 2 within this volume, 'The temple in the Christian tradition before Bede', p. 40.

[9] *Luc.*, p. 349 (= *Marc.*, p. 580) quotes Gregory, *Homiliae in Evangelia*, ed. R. Étaix, CCSL 141, II.XXXIX.7 p. 386 'Templum quoque et domus Dei est ipsa mens atque conscientia fidelium'. Also *Luc.*, p. 207 (= *Marc.*, p. 545); compare Jerome, *In Matheum*, eds D. Hurst and M. Adriaen, CCSL 77, p. 149.

[10] *Cant.*, p. 279; *Sam.*, pp. 11, 109; *Luc.*, p. 311. He also read the ark as faith, which should be kept within the pure heart or conscience: *Sam.*, pp. 45, 54.

often appears in Insular hagiography to emphasize the transitory nature of the body.[11] But Bede still chose to highlight the temple image's application to both bodily and mental purity. Christians could expect condemnation if they did 'not keep the temples of their own hearts and bodies worthy for God to inhabit'.[12] Body and mind ought always to remain in harmony according to Bede; he often spoke of the two in one breath.[13]

Paul used the image of the body as temple to argue for sexual purity, and such an interpretation seems to have been popular amongst some Anglo-Saxons.[14] While Bede did use this verse to condemn dancing, he more usually went beyond any narrowly physical interpretation—maintaining his interest in the linked nature of both heart and body.[15] He did once in *On the Tabernacle* directly link the temple of the individual to *castitas*, but the word clearly signified something more extensive than avoiding intercourse with prostitutes since it concerned restraining 'both the flesh from lascivious impulses and the heart from enticing thoughts'.[16] The mixture of Pauline and patristic elements in Bede's moral use of the temple image thus seems clear, and neither bodily nor spiritual purity alone is dominant. This distinctive mixture of the physical and the interior appears throughout the discussion that follows.

When considering the moral application of the temple image, Bede's homilies may seem likely to provide more fruitful ground for study than his commentaries. Questions still exist over the intended audience and register of the homilies: some scholars argue for a primarily monastic audience, with occasional lay participation, while others suggest that Bede addressed a mixture of clergy and laity. But a scholarly consensus exists, recognizing that the homilies differ from the commentaries in their more explicitly moralizing tone, their more personal focus, and in addressing the audience directly.[17] It is possible that the homilies were composed 'for actual oral delivery', though

---

[11] Adomnán, *Vita S. Columbae*, eds and trans. Alan Orr Anderson and Marjorie Ogilvie Anderson, *Adomnan's Life of Columba* (Oxford, 1991), III.23 pp. 226–7; *HE*, IV.29 pp. 440–1; *VCP*, XXVIII pp. 250–51. 2 Peter 1.14.

[12] *Ezra.*, p. 336 'ne templa cordium uel corporum suorum Deo inhabitatore digna seruarent'; trans. DeGregorio, p. 150. Also *Ezra.*, p. 305.

[13] *Hom.*, II.1 p. 189; *Temp.*, p. 231; *Tab.*, pp. 43, 113. See Scott DeGregorio, 'The Venerable Bede on Prayer and Contemplation', *Traditio* 54 (1999), pp. 1–39, at 9 and 16.

[14] 1 Corinthians 6.19; M. Tangl (ed.), *Die Briefe des Heiligen Bonifatius und Lullus*, MGH Epistolae Selectae 1, 73 pp. 148–9; Aldhelm, *Carmen de Virginitate*, ed. R. Ehwald, MGH Auctores Antiquissimi 15, p. 359; Aldhelm, *Prosa de Virginitate*, in the same volume, XLV p. 299.

[15] *Ezra.*, p. 272; *Hom.*, I.23 p. 165, II.23 p. 352.

[16] *Tab.*, p. 45 'et carnem a lasciuis motibus et cor ab illecebrosis refrenemus cogitationibus'; trans. Holder, p. 49.

[17] A. G. P. van der Walt, 'The Homiliary of the Venerable Bede and Early Medieval Preaching' (PhD thesis, University of London, 1980), pp. 52–8, 73–5, 208–11, 217–18; Eric Jay Del Giacco, 'Exegesis and Sermon: A Comparison of Bede's Commentary and Homilies on Luke', *Medieval Sermon Studies* 50 (2006), pp. 9–29.

their occasionally complex and artistic prose suggests that Bede revised them with an eye towards a reading audience.[18] But regardless of whether it was a reading or listening audience, in the homilies Bede attempted to make the biblical text immediate and relevant to his audience.[19] We might expect the moral focus on the individual as temple to play a major role in such texts, and indeed Bede frequently reminded his readers/hearers that they ought to become temples of the Lord.[20] However, this individual focus never appears at the expense of the social: if one wishes to see God in the heavenly temple then one must work untiringly to build up his house of the Church.[21] This may indicate that Bede had a bias towards the collective interpretation of the temple image, even in the homilies. But primarily it reminds us that, for Bede, individual morality had to make sense in a social context and had to express itself in practical works.

In the homilies Bede warned Christians to purify themselves and to abandon the kind of sinfulness that would lead God to reject them as a temple in which to dwell: 'Let us then cleanse the temples of our bodies and hearts, so that the Spirit of God may deign to dwell in us'.[22] Bede also suggested that God's indwelling in the heart allowed him to examine it in greater detail; therefore, the individual ought to make sure their heart stayed pure lest something worthy of reprobation be found.[23] Here he presented God as judge, an *internus arbiter* examining the most personal aspects of the soul.[24] Sometimes a homily teaches quite practical moral lessons: Christians ought to make sure they do not do anything inappropriately worldly in a church.[25] Other times Bede focused on the inner moral disposition of the believer: Christ builds his house with deep foundations on rock, as also he seeks to root out 'whatever base drives he found in the hearts of his faithful' so that he can build them into an 'unshakeable dwelling-place'.[26] In the homilies, as in his work more generally, Bede never directed the image of temple toward an explicit

---

[18] Del Giacco, 'Exegesis and Sermon', p. 14; Verity Allan, 'Theological Works of the Venerable Bede and their Literary and Manuscript Presentation, with special reference to the Gospel Homilies' (MLitt thesis, University of Oxford, 2006), pp. 61–86.

[19] Lawrence T. Martin, 'The Two Worlds in Bede's Homilies: The Biblical Event and the Listeners' Experience', in *De Ore Domini: Preacher and Word in the Middle Ages*, eds Thomas L. Amos et al. (Kalamazoo MI, 1989), pp. 27–40.

[20] *Hom.*, I.23 p. 165, I.25 p. 183, II.15 pp. 284–5.

[21] *Hom.*, II.24 p. 367.

[22] *Hom.*, II.1 p. 192 'mundemus templa corporum cordiumque nostrorum ut spiritus Dei habitare dignetur in nobis'; trans. Martin and Hurst, II, p. 12. Also *Hom.*, II.12 p. 265, II.24 p. 359.

[23] *Hom.*, II.1 p. 186, II.24 p. 359. Also *Marc.*, p. 576.

[24] *Hom.*, II.25 p. 371; compare Gregory, *Moralia in Iob*, ed. M. Adriaen, CCSL 143+A+B, VII. X.10 p. 341.

[25] *Hom.*, II.1 p. 185.

[26] *Hom.*, II.25 p. 372 'in corde suorum fidelium quicquid terrenae intentionis inuenit funditus exstirpare studuit . . . inconcussam mansionem possit habere'; trans. Martin and Hurst, II, p. 260.

exhortation to avoid sexual and bodily sin in the way Augustine did when addressing a lay audience.[27]

Talk of purity and the indwelling of God calls to mind the cleansing waters of baptism through which the Spirit descended upon the individual Christian. Bede certainly on occasion stated that 'we have become the temple of God by our baptism' or that those who receive the faith become a temple of the Creator.[28] Generally, however, he followed discussions of baptism with explanation of how this unique act requires the individual to follow it with constant acts of moral purification, through the tears of compunction or good works.[29] One cannot repeat baptism and so the purity gained through it must be constantly guarded and if lost only a difficult process of penance can restore it.[30] The Christian journey through the desert of life began with baptism, with other sacraments serving as way stations along the path—from baptism's cleansing waters one went on to burn as a holocaust with the fire of the Spirit at confirmation, or to consecrate oneself by sacrifice at the eucharistic altar.[31] One becomes a temple, therefore, through active and ongoing participation in the sacramental life of the Church. Moral purity requires effort beyond simple reception of the sacraments of initiation since Bede believed strongly in a constant process of growth continuing throughout life: he repeated the Gregorian idea that nobody suddenly becomes perfect throughout the temple trilogy.[32]

When the individual became a temple the heart became an altar, aflame with the love of God. Bede used this image a number of times: when connected with the altar of incense the image usually refers to the sacrifice of prayers (a link between incense and prayers was established by Psalms 140.2); when connected with the altar of holocausts to the sacrifice of good works.[33] Here Bede drew upon the contrast between the contemplative and active lives, but

---

[27] E.g. Augustine, *Sermones*, PL 38, CCLXXVIII.7 col. 1271, which Bede knew: *Excerpts from the Works of Saint Augustine on the Letters of the Blessed Apostle Paul*, trans. David Hurst (Kalamazoo MI, 1999), p. 131.

[28] *Hom.*, II.1 p. 186 'sumus in baptismo templum Dei facti'; trans. Martin and Hurst, II, p. 4. Also *Ezra.*, p. 359; *Hom.*, II.17 p. 306; *Sam.*, p. 66. See also Ch. 6 within this volume, 'The temple as which Church?', p. 150.

[29] *Tab.*, pp. 53, 136; *Temp.*, pp. 207–14. Jennifer O'Reilly, 'Exegesis and the Book of Kells: The Lucan Genealogy', in *The Book of Kells: Proceedings of a Conference at Trinity College Dublin, 6–9 September 1992*, ed. Felicity O'Mahony (Aldershot, 1994), pp. 344–97, at 389–90.

[30] *Ezra.*, pp. 305, 321.

[31] *Temp.*, p. 214; *Cant.*, p. 322; *Hom.*, I.14 pp. 101–2, I.18 p. 130; *Gen.*, p. 128.

[32] *Ezra.*, p. 390; *Tab.*, p. 137; *Temp.*, p. 225; compare Gregory, *Homiliae in Hiezechihelem Prophetam*, ed. M. Adriaen, CCSL 142, II.III.3 p. 238. Jennifer O'Reilly, 'Bede on Seeing the God of Gods in Zion', in *Text, Image, Interpretation: Studies in Anglo-Saxon Literature and its Insular Context in Honour of Eamonn Ó Carragáin*, eds Alastair Minnis and Jane Roberts (Turnhout, 2007), pp. 3–29; Arthur G. Holder, 'The Venerable Bede on the Mysteries of Our Salvation', *American Benedictine Review* 421 (1991), pp. 140–62, at 150–54.

[33] *Tab.*, pp. 76, 132; *Temp.*, pp. 224–5; *Ezra.*, p. 266; *Hom.*, II.19 p. 324, II.25 p. 376; *Marc.*, p. 556. Giovanni Caputa, *Il Sacerdozio dei Fedeli secondo San Beda: un itinerario di maturità cristiana* (Vatican City, 2002), pp. 252–8; Scott DeGregorio, 'The Venerable Bede and Gregory

did not stick to it consistently. When speaking of the altar of holocausts, the fire of which God ordered to be perpetual, Bede declared: 'But the fire of love by which the elect are kindled to offer God sacrifices of *prayers or good deeds* will never go out from the altar, that is, from their hearts'.[34] Action and contemplation form not so much contrasts as points on a continuum: all moral forms of behaviour, from the tears of compunction to chastity to almsgiving, count as offerings to God.[35] And even though Bede usually saw the altar in terms of the heart (implying that the sacrifice was interior and spiritual), on occasion he referred it to both the hearts and bodies of the elect; while he could dismiss the sacrifices of the temple cult as overly material, Bede contrasted them not with faith alone but also with the works of faith.[36] Thus the whole self, body and soul, formed the altar on which the Christian offered the 'libations of the virtues'.[37]

Bede made important contributions to the history of the concept of the four cardinal virtues and this quartet joins the many other fours that appear in his temple commentaries.[38] Prudence, fortitude, temperance, and justice were the four principal virtues 'in which each believer, if he is not to be a believer in vain, must be formed', Bede stated.[39] The numerous rectangular altars and tables of these texts gave him a way to mention the four virtues, alongside the four corners of the world and the four gospels.[40] Most interestingly, he conceived these virtues as being the foundations on which 'every edifice of good action rests'.[41] Virtues for Bede were not merely states of mind; they provided the basis of virtuous action in the world.[42] Because of this Bede followed Gregory in seeing the relationship of the numbers three (faith in the Trinity) and four (the cardinal virtues) as indicative of the necessity of both faith and action in the individual Christian. Hence the Jews completed the

---

the Great: Exegetical Connections, Spiritual Departures', *EME* 18 (2010), pp. 43–60, at 58, contrasts Bede and Gregory's interpretation of holocausts.

[34] *Gen.*, p. 180 'Sed ignis dilectionis quo electi accenduntur ad offerenda Deo sacrificia *orationum siue actionum bonarum* numquam deficiet de altari, id est de cordibus eorum, quae illo mosaico altari designabantur'; adapted from trans. Kendall, pp. 257–8. My emphasis.

[35] *Apoc.*, p. 425; *Tab.*, p. 71; *Temp.*, p. 172; *Hom.*, I.18 p. 133.

[36] *Marc.*, pp. 590–91.

[37] *Tab.*, pp. 76, 126 'uirtutum libamina'.

[38] Jasmijn Bovendeert, 'Beda's deugdenkwartet', *Madoc: Tijdschrift over de Middeleeuwen* 19 (2005), pp. 36–46; István P. Bejczy, *The Cardinal Virtues in the Middle Ages: A Study in Moral Thought from the Fourth to the Fourteenth Century* (Leiden, 2011), pp. 47–8. The classic work is Sybill Mähl, *Quadriga Virtutum: Die Kardinaltugenden in der Geistesgeschichte der Karolingerzeit* (Cologne, 1969), pp. 30–34 for Bede.

[39] *Temp.*, p. 221 'quattuor cardinales uirtutes quibus quisque fidelis, si non frustra fidelis est, debet institui'; trans. Connolly, p. 101.

[40] Bovendeert, 'Beda's deugdenkwartet', pp. 43–5; e.g. *Tab.*, p. 77.

[41] *Temp.*, p. 189 'omnis bonorum actuum structura innititur'; trans. Connolly, p. 60. Compare Gregory, *Moralia*, II.XLIX.76 p. 105.

[42] Also *Tab.*, p. 46.

rebuilding of the temple, discussed in *On Ezra and Nehemiah*, in the twelfth month ($12 = 3 \times 4$) because the grace of the Holy Spirit enters into the mind of the elect so that they might achieve both faith and works.[43]

The four colours of the priestly garments also appear frequently in Bede's temple commentaries, providing another moral quartet.[44] Throughout *On the Tabernacle* Bede provided a consistent interpretation of these: blue refers to 'the mind that is desiring things above', purple to 'the flesh that is subject to afflictions', scarlet twice-dyed to the twofold love of God and neighbour, and white linen to 'the purified flesh that is shining with chastity'.[45] *On the Temple* provides the same basic interpretation while linking purple rather more specifically with Christ's blood (and the need to imitate his passion) and presenting white in a more general fashion as 'the chastening of our flesh'.[46] The combination of internal and external virtues remains, however, as the mind and body both prove necessary to fulfil all these virtues—not that Bede insisted that all Christians had to display them entirely in themselves. Within the overall Christian community they all appeared—the saints may excel in one specific virtue, together forming the rich diversity of the Church.[47] It proves hard not to note the ascetic leanings of Bede's interpretation of the colours: quoting a long section from Gregory on the four colours, Bede could not let the interpretation of purple as kingly control over the vices stand alone, so he added his preferred reading of purple as 'the spilling of one's blood for Christ, or as the endurance of many afflictions'.[48] Physical suffering was rarely far away when Bede thought of this colour.[49]

For Bede, all Christians require the cardinal virtues, although they have an especial importance for preachers.[50] All the virtues represented by the four colours must be displayed by the priest or *doctor* since they were all mixed together in the priestly robes.[51] Such statements remind us of Bede's utter

---

[43] *Ezra.*, p. 299; also *Tab.*, pp. 104, 112; Bejczy, *Cardinal Virtues*, p. 32. This interpretation of twelve seems almost entirely specific to Bede and Gregory: Heinz Meyer and Rudolf Suntrup, *Lexikon der Mittelalterlichen Zahlenbedeutungen* (Munich, 1987), p. 627.

[44] *Sam.*, pp. 214–15, associates the colours with the virtues without going into details.

[45] *Tab.*, pp. 45–6: p. 46 'in bysso retorta caro castitate renitens, in hyacintha mens superna desiderans, in purpura caro passionibus subiacens, in cocco bis tincto mens inter passiones Dei et proximi dilectione praefulgens'; trans. Holder, p. 50. Also *Tab.*, pp. 11, 89.

[46] *Temp.*, p. 188 'castigationem nostrae carnis'; trans. Connolly, p. 59.

[47] *Tab.*, pp. 89–90.

[48] *Tab.*, p. 99 'ut superius dictum est in purpureo colore possit ipsa effusio sanguinis pro Christo uel diuersarum tolerantia pressurarum intellegi...'; trans. Holder, p. 113; compare Gregory, *Regula Pastoralis*, PL 77, II.3 col. 29. Gregory accepted the bloody interpretation of purple elsewhere: *Moralia*, XXX.VI.24 p. 1507.

[49] George Henderson, *Vision and Image in Early Christian England* (Cambridge, 1999), pp. 122–35.

[50] *Temp.*, pp. 215, 221; Bejczy, *Cardinal Virtues*, p. 34. See also Mähl, *Quadriga Virtutum*, pp. 31–3.

[51] *Tab.*, pp. 100–101.

loyalty to the Church's institutional hierarchy but, while some Christians rank higher than the rest, Bede had no doubt that God inhabited all the elect.[52] Not 'only ministers of the altar', but 'all the faithful', share in the participation in Christ's priesthood opened up through the Spirit in baptism.[53] Thus, while priests ought to take care to maintain purity in their body and mind when they celebrate the sacraments of the Lord, so too ought the laity when receiving those same sacraments.[54] Bede extended the moral significance of becoming a temple worthy of God to all Christians; the laity as well as the clergy had to work to so consecrate themselves. Obviously the standard of life to which Christ called the latter lay far above that expected of the former. For Bede 'the leaders and teachers of the Holy Church transcend the common life of the elect by the exceptional eminence of their minds'.[55] Priests who sin can re-enter the Church through penance just like anybody else, but some sins are so heinous that the sinner 'cannot recover' the grade of priest.[56]

Bede would not have seen this hierarchy as denying the bonds of charity between clerics and laity, nor, as Hollis has argued, as creating superhuman saints removed from the common people.[57] As we will go on to see, the need to shape an elite into sufficiently exalted examples clearly underlay Bede's rigorous demands for dignity from preachers and priests. This elite could only remain pure by remaining humble and Bede repeatedly emphasized the importance of humility for the holiest of Christians.[58] From reading Gregory, Bede knew that humility required the saint to return to the active world rather than to exalt themselves above it.[59] Christ entered the temple to perform acts of mercy because he valued these higher than ritual sacrifices.[60] The incarnation became the supreme act of mercy because it involved an acceptance of human suffering and thus, for Bede, the saint embraced suffering rather than rose above it.

---

[52] *Ezra.*, p. 381. For Bede's inclusivity towards the laity: Caputa, *Sacerdozio dei Fedeli*, pp. 276–7.

[53] *Tab.*, p. 138 'Non . . . soli altaris ministri . . . Ammonemus omnes fideles mystico sacerdotum nomine censeri'; trans. Holder, p. 161. Also *Temp.*, pp. 207, 211.

[54] *Tab.*, pp. 138–9.

[55] *Tab.*, p. 96 'praesules ac doctores sanctae ecclesiae communem uitam electorum singulari mentis culmine transcendere'; trans. Holder, p. 110.

[56] *Ezra.*, p. 256 'gradus sui quem repetere nequeunt'; trans. DeGregorio, p. 30.

[57] Stephanie Hollis, *Anglo-Saxon Women and the Church: Sharing a Common Fate* (Woodbridge, 1992), pp. 120–29, who contrasts Bede with the Whitby *Vita Gregorii*, ed. and trans. Bertram Colgrave, *The Earliest Life of Gregory the Great, By an Anonymous Monk of Whitby* (Cambridge, 1985).

[58] Humility necessary for the chaste: *Tab.*, p. 120; humility necessary for the learned: *Hom.*, I.19 p. 138; Eosterwine provided a model of monastic humility: *HA*, 8 pp. 40–43. Mary Thomas Aquinas Carroll, *The Venerable Bede: His Spiritual Teachings* (Washington DC, 1946), pp. 223–7.

[59] Carole Straw, *Gregory the Great: Perfection in Imperfection* (Berkeley CA, 1988), pp. 20, 188–91.

[60] *Hom.*, I.21 pp. 152–3.

Ascetic zeal has sometimes been considered characteristic of 'Celtic' Christianity, but if so, Roman-leaning Anglo-Saxons such as Wilfrid did not reject it.[61] While Carroll has tried to separate the ascetic behaviour recounted in Bede's writings from the spirituality of the man himself, it seems best to acknowledge that his work represents worldly suffering highly positively as a way of replicating in the Christian the engagement with humanity which the incarnation brought about in the body of Christ.[62] On occasion Bede described the process by which individuals became part of the heavenly temple, using such imagery to describe the beneficial way suffering shaped people. The hammering of the materials of the temple reminded him of how suffering prepared the Christian 'hammered by adversities' for heaven.[63] For all who wish to live godly lives in Christ 'it is through the blows of suffering that they make progress toward the grace of immortality, just as metal is stretched out by being smitten'.[64] The flames of tribulations humble and thereby strengthen those who are materials for the heavenly temple.[65]

Here Bede understood the physical building of the temple as the worldly sufferings of Christians; these sufferings prepared them for entry into eternal life. This interest in pain and suffering achieves its purest expression in Bede's *Martyrology*—a highly original text and the first narrative martyrology, though unfortunately still awaiting a final critical edition.[66] Bede's own comments on the *Martyrology* show his interest in providing details about how the saints 'overcame the world' in suffering and death rather than in telling their wider life story.[67] And indeed the detail of the descriptions of torture and death of which the work mainly consists remains its most striking feature.[68] In

---

[61] Sarah Downey, 'Too Much of Too Little: Guthlac and the Temptation of Excessive Fasting', *Traditio* 63 (2008), pp. 89–127, at 125–6. *VW*, XXI pp. 44–5; W. Trent Foley, *Images of Sanctity in Eddius Stephanus' Life of Bishop Wilfrid, An Early English Saint's Life* (Lampeter, 1992), pp. 42–6; Simon Coates, 'The Role of Bishops in the Early Anglo-Saxon Church: A Reassessment', *History* 81 (1996), pp. 177–96, at 183–91.

[62] Carroll, *Spiritual Teachings*, p. 231. The idea that the Christian's sufferings replicated and imitated those of Christ has a long history, especially in relation to martyrdom: Candida R. Moss, *The Other Christs: Imitating Jesus in Ancient Christian Ideologies of Martyrdom* (Oxford, 2010).

[63] *Temp.*, p. 165 'tundimur aduersitatibus'; trans. Connolly, p. 28. Also *Tab.*, p. 42; compare Gregory, *Regula Pastoralis*, III.12 col. 68.

[64] *Tab.*, p. 36 'ipsi quasi metallum feriendo dilatatum per passionis contumelias ad immortalitatis gratiam proficiunt'; trans. Holder, p. 38. Compare Gregory, *In Hiezechihelem*, I.VI.8 p. 71.

[65] *Gen.*, p. 160; *Temp.*, p. 223; compare Gregory, *Regula Pastoralis*, III.13 col. 71.

[66] One can find a good though rather unhelpfully structured Latin text edited by Henri Quentin, *Les Martyrologes Historiques du Moyen Age* (Paris, 1908), pp. 57–112. Based on Quentin's text, and checked against the earliest manuscripts, is the English translation by Felice Lifshitz in *Medieval Hagiography: An Anthology*, ed. Thomas Head (London, 2001), pp. 169–97.

[67] *HE*, V.24 pp. 570–71 'mundum uicerint'.

[68] On suffering in the *Martyrology*: Peter Dendle, 'Pain and Saint-Making in *Andreas*, Bede, and the Old English Lives of St. Margaret', in *Varieties of Devotion in the Middle Ages and Renaissance*, ed. Susan C. Karant-Nunn (Turnhout, 2003), pp. 39–52, at 44–8. On the background to this understudied text: Michael Lapidge, 'Acca of Hexham and the Origin of the Old English Martyrology', *Analecta Bollandiana* 123 (2005), pp. 29–78.

its terse and direct account, the *Martyrology* epitomizes an aspect of Bede's view of sanctity that runs throughout his hagiographical work. Bede's *Life of Cuthbert* highlights the importance of suffering to the making of a saint, especially in its focus on illnesses, which by visiting agony upon the body purify the soul: 'Almighty God might, by chastisement, purify His servant from all blemish of worldly weakness'.[69] This trope also features in Bede's historical writings where he saw physical illnesses as blessings so that a saint's 'virtue might be made perfect in weakness' (2 Corinthians 12.9)—an idea he cited in reference to the illnesses of Æthelburh, Hild, and Benedict Biscop.[70] The great plague, which killed many religious in seventh-century England, actually contributed to building the temple, transferring through death 'the living stones of the church from their earthly sites to the heavenly building'.[71] Small wonder then that on his own deathbed Bede is said to have rejoiced in his suffering and weakness.[72]

Bede certainly reflected here the importance of suffering in the thought of Gregory the Great.[73] The preface to *On the Temple* shows that he did not thoughtlessly copy this theme, but engaged thoughtfully with it. The preface focuses on the suffering and exile of this life: Bede suggested that the image of the temple would help the Christian understand the nature of earthly suffering and thus help them accept 'the present worries of temporal affairs' and appreciate their salutary effects.[74] Bishop Acca, the probable dedicatee of the work, may have been in political exile at the time since the Moore Continuation of the *Ecclesiastical History* states that he was driven from his see in 731, the same year as an attempted coup against King Ceolwulf; hence the commentary could be a consolation for very real earthly tribulations.[75] Bede invited Acca to see his suffering in the context of that of the saints who had come before him: patience comes from studying their examples, at the pinnacle of which rests Christ himself. The sufferings of the just, and of Acca himself, make sense because 'even he who lived his life here below without

---

[69] Esp. *VCP*, XXXVII pp. 274–5 'Ut enim omnipotens Deus famulum suum ab omni labe mundanae fragilitatis ad purum castigaret . . .'; W. Trent Foley, 'Suffering and Sanctity in Bede's *Prose Life of St. Cuthbert*', *JTS* 50 (1999), pp. 102–16.

[70] *HE*, IV.9 pp. 360–61, IV.23 pp. 410–13; *HA*, 13 pp. 50–51; see also *HE*, II.1 pp. 128–9 on Gregory's illness.

[71] *HE*, IV.3 pp. 338–9 'Superuenit namque clades diuinitus missa, quae per mortem carnis uiuos ecclesiae lapides de terrenis sedibus ad aedificium caeleste transferret'.

[72] Cuthbert, *Epistola de Obitu Bedae*, eds and trans. Bertram Colgrave and R. A. B. Mynors, in *Bede's Ecclesiastical History of the English People* (Oxford, 1969), pp. 579–87, at 582–3.

[73] Foley, 'Suffering and Sanctity', pp. 107–9.

[74] *Temp.*, pp. 143–5: p. 144 'praesentes rerum temporalium angores'; trans. Connolly, p. 2.

[75] *HE*, pp. 572–3. Questioning the traditional assumption that, while Ceolwulf's deposition proved temporary, Acca's was permanent, implying that Acca may have been opposed to the king: Lapidge, 'Acca of Hexham', pp. 68–9; N. J. Higham, *(Re-)Reading Bede: The* Ecclesiastical History *in Context* (London, 2006), pp. 63–4; Christopher Grocock and I. N. Wood, *Abbots of Wearmouth and Jarrow* (Oxford, 2013), p. xlvii.

fault, did not depart from this life without chastisement, and he who appeared in the world to heal the sick and raise the dead, chose to return from the world in the weakness of death'.[76] Christ's suffering thus provided an example to be followed by humans.[77]

On the Temple, therefore, frames the ascetic themes that appear throughout the text in the context of Christ's own suffering via the incarnation. Christ's undeserved suffering is a mark of his sympathy with humankind; working divine redemption through afflicted humanity, he added 'his consolation' to 'our toil'.[78] As members of Christ's body, Christians must offer their own bodies as living sacrifices and Bede consistently saw martyrdom in this light.[79] Christian suffering depends on the passion: having offered himself up, Christ, the high priest, exited from the Holy of Holies so that the apostles could enter and offer their own sacrifices.[80] David sacrificing animals as the ark entered Jerusalem symbolized Christ who through the martyrs 'openly manifests both himself and the example of his incarnation and passion'. David did this wearing the priest's linen ephod because he showed the 'truth of human flesh which is triumphant amidst scourgings'.[81] The true flesh of the incarnation, offered up in sacrifice, has here blurred into the bodies of other humans offered as victims by Christ in a manner that we also see in Irish exegesis.[82] Bede's saints did not remain removed from suffering in some superhuman fashion, but rather suffered because human: just as human as Christ was when he suffered, making hope of redemption part of earthly pain.[83] The Christian as temple provides the mirror image of Christ as temple, different but yet in the end similar: 'he became the temple of God by assuming human nature and we become the temple of God *through his Spirit dwelling in us*'.[84]

---

[76] *Temp.*, p. 143 'neque ille hinc sine flagello exiit qui hic sine uitio uixit quique ad sanandos infirmos mortuosque suscitandos apparuit in mundo ipse ad praemonstrandum nobis exemplum patientiae per infirmitatem mortis uoluit redire de mundo'; trans. Connolly, pp. 1–2. The first part of Bede's statement bears similarities to a number of comments by Gregory but seems closest to *Regula Pastoralis*, III.12 col. 69. Also *Abac.*, pp. 382–3.

[77] Carroll, *Spiritual Teachings*, pp. 187–8.

[78] *Temp.*, p. 173 'Ieiunando etenim ostendebat nostrum in se laborem manducando autem et bibendo cum discipulis ostendebat in nobis suam consolationem'; trans. Connolly, p. 39.

[79] *Hom.*, II.23 p. 352. For martyrdom as sacrifice: Bede, *Martyrologium*, pp. 63, 73, 99; *Ret.*, p. 133; *Sam.*, pp. 53–4; *Hom.*, II.22 p. 347; *Gen.*, p. 128.

[80] *Hom.*, II.19 p. 323.

[81] *VIII Q.*, VIII p. 73 '*Boves et arietes immolans* [2 Kings 6.13], hoc est, eos qui aream domini triturant et ouium eius ducatum gerunt martyrii sanguine coronans, et ipse quoque suae incarnationis et passionis exemplum . . . manifestans. Hoc enim significat quod et ipse *David accinctus erat ephod lineo* [2 Kings 6.14]. Nam linum quod de terra procreatum multiplici labore ad candorem uestis peruenit, ueritatem humanae carnis inter flagella triumphantis ostendit'; trans. Arthur G. Holder in *Bede: A Biblical Miscellany* (Liverpool, 1999), p. 164.

[82] *Tractatus Hilarii in Septem Epistolas Canonicas*, ed. R. E. McNally, CCSL 108B, p. 89.

[83] See Hollis, *Anglo-Saxon Women*, p. 120.

[84] *Temp.*, p. 147 'ille templum Dei per assumptam humanitatem factus est et nos templum Dei *per inhabitantem spiritum eius in nobis* [Romans 8.11] efficimur'; trans. Connolly, p. 5.

We thus arrive at one of the most important of all the moral precepts that appear in Bede's temple commentaries: the *imitatio Christi*. As high priest Christ did more than just provide an example. His sacrifice came to its fulfilment when the Spirit descended on the Church, the same Spirit that burns as fire on the altar of each Christian.[85] In other words, Christians (members of the high priest) only offer their faith and works as purifying sacrifices because of Christ's action.[86] The emphasis in the above paragraphs on the actions and virtues of the individual should not imply that Bede believed that any of these things could be possible without God's grace. He had no doubt that the Christian depended on the Lord for everything good which they could achieve. But building the individual into a pure temple required a joint effort between God and man: the house of the Lord was constructed from living stones and what differentiated living from dead stones was cooperation with Christ's work as master builder.[87] Such cooperation still depended on grace, of course; but for Bede grace was not passively received, it had to be actively made real in one's life through works.[88]

The holistic process required to become a temple of the Lord seems clear. One cannot be simply made into a dwelling place for the divine, though one must receive grace and the sacraments. Having done so, however, the individual should actively live the Christian life in a way which involves both body and soul. The divine indwelling does not allow the faithful individual to escape humanity, rather they actually have to re-engage with it on the model of the incarnate Christ. Bede's temple commentaries display no real interest in the individual as an interior soul existing alone before God; the monastic context in which he wrote, where active prayer and work formed part of the daily routine, may be an important context for Bede's attitude to individual spirituality.[89] But theologically, I think, he imagined what a Christian ought to be by looking at what Christ had been. The Saviour provides the foundation on which all the living stones of the Church rest both collectively and as individuals.[90] No temple can be built of mismatched stones, of course, and a certain degree of uniformity proves necessary for individuals to participate in the life of the Church. That uniformity is imposed by means of imitation.

---

[85] *Act.*, pp. 14–15; *Marc.*, p. 556; *Ezra.*, pp. 265, 270.

[86] *EpCath.*, pp. 235–6.   [87] *EpCath.*, pp. 234–5.

[88] Aaron J. Kleist, *Striving with Grace: Views of Free Will in Anglo-Saxon England* (Toronto, 2008), p. 75; Stephanie Clark, 'Theorizing Prayer in Anglo-Saxon England: Bede and Ælfric', (PhD dissertation, University of Ilinois at Urbana-Champaign, 2011), p. 81.

[89] Scott DeGregorio, 'Bede, the Monk, as Exegete: Evidence from the Commentary on Ezra-Nehemiah', *RB* 115 (2005), pp. 343–69; Clark, 'Theorizing Prayer', pp. 87–107.

[90] *Temp.*, pp. 147, 154; *Hom.*, II.25 p. 374; *Apoc.*, p. 527. Bede, of course, cited 1 Corinthians 3.11 on Christ as the foundation of the temple Church.

IMITATION

Imitation and example play an important part in the Christian life as imagined by Bede. For example, Bede's claim that in his commentaries he 'followed in the footsteps of the Fathers' has often been quoted: in the past to support the image of Bede as an unoriginal conduit of patristic knowledge; more recently to establish Bede's own self-conception as a Church Father.[91] We should note, however, that the phrase 'following in the footsteps' appears frequently in his work to express the idea of imitating an illustrious example such as Christ or the apostles.[92] This meaning had long been accepted by the Church Fathers, as Bede knew.[93] Bede's claim to follow the Fathers' footsteps constitutes, therefore, a claim to be their imitator, following the example of previous Christians as any pious individual should.

The concept of imitation has a long history in the Christian tradition. The New Testament emphasized the imitation of Christ, and hagiography showed how saints both imitated previous models and were themselves examples to be followed.[94] Medieval and late antique individuals saw nothing strange about seeking to imitate both living and textual models. Bede put forward a number of different figures as examples worthy of imitation by Christians. Christ obviously provided the most glorious such example, but before looking at the *imitatio Christi*, I want to look at Bede's use of other models for imitation, namely other human beings and angels. The faithful ought always to look upon the examples of those who are better than them, for by studying those greater they can themselves improve.[95] Imitation in fact plays a significant role in Bede's reform rhetoric—he urged *doctores* to make themselves into examples and encouraged *auditores* to imitate them. He constantly reiterated the point that the leaders of the Church should always teach their disciples by 'word and example'; indeed this forms almost the only use of the theme of imitation in *On Ezra and Nehemiah*.[96]

The vestments of the Jewish priesthood symbolized the virtue of the Church's teachers, which had to be performed outwardly and displayed for imitation. The rational/breastplate bore twelve gemstones, inscribed with the names of the twelve tribes; in like manner the Christian *rector* 'searches out the

---

[91] See Roger Ray, 'Who Did Bede Think He Was?', in *Innovation and Tradition in the Writings of the Venerable Bede*, ed. Scott DeGregorio (Morgantown WV, 2006), pp. 11–35, at 11–19. The phrase appears repeatedly: *Temp.*, p. 191; *Cant.*, p. 180; *Act.*, p. 3; *Hom.*, II.11 p. 258.

[92] *Apoc.*, p. 527; *Hom.*, I.13 p. 94, II.2 p. 193; *Temp.*, pp. 205–6.

[93] Augustine, *De Sancta Virginitate*, ed. J. Zycha, CSEL 41, XXVII p. 264, quoted at *Apoc.*, p. 423; Gregory, *In Evangelia*, I.II.8 p. 17, quoted at *Luc.*, p. 332 (= *Marc.*, p. 570).

[94] See 1 Corinthians 4.16, 2 Thessalonians 3.7–9, 1 Timothy 4.12, 1 Peter 5.3. Henri Crouzel, 'L'imitation et la "suite" de Dieu et du Christ dans les premiers siècles chrétiens, ainsi que leurs sources gréco-romaines et hébraïques', *Jahrbuch für Antike und Christentum* 21 (1978), pp. 7–41; Peter Brown, 'The Saint as Exemplar in Late Antiquity', *Representations* 2 (1983), pp. 1–25.

[95] E.g. *Tab.*, p. 80.   [96] *Ezra.*, pp. 264, 279, 321–2, 381; *Temp.*, p. 199; *Gen.*, p. 160.

life of the saints . . . considering how they are adorned with many works of virtues, and is eager to gather them all together in the hidden recesses of his breast by meditating on them, and to bring them forth by putting them into action'.[97] He does not simply order Christians to do what is righteous, but acts it out so that the audience may see, understand, and imitate it; in this way Ezra succeeded in bringing the Jewish people to repentance for their sins, not by telling them to grieve but by himself presenting an example of sorrow.[98] For Bede, one taught as much by displaying virtue as by explaining it. All the faithful should present their good deeds as an example to others since people 'hasten to imitate the hearts of the neighbours when they see them burning with piety'.[99] This explains Bede's insistence on the need for moral perfection amongst teachers. They live virtuously as much for their audience's sake as for their own; 'the examples of those who seem to be endowed with the garb of religion' can actually block the good desires of common people, if those examples prove noxious.[100] Similarly heretics and false Christians, just like *doctores*, go about their work using both words and examples.[101]

Augustine, while aware of the power of example in preaching, thought that an immoral teacher could still theoretically provide useful teaching.[102] The importance of the living example of virtue came to Bede from Gregory rather, who believed it impossible to teach well without living well as an example to others.[103] However, Bede's experience of monasticism, as much as his patristic reading, probably convinced him of the centrality of example to teaching since the imitation by students of the living exemplar of their teacher likely served an important role in the kind of monastic education practised at Wearmouth-Jarrow. Monastic teaching did not depend simply on the study of texts; rather the personal relationship between pupil and pedagogue proved essential, especially to the moral formation of the novice.[104] Novices also learnt from

---

[97] *Tab.*, p. 103 'sanctorum uitam rector inspiciens quibus maxime uirtutum operibus floruerint sedula inquisitione scrutatur et haec cuncta in abditis sui pectoris meditando colligere atque operando proferre satagit'; trans. Holder, p. 119. Also *Apoc.*, p. 527.

[98] *Ezra.*, pp. 328–9.

[99] *Tab.*, p. 81 'omnes qui feruentia pietate corda proximorum uidentes imitari festinant'; trans. Holder, p. 91.

[100] *Ezra.*, p. 360 'ne possint implere quod cupiunt . . . exemplis retardantur eorum qui habitu religionis uidentur esse praediti'; trans. DeGregorio, p. 184.

[101] *Ezra.*, p. 387; *Tab.*, p. 57.

[102] Augustine, *De Doctrina Christiana*, ed. and trans. R. P. H. Green (Oxford, 1995), IV.151–63 pp. 276–83; Ray, 'Who did Bede think he was?', p. 23, argues that Bede did not have access to Book IV of *Doctrina*; but see Alan Thacker, *Bede and Augustine of Hippo: History and Figure in Sacred Text*, Jarrow Lecture (Jarrow, 2005), p. 10.

[103] Gregory, *Regula Pastoralis*, I.2 col. 15–16, II.3 col. 28–30, III.4 col. 54.

[104] Catherine Cubitt, 'Monastic Memory and Identity in Early Anglo-Saxon England', in *Social Identity in Early Medieval Britain*, eds William O. Frazer and Andrew Tyrrell (London, 2000), pp. 253–76, at 262–4; Faith Wallis, *Bede: On the Reckoning of Time* (Liverpool, 1999), pp. xxviii–xxix.

participating in the communal life of the brethren, all of whom had a duty to provide an example to the young.[105] Catherine Cubitt has suggested that at Wearmouth-Jarrow the 'rule' did not consist of a written text, but rather of oral tradition based on memories of the lives of the early abbots who provided 'models of the monastic life', held up as examples to the brothers in the community who imitated these teachers.[106]

This certainly matches the use of Biscop which Bede made in his homily on Wearmouth-Jarrow's founder. He presented Biscop as someone in whose footsteps the whole community sought to follow.[107] Bede outlined how Biscop had learnt the rules of all the religious houses he had travelled to and then passed these on to his own community; those brothers who had known Biscop in turn delighted in talking about him to the newer members of the monastery.[108] In this way ancient examples were fed down to the present through a chain of imitation and teaching. This seems quite similar to *On the Tabernacle*, where Bede declared that the *rector* of the Church must internalize the examples of the Fathers in his own heart and then display the same virtues for the edification of his audience 'so that he may always be holding out heavenly models for his hearers to follow, whether his own or those of the fathers'.[109] Just as a community might come to follow a 'rule' from imitating the examples of their founder members, so too, Bede suggested, Christians formed themselves according to the 'rule' of righteousness by following the examples of the elect of previous generations.[110]

But teachers do not necessarily always derive the 'rule' of how to be a good Christian from living examples, they also learn it from studying scripture and the accounts of the saints. Texts do clearly play a role in passing down examples through the generations. Rhetorically trained Christian authors had long before adapted to their own needs the use of textual *exempla* for ethical instruction in classical education and literature. The *exemplum* went on to become a popular later medieval genre, one which had its origins in Gregory the Great's fondness for exemplary anecdotes.[111] Bede had read Gregory's own *exempla* in the pope's homilies on the gospels and *Dialogues* (assuming, as Bede did, that this was a genuine Gregorian work[112]) with the

---

[105] Jean Leclercq, 'Pedagogie et formation spirituelle du VIe au IXe siècle', *Settimane di studio del Centro italiano di studi sull'alto medioevo* 19 (1972), pp. 255–90, at 262, 267–9.

[106] Cubitt, 'Monastic Memory and Identity', pp. 273–5 (quotation at p. 275).

[107] *Hom.*, I.13 p. 94.   [108] *Hom.*, I.13 pp. 93–4.

[109] *Tab.*, p. 101 'auditoribus suis semper caelestia siue sua siue patrum exempla quae sequantur proponat'; trans. Holder, p. 116. Also *Temp.*, p. 155; *Tab.*, p. 57.

[110] *Temp.*, pp. 155, 203, 223.

[111] Claude Bremond et al., *L''Exemplum'*, Typologie des Sources du Moyen Âge Occidental 40, 2nd ed. (Turnhout, 1996), pp. 48–50.

[112] For recent contributions on both sides of the debate concerning the *Dialogues*: Francis Clark, *The 'Gregorian' Dialogues and the Origins of Benedictine Monasticism* (Leiden, 2003); Marilyn Dunn, *The Christianization of the Anglo-Saxons c.597–c.700: Discourses of Life, Death*

accompanying defence of examples as a powerful tool for education.[113] Interestingly then, Bede's own homilies, excluding *Homily* I.13 on Biscop, lack non-biblical *exempla* of the kind Gregory used—suggesting that Bede intended his homilies for a more solidly monastic audience than did Gregory.[114]

In *On the Temple*, Bede did speak of the moral benefits of 'contemplating the life, sufferings, and teaching of the saints, or reading of them', which might seem suggestive of the kind of *exempla* one finds in the *Dialogues*.[115] But in general when he spoke of reading about the saints in this way Bede primarily thought about biblical accounts of the Old Testament elect and the apostles.[116] On the rare occasions when he explicitly stated that a biblical passage ought to be interpreted literally, it was because the text provided a model for imitation.[117] In *On the Temple* especially, Bede spoke of reading the Bible 'in the historical sense', the sense which displays 'for our imitation the actions of the righteous'.[118] The *Ecclesiastical History* begins with a defence of history as the source of examples for imitation: 'Should history tell of good men and their good estate, the thoughtful listener is spurred on to imitate the good'.[119] Bede probably undertook the writing of *On the Temple* and the *History* at the same time, so the similarity of the idea of history in the two works seems unlikely to be a coincidence. Bede's understanding of historical interpretation as providing examples for imitation indicates, perhaps, the experience of writing his own exemplary historical account.[120]

So far we have considered examples concerning how humans teach and are taught through pious imitation. Bede's temple commentaries, however, devote a significant amount of time to a different type of imitation: that of the angels by humans. Luke's gospel suggests that humanity will become like the angels in heaven, and Bede referred frequently to this link between the two orders

---

and Afterlife (London, 2009), pp. 157–86 (which argues for an Anglo-Saxon origin); Adalbert de Vogüé, 'Grégoire le Grand est-il l'auteur des *Dialogues*?', *Revue d'Histoire Ecclésiastique* 99 (2004), pp. 158–61.

[113] Gregory, *In Evangelia*, II.XXXIX.10 p. 390; Gregory, *Dialogi*, ed. A. de Vogüé, 3 vols (Paris, 1978–80), I.prol.9 II, p. 16.

[114] Joseph Albert Mosher, *The Exemplum in the Early Religious and Didactic Literature of England* (New York, 1911), p. 25; see also Walt, 'Homiliary of the Venerable Bede', pp. 204–5.

[115] *Temp.*, p. 164 'cum uitam passiones doctrinam sanctorum cernentes siue in scripturis legentes ad bene faciendum exemplo excitamur eorum'; trans. Connolly, p. 28.

[116] *Tab.*, p. 97; *Temp.*, pp. 209, 223, 231.

[117] *Ezra.*, pp. 360, 368; *Sam.*, pp. 130, 136.

[118] *Temp.*, p. 229 'diuinae litterae iuxta historicum sensum . . . iustorum nobis actus in exemplum proponunt'; trans. Connolly, p. 112.

[119] *HE*, praef. pp. 2–3 'Siue enim historia de bonis bona referat, ad imitandum bonum auditor sollicitus instigatur . . .'.

[120] See Calvin B. Kendall, 'Imitation and the Venerable Bede's *Historia Ecclesiastica*', in *Saints, Scholars, and Heroes: Studies in Medieval Culture in Honour of Charles W. Jones*, eds Margot H. King and Wesley Stevens, 2 vols (Collegeville MN, 1979), I, pp. 161–90.

of the faithful.[121] The gospel text suggests that humans will become similar to angels by abandoning sexuality and this led to the common Christian belief that virgins on earth already lived the 'angelic life'. The traditional view of monasticism as an imitation of the angels thus developed, though in practice the connection often proved a complicated one.[122] Bede clearly took this association for granted and in his early work on the Apocalypse stated that the saints made themselves a sacrifice to God by angelic chastity.[123] His fellow Anglo-Saxon, Aldhelm, similarly associated virginity with the imitation of angels.[124] It has recently been argued that Bede considered chastity as essential to angelic imitation, which was therefore effectively limited to monks.[125] But in *On the Temple* when Bede said that humans should imitate the angels' *castitas*, he clearly thought about something more than sexual chastity since one achieved this 'by vigils and the divine praises, by sincere love of the creator and the neighbour'.[126] When Bede had to interpret Luke 20.34–6 itself he, rather strikingly, made no reference at all to monasticism or dedicated virgins.[127]

When God revealed the model of the tabernacle on Mount Sinai, Moses saw, Bede declared, the life of the angels, which all human existence on earth ought to try to imitate.[128] Bede passionately called upon his reader to imitate the angels:

> They love God and their neighbours; imitate this. They come to the aid of the unfortunate . . . ; imitate this. They are humble, they are gentle, they are peaceable toward one another, they obey the divine commands; how well would you do to imitate this! They neither speak, nor do, nor think anything that is evil, or useless, or unjust, but assist at the divine praises with speech and thought that are unwearied; as far as you are able, imitate this.[129]

Living a life perfectly loving God and neighbour clearly played a more important role in imitation of the angels than simply refraining from sex for

---

[121] Luke 20.34–6; *Ezra.*, p. 384; *Temp.*, p. 147; *Tab.*, p. 70.

[122] Ellen Muehlberger, 'Ambivalence about the Angelic Life: The Promise and the Perils of an Early Christian Discourse of Asceticism', *Journal of Early Christian Studies* 16 (2008), pp. 447–78; Conrad Leyser, 'Angels, Monks, and Demons in the Early Medieval West', in *Belief and Culture in the Middle Ages: Studies Presented to Henry Mayr-Harting*, eds Richard Gameson and Henrietta Leyser (Oxford, 2001), pp. 9–22.

[123] *Apoc.*, p. 421. Also *Hom.*, I.13 p. 94; *Tab.*, pp. 58–9; *Temp.*, p. 163; *Sam.*, p. 237.

[124] Aldhelm, *Prosa de Virginitate*, XVIII pp. 246–7.

[125] Richard Sowerby, 'Angels in Anglo-Saxon England, 700–1000' (DPhil thesis, University of Oxford, 2013), pp. 70–71; Dr Sowerby's book is forthcoming.

[126] *Temp.*, p. 184 'uigiliis ac laudibus diuinis dilectione sincera conditoris et proximi'; trans. Connolly, p. 54.

[127] *Luc.*, pp. 358–9.   [128] *Tab.*, p. 69.

[129] *Tab.*, p. 13 'diligunt Deum et proximos, hoc imitare; subueniunt miseris . . . hoc imitare; humiles sunt mites sunt inuicem pacati sunt diuinis parent iussis, hoc in quantum uales imitare; nihil mali nihil otiose nihil iniuste loquuntur agunt cogitant diuinis indefessi laudibus uerbo et mente assistunt, hoc quantum potes imitare'; trans. Holder, pp. 10–11.

Bede; as the perfect tabernacle in which God never ceased to dwell, the angels provided a model for the faithful who wished to become temples of God.[130] This view seems closer to that of Gregory the Great, than to the usual monastic interpretation.[131] Gregory, like Bede, saw angels and humans as fellow members of the universal Church: both shared the belief that angels visited human celebrations of the Mass and that they could have close relationships with the saints on earth.[132] The house of God consisted of both angels and humans, the earthly and heavenly members balancing each other—in these circumstances Gregory felt that all humans needed to imitate angels.[133] Difference and diversity existed amongst both humans and angels but unity founded in love overrode any differences.[134] Such an outlook provides the background, it seems to me, for Bede's understanding of angelic exemplarity. The angels themselves were Christians, a more perfect order of Christians than humans, however, and consequently worthy of imitation just like the saints.

In *On the Temple* Bede stated that the angels had 'preserved ever untarnished in themselves the image of their creator'; in heaven humans will become like angelic spirits as 'angels ever remain in their creator's likeness according to which they were made, and on the other hand, the human elect receive his image which they had lost by sinning'.[135] This suggests that the primary difference between angels and human Christians lies in the fact that the former never fell. When humans imitate the angels, they in fact form themselves according to their lost image of God. I would be cautious about hanging too much on one quotation from a single work of Bede's, but *On the Tabernacle* also contains the claim regarding the angels that 'being created free from sin they always preserve the undefiled purity of their creation'.[136] Although Bede did not explicitly mention the divine image here, he utilized

---

[130] *Ezra.*, p. 382; *Tab.*, p. 12; *Temp.*, pp. 179–81.

[131] For other studies of Gregory's influence on Anglo-Saxon views of angels, differing sometimes from my interpretation: Jane Hawkes, 'Gregory the Great and Angelic Mediation: The Anglo-Saxon Crosses of the Derbyshire Peaks', in *Text, Image, Interpretation: Studies in Anglo-Saxon Literature and its Insular Context in Honour of Eamonn Ó Carragáin*, eds Alastair Minnis and Jane Roberts (Turnhout, 2007), pp. 431–48; Thomas Pickles, 'Angel Veneration on Anglo-Saxon Stone Sculpture from Dewesbury (West Yorkshire), Otely (West Yorkshire) and Halton (Lancashire): Contemplative Preachers and Pastoral Care', *Journal of the British Archaeological Association* 162 (2009), pp. 1–28.

[132] Gregory, *Dialogi*, IV.60.3 III, p. 202; *Hom.*, II.10 p. 249.

[133] Gregory, *In Evangelia*, II.XXXIV.11 p. 309; Gregory, *In Hiezechihelem*, II.II.15 p. 236. Leyser, 'Angels, Monks, and Demons', p. 21; Sowerby, 'Angels in Anglo-Saxon England', pp. 66–9.

[134] Gregory, *In Evangelia*, II.XXXIV.14 pp. 313–14.

[135] *Temp.*, p. 179 'habentes inuiolatam in se sui conditoris imaginem seruata in perpetuo sanctitate . . . angeli sancti in imagine sui conditoris ad quam facti sunt semper manent et electi homines imaginem eius quam peccando amiserant recipiunt'; trans. Connolly, p. 47.

[136] *Tab.*, p. 71 'spiritus angelici . . . absque peccato conditi intemeratam suae conditionis puritatem semper custodiunt'; trans Holder, p. 80.

the same idea of the angels preserving the Edenic purity, which was associated with that image and which humans strive to regain.

This brings us to imitation of the divine and imitation as a way to draw close to the divine. The imitation of Christ as a theme reaches back to the very origins of Christian thought and it went on to achieve its greatest flourishing centuries after Bede.[137] Indeed, often historians have claimed that the early Middle Ages focused on Christ's inimitable divinity, a theology of imitation centring on his humanity only developing from the tenth century with the perceived growth of 'affective piety'.[138] Nonetheless, Bede made quite explicit use of the theme on numerous occasions in his commentaries. Every Christian baptism is 'celebrated on the model' of the Lord's baptism.[139] The saints 'make an effort to consider carefully and to imitate as far as they can those works of the Lord and Saviour himself that he performed in the flesh'.[140] Indeed, without imitating the passion of Christ one cannot become a preacher.[141] Much of this focus on imitating Christ emphasizes specifically the example of his suffering and death, as previously suggested. Not only martyrs could imitate this: Bede reminded his brothers that they would earn the same reward as the martyrs if they made their bodies a living sacrifice.[142] Christians follow the example of the passion when they patiently endure the trials of this world or when they reject earthly matters for the higher reality, or even when they simply act virtuously.[143] Bede declared that 'all those who enter the Holy Church are initiated in the faith and sacraments of the Lord's passion in such a way that they understand that they must always live in imitation of it as well'.[144] Such usage of the *imitatio Christi* probably reflects both Bede's reading of authors such as Augustine and the influence of the ascetic environment of Insular monasticism.[145]

---

[137] See Giles Constable, *Three Studies in Medieval Religious and Social Thought* (Cambridge, 1995), Section 2: 'The Ideal of the Imitation of Christ'.

[138] Phyllis G. Jestice, 'A New Fashion in Imitating Christ: Changing Spiritual Perspectives around the Year 1000', in *The Year 1000: Religious and Social Response to the Turning of the First Millennium*, ed. Michael Frassetto (New York, 2002), pp. 165–85, at 166–7. For a critique of the traditional view of affective piety: Scott DeGregorio, 'Affective Spirituality: Theory and Practice in Bede and Alfred the Great', *Essays in Medieval Studies* 22 (2005), pp. 129–39.

[139] *Temp.*, p. 222 'omne fidelium baptisma quo domino consecrantur in exemplum celebratur baptismatis illius'; trans. Connolly, p. 103.

[140] *Ezra.*, p. 280 'ipsius domini et saluatoris ea quae per carnem gessit opera diligenter considerare et in quantum sufficiunt imitari satagunt'; trans. DeGregorio, p. 66.

[141] *Ezra.*, p. 367.   [142] *Hom.*, II.21 p. 341.

[143] *Temp.*, pp. 143, 174–5; *Tab.*, pp. 78–9; *Ezra.*, p. 305.

[144] *Tab.*, p. 53 'omnes qui sanctam intrant ecclesiam ita fide et sacramentis dominicae passionis initiantur ut in huius quoque imitatione sibi semper esse uiuendum intellegant'; trans. Holder, pp. 58–9.

[145] J. N. D. Kelly, *Early Christian Doctrines*, 5th ed. (London, 1977), pp. 393–4; Michael W. Herren and Shirley Ann Brown, *Christ in Celtic Christianity: Britain and Ireland from the Fifth to the Tenth Century* (Woodbridge, 2002), pp. 140–50.

Not just the content, but even the form of Bede's versions of the *Life of Cuthbert* displays how the saint's life mimicked that of God made flesh.[146] Both the verse and prose versions consist of forty-six chapters. Indeed when new material became available to him, Bede declined to add to his prose life since it 'had seemed scarcely fitting and proper to insert new matter or add to a work which was planned and complete'.[147] Walter Berschin relates this to the numerological significance of forty-six: a reference to the incarnate Christ as the true temple.[148] The Christian becomes a temple of God, by imitating Christ, the temple of God. Imitation provides the means by which one becomes a member of Christ: the human priest mediates the true high priest to Christians through his own virtues and faith, copying of which makes one a participant in Christ's priesthood.[149] The image of the altar of the heart situates the sacrificial role of the temple within the Christian and even though the sacrifices of which Bede spoke were not always bloody, the example of Christ always lay in the background. The perfect teacher builds faith in the Lord's passion as an altar in the human heart; following Christ's example, Christians then mortify their own bodies.[150] The idea that the Christian ought to make their body a 'living sacrifice' (Romans 12.1), especially in order to participate in Christ's priesthood, came easily to Bede's pen.[151] Gregory provided a key inspiration to Bede here, as can be seen in his description of Cuthbert celebrating the Mass, which repeats ideas frequently enunciated by Gregory: 'he would himself imitate the rite he was performing, that is to say, he would sacrifice himself to God in contrition of heart'.[152] Imitation of Christ arises from the performance of the sacrament but extends beyond the act so that the Christian becomes a sacrifice in every aspect of their being.

The faithful offer themselves to God, and all Bede's interest in imitation has this end of reaching God as its goal. We have already seen that angelic

---

[146] On the content of the life: Richard Bailey, '*In Medio Duorum Animalium*: Habbakuk, the Ruthwell Cross and Bede's Life of St Cuthbert', in *Listen, O Isles, unto me: Studies in Medieval Word and Image in Honour of Jennifer O'Reilly*, eds Elizabeth Mullins and Diarmuid Scully (Cork, 2011), pp. 243–52, at 249–50.

[147] *VCP*, prol. pp. 144–5 '... deliberato ac perfecto operi noua interserere, uel supradicere minus congruum atque indecorum esse constaret'. Bede, *Vita Cuthberti (Metrica)*, ed. W. Jaager, *Bedas metrische Vita Sancti Cuthberti* (Leipzig, 1935).

[148] Walter Berschin, '*Opus deliberatum ac perfectum*: Why did the Venerable Bede write a second prose life of St. Cuthbert?', in *St Cuthbert, His Cult and His Community until AD 1200*, eds Gerald Bonner et al. (Woodbridge, 1989), pp. 95–102; see Ch. 5 within this volume, 'The temple as Christ', p. 102.

[149] *Tab.*, p. 104.   [150] *Sam.*, p. 123.

[151] *Apoc.*, pp. 259, 425; *Tab.*, pp. 125, 138; *Temp.*, p. 194; *Ezra.*, pp. 242, 264.

[152] *VCP*, XVI pp. 212–13 'imitaretur ipse quod ageret, se ipsum uidelicet Deo in cordis contritione mactando'; see also *Prov.*, p. 160; Gregory, *In Evangelia*, II.XXXVII.9 p. 355; Straw, *Gregory the Great*, pp. 158–60. For the Christian life as a living sacrifice more generally in Gregory: *In Hiezechihelem*, II.VIII.16 pp. 348–9, II.X.19 pp. 394–5; Straw, *Gregory the Great*, pp. 179–93.

imitation could be seen as nothing more than divine imitation at one remove, since angels never lost the divine image. Obviously all Christians desire the restoration of that image; their virtuous lives in the present aim at receiving it again. And when one has regained it: 'We do not conceal in secret the fact that we have received it, but we openly make it known to everyone by word and deed', so that they too might imitate it.[153] Christians follow the examples of the saints because they are the temple in whom the Lord dwells.[154] Teachers, Bede stated, ought to 'set before our hearers for imitation those whom we know to cling in a special way . . . to the Lord'.[155] The examples preachers display in their words and deeds, therefore, do not necessarily belong to them—they themselves have imitated the apostles and prophets. But imitation of even the most illustrious human exemplar always aims at getting closer to the Lord, who supplies the only justification for imitation of humans at all.

This may explain another feature of Bede's use of the theme of imitation: the limitations of example. Sometimes he qualified the idea of angelic imitation by suggesting that humans should imitate angels *insofar as they are able*; one can only achieve so much in this earthly life.[156] This, however, does not indicate any perceived ontological gap between angels and humans since imitating other humans does not prove straightforward either. Anyone who desires to do so cannot simply copy the miracles and exceptional displays of virtue performed by the saints.[157] In Bede's hierarchical vision of the Church, the carnal cannot imitate all the virtues which the perfect display. But the imperfect should still gaze on those examples, and the perfect should still display their goodness declaring, with Paul (1 Corinthians 11.1), 'Be imitators of us, as we also are of Christ'.[158] Bede accepted the imperfection of all imitation but did not seem to think that this undermined the importance of example. With God himself as the supreme example such an outlook seems only reasonable, for in this life Christ can only be imitated to a limited extent.[159]

Does no possibility of perfect imitation exist then? We ought to remember Bede's acute sense of the forward movement of the Christian life, the

---

[153] *Tab.*, p. 114 'hanc nos recepisse non in secreto celamus sed cunctis palam factis et uoce promulgamus'; trans. Holder, p. 131.

[154] *Luc.*, p. 66.

[155] *Temp.*, pp. 155–6 'eos nostris auditoribus imitandos proponere quos . . . specialiter domino adhaerere nouerimus'; trans. Connolly, p. 16.

[156] *Tab.*, pp. 69, 84; *Temp.*, pp. 163, 184, 187. Sowerby, 'Angels in Anglo-Saxon England', pp. 77–8.

[157] *Ezra.*, pp. 315–16.

[158] *Ezra.*, p. 375; *Temp.*, pp. 195–6 'Dirigunt enim uisus a longe in templum Dei cum uitam sublimium discere et ammirari sedulo gaudent et quos uirtutis imitatione sequi nequeunt piae uenerationis amplectuntur affectu . . . perfecti . . . dicere suis auditoribus possint, *Imitatores nostri estote sicut et nos Christi*'; trans. Connolly, p. 71.

[159] E.g. *Tab.*, p. 36.

importance of progress between the earthly and heavenly Churches, which we have seen in his use of the temple image.[160] The exile's longing for the homeland, for the heavenly temple, but also for the temple which is Christ himself, seems ever present in these works. But such longing only makes sense if its fulfilment proves reasonable and possible. The completion of the temple marks the moment when the pilgrimage ends and Christian souls find themselves in the heavenly and eternal Church.[161] Christians then, as the holocausts offered to mark the temple's dedication, become like the angels because 'the flame of true love with which the angelic powers now burn will engulf their minds also, as they behold the vision of their Redeemer'.[162] The vision of the Creator, seen at last face to face and not in pale imitations, hangs over all the work of Bede as the final end towards which the soul strives, and, like the Fathers before him, Bede described eternal bliss as seeing God himself.[163]

Centuries before, Augustine had devoted substantial thought to understanding the vision of God, arguing that it should be understood in a moral rather than material fashion.[164] God will be seen in eternity when he becomes 'all in all' (1 Corinthians 15.28). The Christian person will look into themselves and see God there; they will look at their neighbours and see God within them.[165] Bede understood the final beatific vision in the very same fashion: in seeing God, the individual in a way becomes one with God.[166] Unsurprisingly for Bede, one cannot forget the communal context—all other elect souls become one with God too, and so in heaven the living stones become like glass, open to each other's gaze in a way impossible during earthly life.[167] In the light of God's glory no difference between individuals exists in heaven; the vision of God has achieved the end of imitation: 'there is no difference of will or thought in the heavenly homeland where all are illumined by one and the same vision and glory of God there present'.[168] The interpretative balancing act that sees the temple as the individual Christ, the individual Christian, and also the collective of all such individuals, makes sense when seen against this background of the inevitable interpenetration of God and all elect souls.

---

[160] See Ch. 4 within this volume, 'Bede's use of the cosmic interpretation', pp. 79–81, 83.

[161] *Temp.*, pp. 232–3.

[162] *Hom.*, II.24 p. 366 'Conpleta ergo dedicationis templi ignis de caelo descendens oblatas domino hostias deuorauit quia . . . flagrantia ueri amoris quo nunc angelicae uirtutes inflammantur eorum quoque mentes uisa specie sui redemptoris absorbet'; trans. Martin and Hurst, II, p. 251.

[163] E.g. *Temp.*, p. 158; *Tab.*, p. 67; *Ezra.*, p. 306; compare Gregory, *In Hiezechihelem*, II.IV.6 p. 263, II.IV.18 p. 271. O'Reilly, 'Seeing the God of Gods', pp. 21–9.

[164] Esp. Augustine, *Epistulae*, ed. A. Goldbacher, CSEL 44, CXLVII (*De Videndo Deo*) pp. 274–331; quoted by Bede at *EpCath.*, pp. 314–15.

[165] Augustine, *DCD*, XXII.29 pp. 861–2.

[166] *Temp.*, p. 179 (quoting 1 John 3.2); God shows himself by inhabiting the elect: *Tab.*, p. 73.

[167] *Apoc.*, p. 531; *Temp.*, p. 227; *Tab.*, p. 33; *Hom.*, II.24 p. 366.

[168] *Temp.*, p. 180 'disparilitas uoluntatum siue cogitatuum in superna patria nulla est ubi una eademque omnes Dei praesentis uisione et gloria illustrantur'; trans. Connolly, p. 48.

When speaking of imitation Bede made constant recourse to visual language. The imperfect follow with their gaze the good examples of the perfect, which are displayed for their benefit.[169] Referring to the outward actions of the saints in *On the Temple*, Bede stated that 'we find help for our salvation from those things which are externally visible whether in word or action or suffering'.[170] The context of the statement makes it all the more significant; Bede moved on to discuss how worldly suffering builds one up for the heavenly temple.[171] He followed this with his exegesis of the door in the side of the temple, involving a discussion of how the sacraments derived from the incarnate Christ.[172] Seeing these few pages as being thematically linked we can here read Bede's explanation as to why external acts, physical suffering and visual examples amongst them, can have a real spiritual power. Like baptism and the eucharist, they derive grace from the reality of God's human body. Relatedly, Bede probably knew well the theological justification of holy images, which understood them as resembling the incarnation in making the divine present to human eyes.[173]

In his homilies Bede certainly displayed an interest in the link between the incarnation and vision. Blinded by the Fall, humans could not see God spiritually; God thus had to make himself visible physically, by entering into human flesh, in order to draw humanity back towards spiritual vision.[174] Thus the vision of God at the end of time only becomes possible for humanity, because they have already seen God through Christ's incarnation. But the incarnation also occurred so that humans would have a model to imitate, a model of perfect humility and of perfect living.[175] The *imitatio Christi*, therefore, becomes one of the consequences, indeed one of the aspects, of the vision of God made possible by the incarnation. And, of course, the incarnation also took place in order to restore the image of God in man[176]—the image which could not be regained until displayed to humanity for imitation. We may here seem to have strayed from the image of the temple but we have in fact

---

[169] *Temp.*, p. 195.

[170] *Temp.*, p. 165 'ex eis quae loquendo uel agendo uel patiendo foras ostendunt auxilium nostrae salutis inuenimus'; trans. Connolly, p. 28.

[171] See within this chapter, 'Morality', p. 164.

[172] *Temp.*, pp. 165–6. See Ch. 5 within this volume, 'The temple as Christ', p. 103.

[173] Barbara Raw, *Trinity and Incarnation in Anglo-Saxon Art and Thought* (Cambridge, 1997), pp. 55–64. Bede on the images at Wearmouth-Jarrow: *HA*, 6 pp. 36–7.

[174] *Hom.*, I.2 pp. 11–12, I.4 p. 28, I.7 pp. 47–8, I.8 p. 55. Raw, *Trinity and Incarnation*, pp. 64–71; Celia Chazelle, 'Christ and the Vision of God: The Biblical Diagrams of the Codex Amiatinus', in *The Mind's Eye: Art and Theological Argument in the Middle Ages*, eds Jeffrey F. Hamburger and Anne-Marie Bouché (Princeton NJ, 2006), pp. 84–111, at 97–8. The theme appears in Gregory: *In Hiezechihelem*, II.IV.20 p. 272; Straw, *Gregory the Great*, pp. 170–72.

[175] *Hom.*, I.4 p. 31, I.6 p. 40, I.16 p. 112, I.19 pp. 135–6.

[176] *Hom.*, I.6 p. 39, I.15 p. 110. For this nexus of ideas surrounding the vision of God, the incarnation, and restoration in Augustine: Carol Harrison, *Beauty and Revelation in the Thought of Saint Augustine* (Oxford, 1992), pp. 192–238.

returned to the theme that has been highlighted repeatedly throughout this study: the importance of the incarnate God. By taking on flesh in the material world, God allowed humanity in the flesh, through the material, to approach unity with the divine.

These five chapters of thematic analysis at the centre of this study have helped us form a clear picture of the internal or theological significance of Bede's use of the temple image. We still have more work to do on the image's external or historical context, but for now it seems worthwhile to reiterate the important interlinking themes of Bede's theological world view: unity and incarnation. Christ's physical and human presence in the world served as the bridge between the otherwise eternally opposed realities of Jew and gentile, heaven and earth, God and humanity—opposites that Bede successfully brought together in the image of the temple. While he may have interpreted the temple as the Church above all else, that understanding rested on the fact that the Church was Christ's body and, therefore, both earthly and transcendent. The individual as the temple only gained meaning because God himself, by assuming a human nature, had become the temple. Cosmic unity, racial unity, doctrinal unity, the unity of person, all interested Bede, who used the Jewish temple as a means to explore and celebrate them. Theologically at the heart of the temple image stands the mystery of the incarnation, that Christ was an individual possessing two natures, as the basis of all such unity.

8

Building Bede's Temple

This book has followed a self-consciously synthetic approach, reading across all of Bede's works for the light they can shed on his use of the image of the Jewish temple. Such a method carries obvious dangers. Reading Bede in this fashion may impose an artificial coherence on his thought, normalize the inconsistencies of his different works, and efface the messiness usually attend-ant on developing ideas over time.[1] 'Bede's thought' as a monolithic and univocal system of ideas is not a historical fact, but an abstraction derived from Bede's writings, inevitably coloured by one's own priorities and precon-ceptions. I defend my chosen methodology on two practical grounds. Firstly, much more work remains to be done to establish a detailed chronology of Bede's writings. Secondly, the complexity of Bede's different uses of the temple image makes a thematic approach most convenient—the alternative being a confusing and repetitious quasi-chronological investigation. Nonetheless, we ought to leaven the artificial synchronicity of the previous chapters with a brief overview exploring how Bede built up his interpretation of the temple image over time. The evidence of broad changes in his approach to and interpret-ation of the temple is important in establishing how Bede came to devote so much of his work to that image. This diachronic approach suggests that events at Wearmouth-Jarrow, centred on the preparation of the Codex Amiatinus, provided the stimulus for and indeed some of the content of Bede's own interpretation of the temple.

DIACHRONIC OVERVIEW

This chapter offers an overview of the relevant works, seeking at most to sketch some key uses of the temple image in each, in particular focusing on developments and new directions in Bede's approach. As pointed out earlier,

---

[1] See Quentin Skinner, *Visions of Politics. Volume 1: Regarding Method* (Cambridge, 2002), pp. 67–72, 78–9.

we cannot establish a detailed chronology into which each text can firmly be placed. The broad chronology I map out seems to be plausible, but the exact position of many individual texts sometimes remains unclear. I have avoided detailed discussion of works for which evidence of date does not exist, such as the *Gospel Homilies*. Many commentators have argued that the sophistication of the homilies means these must be late compositions, but such claims remain unsubstantiated.[2] We can perhaps place individual homilies chronologically relative to other works (as later demonstrated),[3] but the detailed scholarship required to do this on a large scale remains undone. The exact dates associated with a few works provide the framework for this relative chronology.

To complicate matters, some of Bede's works have recently been radically redated—or undated. Most importantly, *On Schemes and Tropes*, once generally thought of as one of Bede's earliest works, now appears to date from Bede's maturity with evidence of composition after 709.[4] Hence, the striking use of the temple image to explain the four senses of scripture in *On Schemes and Tropes* probably came after many years of thought about the temple.[5] The centrality of the Jewish temple for Bede's approach to scripture, which it seems to imply, cannot therefore be assumed to have always been the case. The apparent lack of concern or respect for the temple in his (early) *On the Holy Places*, where Bede seems deliberately to have toned down Adomnán's admiration (in the work that was the Northumbrian's major source) for the magnificence of the temple's construction or the fame of its location, supports such an assumption.[6]

Already, however, in Bede's earliest work of exegesis (the *Explanation of the Apocalypse*) we find an interest in the temple image. Of course, the image does play a significant role in the final book of the Bible and had been dealt with by Bede's predecessors, Primasius and Tyconius, on whom he drew extensively.[7] But Bede made a number of, brief and insubstantial it must be granted, comments on the temple image that seem independent of his sources.[8]

[2] A. G. P. van der Walt, 'The Homiliary of the Venerable Bede and Early Medieval Preaching' (PhD thesis, University of London, 1980), p. 270; Lawrence T. Martin, 'Introduction', in *Bede the Venerable: Homilies on the Gospels*, vol. 1 (Kalamazoo MI, 1991), pp. xi–xxiii, at xi.

[3] See within this chapter, pp. 189–90.

[4] Arthur G. Holder, '(Un)Dating Bede's *De arte metrica*', in *Northumbria's Golden Age*, eds Jane Hawkes and Susan Mills (Stroud, 1999), pp. 390–95; Carmela Vircillo Franklin, 'The Date of Composition of Bede's *De Schematibus et Tropis* and *De Arte Metrica*', *RB* 110 (2000), pp. 199–203.

[5] *DST*, II.11 pp. 168–9 (quoted in Ch. 2 within this volume, 'The intellectual context at Wearmouth-Jarrow', pp. 27–8).

[6] Bede, *De Locis Sanctis*, ed. J. Fraipont, CCSL 175, II.3 p. 257; see also Adomnán, *De Locis Sanctis*, ed. L. Bieler, CCSL 175, I.I.14 p. 186.

[7] Gerald Bonner, *Saint Bede in the Tradition of Western Apocalyptic Commentary*, Jarrow Lecture (Jarrow, 1966); Gryson's comments in CCSL 121A, pp. 153–66.

[8] *Apoc.*, pp. 367–9 seems to be an original interpretation of Bede's; *Apoc.*, pp. 289, 337, reference the temple without obvious sources in the biblical text or previous commentary.

In particular, Bede discussed Christ's sacrificial priesthood (twice adding his distinctive phrase 'the altar of the cross' to Primasius' discussion) and the participation of all Christians in that priesthood on a number of occasions.[9] This interest may explain why in three places Bede made references to the garments of the Jewish high priest, which do not seem to be borrowed from any previous exegesis of the Apocalypse or indeed to be demanded by the scriptural text.[10] The vestments to which he would devote so much time in *On the Tabernacle* were already on Bede's mind, but strikingly he ignored the architectural links between the Heavenly Jerusalem and the desert tabernacle.[11] Bede probably chose to comment on the Apocalypse because of its direct relevance to the eschatological debates which his contemporary scientific works addressed;[12] nonetheless the significance of Christ's priesthood and its consequences clearly already engaged him.

His first commentary also displays a concern to contrast the limitations and narrowness of the Jewish temple, enclosed within the walls of a single city, with the global spread of the temple Church that reveals the incarnate Christ.[13] This implies a rather negative view of the physical temple in Jerusalem which, as we saw in Chapter 3 within this volume, Bede does seem to have evinced in his earlier works in particular.[14] He wrote the *Verse Life of Cuthbert* and the *Explanation of the Apocalypse* with an Anglo-Saxon audience in mind and this probably explains Bede's denigration of the distant and exclusive temple. The commentary on Acts both sneers at the golden finery of the temple and situates it within a progressive model,[15] yet in general there is little sense of Bede having been hugely interested in the temple image in this work: the vast majority of his comments respond directly to the plain biblical text. In his only elaborate use of the image, Bede explained (seemingly originally) how Matthias became an apostle by drawing lots, on the model of the Jewish priesthood, interpreting the fire descending on the disciples at Pentecost as the consummation of Christ's paschal sacrifice which brought an end to the old dispensation by completing its rites.[16] This commentary's uses of the image consign the temple cult to the past: the temple became obsolete just like the tabernacle before it; the Jewish custom of drawing lots was no longer necessary once the Spirit had descended on the Church.

---

[9] Christ: *Apoc.*, pp. 245, 335; compare Primasius, *Commentarius in Apocalypsin*, ed. A. W. Adams, CCSL 92, pp. 17, 135–6. Priesthood of believers: *Apoc.*, pp. 239, 247–9, 509 (compare Primasius, *Apocalypsin*, p. 278; Augustine, *DCD*, XX.10 pp. 719–20).

[10] *Apoc.*, pp. 311, 527, 559.

[11] Faith Wallis, *Bede: Commentary on Revelation* (Liverpool, 2013), p. 37.

[12] Wallis, *Bede: Commentary on Revelation*, pp. 43–51.

[13] *Apoc.*, pp. 385, 443.

[14] See Ch. 3 within this volume, 'The house made by human hands', pp. 58–9.

[15] See Ch. 3 within this volume, 'The house made by human hands', p. 54.

[16] *Act.*, pp. 14–15.

Bede sent *On Acts* to Acca of Hexham early in the latter's episcopate along with his commentary on the first letter of John, his exegesis of which remains practically untouched by the temple image; two brief references come from Augustine's earlier work on the letter.[17] Bede's writings on the remaining Catholic Epistles may not necessarily date from this time, but on the whole they consistently display little interest in the temple image.[18] The commentary on the first letter of Peter provides, unsurprisingly, the exception. 1 Peter 2.4–9 contains much temple imagery and Bede interpreted these verses generally as referring to the transference of election from Old Testament Israel to the gentile Church; possibly for the first time he used the imagery of rows of stones placed on each other to symbolize the mutually supporting generations of the faithful, being taught by those before them and teaching those after them in turn.[19] But here, as in *On the Seven Catholic Epistles* more generally, scripture, rather than the exegete's interests, primarily determined the use of the temple image.

Bede's writings in the first decade of the eighth century therefore engaged with the temple image, but as a fairly minor theme over all. Some aspects of the image were already important—especially ideas related to the priesthood of Christ;[20] on the other hand, Bede viewed the historical and material temple with some distaste. Most importantly, the temple image did not actively fascinate Bede before 710 and little evidence suggests that he chose to comment on these parts of the New Testament because of any temple imagery they contained. The early commentaries all share an interest in the post-incarnation development of the Church where there could be little place for the Jewish temple;[21] Bede clearly felt that Augustine had adequately dealt with the Pauline letters and so never directly commented on the most important New Testament texts for the temple image.[22] Acca's patronage subsequently opened up a new phase in Bede's career. It marked the monk of Wearmouth-Jarrow clearly as a Northumbrian author of some importance and his diocesan bishop rapidly demanded new and bigger commentaries.

The massive commentary on Luke's gospel written at Acca's request reveals an author increasingly engaging with the temple image. Of course, the temple

---

[17] *EpCath.*, pp. 310, 313; compare Augustine, *In Iohannis Epistolam ad Parthos Tractatus*, PL 35, IX.1 col. 2045, VII.9 col. 2033.

[18] There are insubstantial comments at *EpCath.*, pp. 190, 257, 341. For the date of this work: Peter Darby, *Bede and the End of Time* (Farnham, 2012), pp. 67–8.

[19] *EpCath.*, pp. 233–8.

[20] Giovanni Caputa, *Il Sacerdozio dei Fedeli secondo San Beda: un itinerario di maturità cristiana* (Vatican City, 2002), pp. 61–6.

[21] John William Houghton, 'Bede's Exegetical Theology: Ideas of the Church in the Acts Commentaries of St. Bede the Venerable' (PhD dissertation, University of Notre Dame, 1994), pp. 45–6.

[22] Bede, *Excerpts from the Works of Saint Augustine on the Letters of the Blessed Apostle Paul*, trans. David Hurst (Kalamazoo MI, 1999).

features in that gospel and Bede followed patristic tradition in considering Christ's priesthood and temple cult as Luke's distinctive theme;[23] nonetheless, the amount of time he devoted to the temple image remains striking. Book Six of *On Luke* even begins with a miniature *On the Temple*, where Bede raced through the figurative meanings of some of its architectural features, while emphasizing that the temple was merely a transitory symbol.[24] Many of his uses of the temple image do not arise from the scriptural text being commented on.[25] For example, mention of Christ's age at the time of his baptism led Bede into probably the longest exegesis of the temple's bronze 'sea' provided by any Christian commentator to date.[26] A discussion of the beatitudes ends with mention of the vestments of the Jewish priests and the declaration that 'to either explain or only describe each' of these garments 'awaits the industry of its own work'.[27] The comment makes clear that Bede had not yet written *On the Tabernacle* (which provides that work), but suggests that he had begun to consider the need for such a book.

Bede seems to have worked out many aspects of his interpretation of the temple image as he wrote *On Luke* sometime between 710 and 716, although he would not write his major temple commentaries until years later. He could have simply drawn the link between the thirty years of Christ's age and the thirty cubits of the bronze sea's circumference, but he preferred to take the opportunity to explore in detail how the latter related to baptism.[28] This distinctively Bedan interpretation also appears briefly in his commentary on the Song of Songs.[29] Bede seems to have brought a pre-existing interest in sacred architecture to his study of Luke's gospel; mentions of the temple image dropped into his exegesis without prompting suggest that the topic already held a fascination for him. Since he wrote *On Luke* in the years immediately before the Codex Amiatinus left Wearmouth-Jarrow, the work on the codex's first quire provides a plausible explanation for this.

In this context it is surely significant that Bede's first attempt to grapple with the detail of the temple's measurements has been dated to around 715, as part

[23] *Luc.*, pp. 9, 71, 88, 402–3, 424–5. Augustine, *De Consensu Evangelistarum*, ed. F. Weihrich, CSEL 43, I.6 pp. 9–10; Ambrose, *Expositio Evangelii Secundum Lucam*, ed. M. Adriaen, CCSL 14, prol.7 p. 5.

[24] *Luc.*, pp. 363–4.

[25] E.g. *Luc.*, pp. 132, 157, 200, 311, 392. *Luc.*, p. 137 does not use the temple image per se, but interprets Exodus 24.13–14 just as Bede would at *Tab.*, p. 7.

[26] *Luc.*, pp. 85–6. *Temp.*, pp. 207–12 is in effect just an expansion of this earlier exegesis.

[27] *Luc.*, pp. 140–41: p. 141 'Quae per singula uel exponere uel solum proponere proprii industriam expectat operis'.

[28] *Luc.*, p. 86.

[29] *Cant.*, p. 322. Neither Gregory, *Regula Pastoralis*, PL 77, II.5 col. 33–34, nor an Irish text preserving earlier exegesis of the sea (*Quaestiones vel Glosae in Evangelio Nomine*, ed. R. E. McNally, CCSL 108B, p. 146), has the baptismal focus that Bede brought to its interpretation.

of his *Thirty Questions on the Book of Kings*. In that work he discussed the question of the height of the temple, interpreted the door on its right-hand side as Christ's wound, and explained the layout of the temple courts—all for the first time.[30] While Bede's interest in numbers long predated 715, he directed no real attention to architectural measurements before becoming fascinated by the temple image; *On the Holy Places* contains some measurements, but surprisingly few over all.[31] *Thirty Questions* includes passing references to two issues clearly relevant to the Codex Amiatinus: Ezra's work in restoring scripture and the diagram of the temple in the Codex Grandior.[32] However, it also complicates the evidence for the influence of the manuscript's production on Bede. Bede's discussions in *Thirty Questions* followed not his own interests, but the specifics of the priest Nothelm's (d. 739) enquiries—a series of seemingly disconnected queries about various details from the Book(s) of Kings.[33] This might imply that factors purely external to Wearmouth-Jarrow determined what Bede addressed. Nonetheless, it seems unlikely that Nothelm asked about the four Books of Kings at the same time as Bede was writing a commentary on the first book purely by coincidence. We can perhaps deduce that he knew of Bede's commentary on Samuel and of Wearmouth-Jarrow's interest in the temple image at this time, and was thus inspired to ask for elucidation on some related points.[34]

Bede followed Augustine in interpreting Samuel's story as signifying the replacement of the old Jewish priesthood with Christ's new priesthood in the Church.[35] This, combined with the important role played by the Ark of the Covenant in 1 Kings, explains much of the use of temple imagery throughout Bede's *On 1 Samuel*, three-quarters completed when Ceolfrith left Wearmouth-Jarrow in June 716. Nonetheless, the exegete's fondness for such imagery remains noteworthy—especially when directed towards discussing the person as the dwelling place or temple of God.[36] Bede does not seem to

---

[30] *Reg.*, XI–XIV pp. 303–7, XVIII pp. 311–13.

[31] For the mathematical ability revealed in Bede's early computistical works: Calvin B. Kendall and Faith Wallis, *Bede: On the Nature of Things and On Times* (Liverpool, 2010), pp. 31–3, 186–7.

[32] *Reg.*, VII pp. 301–2, XVIII p. 312. See Ch. 4 within this volume, 'The Codex Amiatinus', pp. 95–6.

[33] Paul Meyvaert, '"In the Footsteps of the Fathers": The Date of Bede's *Thirty Questions on the Book of Kings* to Nothelm', in *The Limits of Ancient Christianity: Essays on Late Antique Thought and Culture in Honour of R. A. Markus*, eds William E. Klingshirn and Mark Vessey (Ann Arbor MI, 1999), pp. 267–86, at 269; *Reg.*, prol. p. 293. Nothelm, for instance, may have drawn Bede's attention to the apparent disparity between 3 Kings 6.2 and 2 Paralipomenon 3.4 on the height of the temple: see Ch. 3 within this volume, 'The house made by human hands', p. 50.

[34] Meyvaert, '"Footsteps of the Fathers"', pp. 276–7.

[35] *Sam.*, pp. 31–4, 67, 137; *Reg.*, I pp. 296–7. Augustine, *DCD*, XVII.4–5 pp. 554–66.

[36] *Sam.*, pp. 21, 58, 66. Imagery of entering the faith as entering the temple is also present: *Sam.*, pp. 18, 32.

have used this interpretation of the temple as individual much in his earliest works, but it grew increasingly common in the years leading up to 716.[37] *On 1 Samuel* may also prove that Bede perfected his interpretation of the tabernacle as the present and the temple as the heavenly Church around this time. He provided an elaborate exegesis of the ark's movements, reading them as a symbol of the diversity within the Church. The various staging posts in the ark's journeying represent different ways of life (contemplation and action, for example), which all implicitly belong to the earthly Church. Arrival in Jerusalem (the 'vision of peace') symbolizes the move from pilgrimage on earth to heaven and the dedication of the temple represents the final resurrection:

> Do not believe that, without the significance of a great mystery, did the ark of the Lord thus move through various places . . . until the time of the dedication of the house of God where it received a perpetual resting place in the Holy of Holies. These things did not happen in vain but as a type of the Church which in the various but peaceful diversity of its members . . . in those who, now leaving the body, escaping the labours of this changeable world, ascend to the vision of eternal peace, it does not stop fighting, through the prayer of those now reigning in the heavenly seat, on behalf of its members in pilgrimage upon the earth, equally struggling against the enemy, until the brilliant glory of the resurrection which is its happy dedication in the heavenly Holy of Holies.[38]

While not actually mentioning the Mosaic tabernacle, the same contrast between the ark's movement and its final stability appears here as in Bede's later temple commentaries. Interestingly, *On the Song of Songs*, upon parts of which Book Four of *On 1 Samuel* seem to draw, appears to make this distinction between the tabernacle and temple: associating the former with the 'present Church' and the latter with the 'eternal house which is in heaven'.[39] Holder has argued that this relationship of *On the Song of Songs* with the commentary on Samuel and its anti-Pelagian character (which indicates perhaps the live question of the Easter Controversy) suggest a date before 716 for the former.[40] *On the Song of Songs* may also be linked to Bede's

---

[37] *Cant.*, p. 279; *Luc.*, pp. 66, 311.

[38] *Sam.*, pp. 59–60 'Non autem absque magni significatione mysterii credas arcam domini sic uaria per loca mutatam . . . usque ad tempora dedicationis domus Dei qua perpetuam in sancto sanctorum sedem mansionis accepit. Nequaquam haec frustra sed in ecclesiae typum gesta cognosce quae in multimoda sed pacatissima suorum diuersitate membrorum . . . in his qui iam de corpore egressi saeculi uariantis euasere labores uisionem aeternae pacis ascendit nec per eos tamen ipsos in caeli iam sede regnantes pro peregrinantibus in terra suis aeque membris et adhuc contra hostem dimicantibus orando certare desistit donec resurrectionis coruscante gloria quae felix eius est dedicatio in caelestia sancta sanctorum'.

[39] *Cant.*, p. 322 'in tabernaculo uel templo Salomonis . . . uel praesentis societatem ecclesiae uel mansionem aeternae domus quae est in caelis possumus ingredi'.

[40] Arthur G. Holder, 'The Anti-Pelagian Character of Bede's Commentary on the Song of Songs', in *Biblical Studies in the Early Middle Ages*, eds Claudio Leonardi and Giovanni Orlandi (Florence, 2005), pp. 91–103, at 100–103.

commentary on Proverbs, which begins by interpreting the building of the temple as referring to the growth of the Church.[41] The dating of these works has by no means been established (Thacker felt that they belong to the latter part of Bede's career, after 716);[42] for our purposes it is significant that no scholarship has sought to date them to the period before 710. While I would argue for a pre-716 date for the commentaries on Proverbs and the Song of Songs (which share with *On Luke* a distinctive etymology of *sinagoga* and *ecclesia*, which Bede does not use in his temple commentaries), making their brief mentions of the temple indications of his growing interest in it in the years running up to the departure of the Codex Amiatinus, they might also simply indicate Bede's post-716 familiarity with the image.[43]

One can construct a reasonably clear image of Bede during these years (*c.*710–716): he wrote long commentaries for a distinguished clerical audience all over England and with an increased focus on the Old Testament. Furthermore, at this time Bede started to form his understanding of the temple, which he would later set forth in detail in his temple commentaries. While he had discussed the temple previously, he had done so primarily when the biblical text demanded it. For example, Bede discussed Christ as the cornerstone linking the Jewish and gentile peoples in his commentaries on Acts and the Catholic Epistles—but only because the image of the cornerstone appeared in those books.[44] In the works of *c.*710–716 the same image appears more frequently and in cases where the scriptural text did not demand it.[45]

Bede's use of the temple image clearly changed over the course of these years. This does not mean that it had achieved its final form by 716. In *On Luke* Bede interpreted the moulds broken to reveal the bronze temple vessels as symbolizing the ceremonies of the Law, replaced by the gospel truth; *On the Temple* eschews this interpretation in favour of one concentrating on the contrast between this life and the next.[46] Bede explained the barrier around the roof of the temple with reference to the death of King Ochozias by falling in both *On the Temple* and *Thirty Questions on Kings*, but the former provides an allegorical interpretation of this, apparently not yet formulated when he

[41] *Prov*, p. 23. For the possible relationship between these two commentaries on 'Solomonic' works: Arthur G. Holder, 'The Feminine Christ in Bede's Biblical Commentaries', in *Bède le Vénérable entre tradition et postérité: The Venerable Bede. Tradition and Posterity*, eds Stéphane Lebecq et al. (Lille, 2005), pp. 109–18, at 115–16.

[42] Alan Thacker, 'Bede and the Ordering of Understanding', in *Innovation and Tradition in the Writings of the Venerable Bede*, ed. Scott DeGregorio (Morgantown WV, 2006), pp. 37–63, at 54–5.

[43] Conor O'Brien, 'Bede on the Jewish Church', in *The Church on its Past*, eds Peter D. Clarke and Charlotte Methuen (Woodbridge, 2013), pp. 63–73, at 69.

[44] *Act.*, p. 26; *EpCath.*, pp. 236–7.

[45] *Sam.*, pp. 64, 167; *Cant.*, pp. 314–15, 317; *Luc.*, p. 355. On the cornerstone: Ch. 4 within this volume, 'The Anglo-Saxons' place in the world', pp. 84–5.

[46] *Luc.*, p. 363; *Temp.*, pp. 223–4.

wrote the latter.[47] Most strikingly perhaps, the historical Jewish temple still shared in Bede's generally negative attitude to Old Testament Judaism before Iona's acceptance of the Roman Easter.[48] Hence, Bede continued to think creatively about the temple image after 716, developing new interpretations or abandoning old ones. Nonetheless, the core of Bede's interest in that image, which reached fruition in the temple commentaries, developed in the years immediately preceding 716.

Looking at some of Bede's major writings from the decade or so after the Codex Amiatinus left Northumbria confirms this. They provide little evidence that the temple image was still an active and exciting research interest for Bede, appearing in all sorts of unexpected contexts; rather the appearances of the temple in the early 720s suggest that Bede had developed, to an advanced stage, a detailed and influential exegesis of it. For instance, in *On Genesis* he brought the exegesis of the temple into his interpretations of Noah's ark and the tower of Babel.[49] Such a decision makes perfect sense but was substantially original to Bede; he seems to have been so comfortable and keen on the detailed architectural interpretation of the temple image by now that he self-consciously modelled his approach to Babel on it.[50] The exegesis of the ark contains a particularly striking statement. There Bede, discussing how Noah could have fitted so many birds and beasts into a boat, rebutted the suggestion coming from Origen, that Moses gave the ark's measurements in geometric cubits—six times as large as standard cubits.[51] This makes no sense, Bede argued, since one must assume that Moses gave measurements in a consistent manner; if he had always used geometric cubits the tabernacle would have been impossibly huge—far too big to be carried around the desert and larger even than Solomon's temple.[52] It seems unlikely that Bede searched through the Pentateuch for every mention of cubits to test Origen's hypothesis. Rather it appears that he knew the tabernacle's measurements so well that he spotted the flaw in the argument.

Bede also drew on the temple image in a similar fashion when writing about non-exegetical topics. In *On the Reckoning of Time* he explained that the temple 'was finished in seven years, and dedicated in the seventh month of the eighth year, as a symbol of the totality of time in which the Church of

---

[47] *Reg.*, XIII pp. 305–6; *Temp.*, pp. 163–4.

[48] See Ch. 3 within this volume, 'The house made by human hands', pp. 56–63; O'Brien, 'Jewish Church', pp. 69–73.

[49] *Gen.*, pp. 107, 109–10, 160. While Noah's ark called to mind the temple image for Bede, the reverse process rarely occurred, suggesting the priority of the temple: *Ezra.*, p. 274.

[50] See Ch. 6 within this volume, 'The temple versus the tower'.

[51] *Gen.*, pp. 111–12 quotes Augustine, *Quaestiones in Heptateuchum*, ed. J. Fraipont, CCSL 33, I.4 p. 3 but the point comes from Origen/Rufinus, *In Genesim Homiliae*, ed. W. A. Baehrens, *Origenes Werke* 6 (Leipzig, 1920), II.2 p. 29.

[52] *Gen.*, p. 112.

Christ, which is made perfect in the future [age], is built up in this world'.[53] Strikingly, this is one of only five allegorical comments in the entire world chronicle, and Bede did not even bother to explain how this spiritual interpretation depended on his scheme of the eight world ages.[54] He seems to have thought such a comment unexceptional in a work of the mid-720s aimed at a Wearmouth-Jarrow audience. By the first half of the 720s, of course, Bede had already embarked on writing the temple commentaries proper: *On the Tabernacle* probably dates from this period.

The evidence suggests that Bede wrote that work shortly after he had commented on Noah's ark in 720.[55] Showing the Law's spiritual meaning to be greater than its literal meaning, Bede used the story of Noah and provided a summary of its exegesis which matches that put forth in *On Genesis*; earlier on he had noted the importance of 'how we should reckon the length of the cubit that Moses employed [in describing] both Noah's ark and the making of the tabernacle'.[56] This suggests that the question of the ark's measurements (and the tabernacle's role in solving it) was fresh in Bede's mind. The temple image does not burst unexpectedly into the text of Bede's writings in the early 720s as it did in the early 710s; instead he channelled his clear interest in the topic into focused study. *On the Tabernacle* thus provides examples of the whole range of approaches to the temple image which we have explored. In it Bede noted for the first time Cassiodorus' responsibility for the ancient picture to which he had access and outlined the exegetical relationship between the tabernacle and temple in more detail than he did anywhere else.[57]

Bede's early interest in the New Testament seems to have diminished by the 720s; the New Testament works he produced in this period, in fact, looked back to the earlier part of his career. In *On Mark* (in which he made reference to the completed *On the Tabernacle*[58]) Bede habitually repeated whole sections of the earlier *On Luke*, though changes between the two works reveal some interesting developments in his thoughts concerning the temple image. While in the earlier commentary, Bede's discussion of the cleansing of the temple was simply taken from Gregory the Great, in *On Mark* he added to this an entirely new and substantially original interpretation: a lecture on appropriate behaviour in a church.[59] Bede asked that 'if the Lord did not wish to be sold in the

---

[53] *DTR*, LXVI pp. 475–6 'templum domino aedificare coepit…quod in figuram uniuersi temporis, quo in hoc saeculo Christi aedificatur ecclesia, quae in futuro perficitur, VII annis perfecit et septimo octaui anni mense dedicauit'; trans. Wallis, p. 172.

[54] See Ch. 3 within this volume, 'History and the figural interpretation of the temple', p. 71.

[55] Bede's account of Noah in *On Genesis* can be securely dated to 720: see Ch. 3 within this volume, 'The house made by human hands', p. 59 n. 82.

[56] *Tab.*, pp. 69, 13 'Quidam solent interrogare cuius quantitatis sit aestimandus cubitus quem Moyses uel in archa Noe uel in factura tabernaculi posuerit'; trans. Holder, p. 11.

[57] *Tab.*, pp. 81, 42–3. [58] *Marc.*, p. 464.

[59] *Luc.*, p. 349; compare Gregory, *Homiliae in Evangelia*, ed. R. Étaix, CCSL 141, II. XXXIX.6–7 p. 386. *Marc.*, pp. 579–80; compare Gregory, *In Evangelia*, I.XVII.13 p. 127; Gregory,

temple those things which he wished to be offered in the temple . . . with how much censure do you think he would have punished if he had found anybody wasting time with laughter or gossip . . . in the shrines consecrated to God?'.[60] A similar link between the temple of Jerusalem and contemporary church buildings had appeared only a few pages earlier, where the fact that Jesus went straight to the temple on entering Jerusalem was taken to be a model for how one ought, on first entering any town or village, to go to the nearest house of prayer to offer thanks to God.[61] It appears that a new interpretation of the temple entered Bede's thought sometime between writing the commentary concerning Luke and that on Mark—probably when Bede had to compose his homily on John's account of the cleansing. The homily's approach is closer to the later *On Mark*, with its condemnation of laughter and gossip in churches, than the earlier *On Luke*. As a work designed to connect with a listening church congregation, the homily (where Bede turns the story of the cleansing against 'those who enter a church, and not only disregard their intention to pray, but also increase the things for which they should have been praying') provides a plausible context for the initial impetus to use the temple image to discuss appropriate behaviour in a church.[62] As I discuss elsewhere, this suggests that Bede composed *Homily* II.1 between *On Luke* and *On Mark*, probably in the decade or so after 715.[63]

Like the commentary on Mark's gospel, Bede's *Retraction on Acts* broke little new ground; Bede aimed to correct and amend some of the comments in his earlier work on the Acts of the Apostles, particularly in light of his improved understanding of Greek. The *Retraction* says little of substance about the temple image, excepting one bravura usage where Bede declared that the shedding of Christ's blood had turned the entire globe into a house of prayer, as the sacrifice of victims had once consecrated the tabernacle and temple to the Lord.[64] This reminds us that he retained his conviction that the material temple was inferior to the universal temple Church, which would embrace Northumbria as well as Jerusalem.[65] Nevertheless, I have shown that

---

In Evangelia, II.XXXIX.7 p. 386. For Bede's use of the story of the cleansing, in the context of earlier and later writers: Emmanuel Bain, 'Les marchands chassés du Temple, entre commentaires et usages sociaux', *Médiévales* 55 (2008), pp. 53–74, esp. 55–9.

[60] *Marc.*, pp. 578–9 'Si ergo dominus nec ea uolebat in templo uenundari quae in templo uolebat offerri . . . quanta putas animaduersione puniret si inuenisset aliquos ibi risui uel uaniloquio uacantes . . . in aedibus Deo sacratis'.

[61] *Marc.*, p. 575.

[62] *Hom.*, II.1 p. 185 'illos diximus qui ecclesiam ingressi non solum intentionem orandi neglegunt uerum etiam ea pro quibus orare debuerant augent'; trans. Martin and Hurst, II, p. 3.

[63] See Conor O'Brien, 'The Cleansing of the Temple in early medieval Northumbria', forthcoming.

[64] *Ret.*, p. 112.

[65] See Paul Hilliard, 'Sacred and Secular History in the Writings of Bede (†735)', (PhD thesis, University of Cambridge, 2007), pp. 195–6.

Bede did change his attitude to the physical temple, at least at the level of emphasis: he recognized that it had to pass away but did so with a new respect for the divinely instituted glorious building.[66] Increasingly, the Northumbrian monk chose to highlight the connections that bound his own time, place, and people with the ancient Jewish temple and its cult.

This blurring of the boundaries between the biblical world of the temple and contemporary Northumbria reached a high point in *On the Temple* and *On Ezra and Nehemiah*—the two works with the best claims to be Bede's final commentaries. Of course, previous exegetical works had also reflected contemporary concerns, but DeGregorio has convincingly argued that this process appears particularly clearly in *On Ezra and Nehemiah*.[67] These final temple commentaries contain strikingly precise references to the Anglo-Saxon world, with mention of monasteries that fail to provide pastoral care, and praise for the members of the Gregorian mission.[68] The long prologue to *On the Temple* unusually avoids discussion of method and argues strongly for the relevance of scriptural meditation to 'us', for correction and consolation in difficult times.[69] *On the Temple* mainly consists of architectural descriptions and measurements and includes little narrative, but the prologue makes clear that Bede considered this apparently static temple image as supremely relevant to his life and that of his contemporaries.

It may seem rather strange then that so little clear use of the temple image appears in the *Ecclesiastical History*, which Bede must have been writing alongside *On the Temple* and *On Ezra and Nehemiah*.[70] But we should not forget that the *Ecclesiastical History* formed not just the culmination of Bede's life's work (once the scholarly consensus); it was also something new, reaching out (at least in theory) to an audience beyond religious communities. The lack of explicit recourse to the temple image in these circumstances makes sense. Scholars have certainly shown that the links between the history and these commentaries are there to be found on close examination.[71] Fundamentally

---

[66] See Ch. 3 within this volume, 'The house made by human hands'.

[67] Scott DeGregorio, 'Bede's *In Ezram et Neemiam* and the Reform of the Northumbrian Church', *Speculum* 79 (2004), pp. 1–25, at 3–20; DeGregorio, *Bede: On Ezra and Nehemiah* (Liverpool, 2006), pp. xxx–xxxvi. For *On 1 Samuel* as a similar kind of response to Bede's contemporary worries: Alan Thacker, 'Bede, the Britons and the Book of Samuel', in *Early Medieval Studies in Memory of Patrick Wormald*, eds Stephen Baxter et al. (Farnham, 2009), pp. 129–47; Darby, *End of Time*, pp. 165–85.

[68] *Ezra.*, p. 303; *Temp.*, p. 218.   [69] *Temp.*, pp. 143–5.

[70] Jennifer O'Reilly, 'The Multitude of Isles and the Corner-stone: Topography, Exegesis, and the Identity of the *Angli* in Bede's *Historia Ecclesiastica*', in *Anglo-Saxon Traces*, eds Jane Roberts and Leslie Webster (Tempe AZ, 2011), pp. 201–27, at 201–2.

[71] O'Reilly, 'Multitude of the Isles'; O'Reilly, 'Introduction', in *Bede: On the Temple*, trans. Seán Connolly (Liverpool, 1995), pp. xxvii–lv, at xxxiv–xxxix; Henry Mayr-Harting, *The Venerable Bede, The Rule of St. Benedict, and Social Class*, Jarrow Lecture (Jarrow, 1976), pp. 13, 20–22; Julia Barrow, 'How Coifi Pierced Christ's Side: A Re-Examination of Bede's *Ecclesiastical History* II, Chapter 13', *JEH* 62 (2011), pp. 693–706.

the *Ecclesiastical History* reveals that Bede's interest in the Insular world had become quite explicit in his later years; the final temple commentaries reflect the same impulse. The importance of the temple image is that it became the site where the synthesis of Bede's world and the biblical past occurred.

The temple image had not always been so significant to Bede and this section has mapped, in part, how the monk's thought and approach to it developed over time. The evidence clearly suggests that Bede was comparatively uninterested in the temple up until sometime after 710, and that in the years before 716 something outside his own exegetical activity drove his fascination with this image. By around 720 a quite well-developed interpretation existed in Bede's mind, influencing how he approached other parts of the Bible; shortly thereafter he embarked on an ambitious project of commentaries dedicated to the temple image. Unsurprisingly, the evidence is not always straightforward: Bede's interest in sacrificial priesthood came much earlier than that in sacred architecture. The current state of the evidence means that any explanation of the development of Bede's thought will only be partial, although no less valid for all that.

Linking this development with the Codex Amiatinus depends on the date of that manuscript, about which some ambiguity exists. Ceolfrith became abbot in 689/690 and could have begun work on his pandects shortly thereafter. However, the argument that the Codex Amiatinus was in fact the first made of Ceolfrith's pandects and was a 'library copy' until being used as a gift for St Peter is extremely unlikely—not least because the codex was likely always meant to be sent to Rome.[72] Richard Marsden has argued persuasively that the Codex Amiatinus was likely to have been the last of the three Bibles made—perhaps in the years immediately before 716.[73] The Wearmouth-Jarrow scriptorium almost certainly did not rush through it all in the first six months of 716: they had time to go through and correct the entire biblical text, something also implied by the words of Bede and the author of the *Life of Ceolfrith*.[74] Nor need it have been produced over a single defined period—costs may have necessitated spacing production out over a number of years.[75] The text could have been produced first and the first quire of illuminations and prefatory matter added only shortly before the manuscript left the monastery.[76]

---

[72] Barbara Apelian Beall, 'The Illuminated Pages of the Codex Amiatinus: Issues of Form, Function and Production' (PhD dissertation, Brown University, 1997), pp. 131–69.

[73] Richard Marsden, *The Text of the Old Testament in Anglo-Saxon England* (Cambridge, 1995), pp. 100–6.

[74] Marsden, *Text of the Old Testament*, pp. 99–100. *HA*, 15 pp. 56–9; *VCeol.*, 20 pp. 98–9.

[75] Richard Gameson, 'The Cost of the Codex Amiatinus', *Notes and Queries* 39 (1992), pp. 2–9, at 6.

[76] Celia Chazelle, 'Christ and the Vision of God: The Biblical Diagrams of the Codex Amiatinus', in *The Mind's Eye: Art and Theological Argument in the Middle Ages*, eds Jeffrey F. Hamburger and Anne-Marie Bouché (Princeton NJ, 2006), pp. 84–111, at 103. There clearly were some detailed preparations for the journey—including in relation to gifts: *VCeol.*, 22 pp. 100–101.

Interestingly, the tabernacle bifolium does not share the same first stitching as the rest of the opening quire, which may suggest that it was a comparatively late addition to the design, though the monks may also have had artistic or spiritual reasons for not wanting to sew the image into a particular place while the manuscript was at Wearmouth-Jarrow.[77] The work and planning that went into the codex probably took place, then, over a number of years sometime before June 716. That would provide a plausible explanation for the spike in interest in the temple image throughout Bede's writings from the half-decade or so before 716.

The use of the temple image in the Codex Amiatinus derived, of course, from the diagrams and designs available to the Wearmouth-Jarrow community in the Codex Grandior.[78] Bede clearly studied these images in some detail, and perhaps had more access to them over the course of his career than he had to the Amiatinus. Hence, Meyvaert has suggested that the temple commentaries are the result of 'the spell cast by these images' on Bede.[79] However, the monk would not have been so interested in Cassiodorus' work if it had not provided the model for the new pandect, which had a special place in Wearmouth-Jarrow's history. And the decision to link Cassiodorus' use of the temple image with the Northumbrian monastery would have been made, not by Bede, but by Ceolfrith. In other words, the importance of the Codex Grandior to the development of Bede's thought on the temple must have been dependent on and secondary to the communal significance of the Codex Amiatinus.

The evidence suggests that the pandect's preparation did not merely spur Bede into interest in the temple image. Rather, many of the details of Bede's interpretation of the temple were formed in that context, albeit not all of them and not without room for further development: in *On Luke*, Bede's reading of the temple vessels is not that of *On the Temple* years later—but his interpretation of the bronze sea effectively is. This suggests that the creation of the Codex Amiatinus provided Bede with specific interpretations and understandings of the temple, probably derived at that time from communal discussion surrounding the opening quire and its meaning. Bede's writings show that talk and debate concerning the Bible and how to understand it played an important role

---

[77] Paul Meyvaert, 'Dissension in Bede's Community Shown by a Quire of the Codex Amiatinus', *RB* 116 (2006), pp. 295–309, at 305–8; Celia Chazelle, 'Painting the Voice of God: Wearmouth-Jarrow, Rome and the Tabernacle Miniature in the Codex Amiatinus', *Quintana* 8 (2009), pp. 15–59, at 44. Jennifer O'Reilly, 'Bede on Seeing the God of Gods in Zion', in *Text, Image, Interpretation: Studies in Anglo-Saxon Literature and its Insular Context in Honour of Eamonn Ó Carragáin*, eds Alastair Minnis and Jane Roberts (Turnhout, 2007), pp. 3–29, at 15, argues for the thematic unity of the codex's opening quire.

[78] See Ch. 4 within this volume, 'The Codex Amiatinus'.

[79] Paul Meyvaert, 'Bede, Cassiodorus and the Codex Amiatinus', *Speculum* 71 (1996), pp. 827–83, at 883.

in contemporary monastic culture. The *Letter to Plegwine* presents the image of Bede and his brother monks debating the lengths of the world ages—an argument grounded in biblical interpretation.[80] As Cuthbert's mentor Boisil was dying (*c*.661), the two men read through John's gospel, and *discussed* it.[81] The letters Bede received from Acca, Nothelm, and the nun who enquired about the *Canticle of Habakkuk*, amongst many others, all indicate a wide culture of discussion concerning matters of exegesis—much of which would have left little or no trace in the historical record. Awareness of the existence of this discursive culture should, as Mark Stansbury has suggested, 'redirect our view of the reading and understanding of texts away from the solitary activity of scholars to the social activity of communities'.[82] At least some of the interpretations to be found in Bede's temple commentaries probably result from just such social activity at Wearmouth-Jarrow.

A MONK AND HIS MONASTERY

Monastic discussion clearly took place between as well as within individual communities. The chronology of Bede's use of the temple image mapped out here could have more than one explanation; for example, the fact that serious interest in the temple appears in his work predominantly after Acca became his patron might prove significant, especially since Stephen's *Life of Wilfrid*, a work written partially at Acca's request, also deploys the image of the temple. Stephen compared Wilfrid restoring the church at York to Christ cleansing the temple; the building of the great stone church at Ripon saw Wilfrid paralleled with Moses constructing the tabernacle and Solomon the temple.[83] In other words, Stephen primarily used the temple image in order to glorify Wilfrid's architectural activities, although he presumably also intended a spiritual significance.[84] This might indicate a 'Wilfridian' approach to the temple which Acca's patronage would have brought to Bede's attention.

---

[80] Bede, *Epistola ad Pleguinam*, ed. C. W. Jones, CCSL 123C, 15 pp. 624–5. The letter was occasioned when Bede had been accused of heresy during discussion (of his works or of issues of scriptural chronology?) in Wilfrid's presence: 1 p. 617.

[81] VCP, VIII pp. 182–3. Also *Ret.*, p. 155, where queries about the meaning of scripture went far beyond Britain.

[82] Mark Stansbury, 'Early-Medieval Biblical Commentaries, Their Writers and Readers', *Frühmittelalterliche Studien* 33 (1999), pp. 49–82, at 50. Also Paul Meyvaert, 'A New Perspective on the Ruthwell Cross: Ecclesia and Vita Monastica', in *The Ruthwell Cross: Papers from the Colloquium sponsored by the Index of Christian Art, Princeton University, 8 December 1989*, ed. Brendan Cassidy (Princeton NJ, 1992), pp. 95–166, at 164.

[83] VW, XVI–XVII pp. 34–7.

[84] Mark D. Laynesmith, 'Stephen of Ripon and the Bible: Allegorical and Typological Interpretations of the *Life of St Wilfrid*', EME 9 (2000), pp. 163–82, at 172–4.

Recent scholarship has reiterated a long-standing belief that Bede would have felt little sympathy for this glorification of physical church buildings, refusing to assign divine significance to any structure not mentioned in the Bible.[85] Indeed, throughout his career, he condemned those who put constructing rich churches above building up the Church of living stones— Gregory the Great proved superior to other popes for this reason.[86] If increased contact with Acca after 710 confronted Bede with a disagreeable use of the temple image, the monk of Jarrow might have decided to engage more with that image in order to satisfy his new patron and redirect Wilfridian attitudes along lines of which Bede approved—Peter Darby has suggested that Bede used his contact with Acca to try and influence the Hexham community concerning chronology in a similar fashion.[87] Early in *On Luke* Bede stated that David provided Solomon with the plans for the temple 'so that, with the state of worship thriving externally, the height of devotion might also increase internally'.[88] The statement seems not dissimilar to Stephen's explanation that Moses had built the tabernacle 'to stir up the faith of the people of Israel for the worship of God'.[89] Towards the end of *On Luke* Bede attacked people who delighted in building in expensive finery when Christ had not had a place to rest his head: 'Let them hear who worry about building houses and showy porticoes, it is intended as a lesson for those who delight in pomps of precious marble and ceilings adorned with gold'.[90] This could be Bede carefully engaging with the temple image as understood by the Wilfridians, agreeing with them in part but also seeking to correct them of a materialistic focus. Stephen's *Life* was completed between 712 and 714 and thus might just have been known to Bede when

---

[85] Clare Stancliffe, 'Disputed episcopacy: Bede, Acca and the relationship between Stephen's *Life of Wilfrid* and the early prose Lives of St Cuthbert', *ASE* 41 (2012), pp. 7–39, at 31; Arthur G. Holder, 'Allegory and History in Bede's Interpretation of Sacred Architecture', *American Benedictine Review* 40 (1989), pp. 115–31; George Hardin Brown, 'The Church as Non-Symbol in the Age of Bede', in *Northumbria's Golden Age*, eds Hawkes and Mills, pp. 359–64.

[86] *HE*, II.1 pp. 128–9; also *Ezra.*, p. 303. Jennifer O'Reilly, 'The Art of Authority', in *After Rome*, ed. Thomas Charles-Edwards (Oxford, 2003), pp. 141–89, at 146–7; O'Reilly, 'Introduction', pp. xlvi–li.

[87] Darby, *End of Time*, pp. 83–91. See also O'Reilly, 'Introduction', p. l; Celia Chazelle, ' "Romanness" in Early Medieval Culture', in *Paradigms and Methods in Early Medieval Studies*, eds Celia Chazelle and Felice Lifshitz (New York, 2007), pp. 81–98, at 91–2, suggests that the Codex Amiatinus was intended to contrast with the highly material *Romanitas* of the cult of Wilfrid.

[88] *Luc.*, p. 21 'ut crescente extrinsecus statu culturae etiam deuotionis interius culmen augesceret'. Also *Hom.*, II.19 p. 320.

[89] *VW*, XVII pp. 34–5 'Sicut enim Moyses tabernaculum seculare manu factum . . . ad concitandam Israhelitico populo culturae Dei fidem'.

[90] *Luc.*, p. 375 'Audiant quibus aedificandarum domorum cura est et ambitiosarum porticuum cogitatur instructio quos pretiosorum marmorum pompa et distincta auro laquearia delectant cognoscant Christum omnium dominum qui locum ubi caput inclinaret non habuit'.

writing *On Luke*.[91] Such an explanation would situate Bede's use of the temple in debate between different communities rather than in consensus within one community.[92]

Problems, however, exist with this line of interpretation. Making a link between actual contemporary locations and the temple or tabernacle of the Old Testament was not unique to the *Life of Wilfrid*, but may have been widespread in the Insular world. The authors of the *Collectio Canonum Hibernensis* (who may present contemporary ideas from Iona) described monastic enclosure as following the model of the temple precincts, with zones of increasing holiness, each more exclusive than the previous—a model which some Irish monasteries may have followed in practice.[93] Adomnán of Iona seems to have held this view of the monastic complex, which may have been widespread throughout the Insular world, with most Anglo-Saxon monasteries having enclosures, even if purely symbolic ones.[94] The fact that both the Columban and Wilfridian *familiae* could have thought of their religious structures in terms of the temple indicates just how common and uncontroversial an attitude this was. The image of the temple infused the liturgy of church dedication and Bede's own homilies for the celebration of the feast of dedication began with this understanding of the church as the Lord's temple—although they moved on to make the utterly conventional point that the congregation was more truly the temple.[95]

The homilies, in fact, make frequent use of this link between the temple and the Christian church. As the place of eucharistic sacrifice, the church directly paralleled the Jewish temple: 'If [Christ] chose to walk in the temple, where the flesh and blood of brute animals used to be offered, much more will he rejoice to visit our house of prayer, where the sacrament of his own body and blood is celebrated.'[96] This link between the eucharist and the temple cult appears a number of times in the homilies, as do more general interpretations

---

[91] Clare Stancliffe, 'Dating Wilfrid's Death and Stephen's *Life*', in *Wilfrid: Abbot, Bishop, Saint; Papers from the 1300th Anniversary Conferences*, ed. N. J. Higham (Donington, 2013), pp. 17–26, at 22–4.

[92] I am grateful to Matthew Kempshall for discussion on this point.

[93] *Collectio Canonum Hibernensis*, ed. Herrmann Wasserschleben, *Die Irische Kanonensammlung* (Leipzig, 1885), XLIV.1–7 pp. 174–6. David H. Jenkins, *'Holy, Holier, Holiest': The Sacred Topography of the Early Medieval Irish Church* (Turnhout, 2010).

[94] Aidan MacDonald, 'Aspects of the Monastic Landscape in Adomnán's *Life of Columba*', in *Studies in Irish Hagiography: Saints and Scholars*, eds John Carey et al. (Dublin, 2001), pp. 15–30. Sarah Foot, *Monastic Life in Anglo-Saxon England, c.600–900* (Cambridge, 2006), pp. 97–106; John Blair, *The Church in Anglo-Saxon Society* (Oxford, 2005), pp. 196–9.

[95] E.g. *Hom.*, II.24 p. 359. See Ch. 2 within this volume, 'The temple in the Christian tradition before Bede', p. 42.

[96] *Hom.*, II.24 p. 358 'Si ergo ambulare uoluit in templo in quo caro et sanguis brutorum animalium offerebatur, multo magis nostram orationis domum ubi carnis ipsius ac sanguinis sacramenta celebrantur uisitare gaudebit'; trans. Martin and Hurst, II, pp. 241–2.

connecting the temple with church buildings.[97] I have examined these examples in more detail elsewhere and concluded that, in fact, Bede and Stephen
of Ripon would have agreed substantially about the link between the temple
and churches.[98] Bede viewed building fine places of worship with some
suspicion as an activity that occasionally distracted one from important
pastoral work, but he also fully accepted that the biblical temple image could
be read as signifying Christian churches.

However, it does not seem probable that Bede came to this understanding of
the temple because Acca convinced him of any Wilfridian interpretation.
The fact that all his uses of this idea, barring that in *On Mark*, appear in
the homilies directs our focus, once again, to Wearmouth-Jarrow. Of course,
no clear proof survives that Bede himself preached these homilies in one of
the monastery's churches. Many were quite possibly purely literary exercises
intended for general use—although the presence of a homily on Benedict
Biscop in the final collection does prove that the community at Wearmouth-
Jarrow was the intended audience for at least some of the homilies.[99] Homilies,
as previously discussed, aimed at making a direct link with their hearers; even
if Bede never delivered his homilies he would have had an imaginary audience
in mind, which would have shaped his expectations. That imaginary audience
must have reflected Bede's own experience of church congregations, and that
experience would primarily, and possibly overwhelmingly, have been of congregations at Wearmouth and Jarrow. Bede's imagined audience probably,
therefore, shared many interests with his own monastic community.

The temple does indeed seem to have been one of those interests. Frequently Bede expressed his pleasure at discussing the details of the Jewish temple
with his brothers who, he suspected, would delight in hearing about it.[100] If he
personally disapproved of an obsession with fine buildings, his sense of
fraternal duty may have encouraged him to preach on subjects appealing to
a community convinced of the temple-like qualities of their stone churches.
Scholars have on occasion suggested that the temple provided a model for
Wearmouth-Jarrow.[101] Certain stone features may particularly have called
the biblical archetype to mind: for instance, a covered walkway (possibly
colonnaded on one side) at Wearmouth was quite probably described as a

---

[97] E.g. *Hom.*, I.14 pp. 101–2, I.18 p. 130, II.4 pp. 207–8, II.16 p. 300.

[98] O'Brien, 'Cleansing of the Temple'.

[99] Lawrence T. Martin, 'Bede and Preaching', in *The Cambridge Companion to Bede*
(Cambridge, 2010), ed. Scott DeGregorio, pp. 156–69, at 162–3. See Ch. 7 within this volume,
'Morality', pp. 158–9.

[100] *Hom.*, II.1 pp. 189–90, II.19 p. 319, II.24 p. 363, II.25 p. 377.

[101] Holder, 'Allegory and History', pp. 123–5; Ian Wood, *The Most Holy Abbot Ceolfrid*,
Jarrow Lecture (Jarrow, 1995), p. 15; Rosemary Cramp et al., *Wearmouth and Jarrow Monastic
Sites*, 2 vols (Swindon, 2005–2006), I, p. 352; Celia Chazelle, 'Art and Reverence in Bede's
Churches at Wearmouth and Jarrow', in *Intellektualisierung und Mystifizierung mittelalterlicher
Kunst*, eds Martin Büchsel and Rebecca Müller (Berlin, 2010), pp. 79–98, at 87.

porticus—a word Bede used to describe the cloister-like structures he imagined surrounding Solomon's temple.[102] The monastery certainly did not mimic the temple exactly, but it would not have needed to do so in order to count as a copy in the medieval mind; a few symbolic features would have been enough to make the link and such architectural mimicry was not uncommon in early Anglo-Saxon England.[103]

One ought never to forget just how unusual stone buildings were in the Anglo-Saxon world of wood; stone did not constitute the norm, even for church buildings.[104] Anglo-Saxons were fascinated and more than a little cowed by grand Roman stone structures. These were, in the language of Old English verse, the 'work of giants'.[105] Bede's explanation as to why the judges of ancient Israel heard cases at the gates of a city may give a glimpse of his own experience of Anglo-Saxon peasants coming to Wearmouth-Jarrow: the judges sat outside the city 'lest peasants or shepherds were struck dumb by the unaccustomed buildings of the city'.[106] The secular and ecclesiastical elite might not have been rendered speechless by stonework, but they remained fascinated with it as Cuthbert's tour of the Roman stonework of Carlisle shows.[107] Bede's community must have been aware that they lived amongst exceptional structures, different from the mundane buildings around them, and would have turned to scripture to express that difference.[108]

Bede's lived experience in this exceptional built environment provides, then, a plausible reason for the ongoing importance of the temple image in his work. If using the Codex Grandior as the model for their own pandects provided the initial impetus for the Wearmouth-Jarrow community to think about the temple, the daily routine amongst their stone churches and structures likely helped to internalize that image as part of their identity. Whatever Bede's

---

[102] Alan Thacker, *Bede and Augustine of Hippo: History and Figure in Sacred Text*, Jarrow Lecture (Jarrow, 2005), pp. 30–31; Éamonn Ó Carragáin, 'The Term *Porticus* and *Imitatio Romae* in Early Anglo-Saxon England', in *Text and Gloss: Studies in Insular Learning and Literature Presented to Joseph Donovan Pheifer*, eds Helen Conrad-O'Briain et al. (Dublin, 1999), pp. 13–34; Cramp, *Monastic Sites*, I, 95–8, 112. *Ezra.*, p. 298; *Temp.*, pp. 192–3.

[103] Richard Krautheimer, 'Introduction to an "Iconography of Mediaeval Architecture"', *Journal of the Warburg and Courtauld Institutes* 5 (1942), pp. 1–33, at 1–20. Richard Bailey, 'St Wilfrid, Ripon and Hexham', in *Studies in Insular Art and Archaeology*, eds Catherine E. Karkov and Robert Farrell (Oxford OH, 1991), pp. 3–25, at 20–22; O'Reilly, 'Art of Authority', p. 149.

[104] Jane Hawkes, '*Iuxta Morem Romanorum*: Stone and Sculpture in Anglo-Saxon England', in *Anglo-Saxon Styles*, eds Catherine E. Karkov and George Hardin Brown (Albany NY, 2003), pp. 69–99.

[105] See 'The Ruin', ed. and trans. Richard Hamer, *A Choice of Anglo-Saxon Verse* (London, 1970), pp. 25–9.

[106] *Prov.*, p. 158 'nec rusticos uel pastores insolita urbis aedificia stupefacerent'.

[107] *VCP*, XXVII pp. 242–5.

[108] See Thomas Pickles, 'Anglo-Saxon Monasteries as Sacred Places: Topography, Exegesis and Vocation', in *Sacred Text—Sacred Space: Architectural, Spiritual and Literary Convergences in England and Wales*, eds Joseph Sterrett and Peter Thomas (Leiden, 2011), pp. 35–55.

misgivings about costly buildings, his account of his monastery remains strikingly materialistic and he probably mimicked the *Liber Pontificalis* in its fascination with construction work and physical displays of wealth.[109] The stone buildings of Wearmouth-Jarrow clearly played an important role in the community's identity, as Nechtan's request to Ceolfrith for experts to build him a stone church attests.[110] If Bede suspected that preaching about the architectural features of the temple would delight and serve as a good means to educate his brother monks, the evidence suggests that he guessed right.

The historian cannot walk amidst the stones of Wearmouth-Jarrow with its early eighth-century inhabitants and experience how such an environment would have shaped, possibly distorted, their self-image. We can, however, piece together some hints concerning the monastery's identity. Bede mourned Ceolfrith's departure in 716 by comparing the abbot with Moses and Aaron;[111] Pope Gregory II made the same comparison in his letter to the new abbot Hwaetberht accepting Wearmouth-Jarrow's gifts and praising the deceased Ceolfrith.[112] Bede wrote before the papal letter arrived and so could not simply have parroted its phrases. Rather, both writers most likely expressed an understanding of Ceolfrith current in Wearmouth-Jarrow at the time of the Codex Amiatinus' departure—one which could have been explained to the pope by those monks who presented the manuscript in Rome. The picture of the tabernacle within the codex, the names of Moses and Aaron written inside the enclosure, might have acted as a symbolic representation of Wearmouth-Jarrow.[113] Benedict Biscop's reported dying words similarly linked the monastery with Old Testament Israel.[114]

Material in the temple commentaries came from locations other than Wearmouth-Jarrow on occasion. Bede's decision to celebrate the leaders of the Roman mission to the English in *On the Temple* would have been perfectly acceptable to his brother monks, but probably arose from contact with Nothelm and Albinus who sought to promote Canterbury's Rome-centred view of the Anglo-Saxon Church.[115] Albinus played an important role in

---

[109] Simon Coates, 'Ceolfrid: History, Hagiography and Memory in seventh- and eighth-century Wearmouth-Jarrow', *Journal of Medieval History* 25 (1999), pp. 69–86, at 73–4; Vicky Gunn, *Bede's Historiae: Genre, Rhetoric and the Construction of Anglo-Saxon Church History* (Woodbridge, 2009), pp. 116–30.

[110] *HE*, V.21 pp. 532–5.

[111] *Sam.*, p. 212; Bede clearly was writing this before news of Ceolfrith's death at Langres had reached Wearmouth-Jarrow.

[112] *VCeol.*, 39 pp. 118–21.

[113] See Chazelle, 'Painting the Voice of God', p. 52. For a rich analysis of how the imagery of Exodus may relate to Ceolfrith's final journey and how it was understood: O'Reilly, 'Seeing the God of Gods', pp. 12–18.

[114] *HA*, 13 pp. 52–3; *VCeol.*, 25 pp. 104–5.

[115] *Temp.*, p. 218. Paul Meyvaert, *Bede and Gregory the Great*, Jarrow Lecture (Jarrow, 1964), p. 10; Meyvaert, '"Footsteps of the Fathers"', pp. 278–9.

urging Bede to write the *Ecclesiastical History* and Nothelm undertook the necessary research in the papal archives in Rome;[116] Nothelm's role as contact between the abbot of Peter and Paul's and Bede, as well as his elevation to the archbishopric in 735, implies that he was sympathetic to Canterbury's inter- ests. Considering that both men must have been in frequent contact with Bede in the years before 731 it is unlikely that they were unaware of *On the Temple*.[117] Indeed, as already noted, Nothelm had enquired concerning the temple image previously, and Bede sent Albinus *On the Temple* shortly after its completion with a letter that underlines his interest in the work.[118]

Canterbury would have found much that appealed in Bede's use of the temple image. The archiepiscopal Church promoted an ideology of a unified Anglo-Saxon Church founded by Rome, a link symbolized in the stone buildings, which made Canterbury an imitation of the eternal city.[119] There is nothing surprising in the discovery that many Anglo-Saxon clerics from the Roman tradition in the late seventh and early eighth centuries had similar opinions—indeed we would expect it. Such general similarities do not negate the lack of specific evidence for interest in the temple image at Canterbury. The published glosses on Exodus from the Canterbury school display no especial interest in the Mosaic tabernacle and provide a purely descriptive commentary on the priestly vestments.[120] While many of the texts associated with the Canterbury school remain unpublished (including glosses on Kings and other potentially relevant books of the Bible), these are related to the purely literal glosses on words found in the Leiden Glossary, which show absolutely no interest in the temple image, and are unlikely to bear much resemblance to Bede's exegetical approach.[121] Many traditional elements of Christian interpretation of the temple image were, no doubt, known at Canterbury.[122] However, we would expect something more than a few

---

[116] *HE*, praef. pp. 2–5. D. P. Kirby, *Bede's* Historia Ecclesiastica Gentis Anglorum: *Its Contemporary Setting*, Jarrow Lecture (Jarrow, 1992), pp. 3–8; Walter Goffart, *The Narrators of Barbarian History (A.D. 550–800): Jordanes, Gregory of Tours, Bede and Paul the Deacon*, 2nd ed. (Notre Dame IN, 2005), pp. 296–7; N. J. Higham, *(Re-)Reading Bede: The* Ecclesiastical History *in Context* (London, 2006), pp. 76–8, questions the influence of Albinus on the *HE*.

[117] Meyvaert, '"Footsteps of the Fathers"', p. 276, argues that contact between Bede and Canterbury concerning the *HE* probably began before 716.

[118] Bede, *Epistola ad Albinum*, ed. Joshua A. Westgard, 'New Manuscripts of Bede's Letter to Albinus', *RB* 120 (2010), pp. 208–15, at 214.

[119] Nicholas Brooks, 'Canterbury and Rome: The Limits and Myth of *Romanitas*', *Settimane di studio del Centro italiano di studi sull'alto medioevo* 49 (2002), pp. 797–832; Blair, *Anglo-Saxon Society*, pp. 66–8.

[120] Bernhard Bischoff and Michael Lapidge, *Biblical Commentaries from the Canterbury School of Theodore and Hadrian* (Cambridge, 1994), pp. 352–9.

[121] J. H. Hessels (ed.), *A Late Eighth-Century Latin-Anglo-Saxon Glossary preserved in the Library of the Leiden University* (Cambridge, 1906), pp. 10–11, 21.

[122] Jane Stevenson, *The 'Laterculus Malalianus' and the School of Archbishop Theodore* (Cambridge, 1995), pp. 136–41; see Ch. 5 within this volume, 'The temple as Christ', p. 102.

traditional interpretations to mark the primary source and impetus behind Bede's exceptional engagement with the temple image.[123] The use of the temple image in Bede's writings probably reflects the influence of a northern Insular context, rather than the interests of Canterbury.

The temple image crops up in Stephen's *Life of Wilfrid* and in Irish writings, which may suggest a common cultural approach to the temple; the ivory carving of the temple in the Franks Casket probably also derives from eighth-century Northumbria.[124] Despite the possible influence of such examples, the Codex Amiatinus, with its images of the tabernacle, Ezra as high priest, and Christ as the heavenly ark, remains the most striking Insular use of the temple image likely to have influenced Bede which I have been able to identify.[125] When evidence survives for the ideology of the community to which Bede belonged it would seem perverse to set it aside in favour of more distant sources. Any discussion concerning the temple's exegesis at Wearmouth-Jarrow would have been part of a wider conversation, but that local discussion provides, I would argue, the most likely source for the ideas found in Bede's temple commentaries.

Holder has argued that the distinctive features of Bede's exegesis, including his interest in the temple image, derive from his individual psychology or mindset: 'There seems to have been something about the balance, harmony, and regularity of architectural design that appealed to his imagination . . .'.[126] Such a viewpoint perpetuates the long tradition of approaching his works with a focus on Bede the man, the individual genius. This in turn belongs to the mainstream of our Romantic-individualist culture; we think of the published text of *The Waste Land* as Eliot's even though formed by a dialogue between the poet and others who criticized, edited, and *contributed*.[127] A critical apparatus allows the reader to see where Bede used the thoughts and words of the Church Fathers. It cannot reconstruct the influence of the communal culture at Wearmouth-Jarrow; historians must use their imagination for that,

---

[123] Canterbury, however, would have been a key staging post if Cosmas Indicopleustes' *Christian Topography* had reached Wearmouth-Jarrow: Ch. 2 within this volume, 'The temple in the Christian tradition before Bede', p. 39.

[124] See Ch. 5 within this volume, 'The temple as Christ', p. 104.

[125] See Ch. 4 within this volume, 'The Codex Amiatinus', pp. 96–100; Ch. 5 within this volume 'The temple as Christ', p. 108 and 'The priesthood of all believers', pp. 105–7; Carol Neuman de Vegvar, 'Remembering Jerusalem: Architecture and Meaning in Insular Canon Table Arcades', in *Making and Meaning in Insular Art*, ed. Rachel Moss (Dublin, 2007), pp. 242–56, at 254, argues that the pillared arcades, which decorate the pandect's canon tables (fols 798r–801r) refer to the Holy Sepulchre and, therefore, may have called the temple image to mind (the Sepulchre being the new temple).

[126] Arthur G. Holder, 'The Venerable Bede on the Mysteries of Our Salvation', *American Benedictine Review* 42 (1991), pp. 140–62, at 162; Holder, 'Allegory and History', p. 120 for quotation.

[127] See T. S. Eliot, *The Waste Land: a Facsimile and Transcript of the Original Drafts including the Annotations of Ezra Pound*, ed. Valerie Eliot (San Diego CA, 1994).

and that obviously is a risky strategy—but I would argue a necessary one in order to advance our knowledge. The evidence, of Bede's use of the temple image and the chronology of that use, suggests important links between the necessarily communal creation of the Codex Amiatinus and Bede's interpretation of the temple. Clear evidence exists to suppose that the brothers of Wearmouth-Jarrow identified closely with the temple image and that some of Bede's works responded to their interests.

Is it plausible to imagine then that Bede's writings contain the results of communal discourse? Older interpretations of Bede as entirely, blissfully, unconnected with other activities at Wearmouth-Jarrow have become less popular, though they are still occasionally aired.[128] In the preface to *On Luke* Bede claimed to be his own *dictator*, notetaker, and copyist during the work's composition.[129] That suggests a lack of support from his community, although Wearmouth-Jarrow's scribes may have been busy working on the Codex Amiatinus at this time or Bede could have treated such work as fulfilling his monastic duty of manual labour.[130] At the end of his life Bede seems to have been no solitary scholar: surrounded, rather, on his deathbed by notetakers and students devoted to the monk and his work.[131] And in a world without modern medical assistance, as Higham points out, failing eyesight probably meant that Bede required help with reading and writing long before 735—the final temple commentaries and the *Ecclesiastical History* may well have been written with extensive support.[132] In such a well-regimented institution as Wearmouth-Jarrow it is unlikely that resources would have been directed to assisting Bede's work unless it was, in some way, 'officially' endorsed.

As a monk Bede belonged to a way of life built on an ideal of absolute obedience, where the individual's interests disappeared into the collective that had 'but one heart and one soul'.[133] His identification with Wearmouth-Jarrow would have been all the closer for his youth on entering the monastery, whether he initially entered simply for reasons of education or as a child oblate, Bede remained at Wearmouth-Jarrow from the age of seven onwards.

---

[128] E.g. Benedicta Ward, *The Venerable Bede*, 2nd ed. (London, 1998), p. 5.

[129] *Luc.*, p. 7 'ipse mihi dictator simul notarius et librarius existerem'.

[130] Foot, *Monastic Life*, pp. 216–18.

[131] Cuthbert, *Epistola de Obitu Bedae*, eds and trans. Bertram Colgrave and R. A. B. Mynors, in *Bede's Ecclesiastical History of the English People* (Oxford, 1969), pp. 579–87, at 580–87. For an overview of Bede's known contacts throughout his scholarly life: Dorothy Whitelock, 'Bede and His Teachers and Friends', in *Famulus Christi: Essays in Commemoration of the Thirteenth Centenary of the Birth of the Venerable Bede*, ed. Gerald Bonner (London, 1976), pp. 19–39.

[132] Higham, *(Re-)Reading Bede*, p. 8.

[133] Acts 4.32; *Tab.*, p. 42; *Temp.*, p. 163; *Gen.*, p. 128; see Ch. 6 within this volume, 'The temple versus the tower', p. 132. For the influence of Bede's monasticism on his exegesis: Scott DeGregorio, 'Bede, the Monk, as Exegete: Evidence from the Commentary on Ezra-Nehemiah', *RB* 115 (2005), pp. 343–69.

The Benedictine ideal was 'a communal life where the individual was lost in the crowd and stripped of those eccentricities which we call personality'.[134] Such an ideal, of course, never matched the reality of the life lived by Bede or any other medieval monk. Recent work has emphasized the importance of secular and family connections within Anglo-Saxon monasticism; in an early medieval context even oblation did not sever the link between the monk and the kin group beyond the monastery.[135] The aristocratic environment of an Anglo-Saxon monastery was one where the habit failed to strip the individual of worldly distinctions or insulate them from external influences. Bede's status as a monk does not in itself make it certain that he would have imbibed a communal ethos or that his writings would put forward the results of communal discourse.

Yet, Bede's case may be somewhat different from that of the average Anglo-Saxon monk. There is reason to doubt that his integration into Wearmouth-Jarrow would have been balanced by continuing loyalties to a kin group outside the monastery. Bede never mentions his parents, rather saying that his relatives sent him to Benedict Biscop—while Alcuin (drawing on oral traditions?) did specify that Bede was sent to the monastery by his *parentes*, the word is ambiguous and could perhaps simply mean relatives.[136] Consequently some scholars have suggested that he may have lost one or both parents; his entry into a religious house could have arisen from his status as an orphan.[137] Such arguments cannot go beyond the tentative. Bede's writings, however, occasionally evidence a distrust of the aristocratic kin group and preference for the spiritual monastic family.[138] His homily in praise of Benedict Biscop highlights especially the rejection of the aristocrat's duty to propagate children according to the flesh and urges the community to see themselves as the founder's 'spiritual children'.[139] Bede's comments on

---

[134] R. W. Southern, *The Making of the Middle Ages* (London, 1967), p. 213. For a more recent statement of a similar interpretation of early-medieval monasticism: Janet Coleman, *Ancient and Medieval Memories: Studies in the Reconstruction of the Past* (Cambridge, 1992), pp. 129–36.

[135] Catherine Cubitt, 'Monastic Memory and Identity in Early Anglo-Saxon England', in *Social Identity in Early Medieval Britain*, eds William O. Frazer and Andrew Tyrrell (London, 2000), pp. 253–76, at 259–61; Mayke de Jong, *In Samuel's Image: Child Oblation in the Early Medieval West* (Leiden, 1996), pp. 219–27.

[136] *HE*, V.24 pp. 566–7. Alcuin, *Versus de Patribus Regibus et Sanctis Euboricensis Ecclesiae*, ed. Peter Godman, *The Bishops, Kings and Saints of York* (Oxford, 1982), pp. 102–3.

[137] Ian Wood, 'The Gifts of Wearmouth and Jarrow', in *The Languages of Gift in the Early Middle Ages*, eds Wendy Davies and Paul Fouracre (Cambridge, 2010), pp. 89–115, at 113; David Pelteret, 'Bede's Women', in *Women, Marriage, and Family in Medieval Christendom: Essays in Memory of Michael M. Sheehan, C.S.B.*, eds Constance M. Rousseau and Joel T. Rosenthal (Kalamazoo MI, 1998), pp. 19–46, at 24–5; Ward, *Venerable Bede*, p. 3. For a different interpretation of Bede's description of his 'oblation': de Jong, *In Samuel's Image*, pp. 48, 213.

[138] Wood, 'Gifts of Wearmouth and Jarrow', pp. 113–14; Mayr-Harting, *Rule of St. Benedict, and Social Class*; Olivier Szerwiniack, 'Frères et sœurs dans l'*Histoire ecclésiastique du peuple anglais* de Bède le Vénérable: De la fratrie biologique à la fratrie spirituelle', *RB* 118 (2008), pp. 239–61.

[139] *Hom.*, I.13 pp. 93–4. Also *HA*, 1 pp. 24–5.

Wearmouth-Jarrow do not sound like those of an individualist or of someone held back by external connections from complete submersion within the spiritual family. The psychological effect on children of being raised within a religious community is difficult to recover—but it must have led frequently to a close identification with the monastery.[140] Bede certainly seems to have been one of the cases where it did so.

We should note that in early medieval society the kind of 'constructed' kinship which Bede used to describe his monastic community was quite common; friendship and kinship existed, for the Anglo-Saxons, on a continuum of interpersonal relations.[141] Clannish, kin-based ties could cut across the new bonds that the Church sought to create in recently converted barbarian societies—but they could also be hijacked and recreated in a religious context. Aldhelm's letter to the clergy of Wilfrid draws on ideas of loyalty familiar from Anglo-Saxon warrior culture, but uses them to uphold the bonds of the religious *familia*.[142] It has been shown that Boniface's missions to the continent drew not on the institutional resources of the Church, but on personal and familial networks of individuals.[143] Nonetheless, Boniface's correspondence also reveals how, when the security of the family was removed, men and women sought to replace it with spiritual bonds. Ecclesiastical connections provided the means by which those without parents or siblings could avoid being alone;[144] such examples may prove helpful when thinking about how the young Bede came to identify with his monastic house.

Thus, the societal norms of Bede's time make it likely that he would have formed the kinds of bonds necessary to integrate tightly into the Wearmouth-Jarrow community. There is little sense in Bede's own writings that personal, individual friendships were a key part of this process for him—rather the emphasis was on the collective.[145] Of perhaps more importance to present

---

[140] On early-medieval oblation and child-rearing in monasteries: de Jong, *In Samuel's Image*; for Anglo-Saxon monasteries as families: Foot, *Monastic Life*, pp. 70–72.

[141] De Jong, *In Samuel's Image*, pp. 205–19; Thomas Charles-Edwards, 'Anglo-Saxon Kinship Revisited', in *The Anglo-Saxons from the Migration Period to the Eighth Century: An Ethnographic Perspective*, ed. John Hines (Woodbridge, 1997), pp. 171–204; Joseph H. Lynch, *Christianizing Kinship: Ritual Sponsorship in Anglo-Saxon England* (Ithaca NY, 1998).

[142] Aldhelm, *Epistulae*, ed. R. Ehwald, MGH Auctores Antiquissimi 15, XII pp. 500–502. For a discussion of Wilfrid's 'fatherhood' as a theme in Stephen's *Life*: W. Trent Foley, *Images of Sanctity in Eddius Stephanus' Life of Bishop Wilfrid, An Early English Saint's Life* (Lampeter, 1992), pp. 53–70.

[143] Rosamond McKitterick, 'Anglo-Saxon Missionaries in Germany: Personal Connections and Local Influences', in McKitterick, *The Frankish Kings and Culture in the Early Middle Ages* (Aldershot, 1995), pp. 1–40.

[144] M. Tangl (ed.), *Die Briefe des Heiligen Bonifatius und Lullus*, MGH Epistolae Selectae 1, 13–14 pp. 18–26, 27 pp. 48–9, 29 pp. 52–3, 49 p. 78.

[145] Brian Patrick McGuire, *Friendship & Community: The Monastic Experience 350–1250* (Kalamazoo MI, 1988), pp. 91–6. For Bede's *HA* as the portrait of a community, rather than of individual abbots: Alan Thacker, 'The Social and Continental Background to early Anglo-Saxon Hagiography' (DPhil thesis, University of Oxford, 1976), pp. 183–7.

purposes is the question of Bede's own individuality as expressed in his writings. The monk of Jarrow was clearly an exceptional individual in many respects and he is unlikely to have been unaware of this. Nonetheless, despite the traditional certainty about ascertaining his personality, Bede himself remains somewhat nondescript, a distant presence in his own writings. A recent study of Bede's prose style has found, in effect, that he had none; preferring to mimic masterfully the styles of the Church Fathers, his prose lacks 'any kind of idiosyncrasy, even of personality'.[146] He could be original on occasion, but would probably not have thanked modern scholars for pointing it out. Bede's writings present us simply with a 'persona of orthodoxy', built up by the reliance on authorities rather than an emphasis on authorial individuality.[147] Witness the careful listing of sources at the beginning of the *Ecclesiastical History*, followed by the disclaimer: 'I humbly beg the reader, if he finds anything other than the truth set down in what I have written, not to impute it to me'.[148]

While the statement is unlikely to be an entirely accurate representation of Bede's level of authorial control it does show that he was comfortable with seeing himself passing on, not merely the wisdom of the Fathers, but also the oral knowledge of his contemporaries.[149] With this in mind it is worthwhile noting the close resemblance between Wearmouth-Jarrow's ideology and world view (as far as we can reconstruct it), and Bede's use of the temple image. We have seen, in the body of this study, how the temple in Bede's writings celebrates the Anglo-Saxon place in the universal Church, ecclesiastical unity, and Roman orthodoxy—all of which obviously form interrelated strands in Wearmouth-Jarrow's outlook as a self-consciously Romanizing Anglo-Saxon monastery formed by the coming together of two separate institutions.[150] This is not to say that Bede never interpreted the temple image in ways which relate to any wider context; Wearmouth-Jarrow did not have an exclusive hold over his ideas as contact with learned clerics in

[146] Richard Sharpe, 'The Varieties of Bede's Prose', *Proceedings of the British Academy* 129 (2005), pp. 339–55, quotation at p. 340.

[147] Paul Hilliard, 'The Venerable Bede as Scholar, Gentile and Preacher', in *Ego Trouble: Authors and their Identities in the Early Middle Ages*, eds Richard Corradini et al. (Vienna, 2010), pp. 101–9, at 103. For Bede's use of authorities: Joyce Hill, *Bede and the Benedictine Reform*, Jarrow Lecture (Jarrow, 1998), pp. 2, 4.

[148] *HE*, praef. pp. 6–7 'Lectoremque suppliciter obsecro ut, siqua in his quae scripsimus aliter quam se ueritas habet posita reppererit, non hoc nobis inputet'.

[149] D. P. Kirby, 'Bede's Native Sources for the *Historia Ecclesiastica*', *Bulletin of the John Rylands Library* 48 (1965–66), pp. 341–71; N. J. Higham, *Bede as an Oral Historian*, Jarrow Lecture (Jarrow, 2011).

[150] See Ch. 4 within this volume, 'The Anglo-Saxons' place in the world', pp. 89–90; Ch. 5 within this volume, 'The temple as Christ', pp. 105–8; and Ch. 6 within this volume, 'The temple versus the tower', p. 138.

Northumbria, Kent, Wessex and elsewhere will have influenced him.[151] Nonetheless, I have shown that good evidence exists for asserting that the influence of Wearmouth-Jarrow was of the greatest importance to Bede's use of the temple image.

A few years ago, Scott DeGregorio urged that more scholars examine how the 'lived experience' of Bede's monasticism influenced and shaped his exegesis.[152] This study, in part, attempts to do just that by arguing that Bede's interpretation of the temple image developed in response to and preserved ideas formed in the midst of that 'lived experience'. It was an experience not lived by Bede alone; the lives and ideas of many monks, most now nameless, constantly intersected with our author's creative career, although the *vestigia* they left in his work can now be barely guessed at. The question of non-textual influences on Bede can never, necessarily, be solved. We can hope perhaps to reread most of the books he read, though situated in a radically different historical and social context, but we can never hear again the conversations Bede heard. The latter, however, were certainly as real and perhaps as influential as the former; the current respect for Bede's originality should not obscure his probable dependence on the institution and people who surrounded him.

In 'Things that Might Have Been' Borges mourned the non-existence of the work Bede could have written on Anglo-Saxon paganism: 'I think of things that might have been and were not. / The treatise on Saxon mythology that Bede did not write...'.[153] It is salutary to remember that the gaps in our knowledge of Bede and his world are perhaps far greater than that knowledge itself, for we do not know what might fill them. Nevertheless, this study has extended our knowledge of Bede's use of the temple image and thereby raised fruitful questions about how we understand Bede as an author and a monk more generally. Returning to Bede's temple itself, the multivalent complexity of the image cannot be captured in a single sentence or two. But we have seen that important connections exist tying together the different uses of the temple image. We are left with a clear picture of how Bede used the temple to promote his vision of cosmic, ecclesiastical, and individual unity through and with Christ, and the more ill-defined possibility that Bede shared that vision with his community.

---

[151] See Ch. 4 within this volume, 'The Anglo-Saxons' place in the world', pp. 87–8 and Ch. 6 within this volume. As well as Acca, Albinus, and Nothelm, Bede corresponded with Daniel of Winchester and Pecthelm with whom he would have shared scriptural interests.

[152] DeGregorio, 'Bede, the Monk', pp. 368–9.

[153] Jorge Luis Borges, 'Things that Might Have Been', trans. Alastair Reid, *New England Review* 15 (1993), p. 101.

Bibliography

1. Manuscripts

Florence, Biblioteca Medicea Laurenziana, MS Amiatino 1.

2. Primary Sources

Adomnán, *De Locis Sanctis*, ed. L. Bieler, CCSL 175, pp. 175–234.

Adomnán, *Vita S. Columbae*, eds and trans. Alan Orr Anderson and Marjorie Ogilvie Anderson, *Adomnan's Life of Columba* (Oxford, 1991).

Aenigmata Eusebii, ed. F. Glorie, CCSL 133, pp. 209–71.

Æthelwulf, *De Abbatibus*, ed. and trans. A. Campbell (Oxford, 1967).

Ailerán, *Interpretatio Mystica Progenitorum Domini Iesu Christi*, PL 80, col. 327–342.

Alcuin, *Carmina*, ed. E. Dümmler, MGH Poetae Latini Medii Aevi 1, pp. 169–351.

Alcuin, *Versus de Patribus Regibus et Sanctis Euboricensis Ecclesiae*, ed. and trans. Peter Godman, *The Bishops, Kings and Saints of York* (Oxford, 1982).

Aldhelm, *Carmen de Virginitate*, ed. R. Ehwald, MGH Auctores Antiquissimi 15, pp. 350–471.

Aldhelm, *Carmina Ecclesiastica*, ed. R. Ehwald, MGH Auctores Antiquissimi 15, pp. 1–32.

Aldhelm, *Epistulae*, ed. R. Ehwald, MGH Auctores Antiquissimi 15, pp. 473–503.

Aldhelm, *Prosa de Virginitate*, ed. R. Ehwald, MGH Auctores Antiquissimi 15, pp. 226–323.

Ambrose, *De Fide*, ed. O. Faller, CSEL 78.

Ambrose, *De Spiritu Sancto*, ed. O. Faller, CSEL 79, pp. 5–222.

Ambrose, *De Virginibus*, ed. and trans. Franco Gori, *Verginità e Vedovanza*, 2 vols (Milan, 1989), I, pp. 99–241.

Ambrose, *Exameron*, ed. C. Schenkl, CSEL 32, pp. 1–261.

Ambrose, *Exhortatio Virginitatis*, ed. and trans. Franco Gori, *Verginità e Vedovanza*, 2 vols (Milan, 1989), II, pp. 197–271.

Ambrose, *Expositio Evangelii Secundum Lucam*, ed. M. Adriaen, CCSL 14.

Arnobius Junior, *Commentarii in Psalmos*, ed. K.-D. Daur, CCSL 25.

Augustine, *Contra Faustum*, ed. J. Zycha, CSEL 25, pp. 249–797.

Augustine, *Contra Iulianum*, PL 44, col. 641–874.

Augustine, *De Baptismo*, ed. M. Petshenig, CSEL 51, pp. 143–375.

Augustine, *De Bono Viduitatis*, ed. J. Zycha, CSEL 41, pp. 303–43.

Augustine, *De Civitate Dei*, eds B. Dombart and A. Kalb, CCSL 47–8.

Augustine, *De Consensu Evangelistarum*, ed. F. Weihrich, CSEL 43.

Augustine, *De Diversis Quaestionibus Octoginta Tribus*, ed. A. Mutzenbecher, CCSL 44A, pp. 11–249.

Augustine, *De Doctrina Christiana*, ed. and trans. R. P. H. Green (Oxford, 1995).

Augustine, *De Genesi ad Litteram*, ed. J. Zycha, CSEL 28.

Augustine, *De Sancta Virginitate*, ed. J. Zycha, CSEL 41, pp. 235–302.

Augustine, *De Trinitate*, ed. W. J. Mountain, CCSL 50.

Augustine, *Enarrationes in Psalmos*, eds E. Dekkers and J. Fraipont, CCSL 38–40.

Augustine, *Epistulae*, ed. A. Goldbacher, CSEL 34, 44, 57, 58.

Augustine, *In Iohannis Epistolam ad Parthos Tractatus*, PL 35, col. 1977–2062.

Augustine, *In Iohannis Evangelium Tractatus*, ed. R. Willems, CCSL 36.

Augustine, *Quaestiones Evangeliorum*, ed. A. Mutzenbecher, CCSL 44B, pp. 1–118.

Augustine, *Quaestiones in Heptateuchum*, ed. J. Fraipont, CCSL 33, pp. 1–377.

Augustine, *Quaestiones XVI in Matthaeum*, ed. A. Mutzenbecher, CCSL 44B, pp. 119–40.

Augustine, *Sermones post Maurinos Reperti*, ed. G. Morin, *Miscellanea Agostiniana*, vol. 1 (Rome, 1930).

Augustine, *Sermones*, PL 38–9.

Bede, *De Die Iudicii*, ed. J. Fraipoint, CCSL 122, pp. 439–44.

Bede, *De Locis Sanctis*, ed. J. Fraipont, CCSL 175, pp. 245–80; trans. W. Trent Foley, *On the Holy Places*, in *Bede: A Biblical Miscellany* (Liverpool, 1999), pp. 1–25.

Bede, *De Natura Rerum*, ed. Charles W. Jones, CCSL 123A, pp. 173–234; trans. Calvin B. Kendall and Faith Wallis, *On the Nature of Things*, in *Bede: On the Nature of Things* and *On Times* (Liverpool, 2010), pp. 69–103.

Bede, *De Schematibus et Tropis*, ed. Calvin B. Kendall, CCSL 123A, pp. 142–71; trans. Gussie Hecht Tannenhaus, 'Bede's *De Schematibus et Tropis*—a translation', *Quarterly Journal of Speech* 48 (1962), pp. 237–53.

Bede, *De Tabernaculo et Vasis eius ac Vestibus Sacerdotum*, ed. D. Hurst, CCSL 119A, pp. 1–139; trans. Arthur G. Holder, *Bede: On the Tabernacle* (Liverpool, 1994).

Bede, *De Templo*, ed. D. Hurst, CCSL 119A, pp. 141–234; trans. Seán Connolly, *Bede: On the Temple* (Liverpool, 1995).

Bede, *De Temporibus*, ed. Charles W. Jones, CCSL 123, pp. 579–611.

Bede, *De Temporum Ratione*, ed. Charles W. Jones, CCSL 123B; trans. Faith Wallis, *Bede: On the Reckoning of Time* (Liverpool, 1999).

Bede, *Epistola ad Albinum*, ed. and trans. J. A. Westgard, 'New Manuscripts of Bede's Letter to Albinus', *Revue bénédictine* 120 (2010), pp. 208–15, at 213–15; ed. Charles Plummer in *Venerabilis Bedae Opera Historica*, vol. 1 (Oxford, 1896), p. 3.

Bede, *Epistola ad Pleguinam*, ed. Charles W. Jones, CCSL 123C, pp. 617–26; trans. Faith Wallis, *Letter to Plegwine*, in *Bede: On the Reckoning of Time* (Liverpool, 1999), pp. 405–15.

Bede, *Epistola ad Ecgbertum Episcopum*, eds and trans. Christopher Grocock and I. N. Wood, *Abbots of Wearmouth and Jarrow* (Oxford, 2013), pp. 123–61.

Bede, *Excerpts from the Works of Saint Augustine on the Letters of the Blessed Apostle Paul*, trans. David Hurst (Kalamazoo MI, 1999).

Bede, *Expositio Actuum Apostolorum*, ed. M. L. W. Laistner, CCSL 121, pp. 3–99; trans. Lawrence T. Martin, *The Venerable Bede: Commentary on the Acts of the Apostles* (Kalamazoo MI, 1989).

Bede, *Expositio Apocalypseos*, ed. Roger Gryson, CCSL 121A; trans. Faith Wallis, *Bede: Commentary on Revelation* (Liverpool, 2013).

Bede, *Expositio in Canticum Abacuc Prophetae*, ed. J. E. Hudson, CCSL 119B, pp. 377–409; trans. Seán Connolly, *Commentary of Bede the Priest on the Canticle of Habakkuk*, in *Bede: On* Tobit *and on the* Canticle of Habakkuk (Dublin, 1997), pp. 65–95.

Bede, *Historia Abbatum*, eds and trans. Christopher Grocock and I. N. Wood, *Abbots of Wearmouth and Jarrow* (Oxford, 2013), pp. 21–75.

Bede, *Historia Ecclesiastica Gentis Anglorum*, eds and trans. B. Colgrave and R. A. B. Mynors, *Bede's Ecclesiastical History of the English People* (Oxford, 1969).

Bede, *Homiliarum Euangelii*, ed. D. Hurst, CCSL 122, pp. 1–403; trans. Lawrence T. Martin and David Hurst, *Bede the Venerable: Homilies on the Gospels*, 2 vols (Kalamazoo MI, 1991).

Bede, *In Cantica Canticorum*, ed. D. Hurst, CCSL 119B, pp. 167–375; partially trans. Arthur Holder, *On the Song of Songs*, in *The Venerable Bede:* On the Song of Songs *and Selected Writings* (Mahwah NJ, 2011), pp. 35–249.

Bede, *In Epistulas Septem Catholicas*, ed. D. Hurst, CCSL 121, pp. 181–342; trans. David Hurst, *Bede the Venerable: Commentary on the Seven Catholic Epistles* (Kalamazoo MI, 1985).

Bede, *In Ezram et Neemiam*, ed. D. Hurst, CCSL 119A, pp. 235–392; trans. Scott DeGregorio, *Bede: On Ezra and Nehemiah* (Liverpool, 2006).

Bede, *In Librum Beati Patris Tobiae*, ed. D. Hurst, CCSL 119B, pp. 1–19; trans. W. Trent Foley, *On Tobias*, in *Bede: A Biblical Miscellany* (Liverpool, 1999), pp. 53–79.

Bede, *In Lucae Euangelium Expositio*, ed. D. Hurst, CCSL 120, pp. 5–425.

Bede, *In Marci Euangelium Expositio*, ed. D. Hurst, CCSL 120, pp. 431–648.

Bede, *In Primam Partem Samuhelis*, ed. D. Hurst, CCSL 119, pp. 5–287.

Bede, *In Principium Genesis*, ed. Charles W. Jones, CCSL 118A; trans. Calvin B. Kendall, *Bede: On Genesis* (Liverpool, 2008).

Bede, *In Proverbia Salomonis*, ed. D. Hurst, CCSL 119B, pp. 23–163.

Bede, *In Regum Librum XXX Quaestiones*, ed. D. Hurst, CCSL 119, pp. 289–322; trans. W. Trent Foley, *Thirty Questions on the Book of Kings*, in *Bede: A Biblical Miscellany*, (Liverpool, 1999), pp. 81–143.

Bede, *Martyrologium*, ed. Henri Quentin, *Les Martyrologes Historiques du Moyen Age* (Paris, 1908), pp. 57–112; trans. Felice Lifshitz, in *Medieval Hagiography: An Anthology*, ed. Thomas Head (London, 2001), pp. 169–97.

Bede, *Retractatio in Actus Apostolorum*, ed. M. L. W. Laistner, CCSL 121, pp. 103–63.

Bede, *VIII Quaestiones*, ed. Michael Gorman, 'Bede's *VIII Quaestiones* and Carolingian Biblical Scholarship', *Revue bénédictine* 109 (1999), pp. 32–74, at 62–74; trans. Arthur G. Holder, *On Eight Questions*, in *Bede: A Biblical Miscellany* (Liverpool, 1999), pp. 145–65.

Bede, *Vita Cuthberti (Metrica)*, ed. W. Jaager, *Bedas metrische Vita Sancti Cuthberti* (Leipzig, 1935).

Bede, *Vita Sancti Cuthberti*, ed. and trans. Bertram Colgrave, *Two Lives of Saint Cuthbert* (Cambridge, 1942), pp. 142–306.

Biblia Sacra Iuxta Vulgatam Versionem, eds R. Weber et al., 2 vols (Stuttgart, 1969).

Caesarius of Arles, *Sermones*, ed. G. Morin, CCSL 103–4.

Cassian, John, *Collationes*, ed. M. Petschenig, CSEL 13.

Cassian, John, *De Incarnatione Contra Nestorium*, ed. M. Petschenig, CSEL 17, pp. 235–391.

Cassiodorus, *Expositio Psalmorum*, ed. M. Adriaen, CCSL 97–8.

Cassiodorus, *Institutiones*, ed. R. A. B. Mynors (Oxford, 1963).

Collectio Canonum Hibernensis, ed. Herrmann Wasserschleben, *Die Irische Kanonensammlung* (Leipzig, 1885).

Columbanus, *Epistulae*, ed. and trans. G. S. M. Walker, *Sancti Columbani Opera* (Dublin, 1957), pp. 2–59.

Commentarius in Epistolas Catholicas Scotti Anonymi, ed. R. E. McNally, CCSL 108B, pp. 1–50.

Cosmas Indicopleustes, *Topographie Chrétienne*, ed. and trans. Wanda Wolska-Conus, 3 vols (Paris, 1968–1973).

Cummian, *De Controversia Paschali*, eds and trans. Maura Walsh and Dáibhí Ó Cróinín, *Cummian's Letter* De Controversia Paschali *and the* De Ratione Conputandi (Toronto, 1988), pp. 55–97.

Cuthbert, *Epistola de Obitu Bedae*, eds and trans. Bertram Colgrave and R. A. B. Mynors, *Bede's Ecclesiastical History of the English People* (Oxford, 1969), pp. 579–87.

The Dream of the Rood, ed. and trans. Richard Hamer, *A Choice of Anglo-Saxon Verse* (London, 1970), pp. 159–71.

Epistle of Barnabas, ed. and trans. Michael W. Holmes, *The Apostolic Fathers: Greek Texts and English Translations*, 3rd ed. (Grand Rapids MI, 2007), pp. 380–441.

Expositio Quatuor Evangeliorum, PL 30, col. 531–590.

Finsterwalder, Paul Willem (ed.), *Die Canones Theodori Cantuariensis und ihre Überlieferungsformen* (Weimar, 1929).

Gildas, *De Excidio Britanniae*, ed. and trans. Michael Winterbottom, *Gildas: The Ruin of Britain and Other Works* (London, 1978), pp. 13–79, 87–142.

Gregory (the Great), *Dialogi*, ed. and trans. A. de Vogüé, *Dialogues*, 3 vols (Paris, 1978–1980).

Gregory (the Great), *Homiliae in Evangelia*, ed. Raymond Étaix, CCSL 141; trans. David Hurst, *Gregory the Great: Forty Gospel Homilies* (Kalamazoo MI, 1990).

Gregory (the Great), *Homiliae in Hiezechihelem Prophetam*, ed. M. Adriaen, CCSL 142.

Gregory (the Great), *Moralia in Iob*, ed. M. Adriaen, CCSL 143+A+B.

Gregory (the Great), *Registrum Epistularum*, ed. D. Norberg, CCSL 140+A.

Gregory (the Great), *Regula Pastoralis*, PL 77, col. 13–128.

Gregory Nazianzen/Rufinus, *Orationes*, ed. A. Engelbrecht, CSEL 46.

Hessels, J. H. (ed.), *A Late Eighth-Century Latin-Anglo-Saxon Glossary preserved in the Library of the Leiden University* (Cambridge, 1906).

The Holy Bible: Douay Version (London, 1956).

Isidore of Seville, *Chronica*, ed. Jose Carlos Martin, CCSL 112.

Isidore of Seville, *De Natura Rerum*, ed. and trans. Jacques Fontaine, *Traité de la Nature* (Bordeaux, 1960).

Isidore of Seville, *Etymologiae sive Origines*, ed. W. M. Lindsay, 2 vols (Oxford, 1911).

Isidore of Seville, *Quaestiones in Vetus Testamentum*, PL 83, col. 207–424.

Jerome, *Commentarii in Hiezechielem*, ed. F. Glorie, CCSL 75.

Jerome, *Commentarius in Ecclesiasten*, ed. M. Adriaen, CCSL 72, pp. 247–361.

Jerome, *Epistulae*, ed. I. Hilberg, CSEL 54–6.

Jerome, *In Amos*, ed. M. Adriaen, CCSL 76, pp. 211–348.

Jerome, *In Danielem*, ed. F. Glorie, CCSL 75A.

Jerome, *In Esaiam*, ed. M. Adriaen, CCSL 73+A.

Jerome, *In Heremiam Prophetam*, ed. S. Reiter, CCSL 74.

Jerome, *In Matheum*, eds D. Hurst and M. Adriaen, CCSL 77.

Jerome, *Liber de Viris Inlustribus*, ed. E. C. Richardson (Leipzig, 1896).

Josephus, Flavius, *Jewish Antiquities*, eds and trans. H. St. J. Thackeray et al., *The Loeb Classical Library: Josephus*, 10 vols (Cambridge MA, 1926–81); (Latin translation of Books I–III only) ed. Franz Blatt, *The Latin Josephus* (Copenhagen, 1958).

Justin Martyr, *Dialogue with Trypho*, trans. G. Reith, *The Writings of Justin Martyr and Athenagoras* (Edinburgh, 1867), pp. 85–283.

Liber Sacramentorum Romanae Aeclesiae Ordinis Anni Circuli, eds Leo Cunibert Mohlberg, Leo Eizenhöffer, and Petrus Siffrin (Rome, 1960).

Mac Airt, Seán and Gearóid Mac Niocaill (eds and trans.), *The Annals of Ulster (to A. D. 1131)*, (Dublin, 1983).

Optatus of Milevis, *Libri Septem*, ed. C. Ziwsa, CSEL 26.

Origen/Rufinus, *In Exodum Homiliae*, ed. W. A. Baehrens, *Origenes Werke* 6 (Leipzig, 1920), pp. 145–279.

Origen/Rufinus, *In Genesim Homiliae*, ed. W. A. Baehrens, *Origenes Werke* 6 (Leipzig, 1920), pp. 1–114.

Origen/Rufinus, *In Leviticum Homiliae*, ed. W. A. Baehrens, *Origenes Werke* 6 (Leipzig, 1920), pp. 280–507.

Origen/Rufinus, *In Numeros Homiliae*, ed. W. A. Baehrens, *Origenes Werke* 7 (Leipzig, 1921), pp. 3–285.

Pauca Problesmata de Enigmatibus ex Tomis Canonicis: Praefatio et Libri de Pentateucho Moysi, ed. G. MacGinty, Corpus Christianorum Continuatio Mediaeualis 173.

Primasius, *Commentarius in Apocalypsin*, ed. A. W. Adams, CCSL 92.

Pseudo-Clement/Rufinus, *Recognitiones*, eds Bernhard Rehm and Georg Strecker, *Die Pseudoklementinen II* (Berlin, 1994).

Quaestiones vel Glosae in Evangelio Nomine, ed. R. E. McNally, CCSL 108B, pp. 133–49.

'The Ruin', ed. and trans. Richard Hamer, *A Choice of Anglo-Saxon Verse* (London, 1970), pp. 25–9.

Sedulius, *Carmen Paschale*, ed. J. Huemer, CSEL 10, pp. 14–154.

Stephen (of Ripon), *Vita Wilfridi*, ed. and trans. Bertram Colgrave, *The Life of Bishop Wilfrid by Eddius Stephanus* (Cambridge, 1927).

Tangl, M. (ed.), *Die Briefe des Heiligen Bonifatius und Lullus*, MGH Epistolae Selectae 1.

Tractatus Hilarii in Septem Epistolas Canonicas, ed. R. E. McNally, CCSL 108B, pp. 51–124.

Tyconius, *Liber Regularum*, ed. F. C. Burkitt, *The Book of Rules of Tyconius* (Cambridge, 1894).

Virgil, *Eclogues*, ed. and trans. Guy Lee (Liverpool, 1980).

Vita Alcuini, ed. W. Arndt, MGH Scriptores 15, pp. 184–97.

Vita Ceolfridi, eds and trans. Christopher Grocock and I. N. Wood, *Abbots of Wearmouth and Jarrow* (Oxford, 2013), pp. 76–121.

Vita Gregorii, ed. and trans. Bertram Colgrave, *The Earliest Life of Gregory the Great, By an Anonymous Monk of Whitby* (Cambridge, 1985).

Werminghoff, A. (ed.), *Concilia Aevi Karolini I*, MGH Legum Sectio 3 Concilia 2.

3. Secondary Literature

Abels, Richard, *Lordship and Military Obligation in Anglo-Saxon England* (London, 1988).

Abels, Richard, 'What has Weland to do with Christ? The Franks Casket and the Acculturation of Christianity in Early Anglo-Saxon England', *Speculum* 84 (2009), pp. 549–81.

Arceo, Alecia, 'Rethinking the Synod of Whitby and Northumbrian Monastic Sites', *Haskins Society Journal* 20 (2008), pp. 19–30.

Auerbach, Erich, '"Figura"', trans. Ralph Manheim, in *Scenes from the Drama of European Literature* (Manchester, 1984), pp. 11–76.

Aulén, Gustaf, *Christus Victor*, trans. A. G. Herbert (London, 1931).

Bailey, Richard, 'St Wilfrid, Ripon and Hexham', in *Studies in Insular Art and Archaeology*, eds Catherine E. Karkov and Robert Farrell (Oxford OH, 1991), pp. 3–25.

Bailey, Richard, '*In Medio Duorum Animalium*: Habbakuk, the Ruthwell Cross and Bede's Life of St Cuthbert', in *Listen, O Isles, unto me: Studies in Medieval Word and Image in Honour of Jennifer O'Reilly*, eds Elizabeth Mullins and Diarmuid Scully (Cork, 2011), pp. 243–52.

Bain, Emmanuel, 'Les marchands chassés du Temple, entre commentaires et usages sociaux', *Médiévales* 55 (2008), pp. 53–74.

Bammel, C. P., 'Law and Temple in Origen', in *Templum Amicitiae: Essays on the Second Temple presented to Ernst Bammel*, ed. William Horbury (Sheffield, 1991), pp. 463–76.

Bankert, Dabney Anderson, Jessica Wegmann, and Charles D. Wright, *Ambrose in Anglo-Saxon England with Pseudo-Ambrose and Ambrosiaster*, Old English Newsletter Subsidia 25 (Kalamazoo MI, 1997).

Barrow, Julia, 'How Coifi Pierced Christ's Side: A Re-Examination of Bede's *Ecclesiastical History* II, Chapter 13', *Journal of Ecclesiastical History* 62 (2011), pp. 693–706.

Bejczy, István P., *The Cardinal Virtues in the Middle Ages: A Study in Moral Thought from the Fourth to the Fourteenth Century* (Leiden, 2011).

Berschin, Walter, '*Opus deliberatum ac perfectum*: Why did the Venerable Bede write a second prose life of St. Cuthbert?', in *St Cuthbert, His Cult and His Community to AD 1200*, eds Gerald Bonner, Clare Stancliffe, and David Rollason (Woodbridge, 1989), pp. 95–102.

Beumer, Johannes, 'Das Kirchenbild in den Schriftkommentaren Bedas des Ehrwürdigen', *Scholastik* 28 (1958), pp. 40–56.

Bischoff, Bernhard, 'Turning-Points in the History of Latin Exegesis in the Early Middle Ages', trans. Colm O'Grady, in *Biblical Studies: The Medieval Irish Contribution*, ed. Martin McNamara, Proceedings of the Irish Biblical Association 1 (Dublin, 1976), pp. 74–160.

Bischoff, Bernhard, and Michael Lapidge, *Biblical Commentaries from the Canterbury School of Theodore and Hadrian* (Cambridge, 1994).

Blair, John, 'Anglo-Saxon Pagan Shrines and their Prototypes', *Anglo-Saxon Studies in Archaeology and History* 8 (1995), pp. 1–28.

Blair, John, 'Debate: Ecclesiastical Organization and Pastoral Care in Anglo-Saxon England', *Early Medieval Europe* 4 (1995), pp. 193–212.

Blair, John, *The Church in Anglo-Saxon Society* (Oxford, 2005).

Bonner, Gerald, *Saint Bede in the Tradition of Western Apocalyptic Commentary*, Jarrow Lecture (Jarrow, 1966).

Bonner, Gerald, 'The Christian Life in the Thought of the Venerable Bede', *Durham University Journal* 63 (1970), pp. 39–55; repr. in Bonner, *Church and Faith in the Patristic Tradition* (Aldershot, 1996).

Bonner, Gerald, 'Introduction', in *Famulus Christi: Essays in Commemoration of the Thirteenth Centenary of the Birth of the Venerable Bede*, ed. Gerald Bonner (London, 1976), pp. 1–4.

Bonner, Gerald, 'Augustine's Conception of Deification', *Journal of Theological Studies* 37 (1986), pp. 369–86.

Bonner, Gerald, 'The Doctrine of Sacrifice: Augustine and the Latin Patristic Tradition', in *Sacrifice and Redemption: Durham Essays in Theology*, ed. S. W. Sykes (Cambridge, 1991), pp. 101–17.

Bonner, Gerald, 'The Pelagian Controversy in Britain and Ireland', *Peritia* 16 (2002), pp. 144–55.

Borges, Jorge Luis, 'Things that Might Have Been', trans. Alastair Reid, *New England Review* 15 (1993), p. 101.

Bovendeert, Jasmijn, 'Beda's deugdenkwartet', *Madoc: Tijdschrift over de Middeleeuwen* 19 (2005), pp. 36–46.

Bracken, Damian, 'Rome and the Isles: Ireland, England and the Rhetoric of Orthodoxy', *Proceedings of the British Academy* 157 (2009), pp. 75–97.

Bremond, Claude, Jacques Le Goff, and Jean-Claude Schmitt, *L'"Exemplum"*, Typologie des Sources du Moyen Âge Occidental 40, 2nd ed. (Turnhout, 1996).

Brooks, Nicholas, *Bede and the English*, Jarrow Lecture (Jarrow, 1999).

Brooks, Nicholas, 'Canterbury and Rome: The Limits and Myth of *Romanitas*', *Settimane di studio del Centro italiano di studi sull'alto medioevo* 49 (2002), pp. 797–832.

Brown, George Hardin, 'The Church as Non-Symbol in the Age of Bede', in *Northumbria's Golden Age*, eds Jane Hawkes and Susan Mills (Stroud, 1999), pp. 359–64.

Brown, George Hardin, 'Ciceronianism in Bede and Alcuin', in *Intertexts: Studies in Anglo-Saxon Culture Presented to Paul E. Szarmach*, eds Viriginia Blanton and Helene Scheck (Tempe AZ, 2008), pp. 319–29.

Brown, George Hardin, *A Companion to Bede* (Woodbridge, 2009).

Brown, George Hardin, 'Bede Both Subject and Superior to the Episcopacy', in *Envisioning the Bishop: Images and the Episcopacy in the Middle Ages*, eds Sigrid Danielson and Evan A. Gatti (Turnhout, 2014), pp. 91–102.

Brown, Michelle P., *The Lindisfarne Gospels: Society, Spirituality and the Scribe* (London, 2003).

Brown, Peter, 'The Saint as Exemplar in Late Antiquity', *Representations* 2 (1983), pp. 1–25.

Brown, Peter, *The Rise of Western Christendom: Triumph and Diversity, A. D. 200–1000*, 2nd ed. (Oxford, 2003).

Brown, Peter, 'What's in a name?', <http://www.ocla.ox.ac.uk/pdf/brown_what_in_name.pdf> [accessed 10 April 2013].

Bruce-Mitford, R. L. S., *The Art of the Codex Amiatinus*, Jarrow Lecture (Jarrow, 1967).

Bynum, Caroline Walker, 'Did the Twelfth Century Discover the Individual?', *Journal of Ecclesiastical History* 31 (1980), pp. 1–17.

Cambridge, Eric, and David Rollason, 'Debate: The Pastoral Organization of the Anglo-Saxon Church: a Review of the "Minster Hypothesis"', *Early Medieval Europe* 4 (1995), pp. 87–104.

Campbell, James, *Essays in Anglo-Saxon History* (London, 1986).

Campbell, James, 'Elements in the Background to the Life of St Cuthbert and his Early Cult', in *St Cuthbert, His Cult and His Community until AD 1200*, eds Gerald Bonner, David Rollason, and Clare Stancliffe (Woodbridge, 1989), pp. 3–19.

Campbell, James, 'Some Considerations on Religion in Early England', in Collectanea Antiqua: *Essays in Memory of Sonia Chadwick Hawkes*, eds Martin Henig and Tyler Jo Smith (Oxford, 2007), pp. 67–73.

Caputa, Giovanni, *Il Sacerdozio dei Fedeli secondo San Beda: un itinerario di maturità cristiana* (Vatican City, 2002).

Caputa, Giovanni, 'Aspects of the Priestly Ministry according to Saint Bede', in *Priests of Christ: In the Church for the World*, eds Giovanni Caputa and Julian Fox (Jerusalem, 2010), pp. 70–95.

Carlton, C. Clarke, '"The Temple that Held God": Byzantine Marian Hymnography and the Christ of Nestorius', *St Vladimir's Theological Quarterly* 50 (2006), pp. 99–125.

Carroll, Mary Thomas Aquinas, *The Venerable Bede: His Spiritual Teachings* (Washington DC, 1946).

Carruthers, Mary, *The Craft of Thought: Meditation, Rhetoric and the Making of Images, 400–1200* (Cambridge, 1998).

Chadwick, Henry, 'Theodore, the English Church and the Monothelete Controversy', in *Archbishop Theodore: Commemorative Studies on his Life and Influence*, ed. Michael Lapidge (Cambridge, 1995), pp. 88–95.

Charles-Edwards, Thomas, 'The Social Background to Irish *Peregrinatio*', *Celtica* 11 (1976), pp. 43–59.

Charles-Edwards, Thomas, 'Anglo-Saxon Kinship Revisited', in *The Anglo-Saxons from the Migration Period to the Eighth Century: An Ethnographic Perspective*, ed. John Hines (Woodbridge, 1997), pp. 171–204.

Charles-Edwards, Thomas, *Early Christian Ireland* (Cambridge, 2000).

Charles-Edwards, Thomas, 'Conclusion', in *After Rome*, ed. Thomas Charles-Edwards (Oxford, 2003), pp. 259–70.

Charles-Edwards, Thomas, *Wales and the Britons 350–1064* (Oxford, 2013).

Charles-Edwards, Thomas, 'Wilfrid and the Celts', in *Wilfrid: Abbot, Bishop, Saint; Papers from the 1300th Anniversary Conferences*, ed. N. J. Higham (Donington, 2013), pp. 243–59.

Chazelle, Celia, 'Ceolfrid's Gift to St Peter: the First Quire of the Codex Amiatinus and the Evidence of its Roman Destination', *Early Medieval Europe* 12 (2004), pp. 129–57.

Chazelle, Celia, 'Christ and the Vision of God: The Biblical Diagrams of the Codex Amiatinus', in *The Mind's Eye: Art and Theological Argument in the Middle Ages*, eds Jeffrey F. Hamburger and Anne-Marie Bouché (Princeton NJ, 2006), pp. 84–111.

Chazelle, Celia, '"Romanness" in Early Medieval Culture', in *Paradigms and Methods in Early Medieval Studies*, eds Celia Chazelle and Felice Lifshitz (New York, 2007), pp. 81–98.

Chazelle, Celia, 'Painting the Voice of God: Wearmouth-Jarrow, Rome and the Tabernacle Miniature in the Codex Amiatinus', *Quintana* 8 (2009), pp. 15–59.

Chazelle, Celia, 'Art and Reverence in Bede's Churches at Wearmouth and Jarrow', in *Intellektualisierung und Mystifizierung mittelalterlicher Kunst*, eds Martin Büchsel and Rebecca Müller (Berlin, 2010), pp. 79–98.

Chazelle, Celia, and Burton Van Name Edwards (eds), *The Study of the Bible in the Carolingian Era* (Turnhout, 2003).

Church, S. D., 'Paganism in Conversion-Age Anglo-Saxon England: The Evidence of Bede's *Ecclesiastical History* Reconsidered', *History* 93 (2008), pp. 162–80.

Clancy, Finbarr G., 'Augustine's Sermons on the Dedication of a Church', *Studia Patristica* 38 (2001), pp. 48–55.

Clark, Elizabeth A., *Reading Renunciation: Asceticism and Scripture in Early Christianity* (Princeton NJ, 1999).

Clark, Francis, *The 'Gregorian' Dialogues and the Origins of Benedictine Monasticism* (Leiden, 2003).

Claussen, M. A., '"Peregrinatio" and "Peregrini" in Augustine's "City of God"', *Traditio* 46 (1991), pp. 33–75.

Clayton, Paul B., *The Christology of Theoderet of Cyrus: Antiochene Christology from the Council of Ephesus (431) to the Council of Chalcedon (451)* (Oxford, 2007).

Coates, Simon, 'The Bishop as Pastor and Solitary: Bede and the Spiritual Authority of the Monk-Bishop', *Journal of Ecclesiastical History* 47 (1996), pp. 601–19.

Coates, Simon, 'The Role of Bishops in the Early Anglo-Saxon Church: A Reassessment', *History* 81 (1996), pp. 177–96.

Coates, Simon, 'Ceolfrid: History, Hagiography and Memory in seventh- and eighth-century Wearmouth-Jarrow', *Journal of Medieval History* 25 (1999), pp. 69–86.

Coleman, Janet, *Ancient and Medieval Memories: Studies in the Reconstruction of the Past* (Cambridge, 1992).

Colgrave, Bertram, 'Bede's Miracle Stories', in *Bede: His Life, Times, and Writings*, ed. A. Hamilton Thompson (Oxford, 1935), pp. 201–29.

Collins, Samuel W., *The Carolingian Debate over Sacred Space* (New York, 2012).

Congar, Yves, *L'Ecclésiologie du Haut Moyen Age: De saint Grégoire le Grand à la désunion entre Byzance et Rome* (Paris, 1968).

Conrad-O'Briain, Helen, 'The Harrowing of Hell in the Canterbury Glosses and its Context in Augustinian and Insular Exegesis', in *Text and Gloss: Studies in Insular Learning and Literature Presented to Joseph Donovan Pheifer*, eds Helen Conrad-O'Briain, Anne Marie d'Arcy, and John Scattergood (Dublin, 1999), pp. 73–88.

Constable, Giles, *Three Studies in Medieval Religious and Social Thought* (Cambridge, 1995).

Corsano, Karen, 'The First Quire of the Codex Amiatinus and the *Institutiones* of Cassiodorus', *Scriptorium* 41 (1987), pp. 3–34.

Cramp, Rosemary, G. Bettess, and F. Bettess, *Wearmouth and Jarrow Monastic Sites*, 2 vols (Swindon, 2005–2006).

Cross, J. E., 'Bede's Influence at Home and Abroad: An Introduction', in *Beda Venerabilis: Historian, Monk & Northumbrian*, eds L. A. J. R. Houwen and A. A. MacDonald (Groningen, 1996), pp. 17–29.

Crouzel, Henri, 'L'imitation et la "suite" de Dieu et du Christ dans les premiers siècles chrétiens, ainsi que leurs sources gréco-romaines et hébraïques', *Jahrbuch für Antike und Christentum* 21 (1978), pp. 7–41.

Cubitt, Catherine, 'Wilfrid's "Usurping Bishops": Episcopal Elections in Anglo-Saxon England, *c.*600–*c.*800', *Northern History* 25 (1989), pp. 18–38.

Cubitt, Catherine, 'Pastoral Care and Conciliar Canons: the Provisions of the 747 Council of *Clofesho*', in *Pastoral Care Before the Parish*, eds John Blair and Richard Sharpe (Leicester, 1992), pp. 193–211.

Cubitt, Catherine, *Anglo-Saxon Church Councils c.650–c.850* (London, 1995).

Cubitt, Catherine, 'Monastic Memory and Identity in Early Anglo-Saxon England', in *Social Identity in Early Medieval Britain*, eds William O. Frazer and Andrew Tyrrell (London, 2000), pp. 253–76.

Cubitt, Catherine, 'The Clergy in early Anglo-Saxon England', *Historical Research* 78 (2005), pp. 273–87.

Daniélou, Jean, 'La Symbolique du Temple de Jerusalem chez Philon et Josephe', in *Le Symbolisme Cosmique des Monuments Religieux*, ed. Giuseppe Tucci (Rome, 1957), pp. 83–90.

Daniélou, Jean, *From Shadows to Reality: Studies in the Biblical Typology of the Fathers*, trans. Wulstan Hibberd (London, 1960).

Darby, Peter, *Bede and the End of Time* (Farnham, 2012).

Darby, Peter, 'Bede, Iconoclasm, and the Temple of Solomon', *Early Medieval Europe* 21 (2013), pp. 390–421.

Davidse, Jan, 'The Sense of History in the Works of the Venerable Bede', *Studi Medievali* 23 (1982), pp. 647–95.

DeGregorio, Scott, 'The Venerable Bede on Prayer and Contemplation', *Traditio* 54 (1999), pp. 1–39.

DeGregorio, Scott, '"Nostrorum socordiam temporum": the Reforming Impulse of Bede's Later Exegesis', *Early Medieval Europe* 11 (2002), pp. 107–22.

DeGregorio, Scott, 'Bede's *In Ezram et Neemiam* and the Reform of the Northumbrian Church', *Speculum* 79 (2004), pp. 1–25.

DeGregorio, Scott, 'Affective Spirituality: Theory and Practice in Bede and Alfred the Great', *Essays in Medieval Studies* 22 (2005), pp. 129–39.

DeGregorio, Scott, 'Bede, the Monk, as Exegete: Evidence from the Commentary on Ezra-Nehemiah', *Revue bénédictine* 115 (2005), pp. 343–69.

DeGregorio, Scott, *Bede: On Ezra and Nehemiah* (Liverpool, 2006).

DeGregorio, Scott, 'Footsteps of His Own: Bede's Commentary on Ezra-Nehemiah', in *Innovation and Tradition in the Writings of the Venerable Bede*, ed. Scott DeGregorio (Morgantown WV, 2006), pp. 143–68.

DeGregorio, Scott, 'Introduction: The New Bede', in *Innovation and Tradition in the Writings of the Venerable Bede*, ed. Scott DeGregorio (Morgantown WV, 2006), pp. 1–10.

DeGregorio, Scott, 'Bede and Benedict of Nursia', in *Early Medieval Studies in Memory of Patrick Wormald*, eds Stephen Baxter, Catherine Karkov, Janet Nelson, and David Pelteret (Farnham, 2009), pp. 158–62.

DeGregorio, Scott, 'Monasticism and Reform in Book IV of Bede's "Ecclesiastical History of the English People"', *Journal of Ecclesiastical History* 61 (2010), pp. 673–87.

DeGregorio, Scott, 'The Venerable Bede and Gregory the Great: Exegetical Connections, Spiritual Departures', *Early Medieval Europe* 18 (2010), pp. 43–60.

DeGregorio, Scott (ed.), *The Cambridge Companion to Bede* (Cambridge, 2010).

Del Giacco, Eric Jay, 'Exegesis and Sermon: A Comparison of Bede's Commentary and Homilies on Luke', *Medieval Sermon Studies* 50 (2006), pp. 9–29.

Dendle, Peter, 'Pain and Saint-Making in *Andreas*, Bede, and the Old English Lives of St. Margaret', in *Varieties of Devotion in the Middle Ages and Renaissance*, ed. Susan C. Karant-Nunn (Turnhout, 2003), pp. 39–52.

Dionisotti, Anna Carlotta, 'On Bede, Grammars, and Greek', *Revue bénédictine* 92 (1982), pp. 111–41.

Dolbeau, François, 'Bède, lecteur des Sermons d'Augustin', *Filologia Mediolatina* 3 (1996), pp. 105–33.

Douglas, Iain M., 'Bede's *De Templo* and the Commentary on Samuel and Kings by Claudius of Turin', in *Famulus Christi: Essays in Commemoration of the Thirteenth Centenary of the Birth of the Venerable Bede*, ed. Gerald Bonner (London, 1976), pp. 325–33.

Downey, Sarah, 'Too Much of Too Little: Guthlac and the Temptation of Excessive Fasting', *Traditio* 63 (2008), pp. 89–127.

Duncan, Archibald A. M., 'Bede, Iona and the Picts', in *The Writing of History in the Middle Ages: Essays Presented to Richard William Southern*, eds R. H. C. Davis and J. M. Wallace-Hadrill (Oxford, 1981), pp. 1–42.

Duncan, Sandra, 'Prophets Shining in Dark Places: Biblical Themes and Theological Motifs in the *Vita Sancti Wilfridi*', in *Wilfrid: Abbot, Bishop, Saint; Papers from the 1300th Anniversary Conferences*, ed. N. J. Higham (Donington, 2013), pp. 80–92.

Dunn, Marilyn, *The Christianization of the Anglo-Saxons c.597–c.700: Discourses of Life, Death and Afterlife* (London, 2009).

The Electronic Sawyer, eds Susan Kelly et al., <www.esawyer.org.uk> [accessed 14 October 2014].

Eliot, T. S., *The Waste Land: a Facsimile and Transcript of the Original Drafts including the Annotations of Ezra Pound*, ed. Valerie Eliot (San Diego CA, 1994).

Fahey, Michael A., 'Augustine's Ecclesiology Revisited', in *Augustine: From Rhetor to Theologian*, eds Timothy D. Barnes, Michael A. Fahey, and Peter Slater (Waterloo, 1992), pp. 173–81.

Farr, Carol, *The Book of Kells: Its Function and Audience* (London, 1997).

Foley, W. Trent, *Images of Sanctity in Eddius Stephanus' Life of Bishop Wilfrid, An Early English Saint's Life* (Lampeter, 1992).

Foley, W. Trent, 'Suffering and Sanctity in Bede's *Prose Life of St. Cuthbert*', *Journal of Theological Studies* 50 (1999), pp. 102–16.

Foley, W. Trent, 'Bede's Exegesis of Passages Unique to the Gospel of Mark', in *Biblical Studies in the Early Middle Ages*, eds Claudio Leonardi and Giovanni Orlandi (Florence, 2005), pp. 105–24.

Foley, W. Trent, and Nicholas J. Higham, 'Bede on the Britons', *Early Medieval Europe* 17 (2009), pp. 154–85.

Folliet, Georges, 'Les trois categories de chrétiens: à partir de Luc (17, 34–36), Matthieu (24, 40–41) et Ézéchiel (14,14)', in *Augustinus Magister: Congrès International Augustinien Paris, 21–24 Septembre 1954* (Paris, 1954), pp. 631–44.

Folliet, Georges, 'Les trois categories de chrétiens: Survie d'un thème augustinien', *L'Année Théologique Augustinienne* 49–50 (1954), pp. 81–96.

Foot, Sarah, 'Anglo-Saxon Minsters: a Review of Terminology', in *Pastoral Care before the Parish*, eds John Blair and Richard Sharpe (Leicester, 1992), pp. 212–25.

Foot, Sarah, 'The Making of *Angelcynn*: English Identity before the Norman Conquest', *Transactions of the Royal Historical Society* 6th series 6 (1996), pp. 25–49.

Foot, Sarah, 'The Role of the Minster in Earlier Anglo-Saxon Society', in *Monasteries and Society in Medieval Britain: Proceedings of the 1994 Harlaxton Symposium*, ed. Benjamin Thompson (Stamford, 1999), pp. 35–58.

Foot, Sarah, *Veiled Women. Volume I: The Disappearance of Nuns from Anglo-Saxon England* (Aldershot, 2000).

Foot, Sarah, *Monastic Life in Anglo-Saxon England c.600–900* (Cambridge, 2006).

Foot, Sarah, *Bede's Church*, Jarrow Lecture 2012 (Jarrow, 2013).

Foot, Sarah, 'Women, Prayer and Preaching in the Early English Church', in *Prayer and Thought in Monastic Tradition: Essays in Honour of Benedicta Ward SLG*, eds Santha Bhattacharji, Dominic Mattos, and Rowan Williams (London, 2014), pp. 59–75.

Foxhall Forbes, Helen, *Heaven and Earth in Anglo-Saxon England: Theology and Society in an Age of Faith* (Farnham, 2013).

Franklin, Carmela Vircillo, 'The Date of Composition of Bede's *De Schematibus et Tropis* and *De Arte Metrica*', *Revue bénédictine* 110 (2000), pp. 199–203.

Franklin, Carmela Vircillo, 'Grammar and Exegesis: Bede's *Liber de schematibus et tropis*', in *Latin Grammar and Rhetoric: From Classical Theory to Medieval Practice*, ed. Carol Dana Lanham (London, 2002), pp. 63–91.

Frantzen, Allen J., 'The Penitentials Attributed to Bede', *Speculum* 58 (1983), pp. 573–97.

Fredriksen, Paula, *Augustine and the Jews: A Christian Defense of Jews and Judaism* (New York, 2008).

Gameson, Richard, 'The Cost of the Codex Amiatinus', *Notes and Queries* 39 (1992), pp. 2–9.

Garrison, Mary, 'The Franks as the New Israel? Education for an identity from Pippin to Charlemagne', in *The Uses of the Past in the Early Middle Ages*, eds Yitzhak Hen and Matthew Innes (Cambridge, 2000), pp. 114–61.

Gittos, Helen, *Liturgy, Architecture and Sacred Places in Anglo-Saxon England* (Oxford, 2013).

Gleason, Michael, 'Bede and his Fathers', *Classica et Mediaevalia* 45 (1994), pp. 223–38.

Goffart, Walter, *The Narrators of Barbarian History (A.D. 550–800): Jordanes, Gregory of Tours, Bede and Paul the Deacon*, 2nd ed. (Notre Dame IN, 2005).

Goffart, Walter, 'Bede's History in a Harsher Climate', in *Innovation and Tradition in the Writings of the Venerable Bede*, ed. Scott DeGregorio (Morgantown WV, 2006), pp. 203–26.

Goodman, Martin, *Rome and Jerusalem: The Clash of Ancient Civilisations* (London, 2008).

Gorman, Michael, 'Theodore of Canterbury, Hadrian of Nisida and Michael Lapidge', *Scriptorium* 50 (1996), pp. 184–92.

Gorman, Michael, 'Bede's *VIII Quaestiones* and Carolingian Biblical Scholarship', *Revue bénédictine* 109 (1999), pp. 32–74.

Gorman, Michael, 'The Myth of Hiberno-Latin Exegesis', *Revue bénédictine* 110 (2000), pp. 42–85.

Gorman, Michael, 'The Canon of Bede's Works and the World of Ps. Bede', *Revue bénédictine* 111 (2001), pp. 399–445.

Gorman, Michael, 'Source Marks and Chapter Divisions in Bede's Commentary on Luke', *Revue bénédictine* 112 (2002), pp. 246–90.

Gorman, Michael, 'The Codex Amiatinus: A Guide to the Legends and Bibliography', *Studi Medievali* 44 (2003), pp. 863–910.

Graves, Michael, '"Judaizing" Christian Interpretations of the Prophets as seen by Saint Jerome', *Vigiliae Christianae* 61 (2007), pp. 142–56.

Greer, Rowan A., *The Captain of Our Salvation: A Study in the Patristic Exegesis of Hebrews* (Tübingen, 1973).

Greer, Rowan A., 'Christ the Victor and the Victim', *Concordia Theological Quarterly* 59 (1995), pp. 1–30.

Grocock, Christopher, and I. N. Wood, *Abbots of Wearmouth and Jarrow* (Oxford, 2013).

Gryson, Roger, *Le Prêtre selon Saint Ambroise* (Louvain, 1968).

Gryson, Roger, 'Les Lévites, Figure du Sacerdoce Véritable, selon Saint Ambrose', *Ephemerides Theologicae Lovanienses* 56 (1980), pp. 89–112.

Gunn, Vicky, *Bede's Historiae: Genre, Rhetoric and the Construction of Anglo-Saxon Church History* (Woodbridge, 2009).

Hamblin, William J., and David Rolph Seely, *Solomon's Temple: Myth and History* (London, 2007).

Hanning, Robert W., *The Vision of History in Early Britain: From Gildas to Geoffrey of Monmouth* (London, 1966).

Harrison, Carol, *Beauty and Revelation in the Thought of Saint Augustine* (Oxford, 1992).

Hart-Hasler, J. N., 'Bede's Use of Patristic Sources: The Transfiguration', *Studia Patristica* 28 (1993), pp. 197–204.

Hawkes, Jane, '*Iuxta Morem Romanorum*: Stone and Sculpture in Anglo-Saxon England', in *Anglo-Saxon Styles*, eds Catherine E. Karkov and George Hardin Brown (Albany NY, 2003), pp. 69–99.

Hawkes, Jane, 'Gregory the Great and Angelic Mediation: The Anglo-Saxon Crosses of the Derbyshire Peaks', in *Text, Image and Interpretation: Studies in Anglo-Saxon Literature and its Insular Context in Honour of Éamonn Ó Carragáin*, eds Alastair Minnis and Jane Roberts (Turnhout, 2007), pp. 431–48.

Heisey, Daniel J., 'Bede's Pepper, Napkins, and Incense', *Downside Review* 129 (2011), pp. 16–30.

Henderson, George, *Vision and Image in Early Christian England* (Cambridge, 1999).

Henson, Herbert Hensley, 'Introduction', in *Bede: His Life, Times, and Writings*, ed. A. Hamilton Thompson (Oxford, 1935), pp. xiii–xvi.

Herbert, Máire, *Iona, Kells, and Derry: The History and Hagiography of the Monastic Familia of Columba* (Oxford, 1988).

Herren, Michael W., 'Irish Biblical Commentaries before 800', in *Roma, Magistra Mundi: Itineraria Culturae Medievalis*, ed. Jacqueline Hamesse, vol. 1 (Louvain, 1998), pp. 391–407.

Herren, Michael W., and Shirley Ann Brown, *Christ in Celtic Christianity: Britain and Ireland from the Fifth to the Tenth Century* (Woodbridge, 2002).

Herrin, Judith, *The Formation of Christendom* (London, 1989).

Higham, N. J., *The Kingdom of Northumbria: AD 350–1100* (Stroud, 1993).

Higham, N. J., *The Convert Kings: Power and Religious Affiliation in early Anglo-Saxon England* (Manchester, 1997).

Higham, N. J., *(Re-)Reading Bede: The* Ecclesiastical History *in Context* (London, 2006).

Higham, N. J., *Bede as an Oral Historian*, Jarrow Lecture (Jarrow, 2011).

Higham, N. J. (ed.), *Wilfrid: Abbot, Bishop, Saint; Papers from the 1300th Anniversary Conferences* (Donington, 2013).

Higham, N. J., 'Bede's Agenda in Book IV of the "Ecclesiastical History of the English People": A Tricky Matter of Advising the King', *Journal of Ecclesiastical History* 64 (2013), 476–93.

Hill, Joyce, *Bede and the Benedictine Reform*, Jarrow Lecture (Jarrow, 1998).

Hill, Joyce, 'Carolingian Perspectives on the Authority of Bede', in *Innovation and Tradition in the Writings of the Venerable Bede*, ed. Scott DeGregorio (Morgantown WV, 2006), pp. 227–49.

Hill, Rosalind, 'Bede and the Boors', in *Famulus Christi: Essays in Commemoration of the Thirteenth Centenary of the Birth of the Venerable Bede*, ed. Gerald Bonner (London, 1976), pp. 93–105.

Hillgarth, J. N., 'L'influence de la *Cité du Dieu* de saint Augustin au Haut Moyen Age', *Sacris Erudiri* 28 (1985), pp. 5–34.

Hilliard, Paul, 'The Venerable Bede as Scholar, Gentile and Preacher', in *Ego Trouble: Authors and their Identities in the Early Middle Ages*, eds Richard Corradini, Matthew Gillis, Rosamond McKitterick, and Irene Van Renswoude (Vienna, 2010), pp. 101–9.

Holder, Arthur G., 'Allegory and History in Bede's Interpretation of Sacred Architecture', *American Benedictine Review* 40 (1989), pp. 115–31.

Holder, Arthur G., 'New Treasures and Old in Bede's "De Tabernaculo" and "De Templo"', *Revue bénédictine* 99 (1989), pp. 237–49.

Holder, Arthur G., 'Bede and the Tradition of Patristic Exegesis', *Anglican Theological Review* 72 (1990), pp. 399–411.

Holder, Arthur G., 'The Venerable Bede on the Mysteries of Our Salvation', *American Benedictine Review* 42 (1991), pp. 140–62.

Holder, Arthur G., 'The Mosaic Tabernacle in Early Christian Exegesis', *Studia Patristica* 25 (1993), pp. 101–6.

Holder, Arthur G., '(Un)Dating Bede's *De arte metrica*', in *Northumbria's Golden Age*, eds Jane Hawkes and Susan Mills (Stroud, 1999), pp. 390–95.

Holder, Arthur G., 'The Patristic Sources of Bede's Commentary on the Song of Songs', *Studia Patristica* 34 (2001), pp. 370–75.

Holder, Arthur G., 'The Anti-Pelagian Character of Bede's Commentary on the Song of Songs', in *Biblical Studies in the Early Middle Ages*, eds Claudio Leonardi and Giovanni Orlandi (Florence, 2005), pp. 91–103.

Holder, Arthur G., 'The Feminine Christ in Bede's Biblical Commentaries', in *Bède le Vénérable entre tradition et postérité: The Venerable Bede. Tradition and Posterity*, eds Stéphane Lebecq, Michel Perrin, and Olivier Szerwiniack (Lille, 2005), pp. 109–18.

Holder, Arthur G., 'Using Philosophers to Think With: The Venerable Bede on Christian Life and Practice', in *The Subjective Eye: Essays in Culture, Religion, and Gender in Honor of Margaret R. Miles*, ed. Richard Valantasis (Eugene OR, 2006), pp. 48–58.

Holder, Arthur G., 'Hunting Snakes in the Grass: Bede as Heresiologist', in *Listen, O Isles, unto me: Studies in Medieval Word and Image in Honour of Jennifer O'Reilly*, eds Elizabeth Mullins and Diarmuid Scully (Cork, 2011), pp. 105–14.

Hollis, Stephanie, *Anglo-Saxon Women and the Church: Sharing a Common Fate* (Woodbridge, 1992).

Hoskins, Paul M., *Jesus as the Fulfillment of the Temple in the Gospel of John* (Milton Keynes, 2006).

Houghton, John William, 'St. Bede among the Controversialists: A Survey', *American Benedictine Review* 50 (1999), pp. 397–422.

Howe, Nicholas, *Writing the Map in Anglo-Saxon England: Essays in Cultural Geography* (New Haven CT, 2008).

Innes, Matthew, '"Immune from Heresy": Defining the Boundaries of Carolingian Christianity', in *Frankland: The Franks and the World of the early Middle Ages. Essays in honour of Dame Jinty Nelson*, eds Paul Fouracre and David Ganz (Manchester, 2008), pp. 101–25.

Irvine, Martin, 'Bede the Grammarian and the Scope of Grammatical Studies in eighth-century Northumbria', *Anglo-Saxon England* 15 (1986), pp. 15–44.

Isaacs, Marie E., *Sacred Space: An Approach to the Theology of the Epistle to the Hebrews* (Sheffield, 1992).

Jenkins, Claude, 'Bede as Exegete and Theologian', in *Bede: His Life, Times, and Writings*, ed. A. Hamilton Thompson (Oxford, 1935), pp. 152–200.

Jenkins, David H., *'Holy, Holier, Holiest': The Sacred Topography of the Early Medieval Irish Church* (Turnhout, 2010).

Jestice, Phyllis G., 'A New Fashion in Imitating Christ: Changing Spiritual Perspectives around the Year 1000', in *The Year 1000: Religious and Social Response to the Turning of the First Millennium*, ed. Michael Frassetto (New York, 2002), pp. 165–85.

Jones, Charles W., *Bedae Pseudepigrapha: Scientific Writings Falsely Attributed to Bede* (Ithaca NY, 1939).

Jones, Charles W., *Bedae Opera de Temporibus* (Cambridge MA, 1943).

Jones, Charles W., 'Some Introductory Remarks on Bede's Commentary on Genesis', *Sacris Erudiri* 19 (1969–70), pp. 115–98.

Jones, Putnam Fennell, *A Concordance to the Historia Ecclesiastica of Bede* (Cambridge MA, 1929).

Jong, Mayke de, *In Samuel's Image: Child Oblation in the Early Medieval West* (Leiden, 1996).

Kaczynski, Bernice M., 'Bede's Commentaries on Luke and Mark and the Formation of a Patristic Canon', in *Anglo-Latin and its Heritage: Essays in Honour of A. G. Rigg on his 64th Birthday*, eds Siân Echard and Gernot R. Wieland (Turnhout, 2001), pp. 17–26.

Kelly, Henry Ansgar, *The Devil at Baptism: Ritual, Theology, and Drama* (Ithaca NY, 1985).

Kelly, J. N. D., *Early Christian Doctrines*, 5th ed. (London, 1977).

Kendall, Calvin B., 'Imitation and the Venerable Bede's *Historia Ecclesiastica*', in *Saints, Scholars, and Heroes: Studies in Medieval Culture in Honour of Charles W. Jones*, eds Margot H. King and Wesley M. Stevens, 2 vols (Collegeville MN, 1979), I, pp. 161–90.

Kendall, Calvin B., 'The Responsibility of *Auctoritas*: Method and Meaning in Bede's Commentary on Genesis', in *Innovation and Tradition in the Writings of the Venerable Bede*, ed. Scott DeGregorio (Morgantown WV, 2006), pp. 101–19.

Kendall, Calvin B., *Bede: On Genesis* (Liverpool, 2008).

Kendall, Calvin B., and Faith Wallis, *Bede: On the Nature of Things* and *On Times* (Liverpool, 2010).

Kessler, Herbert L., 'Through the Temple Veil: The Holy Image in Judaism and Christianity', *Kairos* 32/33 (1990–91), pp. 53–77.

King, Margot H., '*Grammatica Mystica*: A Study of Bede's Grammatical Curriculum', in *Saints, Scholars, and Heroes: Studies in Medieval Culture in Honour of Charles W. Jones*, eds Margot H. King and Wesley Stevens, 2 vols (Collegeville MN, 1979), I, pp. 145–59.

Kirby, D. P., 'Bede's Native Sources for the *Historia Ecclesiastica*', *Bulletin of the John Rylands Library* 48 (1965–66), pp. 341–71.

Kirby, D. P., 'Bede and the Pictish Church', *Innes Review* 24 (1973), pp. 6–25.

Kirby, D. P., 'King Ceolwulf of Northumbria and the *Historia Ecclesiastica*', *Studia Celtica* 14–15 (1979–80), pp. 168–73.

Kirby, D. P., *Bede's* Historia Ecclesiastica Gentis Anglorum: *Its Contemporary Setting*, Jarrow Lecture (Jarrow, 1992).

Kirby, D. P., 'The Genesis of a Cult: Cuthbert of Farne and Ecclesiastical Politics in Northumbria in the Late Seventh and Early Eighth Centuries', *Journal of Ecclesiastical History* 46 (1995), pp. 383–97.

Kleist, Aaron J., *Striving with Grace: Views of Free Will in Anglo-Saxon England* (Toronto, 2008).

Knappe, Gabriele, 'Classical Rhetoric in Anglo-Saxon England', *Anglo-Saxon England* 27 (1998), pp. 5–29.

Knibbs, Eric, 'The Manuscript Evidence for the *De Octo Quaestionibus* ascribed to Bede', *Traditio* 63 (2008), pp. 129–83.

Knowles, David, *Saints and Scholars: Twenty-five Medieval Portraits* (Cambridge, 1962).

Kramer, Joanna, '"Ðu eart se weallstan": Architectural Metaphor and Christological Imagery in the Old English *Christ I* and the Book of Kells', in *Source of Wisdom: Old English and Early Medieval Latin Studies in Honour of Thomas D. Hill*, eds Charles D. Wright, Frederick M. Biggs, and Thomas N. Hall (Toronto, 2007), pp. 90–112.

Krautheimer, Richard, 'Introduction to an "Iconography of Mediaeval Architecture"', *Journal of the Warburg and Courtauld Institutes* 5 (1942), pp. 1–33.

Kühnel, Bianca, 'Jewish Symbolism of the Temple and the Tabernacle and Christian Symbolism of the Holy Sepulchre and the Heavenly Jerusalem', *Jewish Art* 12/13 (1986–87), pp. 147–68.

Ladner, Gerhart B., 'The Symbolism of the Biblical Corner Stone in the Mediaeval West', *Mediaeval Studies* 4 (1942), pp. 43–60.

Laistner, M. L. W., 'Bede as a Classical and a Patristic Scholar', *Transactions of the Royal Historical Society* 4th series 16 (1933), pp. 69–94.

Laistner, M. L. W., 'The Library of the Venerable Bede', in *Bede: His Life, Times, and Writings*, ed. A. Hamilton Thompson (Oxford, 1935), pp. 237–66.

Laistner, M. L. W., *Bedae Venerabilis: Expositio Actuum Apostolorum et Retractatio* (Cambridge MA, 1939).

Laistner, M. L. W., and H. H. King, *A Hand-List of Bede Manuscripts* (Ithaca NY, 1943).

Lake, Stephen, 'Knowledge of the Writings of John Cassian in early Anglo-Saxon England', *Anglo-Saxon England* 32 (2003), pp. 27–41.

Lang, James, 'The Imagery of the Franks Casket', in *Northumbria's Golden Age*, eds Jane Hawkes and Susan Mills (Stroud, 1999), pp. 247–55.

Lapidge, Michael, and Michael Herren, *Aldhelm: The Prose Works* (Cambridge, 1979).

Lapidge, Michael, 'Anglo-Latin Literature', repr. in Lapidge, *Anglo-Latin Literature 600–899* (London, 1996), pp. 1–36.

Lapidge, Michael, 'Bede's Metrical *Vita S. Cuthberti*', in *St Cuthbert, His Cult and His Community until AD 1200*, eds Gerald Bonner, David Rollason, and Clare Stancliffe, (Woodbridge, 1989), pp. 77–93.

Lapidge, Michael, 'Acca of Hexham and the Origin of the Old English Martyrology', *Analecta Bollandiana* 123 (2005), pp. 29–78.

Lapidge, Michael, *The Anglo-Saxon Library* (Oxford, 2006).

Lapidge, Michael, 'Beda Venerabilis', in *La Trasmissione dei Testi Latini del Medioevo/ Medieval Latin Texts and their Transmission*, eds Paolo Chiesa and Lucia Castaldi, vol. 3 (Florence, 2008), pp. 44–137.

Lapidge, Michael, 'Introduzione', in *Beda: Storia degli Inglesi*, ed. Michael Lapidge and trans. Paolo Chiesa, vol. 1 (Rome, 2008), pp. xiii–lxxxi.

Lapidge, Michael (ed.), *Bede and His World*, 2 vols (Aldershot, 1994).

Laynesmith, Mark, 'Stephen of Ripon and the Bible: Allegorical and Typological Interpretations of the *Life of St Wilfrid*', *Early Medieval Europe* 9 (2000), pp. 163–82.

Laynesmith, Mark, 'Anti-Jewish Rhetoric in the *Life of Wilfrid*', in *Wilfrid: Abbot, Bishop, Saint; Papers from the 1300th Anniversary Conferences*, ed. N. J. Higham (Donington, 2013), pp. 67–79.

Leclercq, Jean, 'Pedagogie et formation spirituelle du VIᵉ au IXᵉ siècle', *Settimane di studio del Centro italiano di studi sull'alto medioevo* 19 (1972), pp. 255–90.

Leclercq, Jean, *The Love of Learning and the Desire for God: A Study of Monastic Culture*, trans. Catherine Misrahi, 3rd ed. (New York, 1982).

Lees, Clare A., and Gillian R. Overing, 'Birthing Bishops and Fathering Poets: Bede, Hild, and the Relations of Cultural Production', *Exemplaria* 6 (1994), pp. 35–65.

Leonardi, Claudio, 'Il Venerabile Beda e la Cultura del Secolo VIII', *Settimane di studio del Centro italiano di studi sull'alto medioevo* 20 (1973), pp. 603–58.

Leyser, Conrad, *Authority and Asceticism from Augustine to Gregory the Great* (Oxford, 2000).

Leyser, Conrad, 'Angels, Monks, and Demons in the Early Medieval West', in *Belief and Culture in the Middle Ages: Studies Presented to Henry Mayr-Harting*, eds Richard Gameson and Henrietta Leyser (Oxford, 2001), pp. 9–22.

Love, Rosalind, 'The Library of the Venerable Bede', in *The Cambridge History of the Book in Britain. Volume 1: c.400–1100*, ed. Richard Gameson (Cambridge, 2012), pp. 606–32.

Loveluck, Christopher, 'Cædmon's World: Secular and Monastic Lifestyles and Estate Organization in Northern England, A.D. 650–900', in *Cædmon's Hymn and Material Culture in the World of Bede*, eds Allen J. Frantzen and John Hines (Morgantown WV, 2007), pp. 150–90.

Lowden, John, *The Octateuchs: A Study in Byzantine Manuscript Illustration* (University Park PA, 1992).

Lubac, Henri de, *Exégèse médiévale: les quatres sens de l'Écriture*, 2 parts in 4 vols (Paris, 1959–1964); partially trans. Mark Sebanc and E. M. Macierowski, *Medieval Exegesis: The Four Senses of Scripture*, 2 vols (Edinburgh, 1998–2000).

Lynch, Joseph H., *Christianizing Kinship: Ritual Sponsorship in Anglo-Saxon England* (Ithaca NY, 1998).

Lynch, Kevin M., 'The Venerable Bede's Knowledge of Greek', *Traditio* 39 (1983), pp. 432–9.

McClure, Judith, 'Bede's Old Testament Kings', in *Ideal and Reality in Frankish and Anglo-Saxon Society: Studies presented to J. M. Wallace-Hadrill*, eds Patrick Wormald, Donald A. Bullough, and Roger Collins (Oxford, 1983), pp. 76–98.

McClure, Judith, 'Bede and the Life of Ceolfrid', *Peritia* 3 (1984), pp. 71–84.

McClure, Judith, 'Bede's *Notes on Genesis* and the Training of the Anglo-Saxon Clergy', in *The Bible in the Medieval World: Essays in Memory of Beryl Smalley*, eds Katherine Walsh and Diana Wood (Oxford, 1985), pp. 17–30.

McCready, William D., *Miracles and the Venerable Bede* (Toronto, 1994).

Mac Carron, Máirín, 'Bede, *Annus Domini* and the *Historia ecclesiastica gentis anglorum*', in *The Mystery of Christ in the Fathers of the Church: Essays in Honour of D. Vincent Twomey SVD*, eds Janet E. Rutherford and David Woods (Dublin, 2012), pp. 116–34.

MacDonald, Aidan, 'Aspects of the Monastic Landscape in Adomnán's *Life of Columba*', in *Studies in Irish Hagiography: Saints and Scholars*, eds John Carey, Máire Herbert, and Padraig Ó Riain (Dublin, 2001), pp. 15–30.

McGuckin, John A., *St. Cyril of Alexandria: The Christological Controversy: Its History, Theology, and Texts* (Leiden, 1994).

McGuire, Brian Patrick, *Friendship & Community: The Monastic Experience 350–1250* (Kalamazoo MI, 1988).

McKelvey, R. J., *The New Temple: The Church in the New Testament* (Oxford, 1969).

McKitterick, Rosamond, 'Anglo-Saxon Missionaries in Germany: Personal Connections and Local Influences', repr. in McKitterick, *The Frankish Kings and Culture in the Early Middle Ages* (Aldershot, 1995), pp. 1–40.

McLeod, Frederick G., *Theodore of Mopsuestia* (London, 2009).

Macy, Gary, *The Hidden History of Women's Ordination: Female Clergy in the Medieval West* (Oxford, 2008).

Maddicott, J. R., 'Two Frontier States: Northumbria and Wessex, c.650–750', in *The Medieval State: Essays Presented to James Campbell*, eds J. R. Maddicott and D. M. Palliser (London, 2000), pp. 25–45.

Mähl, Sybill, *Quadriga Virtutum: Die Kardinaltugenden in der Geistesgeschichte der Karolingerzeit* (Cologne, 1969).

Major, Tristan, 'Words, Wit, and Wordplay in the Latin Works of the Venerable Bede', *Journal of Medieval Latin* 22 (2012), pp. 185–219.

Márkus, Gilbert, 'Pelagianism and the "Common Celtic Church"', *Innes Review* 56 (2005), pp. 165–213.

Markus, R. A., *Bede and the Tradition of Ecclesiastical Historiography*, Jarrow Lecture (Jarrow, 1975).

Markus, R. A., 'Gregory the Great's *Rector* and His Genesis', in *Grégoire Le Grand*, eds Jacques Fontaine, Robert Gillet, and Stan Pellistrandi (Paris, 1986), pp. 137–46.

Markus, R. A., *Saeculum: History and Society in the Theology of St Augustine*, rev. ed. (Cambridge, 1988).

Markus, R. A., *The End of Ancient Christianity* (Cambridge, 1990).

Markus, R. A., 'The Jew as a Hermeneutic Device: The Inner Life of a Gregorian Topos', in *Gregory the Great: A Symposium*, ed. John C. Cavadini (London, 1995), pp. 1–15.

Markus, R. A., *Signs and Meanings: World and Text in Ancient Christianity* (Liverpool, 1996).

Markus, R. A., 'Gregory the Great's Pagans', in *Belief and Culture in the Middle Ages: Studies Presented to Henry Mayr-Harting*, eds Richard Gameson and Henrietta Leyser (Oxford, 2001), pp. 23–34.

Markus, R. A., 'Living within Sight of the End', in *Time in the Medieval World*, eds Chris Humphrey and W. M. Ormrod (York, 2001), pp. 23–34.

Marsden, Richard, 'Job in his Place: The Ezra Miniature in the Codex Amiatinus', *Scriptorium* 49 (1995), pp. 3–15.

Marsden, Richard, *The Text of the Old Testament in Anglo-Saxon England* (Cambridge, 1995).

Marsden, Richard, '*Manus Bedae*: Bede's Contribution to Ceolfrith's Bibles', *Anglo-Saxon England* 27 (1998), pp. 65–85.

Marsden, Richard, 'Amiatinus in Italy: The Afterlife of an Anglo-Saxon Book', in *Anglo-Saxon England and the Continent*, eds Hans Sauer and Joanna Storey, with Gaby Waxenberger (Tempe AZ, 2011), pp. 217–39.

Martin, Lawrence T., 'The Two Worlds in Bede's Homilies: The Biblical Event and the Listeners' Experience', in *De Ore Domini: Preacher and Word in the Middle Ages*, eds Thomas L. Amos, Eugene A. Green, and Beverly Mayne Kienzle (Kalamazoo MI, 1989), pp. 27–40.

Martin, Lawrence T., 'Introduction', in *Bede the Venerable: Homilies on the Gospels*, vol. 1 (Kalamazoo MI, 1991), pp. xi–xxiii.

Martin, Lawrence T., 'Bede and Preaching', in *The Cambridge Companion to Bede*, ed. Scott DeGregorio (Cambridge, 2010), pp. 156–69.

Mayr-Harting, Henry, *The Venerable Bede, The Rule of St. Benedict, and Social Class*, Jarrow Lecture (Jarrow, 1976).

Mayr-Harting, Henry, *The Coming of Christianity to Anglo-Saxon England*, 3rd ed. (London, 1991).

Mayr-Harting, Henry, 'Bede's Patristic Thinking as an Historian', in *Historiographie im frühen Mittelalter*, eds A. Scharer and G. Scheibelreiter (Vienna, 1994), pp. 367–74.

Merrills, A. H., *History and Geography in Late Antiquity* (Cambridge, 2005).

Meyer, Heinz, and Rudolf Suntrup, *Lexikon der Mittelalterlichen Zahlenbedeutungen* (Munich, 1987).

Meyvaert, Paul, 'Diversity within Unity, a Gregorian Theme', *The Heythrop Journal* 4 (1963), pp. 141–62.

Meyvaert, Paul, *Bede and Gregory the Great*, Jarrow Lecture (Jarrow, 1964).

Meyvaert, Paul, 'Bede the Scholar', in *Famulus Christi: Essays in Commemoration of the Thirteenth Centenary of the Birth of the Venerable Bede*, ed. Gerald Bonner (London, 1976), pp. 40–69.

Meyvaert, Paul, 'A New Perspective on the Ruthwell Cross: Ecclesia and Vita Monastica', in *The Ruthwell Cross: Papers from the Colloquium sponsored by the Index of Christian Art, Princeton University, 8 December 1989*, ed. Brendan Cassidy (Princeton NJ, 1992), pp. 95–166.

Meyvaert, Paul, 'Bede, Cassiodorus and the Codex Amiatinus', *Speculum* 71 (1996), pp. 827–83.

Meyvaert, Paul, '"In the Footsteps of the Fathers": The Date of Bede's *Thirty Questions on the Book of Kings* to Nothelm', in *The Limits of Ancient Christianity: Essays on Late Antique Thought and Culture in Honour of R. A. Markus*, eds William E. Klingshirn and Mark Vessey (Ann Arbor MI, 1999), pp. 267–86.

Meyvaert, Paul, 'Discovering the Calendar (*Annalis Libellus*) attached to Bede's own Copy of *De Temporum Ratione*', *Analecta Bollandiana* 120 (2002), pp. 5–64.

Meyvaert, Paul, 'The Date of Bede's *In Ezram* and his Image of Ezra in the Codex Amiatinus', *Speculum* 80 (2005), pp. 1087–133.

Meyvaert, Paul, 'Dissension in Bede's Community shown by a Quire of the Codex Amiatinus', *Revue bénédictine* 116 (2006), pp. 295–309.

Michelet, Fabienne, *Creation, Migration, and Conquest: Imaginary Geography and Sense of Space in Old English Literature* (Oxford, 2006).

Molyneux, George, 'Did the English really think they were God's elect in the Anglo-Saxon period?', *Journal of Ecclesiastical History* 65 (2014), pp. 721–37.

Moorhead, John, 'Bede on the Papacy', *Journal of Ecclesiastical History* 60 (2009), pp. 217–32.

Morris, Colin, *The Discovery of the Individual, 1050–1200* (London, 1972).

Morris, Richard, *Journeys from Jarrow*, Jarrow Lecture (Jarrow, 2004).

Mosher, Joseph Albert, *The Exemplum in the Early Religious and Didactic Literature of England* (New York, 1911).

Moss, Candida R., *The Other Christs: Imitating Jesus in Ancient Christian Ideologies of Martyrdom* (Oxford, 2010).

Muehlberger, Ellen, 'Ambivalence about the Angelic Life: The Promise and the Perils of an Early Christian Discourse of Asceticism', *Journal of Early Christian Studies* 16 (2008), pp. 447–78.

Muller, Earl C., 'The Priesthood of Christ in Book IV of the *De trinitate*', in *Augustine: Presbyter Factus Sum*, eds Joseph T. Lienhard, Earl C. Muller, and Roland J. Teske (New York, 1993), pp. 135–49.

Nees, Lawrence, 'Problems of Form and Function in Early Medieval Illustrated Bibles from Northwest Europe', in *Imaging the Early Medieval Bible*, ed. John Williams (University Park PA, 1999), pp. 121–77.

Neuman de Vegvar, Carol, *The Northumbrian Renaissance: A Study in the Transmission of Style* (London, 1987).

Neuman de Vegvar, Carol, 'Converting the Anglo-Saxon Landscape: Crosses and their Audiences', in *Text, Image, Interpretation: Studies in Anglo-Saxon Literature and its Insular Context in Honour of Eamonn Ó Carragáin*, eds Alastair Minnis and Jane Roberts (Turnhout, 2007), pp. 407–29.

Neuman de Vegvar, Carol, 'Remembering Jerusalem: Architecture and Meaning in Insular Canon Table Arcades', in *Making and Meaning in Insular Art*, ed. Rachel Moss (Dublin, 2007), pp. 242–56.

Neville, Jennifer, *Representations of the Natural World in Old English Poetry* (Cambridge, 1999).

Newlands, Carole E., 'Bede and Images of Saint Cuthbert', *Traditio* 52 (1997), pp. 73–109.

Ó Carragáin, Éamonn, *The City of Rome and the World of Bede*, Jarrow Lecture (Jarrow, 1994).

Ó Carragáin, Éamonn, 'The Term *Porticus* and *Imitatio Romae* in Early Anglo-Saxon England', in *Text and Gloss: Studies in Insular Learning and Literature presented to Joseph Donovan Pheifer*, eds Helen Conrad-O'Briain, Anne Marie D'Arcy, and John Scattergood (Dublin, 1999), pp. 13–34.

Ó Carragáin, Éamonn, *Ritual and the Rood: Liturgical Images and the Old English Poems of the Dream of the Rood Tradition* (London, 2005).

Ó Carragáin, Éamonn, 'The Wearmouth Icon of the Virgin (A.D. 679): Christological, Liturgical, and Iconographic Contexts', in *Poetry, Place, and Gender: Studies in Medieval Culture in Honour of Helen Damico*, ed. Catherine E. Karkov (Kalamazoo MI, 2009), pp. 13–37.

Ó Corráin, Donnchadh, Liam Breatnach, and Aidan Breen, 'The Laws of the Irish', *Peritia* 3 (1984), pp. 382–438.

Ó Cróinín, Dáibhí, 'The Irish Provenance of Bede's *Computus*', *Peritia* 2 (1983), pp. 238–42.

Ó Cróinín, Dáibhí, 'Rath Melsigi, Willibrord, and the Earliest Echternach Manuscripts', *Peritia* 3 (1984), pp. 17–49.

Ó Cróinín, Dáibhí, '"New Heresy for Old": Pelagianism in Ireland and the Papal Letter of 640', *Speculum* 60 (1985), pp. 505–16.

Ó Cróinín, Dáibhí, 'Bischoff's Wendepunkte Fifty Years On', *Revue bénédictine* 110 (2000), pp. 204–37.

O'Brien, Conor, 'A Quotation from Origen's *Homilies on Leviticus* in Bede's Commentary on Luke's Gospel', *Notes and Queries* 60 (2013), pp. 185–6.

O'Brien, Conor, 'Bede on the Jewish Church', in *The Church on its Past*, eds Peter D. Clarke and Charlotte Methuen (Woodbridge, 2013), pp. 63–73.

O'Brien, Conor, 'Exegesis as Argument: The Use of Ephesians 2, 14 in Cummian's *De Controversia Paschali*', *Cambrian Medieval Celtic Quarterly* 67 (2014), pp. 73–81.

O'Brien, Conor, 'The Cleansing of the Temple in early medieval Northumbria', forthcoming.

O'Loughlin, Thomas (ed.), *The Scriptures and Early Medieval Ireland* (Turnhout, 1999).

Olsen, Glenn, 'Bede as Historian: The Evidence from his Observations on the Life of the First Christian Community at Jerusalem', *Journal of Ecclesiastical History* 33 (1982), pp. 519–30.

Olsen, Glenn W., 'From Bede to the Anglo-Saxon Presence in the Carolingian Empire', *Settimane di studio del Centro italiano di studi sull'alto medioevo* 32 (1984), pp. 305–82.

Oort, Johannes van, *Jerusalem and Babylon: A Study of Augustine's City of God and the Sources of his Doctrine of the Two Cities* (Leiden, 1991).

O'Reilly, Jennifer, 'Exegesis and the Book of Kells: The Lucan Genealogy', in *The Book of Kells: Proceedings of a Conference at Trinity College Dublin, 6–9 September 1992*, ed. Felicity O'Mahony (Aldershot, 1994), pp. 344–97.

O'Reilly, Jennifer, 'Introduction', in *Bede: On the Temple*, trans. Seán Connolly (Liverpool, 1995), pp. xvii–lv.

O'Reilly, Jennifer, 'Patristic and Insular Traditions of the Evangelists: Exegesis and Iconography', in *Le Isole Britanniche e Roma in Età Romanobarbarica*, eds A. M. Luiselli Fadda and É. Ó Carragáin (Rome, 1998), pp. 49–94.

O'Reilly, Jennifer, 'The Library of Scripture: Views from Vivarium and Wearmouth-Jarrow', in *New Offerings, Ancient Treasures: Studies in Medieval Art for George Henderson*, eds Paul Binski and William Noel (Stroud, 2001), pp. 3–39.

O'Reilly, Jennifer, 'The Art of Authority', in *After Rome*, ed. Thomas Charles-Edwards (Oxford, 2003), pp. 141–89.

O'Reilly, Jennifer, 'Islands and Idols at the Ends of the Earth: Exegesis and Conversion in Bede's *Historia Ecclesiastica*', in *Bède Le Vénérable Entre Tradition et Postérité: The Venerable Bede. Tradition and Posterity,* eds Stéphane Lebecq, Michel Perrin, and Olivier Szerwiniack (Lille, 2005), pp. 119–45.

O'Reilly, Jennifer, 'Bede on Seeing the God of Gods in Zion', in *Text, Image, Interpretation: Studies in Anglo-Saxon Literature and its Insular Context in Honour of Éamonn Ó Carragáin*, eds Alastair Minnis and Jane Roberts, (Turnhout, 2007), pp. 3–29.

O'Reilly, Jennifer, '"All that Peter Stands For": The *Romanitas* of the *Codex Amiatinus* Reconsidered', *Proceedings of the British Academy* 157 (2009), pp. 367–95.

O'Reilly, Jennifer, 'The Multitude of Isles and the Corner-stone: Topography, Exegesis, and the Identity of the *Angli* in Bede's *Historia Ecclesiastica*', in *Anglo-Saxon Traces*, eds Jane Roberts and Leslie Webster (Tempe AZ, 2011), pp. 201–27.

Orton, Fred, and Ian Wood with Clare A. Lees, *Fragments of History: Rethinking the Ruthwell and Bewcastle Monuments* (Manchester, 2007).

Page, R. I., 'Anglo-Saxon Paganism: The Evidence of Bede', in *Pagans and Christians: The Interplay between Christian Latin and Traditional Germanic Cultures in Early Medieval Europe*, eds T. Hofstra, L. A. J. R. Houwen, and A. A. MacDonald (Groningen, 1995), pp. 99–129.

Palmer, James, *Anglo-Saxons in a Frankish World, 690–900* (Turnhout, 2009).

Parkes, Malcolm, *The Scriptorium of Wearmouth-Jarrow*, Jarrow Lecture (Jarrow, 1982).

Pelteret, David, 'Bede's Women', in *Women, Marriage, and Family in Medieval Christendom: Essays in Memory of Michael M. Sheehan, C.S.B.*, eds Constance M. Rousseau and Joel T. Rosenthal (Kalamazoo MI, 1998), pp. 19–46.

Petroff, Valery V., 'The *De Templo* of Bede as the Source of an Ideal Temple Description in Eriugena's *Aulae Siderae*', *Recherches de théologie et philosophie médiévales* 65 (1998), pp. 97–106.

Pfaff, Richard W., 'Bede Among the Fathers? The Evidence from Liturgical Commemoration', *Studia Patristica* 28 (1993), pp. 225–9.

Pfaff, Richard W., *The Liturgy in Medieval England: A History* (Cambridge, 2009).

Piano, Natacha, 'De la porte close du temple de Salomon à la porte ouverte du Paradis', *Studi Medievali* 50 (2009), pp. 133–57.

Picard, Jean-Michel, 'Bede, Adomnán, and the writing of history', *Peritia* 3 (1984), pp. 50–70.

Picard, Jean-Michel, 'Bède et ses sources irlandaises', in *Bède le Vénérable entre Tradition et Postérité: The Venerable Bede. Tradition and Posterity*, eds Stéphane Lebecq, Michel Perrin, and Olivier Szerwiniack (Lille, 2005), pp. 43–61.

Pickles, Thomas, 'Angel Veneration on Anglo-Saxon Stone Sculpture from Dewesbury (West Yorkshire), Otely (West Yorkshire) and Halton (Lancashire): Contemplative Preachers and Pastoral Care', *Journal of the British Archaeological Association* 162 (2009), pp. 1–28.

Pickles, Thomas, 'Anglo-Saxon Monasteries as Sacred Places: Topography, Exegesis and Vocation', in *Sacred Text—Sacred Space: Architectural, Spiritual and Literary Convergences in England and Wales*, eds Joseph Sterrett and Peter Thomas (Leiden, 2011), pp. 35–55.

Plummer, Charles, *Venerabilis Baedae Opera Historica*, 2 vols (Oxford, 1896).

Rabin, Andrew, 'Historical recollections: rewriting the world in Bede's *De Temporum Ratione*', *Viator* 36 (2005), pp. 23–39.

Ramirez, Janina, '*Sub culmine gazas*: The Iconography of the *Armarium* on the Ezra Page of the Codex Amiatinus', *Gesta* 48 (2009), pp. 1–18.

Raw, Barbara, *Trinity and Incarnation in Anglo-Saxon Art and Thought* (Cambridge, 1997).

Ray, Roger, 'Bede, the Exegete, as Historian', in *Famulus Christi: Essays in Commemoration of the Thirteenth Centenary of the Birth of the Venerable Bede*, ed. Gerald Bonner (London, 1976), pp. 125–40.

Ray, Roger, 'What do we know about Bede's Commentaries?', *Recherches de Théologie ancienne et médiévale* 49 (1982), pp. 5–20.

Ray, Roger, 'Bede and Cicero', *Anglo-Saxon England* 16 (1987), pp. 1–15.

Ray, Roger, 'Who Did Bede Think He Was?', in *Innovation and Tradition in the Writings of the Venerable Bede*, ed. Scott DeGregorio (Morgantown WV, 2006), pp. 11–35.

Repsher, Brian, *The Rite of Church Dedication in the Early Medieval Era* (Lampeter, 1998).

Revel-Neher, Elisabeth, 'La page double du Codex Amiatinus et ses rapports avec les plans du tabernacle dans l'art juif et dans l'art byzantin', *Journal of Jewish Art* 9 (1982), pp. 6–17.

Riché, Pierre, *Education and Culture in the Barbarian West: from the Sixth through Eighth Century*, trans. John J. Contreni (Columbia SC, 1978).

Rollason, David, 'Hagiography and Politics in Early Northumbria', in *Holy Men and Holy Women: Old English Prose Saints' Lives and Their Contexts*, ed. P. E. Szarmach (Albany NY, 1996), pp. 95–114.

Rollason, David, 'Monasteries and Society in Early Medieval Northumbria', in *Monasteries and Society in Medieval Britain: Proceedings of the 1994 Harlaxton Symposium*, ed. Benjamin Thompson (Stamford, 1999), pp. 59–74.

Rollason, David, *Bede and Germany*, Jarrow Lecture (Jarrow, 2001).

Rowland, Christopher, 'The Temple in the New Testament', in *Temple and Worship in Biblical Israel*, ed. John Day (London, 2005), pp. 469–83.

Rowley, Sharon M., 'Reassessing Exegetical Interpretations of Bede's *Historia Ecclesiastica Gentis Anglorum*', *Literature and Theology* 17 (2003), pp. 227–43.

Rowley, Sharon M., 'Bede in later Anglo-Saxon England', in *The Cambridge Companion to Bede*, ed. Scott DeGregorio (Cambridge, 2010), pp. 216–28.

Roy, Gopa, 'The Anglo-Saxons and the Shape of the World', in *Essays on Anglo-Saxon and Related Themes in Memory of Lynne Grundy*, eds Jane Roberts and Janet Nelson (London, 2000), pp. 455–81.

Russell, James C., *The Germanization of Early Medieval Christianity* (Oxford, 1994).

Sanchis, Dominique, 'Le symbolisme communautaire du temple chez Saint Augustin', *Revue d'Ascétique et de Mystique* 37 (1961), pp. 3–30 and 137–47.

Sanders, E. P., 'Jerusalem and its Temple in Early Christian Thought and Practice', in *Jerusalem: Its Sanctity and Centrality to Judaism, Christianity, and Islam*, ed. Lee I. Levine (New York, 1999), pp. 90–103.

Scheil, Andrew P., *The Footsteps of Israel: Understanding Jews in Anglo-Saxon England* (Ann Arbor MI, 2004).

Schenck, Kenneth L., *Cosmology and Eschatology in Hebrews: The Settings of the Sacrifice* (Cambridge, 2007).

Schüssler Fiorenza, Elisabeth, 'Cultic Language in Qumran and in the NT', *Catholic Biblical Quarterly* 38 (1976), pp. 159–77.

Scully, Diarmuid, 'Introduction', in *Bede: On* Tobit *and on the* Canticle of Habakkuk, trans. Seán Connolly (Dublin, 1997), pp. 17–37.

Scully, Diarmuid, 'Bede, Orosius and Gildas on the Early History of Britain', in *Bède Le Vénérable Entre Tradition et Postérité: The Venerable Bede. Tradition and Posterity*, eds Stéphane Lebecq, Michel Perrin, and Olivier Szerwiniack (Lille, 2005), pp. 31–42.

Scully, Diarmuid, 'Bede's *Chronica Maiora*: Early Insular History in a Universal Context', *Proceedings of the British Academy* 157 (2009), pp. 47–73.

Scully, Diarmuid, 'Location and Occupation: Bede, Gildas, and the Roman Vision of Britain' in *Anglo-Saxon Traces*, eds Jane Roberts and Leslie Webster (Tempe AZ, 2011), pp. 243–72.

Sharpe, Richard, 'Some Problems concerning the Organization of the Church in Early Medieval Ireland', *Peritia* 3 (1984), pp. 230–70.

Sharpe, Richard, 'The Varieties of Bede's Prose', *Proceedings of the British Academy* 129 (2005), pp. 339–55.

Siemens, James, *The Christology of Theodore of Tarsus: The* Laterculus Malalianus *and the Person and Work of Christ* (Turnhout, 2010).

Siemens, James, 'Another Book for Jarrow's Library? Coincidences in Exegesis between Bede and the *Laterculus Malalianus*', *Downside Review* 132 (2013), pp. 15–34.

Simonetti, Manlio, *Biblical Interpretation in the Early Church: An Historical Introduction to Patristic Exegesis*, trans. John A. Hughes, eds Anders Bergquist and Marcus Bockmuehl (Edinburgh, 1994).

Sims-Williams, Patrick, *Religion and Literature in Western England, 600–800* (Cambridge, 1990).

Skinner, Quentin, *Visions of Politics. Volume 1: Regarding Method* (Cambridge, 2002).

Smalley, Beryl, *The Study of the Bible in the Middle Ages*, 3rd ed. (Oxford, 1983).

Smetana, Cyril, 'Paul the Deacon's Patristic Anthology', in *The Old English Homily & its Backgrounds*, eds Paul E. Szarmach and Bernard F. Huppé (Albany NY, 1978), pp. 75–97.

Smith, Lesley, *The* Glossa Ordinaria: *The Making of a Medieval Bible Commentary* (Leiden, 2009).

Smyth, Marina, *Understanding the Universe in Seventh-Century Ireland* (Woodbridge, 1996).

Southern, R. W., *The Making of the Middle Ages* (London, 1967).

Southern, R. W., *Medieval Humanism and Other Studies* (Oxford, 1970).

Spiegel, Flora, 'The *tabernacula* of Gregory the Great and the Conversion of Anglo-Saxon England', *Anglo-Saxon England* 36 (2007), pp. 1–13.

Spijker, Ineke van 't, 'Introduction', in *The Multiple Meaning of Scripture: the Role of Exegesis in early Christian and Medieval Culture*, ed. Ineke van 't Spijker (Leiden, 2009), pp. 1–12.

Stancliffe, Clare, 'Early "Irish" Biblical Exegesis', *Studia Patristica* 12 (1975), pp. 361–70.

Stancliffe, Clare, 'Cuthbert and the Polarity between Pastor and Solitary', in *St Cuthbert, His Cult and His Community until AD 1200*, eds Gerald Bonner, Clare Stancliffe, and David Rollason (Woodbridge, 1989), pp. 21–44.

Stancliffe, Clare, *Bede, Wilfrid, and the Irish*, Jarrow Lecture (Jarrow, 2003).

Stancliffe, Clare, *Bede and the Britons*, Whithorn Lecture 2005 (Whithorn, 2007).

Stancliffe, Clare, 'Creator and Creation: A Preliminary Investigation of Early Irish Views and their Relationship to Biblical and Patristic Traditions', *Cambrian Medieval Celtic Studies* 58 (2009), pp. 9–27.

Stancliffe, Clare, '"Charity with Peace": Adomnán and the Easter Question', in *Adomnán of Iona: Theologian, Lawmaker, Peacemaker*, eds Jonathan M. Wooding, Rodney Aist, Thomas Owen Clancy, and Thomas O'Loughlin (Dublin, 2010), pp. 51–69.

Stancliffe, Clare, 'Disputed episcopacy: Bede, Acca and the relationship between Stephen's *Life of Wilfrid* and the early prose Lives of St Cuthbert', *Anglo-Saxon England* 41 (2012), pp. 7–39.

Stancliffe, Clare, 'Dating Wilfrid's Death and Stephen's *Life*', in *Wilfrid: Abbot, Bishop, Saint; Papers from the 1300th Anniversary Conferences*, ed. N. J. Higham (Donington, 2013), pp. 17–26.

Stansbury, Mark, 'Early-Medieval Biblical Commentaries, Their Writers and Readers', *Frühmittelalterliche Studien* 33 (1999), pp. 49–82.

Stevens, Wesley M., *Bede's Scientific Achievement*, Jarrow Lecture (Jarrow, 1985).

Stevenson, Gregory, *Power and Place: Temple and Identity in the Book of Revelation* (Berlin, 2001).

Stevenson, Jane, *The 'Laterculus Malalianus' and the School of Archbishop Theodore* (Cambridge, 1995).

Straw, Carole, *Gregory the Great: Perfection in Imperfection* (Berkeley CA, 1988).

Sutcliffe, E. F., 'The Venerable Bede's Knowledge of Hebrew', *Biblica* 16 (1935), pp. 300–6.

Szerwiniack, Olivier, 'Frères et sœurs dans l'*Histoire ecclésiastique du peuple anglais* de Bède le Vénérable: De la fratrie biologique à la fratrie spirituelle', *Revue bénédictine* 118 (2008), pp. 239–61.

Terrian, Marie-Pierre, 'Religious Architecture and Mathematics during the Late Antiquity', in *Mathematics and the Divine: A Historical Study*, eds T. Koetsier and L. Bergmans (Amsterdam, 2005), pp. 147–60.

Thacker, Alan, 'Bede's Ideal of Reform', in *Ideal and Reality in Frankish and Anglo-Saxon Society: Studies presented to J. M. Wallace-Hadrill*, eds Patrick Wormald, Donald Bullough, and Roger Collins (Oxford, 1983), pp. 130–53.

Thacker, Alan, 'Lindisfarne and the Origins of the Cult of St Cuthbert', in *St Cuthbert, His Cult and His Community until AD 1200*, eds Gerald Bonner, David Rollason, and Clare Stancliffe (Woodbridge, 1989), pp. 103–22.

Thacker, Alan, 'Monks, Preaching and Pastoral Care in early Anglo-Saxon England', in *Pastoral Care Before the Parish*, eds John Blair and Richard Sharpe (Leicester, 1992), pp. 137–70.

Thacker, Alan, 'Bede and the Irish', in *Beda Venerabilis: Historian, Monk & Northumbrian*, eds L. A. J. R. Houwen and A. A. MacDonald (Groningen, 1996), pp. 31–59.

Thacker, Alan, *Bede and Augustine of Hippo: History and Figure in Sacred Text*, Jarrow Lecture (Jarrow, 2005).

Thacker, Alan, 'Bede and the Ordering of Understanding', in *Innovation and Tradition in the Writings of the Venerable Bede*, ed. Scott DeGregorio (Morgantown WV, 2006), pp. 37–63.

Thacker, Alan, 'Bede, the Britons and the Book of Samuel', in *Early Medieval Studies in Memory of Patrick Wormald*, eds Stephen Baxter, Catherine Karkov, Janet Nelson, and David Pelteret (Farnham, 2009), pp. 129–47.

Thacker, Alan, 'Priests and Pastoral Care in Early Anglo-Saxon England', in *The Study of Medieval Manuscripts of England: Festschrift in Honor of Richard W. Pfaff*, eds George Hardin Brown and Linda Ehrsam Voigts (Tempe AZ, 2010), pp. 187–208.

Thomas, Benjamin, 'Priests and Bishops in Bede's Ecclesiology: the use of sacerdos in the *Historia Ecclesiastica Gentis Anglorum*', *Ecclesiology* 6 (2010), pp. 68–93.

Tugène, Georges, 'L'histoire "ecclésiastique" du peuple anglais: Réflexions sur le particularisme et l'universalisme chez Bède', *Recherches augustiniennes* 17 (1982), pp. 129–72.

Tugène, Georges, *L'idée de nation chez Bède le Vénérable* (Paris, 2001).

Tugène, Georges, 'Le thème des deux peuples dans le *De Tabernaculo* de Bède', in *Bède Le Vénérable Entre Tradition et Postérité: The Venerable Bede. Tradition and Posterity*, eds Stéphane Lebecq, Michel Perrin, and Olivier Szerwiniack (Lille, 2005), pp. 73–84.

Turner, H. E. W., *The Patristic Doctrine of Redemption: A Study of the Development of Doctrine during the First Five Centuries* (London, 1952).

Veitch, Kenneth, 'The Columban Church in northern Britain, 664–717: a reassessment', *Proceedings of the Society of Antiquaries of Scotland* 127 (1997), pp. 627–47.

Vogüé, Adalbert de, 'Grégoire le Grand est-il l'auteur des *Dialogues*?', *Revue d'Histoire Ecclésiastique* 99 (2004), pp. 158–61.

Wallis, Faith, *Bede: On the Reckoning of Time* (Liverpool, 1999).

Wallis, Faith, 'Cædmon's Created World and the Monastic Encyclopedia', in *Cædmon's Hymn and Material Culture*, eds Allen J. Frantzen and John Hines (Morgantown WV, 2007), pp. 80–110.

Wallis, Faith, *Bede: Commentary on Revelation* (Liverpool, 2013).

Walt, A. D. P. van der, 'Reflections of the Benedictine Rule in Bede's Homiliary', *Journal of Ecclesiastical History* 37 (1986), pp. 367–76.

Walterspacher, Ralph, 'Book V of Bede's *Historia ecclesiastica gentis Anglorum*: Perspective on Salvation History and Eschatology', *Archa Verbi: Yearbook for the Study of Medieval Theology* 1 (2004), pp. 11–24.

Ward, Benedicta, 'Miracles and History: A Reconsideration of the Miracle Stories used by Bede', in *Famulus Christi: Essays in Commemoration of the Thirteenth Centenary of the Birth of the Venerable Bede*, ed. Gerald Bonner (London, 1976), pp. 70–76.

Ward, Benedicta, *Bede and the Psalter*, Jarrow Lecture (Jarrow, 1991).

Ward, Benedicta, *The Venerable Bede*, 2nd ed. (London, 1998).

Wardle, Timothy, *The Jerusalem Temple and Early Christian Identity* (Tübingen, 2010).

Wehlau, Ruth, *'The Riddle of Creation': Metaphor Structures in Old English Poetry* (New York, 1997).

Westgard, Joshua A., 'Bede and the Continent in the Carolingian Age and Beyond', in *The Cambridge Companion to Bede*, ed. Scott DeGregorio (Cambridge, 2010), pp. 201–15.

Westgard, Joshua A., 'New Manuscripts of Bede's Letter to Albinus', *Revue bénédictine* 120 (2010), pp. 208–15.

White, H. J., 'The Codex Amiatinus and its Birthplace', *Studia Biblica et Ecclesiastica* 3 (1890), pp. 273–308.

Whitehead, Christiana, *Castles of the Mind: A Study of Medieval Architectural Allegory* (Cardiff, 2003).

Whitelock, Dorothy, *After Bede*, Jarrow Lecture (Jarrow, 1960).

Whitelock, Dorothy, 'Bede and His Teachers and Friends', in *Famulus Christi: Essays in Commemoration of the Thirteenth Centenary of the Birth of the Venerable Bede*, ed. Gerald Bonner (London, 1976), pp. 19–39.

Wilken, Robert L., *'In novissimis diebus*: Biblical Promises, Jewish Hopes and Early Christian Exegesis', *Journal of Early Christian Studies* 1 (1993), pp. 1–19.

Willmes, Ansgar, 'Bedas Bibelauslegung', *Archiv für Kulturgeschichte* 44 (1962), pp. 281–314.

Winterbottom, Michael, 'Bede's Homily on Benedict Biscop (*Hom.* i.13)', *Journal of Medieval Latin* 21 (2011), pp. 35–51.

Wolska, Wanda, *La Topographie Chrétienne de Cosmas Indicopleustès: Théologie et Science au VIe siècle* (Paris, 1962).

Wood, Ian, 'Ripon, Francia and the Franks Casket in the Early Middle Ages', *Northern History* 26 (1990), pp. 1–19.

Wood, Ian, *The Most Holy Abbot Ceolfrid*, Jarrow Lecture (Jarrow, 1995).

Wood, Ian, 'Bede's Jarrow', in *A Place to Believe In: Locating Medieval Landscapes*, eds Clare A. Lees and Gillian R. Overing (University Park PA, 2006), pp. 67–84.

Wood, Ian, 'Monasteries and the Geography of Power in the Age of Bede', *Northern History* 45 (2008), pp. 11–25.

Wood, Ian, 'The Foundation of Bede's Wearmouth-Jarrow', in *The Cambridge Companion to Bede*, ed. Scott DeGregorio (Cambridge, 2010), pp. 84–96.

Wood, Ian, 'The Gifts of Wearmouth and Jarrow', in *The Languages of Gift in the Early Middle Ages*, eds Wendy Davies and Paul Fouracre (Cambridge, 2010), pp. 89–115.

Wood, Ian, 'Entrusting Western Europe to the Church, 400–750', *Transactions of the Royal Historical Society* 6th Series 23 (2013), pp. 37–73.

Wood, Jamie, *The Politics of Identity in Visigothic Spain: Religion and Power in the Histories of Isidore of Seville* (Leiden, 2012).

Woolf, Rosemary, 'Doctrinal Influences on *The Dream of the Rood*', *Medium Aevum* 27 (1958), pp. 137–53.

Wormald, Patrick, 'Bede and Benedict Biscop', repr. in Wormald, *The Times of Bede: Studies in Early English Christian Society and its Historian*, ed. Stephen Baxter (Oxford, 2006), pp. 3–29.

Wormald, Patrick, 'Bede, *Beowulf* and the Conversion of the Anglo-Saxon Aristocracy', repr. in Wormald, *The Times of Bede: Studies in Early English Christian Society and its Historian*, ed. Stephen Baxter (Oxford, 2006), pp. 30–105.

Wormald, Patrick, 'Bede and the Conversion of England: The Charter Evidence', repr. in Wormald, *The Times of Bede: Studies in Early English Christian Society and its Historian*, ed. Stephen Baxter (Oxford, 2006), pp. 135–66.

Wormald, Patrick, 'The Venerable Bede and the "Church of the English"', repr. in Wormald, *The Times of Bede: Studies in Early English Christian Society and its Historian*, ed. Stephen Baxter (Oxford, 2006), pp. 207–28.

Wright, Neil, 'Bede and Vergil', *Romanobarbarica* 6 (1982), pp. 361–79.

Yorke, Barbara, *Nunneries and the Anglo-Saxon Royal Houses* (London, 2003).

Yorke, Barbara, *Rex Doctissimus: Bede and King Aldfrith of Northumbria*, Jarrow Lecture (Jarrow, 2009).

Yorke, Barbara, 'Adomnán at the Court of King Aldfrith', in *Adomnán of Iona: Theologian, Lawmaker, Peacemaker*, eds Jonathan M. Wooding, Rodney Aist, Thomas Owen Clancy, and Thomas O'Loughlin (Dublin, 2010), pp. 36–50.

Young, Frances M., *Biblical Exegesis and the Formation of Christian Culture* (Cambridge, 1997).

4. Unpublished Theses

Allan, Verity, 'Theological Works of the Venerable Bede and their Literary and Manuscript Presentation, with special reference to the Gospel Homilies' (MLitt thesis, University of Oxford, 2006).

Beall, Barbara Apelian, 'The Illuminated Pages of the Codex Amiatinus: Issues of Form, Function and Production' (PhD dissertation, Brown University, 1997).

Clark, Stephanie, 'Theorizing Prayer in Anglo-Saxon England: Bede and Ælfric', (PhD dissertation, University of Ilinois, Urbana-Champaign, 2011).

Fleming, Damian, '"The Most Exalted Language": Anglo-Saxon Perceptions of Hebrew' (PhD thesis, University of Toronto, 2006).

Hilliard, Paul, 'Sacred and Secular History in the Writings of Bede (†735)' (PhD thesis, University of Cambridge, 2007).

Holder, Arthur G., 'Bede's Commentaries on the Tabernacle and the Temple' (PhD dissertation, Duke University, 1987).

Houghton, John William, 'Bede's Exegetical Theology: Ideas of the Church in the Acts Commentaries of St. Bede the Venerable' (PhD dissertation, University of Notre Dame, 1994).

Sowerby, Richard, 'Angels in Anglo-Saxon England, 700–1000', (DPhil thesis, University of Oxford, 2013).

Thacker, Alan, 'The Social and Continental Background to early Anglo-Saxon Hagiography' (DPhil thesis, University of Oxford, 1976).

Walt, A. G. P. van der, 'The Homiliary of the Venerable Bede and Early Medieval Preaching' (PhD thesis, University of London, 1980).

Index

For reasons of space this index only includes references to works of Bede from the body of the text; no attempt has been made to record references in the footnotes unless part of a substantive discussion. Figures are indicated by the use of *italic* type.